THE RED STAR Al

JAMES REARDON-ANDERSON

(*Editor*)

The Red Star and the Crescent

China and the Middle East

جـامـعـة جـورجـتـاون قـطـر
GEORGETOWN UNIVERSITY QATAR

Center *for* International *and* Regional Studies

OXFORD
UNIVERSITY PRESS

OXFORD

UNIVERSITY PRESS

Oxford University Press is a department of the
University of Oxford. It furthers the University's objective
of excellence in research, scholarship, and education
by publishing worldwide.

Oxford   New York

Auckland   Cape Town   Dar es Salaam   Hong Kong   Karachi
Kuala Lumpur   Madrid   Melbourne   Mexico City   Nairobi
New Delhi   Shanghai   Taipei   Toronto

With offices in

Argentina   Austria   Brazil   Chile   Czech Republic   France   Greece
Guatemala   Hungary   Italy   Japan   Poland   Portugal   Singapore
South Korea   Switzerland   Thailand   Turkey   Ukraine   Vietnam

Oxford is a registered trade mark of Oxford University Press
in the UK and certain other countries.

Published in the United States of America by
Oxford University Press
198 Madison Avenue, New York, NY 10016

Library of Congress Cataloging-in-Publication Data is available
James Reardon-Anderson.
The Red Star and the Crescent: China and the Middle East.
ISBN: 9780190877361

Printed in India on acid-free paper

CONTENTS

CONTENTS

PART IV

DOMESTIC FACTORS IN CHINA-MIDDLE EAST RELATIONS

ABOUT THE CONTRIBUTORS

Mohammed Turki Al-Sudairi is a PhD candidate at the University of Hong Kong, specializing in comparative politics and cultural security practices in China and Saudi Arabia. He has published extensively on various aspects of China's relationship with the Middle East.

Jon B. Alterman is Senior Vice President, Brzezinski Chair in Global Security and Geostrategy, and Director of the Middle East Program at the Center for Strategic and International Studies in Washington. He is the author or co-author of four books on the Middle East, including (with John Garver) *The Vital Triangle: China, the United States and the Middle East* (Washington, DC: CSIS, 2008), and the editor of five more.

Altay Atlı is a research associate at Sabancı University's Istanbul Policy Center, and an adjunct professor teaching courses on international political economy, Asian economies and international relations in the Asia Pacific. Having studied in Turkey and Australia, Dr. Atlı obtained his Ph.D. from Boğaziçi University, and was affiliated with this university's Asian Studies Center as well as Shanghai University's Center for Global Studies. He also worked as research coordinator at Turkey's Foreign Economic Relations Board (DEİK), and continues to provide training and consulting services for the business community. Dr. Atlı is an expert member at the China Network of Turkish Industry and Business Association (TÜSİAD) and a columnist at the Hong Kong based international news and opinion portal *Asia Times*. More details on his work can be found in his personal web site www.altayatli.com.

Stephen Blank is Senior Fellow at the American Foreign Policy Council, formerly Professor of National Security Affairs at the US Army War College. He is author of *Russo-Chinese Energy Relations: Politics in Command* (London, UK:

Global Markets Briefing, 2006), among various other books and articles on Russian policy in the Caucasus, Europe, Asia, and defense policy.

James M. Dorsey is a senior fellow at the S. Rajaratnam School of International Studies and Nanyang Technological University, co-director of the University of Würzburg's Institute for Fan Culture, and the author of *The Turbulent World of Middle East Soccer* (Oxford: Oxford University Press, 2014) and a blog with the same title, and *Comparative Political Transitions between Southeast Asia and the Middle East and North Africa* (New York: Palgrave Macmillan, 2016), co-authored with Teresita Cruz-del Rosario.

John Garver is emeritus professor with the Sam Nunn School of International Affairs at Georgia Institute of Technology. His most recent publication is *China's Quest, The Foreign Relations of the People's Republic of China* (Oxford: Oxford University Press, 2016).

Mehran Kamrava is Professor and Director of the Center for International and Regional Studies at Georgetown University's School of Foreign Service in Qatar. He is the author of a number of journal articles and books, including, most recently, *The Impossibility of Palestine: History, Geography, and the Road Ahead* (New Haven, CT: Yale University Press, 2016); *Qatar: Small State, Big Politics* (New York: Cornell University Press, 2015); *The Modern Middle East: A Political History since the First World War*, 3rd edn (Oakland, CA: University of California Press, 2013); and *Iran's Intellectual Revolution* (Cambridge: Cambridge University Press, 2008).

James Reardon-Anderson is Sun Yat-sen Professor of Chinese Studies and Dean of the Georgetown University School of Foreign Studies in Qatar. He is the author of five books on the history and politics of China, most recently *Reluctant Pioneers: China's Northward Expansion* (Stanford, CA: Stanford University Press, 2005).

Joseph Sassoon is an Associate Professor at Georgetown University and holds the al-Sabah Chair in Politics and Political Economy of the Arab World. He is also a Senior Associate Member at St Antony's College, Oxford. During the academic year 2014–2015 he was chosen as Fellow at the Woodrow Wilson Center for International Scholars in Washington, DC. His most recent book is *Anatomy of Authoritarianism in the Arab Republics* (Cambridge: Cambridge University Press, 2016). In 2013, his book on the Ba'th Party, *Saddam Hussein's Ba'th Party: Inside An Authoritarian Regime* (Cambridge: Cambridge

University Press, 2012), won the prestigious British-Kuwait Prize for the best book on the Middle East.

Andrew Scobell is Senior Political Scientist at the RAND Corporation and Adjunct Professor of Asian Studies at Georgetown University's Edmund A. Walsh School of Foreign Service. He is author (with Andrew J. Nathan) of *China's Search for Security* (New York: Columbia University Press, 2012); *China's Use of Military Force: Beyond the Great Wall and the Long March* (Cambridge: Cambridge University Press, 2003); more than a dozen monographs and reports, as well as many journal articles and book chapters. He has also edited or co-edited more than a dozen volumes on various aspects of security in the Asia-Pacific region, including (with Phillip Saunders) *PLA Influence on China's National Security Policymaking* (Stanford, CA: Stanford University Press, 2015).

Andrew Small is a senior transatlantic fellow with the German Marshall Fund's Asia program, which he established in 2006. His research focuses on US-China relations, Europe-China relations, Chinese policy in South Asia, and border developments in China's foreign and economic policy. His articles have appeared in a number of journals and media outlets, including *The New York Times, Foreign Affairs, Foreign Policy,* and the *Washington Quarterly.* He is the author of *The China-Pakistan Axis: Asia's New Geopolitics* (London: Hurst; New York: Oxford University Press, 2015).

Degang Sun is Professor of the Middle East Studies Institute, Shanghai International Studies University, China. His research interests are great powers and the Middle East, Middle East security, and China's policy toward the Middle East. His latest articles (with Yahia H. Zoubir) are "China's Response to the Revolts in the Arab World: A Case of Pragmatic Diplomacy," *Mediterranean Politics,* vol. 19, no. 1 (2014); and "China's Economic Diplomacy towards the Arab Countries: challenges ahead?" *Journal of Contemporary China,* vol. 24, no. 95 (2015). He is also the co-editor of *Building a New Silk Road: China and the Middle East in the 21st Century* (Beijing: World Affairs Press, 2014).

ACKNOWLEDGMENTS

This volume is a product of the research and publication program of the Center for International and Regional Studies (CIRS) of Georgetown University in Qatar. A number of specialists and scholars helped identify original research questions related to the study of China and the Middle East and shaped the intellectual discussions that led to the volume before you. In addition to the authors that appear in this book, these contributors include Osama Abi-Mershed, Jacqueline Armijo, Zahra Babar, Victor Cha, Manochehr Dorraj, Tugrul Keskin, Liao Baizhi, Oriana Mastro, Michael McCall, Irfan Nooruddin, Pan Guan, Yitzhak Shichor, Wu Bingbing, and Casimir Yost. The staff of CIRS, especially the director, Mehran Kamrava, and the associate director of research, Zahra Babar, guided the project at each stage and deserve much credit for the final product. Grateful acknowledgment goes to Qatar Foundation for Education, Science and Community Development, whose inspiration and support makes this series of scholarly publications, and much else, possible.

INTRODUCTION

CHINA AND THE MIDDLE EAST

James Reardon-Anderson

This book brings together recent scholarship on China's relations with the Middle East and more narrowly the Persian (or Arabian) Gulf—a topic that has hitherto attracted too little attention from policy-makers and scholars. The most important reason for this new-found focus is a new confluence of interests: China needs oil and gas, and the major oil producers in the Gulf need the Chinese market. Despite the decline in China's economic growth, its residents remain dependent on imports of energy, and the world's biggest suppliers are in the Gulf. Currently, more than half of China's crude oil imports come from the Gulf—the leading suppliers being (in order) Saudi Arabia, Oman, Iran, and Iraq. One can imagine that the details of this picture will change, as China's economy, world oil prices, and supply lines fluctuate, but it is highly unlikely that China's dependence on Middle East oil (and secondarily natural gas) will decline any time soon. No significant decline in China's needs is likely to occur within the lifetime of Chinese President Xi Jinping's administration, which will run to the early 2020s and perhaps beyond.

It is not that the Middle East has been or is likely to be the highest priority for Chinese policy-makers. It is understandable that in the past, and more likely that in the future, Beijing has paid and will pay more attention to the

Great Powers—the United States, Russia, and Europe—and that China has been and will remain a regional rather than a global power, whose historical traditions and immediate interests reside on the country's periphery—both land borders and surrounding waters. Yet beyond these priorities, the Middle East is and is likely to remain a focus of China's attention.

The same might be said of the countries in the Middle East. Until recently, China meant little to this region, which has been, and to a large extent remains, focused on its own problems and beholden to its main patron and protector, the United States. But things have changed in recent years, as the phenomenal growth of the Chinese economy has created a corresponding demand for energy and the United States has been both distracted from and demonstrably less able to provide the leadership that countries in the region have come to expect or hope for. Countries in the Gulf that lead the world in petroleum reserves, production, and exports, now and in the future, will see China as an important (currently their single largest) market. As the demand for oil imports into the US falls, and as world prices decline, the petroleum exporting countries of the Gulf increasingly "look east" to China, and also to East, Southeast, and South Asia as the most promising markets. In recent years (2013 and 2014), the percentage of crude oil exports that went from the major Gulf producers to Asia were: from Iraq 58 percent, from Saudi Arabia 68 percent, and from Iran 80 percent. In all cases, China now occupies and is likely to remain the region's largest market, while the overall shift in oil exports to the east reinforces the structure of regional and global security arrangements. Although the numbers and other details may fluctuate, there is little reason to think that energy trade, which now dominates all aspects of Sino-Middle East relations, will change any time soon. This is the bedrock of the relationship; the major policy choices involve how to deal with this fact.

While energy trade is by far the most important consideration, this topic has been described elsewhere, so the chapters in this volume are designed to deal more with the implications of trade than with the trade itself, and to explore resultant or tangential issues. One of these issues is how to deal with the other great powers that are external to the region, most notably the United States. Despite recent developments, the US remains the principal keeper of security within the region and of the supply lines that connect the Gulf to its eastern (and all other) markets. The Gulf states and the Chinese recognize that they depend on the US for regional stability and secure supply lines. The Chinese may chafe at the assertion that they are "free riders," enjoying the fruits of this trade without paying their share to protect it. But both Beijing and states within the region are acutely aware that they need the American security presence, as well as a positive relationship with the United States, and this realization places constraints on policy-makers on all sides.

Finally, an issue that weighs heavily on both China and its partners in the Middle East is Islamic extremism or, as others see it, the rights of Muslims in China (and elsewhere) to practice their religious and cultural traditions. For China, this means limiting outside support for the Uyghurs, a Turkic and Islamic minority in China's far western region of Xinjiang, not quite adjacent but near enough to the countries of the Middle East, whom Beijing views as a source of the "three evils"—separatism, extremism, and terrorism. For those who sympathize with the Uyghurs, it means supporting their legitimate rights to practice Islam and sustain their linguistic and cultural traditions.

This book has been designed as a conversation among the authors. We have tried to avoid either extreme: of forcing the contributors' diverse approaches into a uniform account of the subject, or inviting a "hundred flowers" that offer color and diversity at the expense of coherence. Our goal, rather, has been to put together a group of chapters that draw on the effort and creativity of the various authors, while at the same time speak to one another in a conversation that makes sense and enriches our understanding. We have approached this goal in two ways: first, by inviting the authors to meet, exchange drafts, and discuss their separate and shared interests as the project proceeded; and second, in the final round, to present them with the three most broad-gauged papers—those by Andrew Scobell, Jon B. Alterman, and Mehran Kamrava—and invite them to engage with the major themes of these papers—agreeing, disagreeing, or showing why they take a different tack.

In the opening chapter, Andrew Scobell explains the apparent mismatch between China's growing interests in the Middle East and the limited resources or efforts it expends to defend these interests. Scobell concludes that there are two major reasons for this mismatch: first, from a geostrategic perspective, China conserves its limited diplomatic and military resources for the primary goals of maintaining security within China and around the country's immediate periphery; and second, from a constructivist perspective, China draws on both a cultural proclivity and historical experience to minimize commitments and the expenditure of resources far from its borders. Scobell argues that with regard to the former geostrategic considerations, China sees greater opportunities and is willing to commit greater resources in the regions that lie between China and the Middle East—namely, Central and South Asia—while viewing the Middle East per se as more remote and thus less central to China's interests. With regard to the latter, constructivist factors, Scobell points out that Chinese culture provides for a low level of trust, especially toward outsiders, and thus a disinclination to form alliances, while placing a higher value on status and symbolism, thus favoring broad statements of principle over concrete actions. Similarly, historical experiences have taught the Chinese to concentrate on the unity of the empire and low cost security arrangements with the surrounding states, while alliances and other forms of partnership have not worked out to China's satisfaction. All of these factors have made Beijing commitment averse.

In the chapter that follows, Jon B. Alterman adopts a similar view of China's goals and policies, as he examines the relationship between China and the United States in the Middle East. Alterman explores the US-China relationship from two angles. First, he compares the roles of the two powers in this region. The US entered the Middle East during the Cold War, when the rivalry with the Soviet Union prompted Washington to seek superiority within the region. Decades later, when the Soviet Union is no more and US global dominance is in decline, Washington has been less expansive and must choose among the objectives that merit the commitment of scarce resources. China, by contrast, has entered this region later, with more limited goals and with a less expansive sense of its own role. As its interests in the region grow, China must decide what tools it will develop to protect those interests. Second, Alterman traces the recent relations between China and the United States in the Middle East. Both countries seek to avoid conflict and maintain stability in this region, while at the same time eyeing each other with some suspicion. The question for China is: How permissive will the US be to China's expansion westward? On the one hand, Washington welcomes China as a "responsible stakeholder" and contributor to the anti-piracy campaign off the coast of Somalia, UN peacekeeping operations, and the like. On the other hand, the US maintains close ties with China's rivals, such as India, Japan, and Australia; has opposed China's efforts to establish the Asian Infrastructure Investment Bank (AIIB); and has excluded China from the Trans Pacific Partnership (TPP), before abandoning this venture itself. The question for the United States is: Will China's growing role undermine or support the US in this region? China needs the US to maintain security of supply lines and poses no fundamental alternative to the Western global order, yet China's growing power can facilitate or complicate Washington's priorities.

In Chapter 3, Mehran Kamrava considers the "China model" and its appeal to regimes and publics in the Middle East, both as a political symbol and as a practical alternative for governmental and economic reform. The "China model," in a crude, symbolic sense of promising rapid economic growth under an authoritarian government overseeing a mixed economy, appeals to those governments and elites in the Middle East that are disillusioned by American failures, annoyed by American lecturing, and who now fear abandonment as Washington grows less assertive abroad and more preoccupied with internal affairs. China, lacking the baggage of long standing engagement in the Middle East and promising trade and aid with no strings attached, appeals to both publics and policy-makers throughout the region. At a deeper analytical level, however, Kamrava finds that the "China model" depends on the effective institutional capacities and public acceptance that are distinct, even unique, features of China and other developmental states in East Asia, where state formation preceded the inclusion of popular classes and where statesmen enjoyed wide latitude in choosing policies and practices. Viewed from this angle, the "China model" appears inapplicable to the states of the Middle East, which were formed later, and whose statesmen must cater to the demands of the popular classes. Comparing these two dimensions, Kamrava concludes that the "China model" acts as a symbol to justify the reign of authoritarian regimes and the attraction of China as an alternative to the United States, whereas there is little potential for any of these states to adopt the actual "China model" as a basis for their own political and economic development.

Part II examines individual states to show how each of them views and deals with the other(s). Three of the authors follow lines similar to those outlined by Andrew Scobell and Jon B. Alterman: that China's approach in the Middle East has been incremental and cautious. From the eastern end of the continent, Sun Degang argues that China sees the Middle East as a "market" and that its military force has entered the region to safeguard China's geo-economic interests, such as energy, investments, and trade. By contrast, Sun points out, China has not sought to establish hard military bases, on the model of the United States and other Western powers. In Beijing's view, economic relations and military dependencies provide greater influence at a lower cost than do hard military bases. China's military ties in the Middle East vary from the long-term to the ad hoc. The former include China's naval fleet to deal with piracy off the coast of Somalia, the newly established logistical base in Djibouti, and UN peacekeeping forces throughout the region. The latter include military exchanges and arms sales, the deployment of security contractors, joint military exercises, the evacuation of overseas Chinese nationals, and participation in UN Security Council missions that serve Beijing's interests. This "soft" military presence, Sun concludes, is unlikely to be replaced with "hard" military bases in the foreseeable future.

Altay Atlı's account of China's relations with Turkey, a newly prominent player in the Middle East, shows how and why China's ambitious and actions remain limited. At the rhetorical level, leaders in both countries have tried to elevate the importance of what some would like to believe is or will become a "strategic partnership." With Turkey's large population and growing economy, its propitious location spanning the east-west highway, and a government that has volatile relations with China's rivals, the United States, Russia, and Europe, this country looks like an ideal target of opportunity as China "marches west." Atlı reports on the aspirations and positive steps that have been adopted by both sides. In the end, however, political conflicts across a number of issues—a broken agreement on missile sales, differences over Syria and other regional issues, and the status and role of the Uyghurs, an ethnic minority in China with close ties to Turkey—have defeated efforts to forge a stronger relationship. The explanation, according to Atlı, is that trade and investment between the parties are too small to gird a "strategic partnership" against the conflicts that beset China's relations with all of the countries in this region. Turkey lacks the oil and gas required to hold China's attention and pay for imports that Turkey would like in return. In the meantime, while Turkey expresses interest in Chinese investment and China appears willing to capitalize on Turkey's position between Europe and Asia, there has been little concrete collaboration between the two countries. With no strong economic ties, political factors periodically toss the relationship up and down.

John Garver's treatment of China's role in the Seven Party talks on Iran's nuclear program paints a quite different picture. Garver argues that Beijing played a more proactive and important role than suggested by the "commitment averse" China described by Scobell and Alterman. He shows that beginning in 2013, policy-makers in Beijing sought to persuade Tehran to seek an agreement with the United States limiting Iran's nuclear weapons capability. President Xi Jinping and other People's Republic of China (PRC) representatives encouraged the Iranians to accept measures demanded by the United States and its European allies to forestall Iran's development of nuclear weapons, in exchange for confirmation of Iran's right to develop nuclear power and non-military nuclear research and a lifting of the economic sanctions that had been imposed on Iran since 2006. Garver concludes that the Chinese played a significant role in bringing about the final agreement reached in 2015, indicating that Beijing has been more confident and assertive than suggested by any of the authors mentioned above. Garver views China as a cautious but rising power in the Persian Gulf, with the construction of a strategic partnership with Iran being an implicit, long-term component of that growing role.

Focusing on Iraq, Joseph Sassoon argues that the jury is still out. In the wake of the American occupation, China has had great success doing exactly what those who describe a cautious, incremental China would expect: that is, maintaining good relations with all parties, while maximizing its economic benefits, in this instance by becoming the leading investor in Iraqi oil production and a leading importer of Iraqi oil. However, Sassoon points out, this short-term success has raised the fundamental question of whether China will be drawn into local conflicts and forced to become more proactive, as it is called on to protect its investments and a large overseas workforce as in the case of Libya, Yemen, and other conflict zones. In Sassoon's view, the Iraqi case illustrates the challenge that China faces in maintaining the "commitment averse" and "soft" military approach proposed by the other authors cited above.

Part III, titled "One Belt, One Road," presents a different approach. "The Silk Road Economic Belt and the 21st-Century Maritime Silk Road" (abbreviated to "One Belt, One Road," or OBOR) is the slogan put forth by China's paramount leader, Xi Jinping, to describe an ambitious strategy for China's expansion westward. As such, it embraces a vision in sharp contrast to the cautious and self-limiting approach, suggested by Scobell and Alterman, of a China that seeks to make and keep friends on all sides, maximize economic returns while minimizing political and military commitments, leave the initiative to others, and respond modestly and only when necessary. It thus points squarely to the fundamental question on the minds of all China watchers: China is rising, but how?

Two authors provide contrasting answers to that question. Stephen Blank sees "One Belt, One Road" as an audacious strategic project that links China to the Middle East, although he is less certain how China will use the linkages spawned by this initiative to advance its interests in the region. To date, most of China's efforts have been focused on Central Asia, but Blank draws the connections to a similar approach to the Middle East. And while recognizing that the enunciation of ambitious goals awaits implementation in a world of constrained resources, he points out that today only China can think and is thinking in these expansive terms. If Blank has it right, then Chinese policy in the Middle East involves some short-term, tactical moves to reassure the United States and other parties, while laying the groundwork for much more ambitious initiatives in the future.

Andrew Small is decidedly less bullish about "One Belt, One Road" in general, and about its application to the Middle East in particular. He points out that the Gulf countries are too rich to need Chinese investment, while others (Small notes in particular Iran and Turkey, which are often seen as potential partners for China) are distracted by other issues, and all are constrained by the need to protect their relations with the United States and other Western powers. While opening up some opportunities, Small concludes that "One Belt, One Road" offers far less than a "transformative" agenda for China in the Middle East.

Finally, Part IV introduces a different way of understanding relations between China and the Middle East. Two authors draw the links between issues within both China and various Middle East countries and the relations between them. Mohammed Al-Sudairi examines the role of Islam in China and Saudi Arabia, both as a political issue and tool and in its broader role in the society and culture of these two countries. Al-Sudairi directs the discussion away from the narrowly political or instrumental view of religion and culture: at one extreme, that it is a common bond that unites the Chinese and Arab peoples along the peaceful path of the "Silk Road" in an embrace marked by harmony and mutual admiration and respect; or at the other extreme, that it is a source of tension, antagonism, and even violence that drives apart the peoples and governments at opposite ends of the continent. In lieu of this preoccupation with politics, he emphasizes the role of Islamic non-state actors and those things that produce broader and deeper "connectivities" between Chinese and Saudi societies.

Finally, James Dorsey links Beijing's domestic policies, designed to deal with the restive Uyghur minority in the north-western region of Xinjiang, with its relations with countries in the Middle East, most notably Iran, Pakistan, Saudi Arabia, and Turkey. Dorsey describes Chinese policies as on the one hand promoting economic development and job opportunities in China's north-west, designed to lure the Uyghurs into a peaceful and productive multi-ethnic Chinese society, similar to the role played by the Muslim Hui minority; while on the other hand, they are cracking down on Uyghur support for the "three evils" of ethnic separatism, religious extremism, and terrorism. This has led, Dorsey argues, to conflicting trends in China's relations with several countries in the Middle East.

In sum, this book attempts to anticipate from different angles the future of China's policies in the Middle East (and by implication elsewhere). It brings together chapters written by leading scholars of Chinese and Middle East international relations in 2017. Inevitably, whenever the book appears, it will miss the most recent events; and in selecting among a range of issues, it will capture some and miss others. Essentially, we wish to point out that our chapters were completed before the election of Donald Trump and have focused on China's approach to the (Arabian or Persian) Gulf, while ignoring some tangential issues (such as China's relations with Israel).

PART I

THE BIG PICTURE

1

CHINA'S SEARCH FOR SECURITY
IN THE GREATER MIDDLE EAST

Andrew Scobell

"China is a powerful state but doesn't act like it [in the Middle East]."[1]

Unnamed Chinese Middle East expert, April 2013

"Even if China becomes a superpower...it still won't play a major role in the Middle East."[2]

Yin Gang, Chinese Academy of Social Sciences, May 2013

One of the most remarkable seismic shifts in the geopolitical landscape of the Middle East since the end of the Cold War has been the increasing involvement of the People's Republic of China (PRC). However, China's activism has been almost exclusively economic; in diplomatic and military arenas, Beijing has been extraordinarily timid in the Middle East.

After decades of near absence and virtual irrelevance, in the twenty-first century the PRC has emerged as a major player and presence in the region, but Beijing's role has been largely focused on economic activities. China's trade with the Middle East has increased more than 600 percent over a ten-year period, growing to $230 billion by 2014; as of 2015, China was the world's largest importer of crude oil—more than half of which comes from the Middle East.[3] Of course this increase in trade is not confined to the Middle East alone; Chinese trade with, for example, Central Asia has also seen tremendous growth, reaching $46 billion in 2012 from only $527 million in 1992.[4] But even in such an environment of general trade expansion, China's increasing economic involvement in the Middle East does stand out. China's annual foreign assistance delivered to the Middle East, according to one estimate, jumped from $151 million in 2001 to $6.8 billion in 2010.[5] Moreover, approximately 550,000 of the some 5 million PRC citizens around the world are located in the Middle East according to one analyst.[6] In contrast, China has only been modestly engaged diplomatically and militarily in the region (see below).

This timidity in the Middle East is in stark contrast to China's greater twenty-first-century assertiveness both in its own neighborhood and in other locales around the world.[7] PRC President Xi Jinping, since assuming office in 2013, has articulated an ambitious agenda, including a more prominent role for China in global affairs. Despite greatly expanded interests in the Middle East, China has yet to allocate substantial security resources and make greater efforts toward protecting its interests in the region. This stark mismatch is a source of frustration to some Chinese analysts.[8]

What are China's paramount interests in the Middle East? China's top interests include access to the region's energy resources, especially petroleum; doing whatever it can in the Middle East to preserve stability at home and peace in its Asia-Pacific neighborhood; expanding its influence in what Beijing regards as a pivotal region of the world; and demonstrating China's status as a global power.[9] Beijing recognizes that the United States is the dominant outside power in the Middle East, and China's involvement in the region necessarily entails elements of cooperation and competition with Washington (the US-China dynamic is addressed in Jon B. Alterman's chapter in this volume).

Explaining the interest-effort mismatch

What explains Beijing's interest-effort mismatch in the Middle East in the early twenty-first century? The answer can be found in a blend of geostrategic and constructivist analysis. China has long viewed the core Middle East region as geographically far removed from China, but in the twenty-first century

Beijing increasingly perceives the Middle East in more expansive terms, to the extent that it is intertwined and enmeshed with China's borderlands and internal affairs. Despite the increased prominence of a "Greater Middle East" to Beijing's worldview and a substantial economic role in the region, China avoids more robust diplomatic and/or military involvement in the Middle East because of learned behaviors and enduring attitudes. More specifically, Beijing is wary of being entrapped by expanded international cooperation due to negative lessons of past relationships and concepts of power as status rather than as action.

This chapter explores why, in the face of escalating threats to Chinese interests in the Middle East, China does not act more assertively in the region. First, this chapter considers which of several leading theories of international relations might be able to explain China's timid approach to the Middle East. Second, this chapter examines the limited level of diplomatic and military efforts that the PRC has applied toward the rump region. Third, the chapter employs a geostrategic analysis to illuminate the logic of China's minimalist approach to the region, introducing the concept of a "Greater Middle East" to underscore Beijing's growing attention to the wider region and the expanding linkages connecting China with this region. Fourth, the chapter adopts a constructivist approach to elucidate how the lessons Beijing has gleaned from the PRC's record of foreign relations shape China's current search for security in the Greater and Lesser Middle East. Finally, the chapter summarizes its main findings.

Testing theories

In this chapter I test four theoretical approaches in international relations theory: offensive realism, defensive realism, constructivism, and geostrategy.[10] Realism, constructivism, and geostrategy have each been fruitfully applied to China's contemporary international relations, although not specifically to China and the Middle East. Thomas Christensen characterizes China as the "high church of realpolitik."[11] Iain Johnston argues that China possesses a "parabellum" or hard realpolitik strategic tradition.[12] Johnston also highlights the utility of constructivism to explain contemporary Chinese international behavior.[13] Meanwhile, Andrew Nathan and Andrew Scobell adopt a geostrategic approach to interpret twenty-first-century Chinese foreign policy.[14] Whatever the approach, there is a consensus among scholars that twenty-first-century Chinese foreign policy is no longer either significantly shaped by nor explained with reference to ideology. While token reference is made to Marxism-Leninism and Mao Zedong thought, current PRC foreign policy is driven by national interests (see, for example, China's defense white papers and the section below titled "Geostrategic interests").

From an offensive realist perspective, one would expect China to employ the instruments of national power proactively and assertively in order to defend forcefully its expanding interests in the Middle East.[15] This might include military conquest and/or occupation of at least portions of the region, the establishment of a network of overseas military bases, and, possibly, the formation of an axis with one or two key states in the region with overlapping interests. Moreover, China would not shy away from the routine use of military muscle to advance its interests in the Middle East.

From a defensive realist perspective, one would also expect China to engage in a vigorous defense of its interests in the Middle East. But, unlike offensive realism, China would be more inclined to adopt a less heavy-handed military approach and more likely to establish alliances and work closely with these allies to protect its interests.[16] So what would constitute an alliance? According to one prominent scholar, an alliance is "a formal or informal relationship of security cooperation between two or more sovereign states." According to Stephen Walt, this alliance definition "assumes some level of commitment" between the states involved.[17]

A constructivist lens is ambiguous about anticipating China's actions beyond expecting Beijing's behavior to evolve and involve adjustments or changes in approach.[18] A state's trajectory on the global stage is not predetermined by structure but guided by process—its interactions with other states. The international system is constructed through the accumulation of multiple interactions.[19] As China learns and adapts, its actions, including military steps, would likely be limited, gradual, or even tentative.

A geostrategic perspective would also anticipate a very modest response, since China's top priority is security within its borders and around its periphery—inside its own home region.[20] China would, therefore, be reluctant to commit sizeable resources to a region far outside its immediate neighborhood.

To date, China's twenty-first-century actions in the Middle East seem to be most consistent with a constructivist and/or geostrategic approach. Of course, Chinese actions are also consistent with the PRC's modest military power projection capabilities and limited diplomatic tools. In spite of these limitations, however, given the growing importance of the region to China, from a realist perspective, one would expect to see at least greater activity and ramped up efforts at security cooperation with other states in the Middle East.

Geostrategically, the PRC has little history or tradition of activism—diplomatic or military—outside its own Asia-Pacific neighborhood. Beijing is wary of being mired in the Middle East morass far from home. From a constructivist perspective, China's learned insecurities and imbued pathologies influence policy choices. An important lesson of the PRC's foreign relations experience is that it must be hyper-vigilant against entangling alliances. Beijing is very cautious about expanding cooperative relations with other states. China has had bad experiences with allies and limited experience of sustained mutually beneficial cooperation with other states. Historical examples include China's close relations with North Vietnam and the Soviet Union, as well as its still-continuing ties to North Korea, all of which will be discussed in detail later on.[21] As a result of lessons learned from these past experiences, China is commitment-averse. In addition, culturally, power tends to be understood in terms of status rather than action.

The next section examines China's recent diplomatic and military activities in the Middle East.

How is China securing its interests in the Middle East?

In recent years, China has expressed growing concern about complex and multiple traditional and non-traditional security threats to its interests at home and abroad.[22] China can either work to counter these threats by throwing more resources at the problem, including diplomatic and military, and/or by acting, either unilaterally or in cooperation with other states or groups of states. "Presence" refers to PRC efforts to allocate resources to the Middle East; and "cooperation" refers to Chinese efforts to work with other states in the region. To date Beijing has promoted security in the Middle East through increased application of effort, but these Chinese actions have been extremely limited: mostly slightly stepped up diplomatic activity, more policy statements, and some token non-combat employments of military forces. However, there has been no effort to do any heavy lifting.

Presence

China has raised its profile in the Middle East security-wise, but this presence has tended to be thin and symbolic. In other words, China spouts high-minded rhetoric and very modest but high-profile diplomatic gestures, and combines this with small but well publicized tangible commitments of resources. Diplomatically, Beijing has been superficially more engaged in the Middle East with prominent visits by senior PRC officials. These included one trip by President Xi Jinping (in 2016) and two trips by his predecessor, President Hu Jintao (in 2006 and 2009). In 2004, China established a multilateral forum called the Sino-Arab Cooperation Forum through which China could engage diplomatically with the members of the Arab League. China also dialogues with the Gulf Cooperation Council. Moreover, Beijing has taken steps to signal that it is paying greater attention to the region: back in 2002, the PRC created the position of special envoy to the Middle East; and in 2013, China released a conspicuous but "bland" formal proposal for Israeli-Palestinian peace.[23] By publicly proclaiming an interest in addressing the Israel-Palestine problem, Beijing has made a grand symbolic gesture that projects to a troubled region the image of an engaged outside power and morally upright state. However, China's involvement in the Middle East peace process has been dubbed "merely diplomatic rhetoric," and "China's impact" has been assessed as having "hardly been felt."[24]

And yet, China has not issued a white paper on the Middle East as it has done for Africa and for other issues of great importance to China. Instead, the Ministry of Foreign Affairs issued a "China's Arab Policy Paper" on 13 January 2016, chock-full of platitudes. The paper did contain one specific policy position: "China supports the Middle East peace process and establishment of an independent state of Palestine with full sovereignty, based on the pre-1967 borders, with East Jerusalem as its capital."[25] PRC President Xi Jinping was slow to make his first trip to the Middle East, although he has visited almost every other region of the world during the first three years of his tenure, including two visits to far-flung Latin America. By chance, Xi's first visit coincided with the issuing of the "Arab Policy Paper": in January 2016, the PRC head of state visited Egypt, Iran, and Saudi Arabia. In Cairo, Xi delivered a formal address at the headquarters of the Arab League; and while in Tehran and Riyadh, Xi worked to strengthen Beijing's enduring relations with each of these Middle East powers and expand economic cooperation.[26] Premier Li Keqiang, meanwhile, has yet to visit the Middle East.[27] The reason for this low-profile approach to the region appears to be that the current Beijing leadership considers the Middle East a byzantine minefield to be navigated with extreme caution.[28] One exception of note, however, to the fairly recent nature of Chinese diplomatic involvement in the Middle East is the case of Egypt, with whom China has had diplomatic ties all the way back to the 1950s.[29]

Military-wise, China's presence includes United Nations Peacekeeping Operations (UNPKO) missions in the Golan Heights since 1990, when five

PRC military observers were dispatched, and the anti-piracy three-vessel PLA Navy flotillas which have patrolled the Gulf of Aden since early 2009. Beyond these involvements, China's military operational activity in the Middle East has mostly been limited to involvement in non-combatant evacuations (NEOs) of PRC citizens from regional states. And even this PLA involvement has been extremely modest. Thus Degang Sun dubs this as China's "soft military footprint" in the Middle East (see Chapter 4). The PLA played a supporting role in the 2011 NEO from Libya and a central role in the smaller scale 2014 NEO from Yemen. In the latter operation, 629 PRC citizens were evacuated by sea by two Chinese Navy vessels.[30] In the former NEO, a PLA Navy frigate served as an escort to civilian vessels carrying PRC nationals and four PLA Air Force transports flew out some of the 36,000 Chinese citizens evacuated. But the lion's share of the heavy lifting in these types of evacuations, including those from Lebanon and Iraq, were civilian efforts coordinated by the PRC Ministry of Foreign Affairs.[31]

Cooperation

In the Middle East, the PRC has skillfully managed to remain a friend to all and enemy of no one. Many of the partnerships are thick and comprehensive but very superficial in terms of "level of commitment." However, at least four of these partnerships have proved quite robust, comprehensive, enduring, and most have a military/security component and include Egypt (since the 1950s), Iran (since the 1970s), Israel (since the 1980s), and more recently Saudi Arabia (since the 1980s). Each of them has involved cooperation in the security realm, often conducted in secret and frequently involving arms sales as well as the sharing of sensitive technology.[32] One noteworthy instance of cooperation is China's involvement in the extended P5+1 negotiations on Iran's nuclear program. While the full extent of China's involvement and level of effort remains difficult to discern, Beijing appears to have played a useful role (see Chapter 6 by John Garver).

Analysis

An examination of China's efforts at military presence and security cooperation in the Middle East to date uncovers a record of superficial and/or shallow commitments and involvements. China's expanding interests in the region beg the question of why its security involvement has not been significantly greater, especially in recent years when Chinese military capabilities have been growing. Why the glaring interest-effort mismatch?

First of all, it is important to note that China has limited security resources to apply to its burgeoning "overseas interests," and these are spread thinly around the globe. And yet, China has one of the largest and most potent armed forces in the world. But Chinese leaders decide how these forces are deployed: with significant domestic responsibilities at home and mostly tasked with missions close to home. Thus, there is significant "domestic drag" upon these security resources because of the high priority of internal security.[33] Beijing has also focused on its immediate neighborhood—the Asia-Pacific—but from a geostrategic perspective, Chinese leaders have learned that the Middle East has become the key out-of-area region for their country. Meanwhile, Chinese leaders are studying how to protect their interests and attempt to overcome being socialized, in order to economize on security efforts beyond China's borders and emphasize symbolism over substance. In addition, as Beijing attempts to cooperate with other states, it is wrestling with how to apply both positive and negative lessons of past cooperative efforts—consistent with a constructivist approach.

Introverted regional power

The PRC has no history of projecting armed force far beyond its borders, and extremely limited experience of sustaining military forces in out-of-area operations.[34] Moreover—with a few key exceptions—the PLA has not stationed military forces abroad for extended periods. The primary exceptions are Korea and Vietnam, both of which are on China's immediate periphery and each shares a land border with the PRC. Sustaining the operation of military forces further afield is virtually virgin territory for the PLA. Two recent instances noted earlier are participation in United Nations Peace Keeping missions around the globe and the anti-piracy flotillas in the Gulf of Aden. For the UNPKO missions, including those in the Middle East, China does not handle its own transportation or logistics. For resupplying its three-vessel naval task force in the Gulf, the PLA has improvised on the fly and has been "learning by doing": purchasing fuel, food, and fresh water during port visits.[35] Any ideas of dispatching and then rotating in larger sized naval, ground, or air units—or even stationing them—in the Middle East are daunting, albeit not insurmountable, challenges. Most PLA units have never been outside China, and operationally the major ongoing challenge most commanders face is how to move their units from one military region in China to another.[36] One notable exception to this pattern of limited military involvement abroad is the recent establishment of a Chinese naval logistics facility in Djibouti in 2015, China's first overseas military outpost. With its strategic placement on the Horn of Africa, this naval outpost not only gives China a solid footing on the African continent itself, but also grants access to the Arabian Peninsula.[37]

Certainly, in recent decades Chinese military and law enforcement agencies have engaged internationally to an unprecedented extent, but this has rarely been sustained or across the board. Perhaps China's ties with North Korea, Pakistan, and the members of the Shanghai Cooperation Organization (SCO) are the most significant instances of defense cooperation. And yet even these are constrained, mostly bilateral, and exercises are on a small scale with levels of interoperability and coordination being quite superficial. China's coordination with North Korea has been minimal, verging on non-existent, even though Pyongyang is formally Beijing's only twenty-first-century military ally.[38] China's military cooperation with Pakistan has been more robust, albeit still relatively modest.[39] In short, China has concentrated its security efforts and resources very close to home—consistent with a geostrategic approach.

Geostrategic linkages

When Chinese leaders gaze out of their Beijing office windows, they see China as the center of a world ringed by four concentric circles. The innermost ring contains all the territory that the PRC controls or claims (including land and maritime areas); the second ring extends just beyond the periphery of these borders to those countries and areas immediately geographically adjacent to the PRC; the third ring encompasses China's larger Asia-Pacific neighborhood (comprising the regions of Northeast Asia, Southeast Asia, Oceania, South Asia, Central Asia); the fourth ring includes the rest of the globe (the Middle East, Europe, Africa, and the Americas).[40]

While the Sino-centric dimension to Beijing's geostrategic perspective should not be unexpected, what might come as a surprise is the level of insecurity with which PRC leaders view the security environments in all four rings. This may be particularly puzzling given that China continues to grow stronger economically, more powerful militarily, and enjoys relatively good or at least cordial relations with virtually every country around its periphery. Indeed, China is arguably more secure in the second decade of the twenty-first century than it has been in some two hundred years. Nevertheless, Chinese leaders see serious national security threats in each of these rings, but the gravest are those located in first ring: domestic dynamics that endanger the rule of the Chinese Communist Party (CCP). Next in importance are those dangers that lurk in the second ring, followed by those that fester in the third ring.

But the greatest fear of Chinese leaders is that threats will combine and interact across rings in ways that aggravate and exacerbate threats to national security and CCP rule. Given the high level of insecurity of Chinese leaders, one might expect them to adopt an autarkic policy. Indeed the simplest way to keep out dangerous foreign influences would be to close off China from the outside world. This was essentially the policy adopted by Mao Zedong for extended portions of his rule (1949–76). China's top priority in the post-Mao era has been sustained economic development; Mao's policy initiative of self-sufficiency and mass mobilization has been discredited because it failed spectacularly, with the Great Leap Forward (1958–61) resulting in mass famine. Post-Mao leaders, by contrast, have adopted a sustained policy of reform and opening to the outside world—what I have dubbed "China's Great Leap Outward."[41]

These threat linkages across rings are especially worrisome in a twenty-first-century world where the magnitude of China's vulnerability is intensified by globalization. The PRC is inextricably enmeshed and intertwined with the global economic system. Despite the deep insecurity that pervades Beijing's corridors of power, retreat or withdrawal from the world is not considered a realistic option. China is reliant on external markets and resources around the globe to keep the country prosperous and its people employed. But sustaining China's economic juggernaut is dependent not just on continued engagement with the outside world; it also requires expanding China's interactions with the second, third, and fourth rings. The unofficial mantra of Xi Jinping is "thinking locally demands acting globally."[42]

The most significant twenty-first-century foreign policy manifestation of this implicit mantra to date is the launching of the Silk Road initiative by PRC President and CCP General Secretary Xi Jinping. More commonly dubbed the "One Belt, One Road" project, it has become the flagship foreign policy effort of the Xi administration—a rubric that encompasses and frames virtually all of China's diplomatic and economic activities.[43] The effort involves the development of a massive network of roads, railways, pipelines, canals, and sea lanes connecting China with the rest of the world—an extremely ambitious undertaking. Other than China itself, the Middle East appears to be the key region geostrategically, as well as the central node in a global web of Silk Road networks.[44]

China and the Greater and Lesser Middle East

The Middle East has become the region of greatest importance outside China's Asia-Pacific neighborhood. Its special status is highlighted by the twenty-first-century Silk Road initiative. Its growing importance to China (especially in geostrategic, economic, and ethno-religious terms) has prompted the region to be perceived as closely intertwined with the Asia-Pacific region. In fact, Chinese citizens are beginning to see the Middle East as an extension of China's border areas and their country's periphery. As a result of the growing importance of the Middle East, Chinese analysts now identify an enlarged area they refer to as the Greater Middle East (*Da Zhong Dong*), which includes not just West Asia and North Africa (*Xi Ya Bei Fei*), but at least portions of Central and South Asia.[45] According to one prominent Shanghai-based Middle East researcher, "Currently [i.e. 2012], the trend in the 'Greater Middle East'—comprising the Middle East, Central Asia and South Asia—toward geopolitical integration becomes more prominent by the day."[46] In this chapter I distinguish between the Greater Middle East and the more circumscribed geographic area that most people consider to be the Middle East. To avoid confusion and clearly differentiate it from the larger conception, I follow the lead of some Chinese analysts and label the latter as the Lesser Middle East (*Xiao Zhong Dong*).[47]

In the twenty-first century, China considers the Middle East much closer to home and more proximate to its Asia-Pacific neighborhood than at any time in centuries—since the time of the Silk Road. Beijing perceives itself bound through ties of commerce and shared ethno-religious linkages. According to Li Weijian of the Shanghai Institutes for International Studies, the Middle East had become "a strategic extension of China's periphery." Writing in 2004, Li explained:

> After the breakup of the Soviet Union ... a group of Islamic countries emerged in Central Asia, and it is an indisputable fact that the geopolitical distance between China and the Middle East shrank at once. China's western region was originally a neighbor of the Middle East and has long since been connected with the Middle East via the Silk Road; the two regions have close affinities and relations along ethnic, religious, and cultural dimensions. As the strategic extension of China's western border region, the trends governing the situation in the Middle East and the region's pan-nationalisms and extremist religious ideological trends have a direct influence on China's security and stability.[48]

Analysts in China, such as Li, have adopted the term "Greater Middle East," which of course originated with the second administration of US President

George W. Bush. The idea appears to resonate in Beijing, because it captures the ethnic, religious, and economic interconnections that enmesh the countries at the core of the Middle East with those on the periphery of the wider region and thence to China.

According to Liu Zhongmin of the Shanghai International Studies University:

> China should view the Middle East's strategic importance in light of the concept of the 'Greater Middle East.' From the perspective of land border security, the Middle East, Central Asia, and South Asia together comprise the geopolitical 'heartland,' directly influencing the security environment of China's northwest. From the perspective of maritime security, the Middle East directly affects the security of China's energy passageways and China's strategic interests in the Indian Ocean.[49]

China's greater dependence on imported energy has raised Beijing's interest in the Middle East. Indeed, as noted earlier, the Lesser Middle East has become the single most important source of Chinese imported petroleum.

For at least two decades, an emerging concern in Beijing has been how to maintain some semblance of stability in the Lesser Middle East. Beijing's thinking has transformed from not caring about conflict or turmoil in the region to a clear preference for peace and order. In an earlier time, upheaval in the Middle East was not seen as a negative, because it served to sap the strength of the United States and Soviet Union and divert the attention of Washington and Moscow away from Beijing and Asia. During the Cold War, leaders such as Mao Zedong and Deng Xiaoping viewed the Middle East as a distant zone of contestation for influence with the two superpowers and rivalry with Taiwan. But by the 2000s, China had a strong preference for a tranquil region, and Chinese analysts expressed a clear desire for the United States to "uphold stability in the [Lesser] Middle East."[50]

But as a geographic construct, the Greater Middle East better captures how Beijing has come to see the Middle East and its greater relevance to twenty-first-century China. The broader conception brings the region more immediacy and proximity to China's wide array of key security concerns.

How is China securing its interests in the Greater Middle East?

Xi Jinping seems to perceive the Middle East as "Greater" and as an extension of China's periphery, as well as a zone of fragile stability stretching from Central and Southern Asia to North Africa and the shores of the

Mediterranean. Moreover, Beijing has become concerned about regime stability in the Lesser Middle East after being essentially "agnostic" for many years.[51] With the advent of the "color revolutions" in former communist states, the emergence of the "Arab Spring" in 2011, and continued turmoil in a range of Lesser Middle Eastern states, this stance has changed dramatically. In addition, the rise of radical Islamic movements such as ISIL out of civil wars in Syria and Iraq has forced China to rethink its preferences. All these dynamics not only threaten China's considerable economic interests in the core Middle East region, including energy supplies, and in the Greater Middle East, including transportation routes, but also are seen to pose a threat to CCP rule. Beijing is worried that these popular and extremist movements may inspire ethnic Han dissidents to push for greater democracy in China proper and Uyghur activists to press for greater autonomy and/or religious freedom in Xinjiang.[52]

Presence

China has been much more active diplomatically and militarily in the Greater Middle East since the 1990s. Diplomatically, China has been most active in Central Asia, with at least annual visits to the region by the PRC president to attend Shanghai Cooperation Organization (SCO) head of state summits. The SCO serves as a key vehicle for PRC diplomatic, military, and economic involvement in the Greater Middle East (see also the "Cooperation" section below). While all the members aside from Russia and China are geographically located in Central Asia, Pakistan, India, Iran, and Afghanistan have been observers since 2005. Sri Lanka has also been participating as a dialogue partner since 2009, and Turkey since 2013.[53]

In South Asia, China has also been diplomatically active, with Xi Jinping visiting a range of countries since becoming PRC president in early 2013, including India, Pakistan, Sri Lanka, and even the lowly Maldives. China is also accredited as an observer in the South Asia Association for Regional Cooperation. More recently, Afghanistan has become another focus of Chinese attention, especially since the drawdown of US and ISAF forces post-2014. Beijing has stepped up its cooperation with Kabul and its level of activism and consultation with key actors, including Islamabad and the Afghan Taliban.[54]

Moreover, since 2002, China has conducted regular military exercises with members of the SCO. These almost annual activities have been both bilateral and multilateral, conducted inside and outside China, and have included military and/or paramilitary forces from all six full members: four Central Asian states (Kazakhstan, Kyrgyzstan, Tajikistan, Uzbekistan) as well as Russia and China (see below).[55] Also in the Greater Middle East, China developed or at least gained access to port facilities, most notably in Gwadar, Pakistan. Then, in November 2015, Beijing announced that it was establishing a naval logistics facility on the shores of the Red Sea in the small African state of Djibouti. China and Djibouti reportedly signed an agreement for a ten-year lease.[56]

Cooperation

China has been far more vigorous in the Greater Middle East, establishing a series of ongoing partnerships with an array of states. Of particular note is Beijing's long-standing military partnership with Islamabad and China's multilateral cooperation in the SCO. China's partnership with Pakistan is probably the PRC's most enduring and functional cooperative bilateral relationship. There has long been an extensive military-to-military relationship. Economic ties have also grown, and Pakistan appears to be a significant part of China's "One Belt, One Road" initiative. During President Xi Jinping's visit to Islamabad in April 2015, he announced that China would invest $46 billion dollars in Pakistan to develop the China-Pakistan Economic Corridor.[57]

Of more recent vintage is the significant Chinese partnership with Russia and four Central Asian states in a multilateral regional entity founded in 2001: the Shanghai Cooperation Organization. Beijing was the driving force behind its establishment and the most important country sustaining it. The SCO has proven to be remarkably resilient and adaptive as a mechanism to manage China's relations with the Central Asian "stans" and Russia in a manner that reassures the smaller member states that China is not seeking overt conquest, domination of the region, or an alliance structure. It also provides some confidence on the part of Russia that Beijing will at least consult and coordinate with Moscow as it increases its influence in this landlocked region that has traditionally been part of Russia's sphere of influence.

China also has military-to-military relations, including field exercises, with an array of other states. Pakistan stands out, in the Greater Middle East, because of the frequency of PLA exercises with the Pakistani armed forces: since 2003, the two militaries have conducted more than fifteen multilateral or bilateral field exercises.[58] Also of note are China's modest but burgeoning security ties with Turkey. Beijing views Ankara as a key regional player, with significant influence penetrating into Central Asia and even western China.

Of course, the fact that Turkey is a member of NATO is not lost on China. But perhaps of greater importance to Beijing is that this country's ethnic kinspeople spill eastward over borders across the Central Asia steppe. According to a prominent Chinese military leader, Turkey is China's most "fearsome and formidable rival" in Central Asia.[59] General Liu Yazhou, the political commissar of the National Defense University, explains: "Turkey is the best example of secularization and democratization in the Islamic and Turkic worlds. Turkey claims to be the ancestral home of all ethnic Turkic peoples [including the Uyghurs]."[60] Turkey, in particular, has been a sanctuary for dissident Uyghurs, and Prime Minister Recep Tayyip Erdoğan appears to have been the only government leader in the Greater Middle East to criticize Beijing publicly for brutal repression in Xinjiang in 2009—reportedly calling Chinese actions "near genocide" (for more on Xinjiang, see the next section).[61] China launched a concerted initiative to repair relations with Turkey and expand security ties. During late September to early October 2010, the PLA participated in the "Anatolian Eagle" military exercises. Then, in 2013, Turkey agreed to purchase an air defense system from China worth more than $US 3 billion. Two years later, however, Ankara scrapped the controversial deal in the face of pressure from other NATO countries.[62]

Geostrategic interests: static at home, expanding abroad

Focusing on Beijing's thinking about the Middle East is useful in illuminating the growing significance of Chinese concerns about "overseas interests." Although much attention has been paid to the PRC's articulation of its (domestic) "core interests," far less attention has been given to its former set of interests. While China's set of core interests are essentially fixed, PRC overseas interests are in flux and of growing importance.[63] Although the PRC had not articulated national interests until the twenty-first century, these have been implicit across time—often expressed in terms of lofty principles. The term "core interests" has become a code word for a series of issues considered of vital importance, which include Tibet, Xinjiang, and Taiwan. Overseas interests are still in the process of being defined, but seem to include the safety of PRC citizens and property, and the safeguarding of access to resources essential to China's economic prosperity.

Core interests, overseas interests: Cold War and beyond

A consuming focus for Beijing since at least the late 1970s has been how to maintain stability both inside China's borders and around its periphery. While

Chinese leaders are still plagued with insecurities in 2017, they do feel some-what more secure at home and along their borders, although certain sectors are still worrisome (Pakistan and North Korea come to mind). While jurisdictions on China's eastern coastal periphery, such as Hong Kong and Taiwan, have proved to be periodic twenty-first-century challenges to Beijing, more persistent problems have emerged in China's western-most regions, and these have become especially challenging since the late 2000s. Unrest and dissent among PRC ethnic minorities—the Uyghurs and Tibetans in particular—have become a thorny issue. Although ethnic minorities constitute less than 8 percent of the PRC's overall population, many—including the Uyghurs and Tibetans—are concentrated in sparsely inhabited and strategically important frontier areas.[64]

While Tibet has tended to be a higher profile and more complex problem for Beijing than Xinjiang—where most Uyghurs are located—this is changing in the twenty-first century. The plight of Tibetans has long attracted considerable international attention, partly because of the charismatic and eloquent Dalai Lama who has headed the Tibetan government-in-exile in India since 1959. Moreover, the Tibet issue was intertwined with an unresolved territorial dispute between China and India. However, the plight of the Uyghurs—a mostly Muslim Turkic ethnic group—has begun to receive far greater international attention because of high-profile episodes of violence and harsh PRC repression in recent years.[65] Moreover, Beijing is alarmed over greater manifestations of discontent by Uyghur and apparent radicalization that has prompted acts of violence across China, and cooperation and coordination between PRC Uyghurs, the Uyghurs diaspora, and Muslim groups in Central Asia, South Asia, and the Lesser Middle East. Uyghurs radicals have reportedly been trained in Pakistan, fought with the Taliban in Afghanistan, and joined the ranks of ISIL in Syria and Iraq. As a result, the PRC has become more vocal about the threat of terrorism and more energized to take action.[66]

Beijing appears to have shifted from an earlier era when China viewed the Lesser Middle East primarily as a key region of contestation between the Cold War superpowers and competition with Taiwan, in which China was simply seeking to become relevant. Today, in a twenty-first-century situation, China's expanding interests make fostering peace and stability in the Greater Middle East its highest priorities.[67]

In the Cold War era, Beijing felt largely closed out of the Lesser Middle East as Washington and Moscow fought for influence and power via regional proxy forces. Moreover, until the 1980s, the PRC's Chinese rival, the Republic of China (ROC) in Taipei, continued to be the "China" diplomatically recognized by many states in the region. Economically, until the 1990s, the PRC was almost non-existent in the Lesser Middle East with the exception of a supplier of bargain-priced and/or hard-to-get weaponry to states such as Iraq, Iran, and Saudi Arabia.[68]

Then, in the weeks and months after the June 1989 Tiananmen massacre, the Lesser Middle East gained sudden prominence for China as Western capitals ostracized Beijing and imposed sanctions on the PRC. China's response was to reach out to developing countries to counter the cold shoulder from developed states. Middle Eastern capitals were central targets of Beijing's counterstrategy in the early 1990s.[69] Moreover, this initiative coincided with growing demand for imported energy resources and commodities as China reinvigorated its economic reform and opening policy.

By the twenty-first century, all states in the Lesser Middle East had broken official ties with Taiwan and established full diplomatic relations with the PRC, which they recognized as the sole legitimate government of China. The PRC is now a key economic actor in countries throughout the region, with modest but significant military relationships with many rump Middle Eastern states. Moreover, a weakened Russia is no longer a major external actor in the Lesser Middle East—with the notable exception of Syria—and the staying power of the United States is being questioned by US allies, partners, and rivals alike.[70]

Constructing a future

China's search for security in the Greater Middle East is driven forward by a geostrategic imperative shaped by the lessons of past Chinese international experience.

Socialized to economy of effort and power of symbolism

China has been socialized to operate by economizing on its level of effort in international affairs, especially beyond its immediate periphery. This is in part because Beijing is accustomed to having limited resources at its disposal and also because China is fearful of over-committing. China is used to operating according to what one scholar has dubbed the "Maxi-Mini principle," which esteems greatest possible benefit to China for least required PRC effort:[71] in short, minimum Chinese output for maximum Chinese gain. Thus, China is used to acting as a perennial "free rider," especially where public goods and the global commons are concerned. As a result, China does not tend to send military forces into situations or locations where they are vulnerable. Moreover, China is prone to taking modest initiatives and then skillfully hyping these contributions. A prime example is China's very limited ongoing three-ship flotilla engaged in anti-piracy operations in the Gulf of Aden.

China is also socialized to value symbolism over substance. This attention to symbolism is culturally learned. Indeed, in Chinese politics, power tends to be defined more in terms of status, rather than in ability or action.[72] In international relations and domestic politics, China tends to emphasize publicly stated principles and grand gestures over actual commitment of resources or real actions. Take for example the much ballyhooed Five Principles of Peaceful Coexistence: these were first articulated in the 1950s and have been routinely resurrected or recycled by Chinese diplomats and foreign policy scholars ever since. Beijing is eager to claim the moral high ground on every issue, but is frequently reluctant to follow through with concrete contributions. China, according to Harry Harding, "can be effusive in its rhetoric and symbolic support."[73] While Beijing's level of commitment does not always stop there, it often does. For PRC leaders, while the external audience is important, the internal audience is of greater significance.[74] The CCP desires to be seen by the Chinese people as the legitimate rulers of the PRC, and, in the minds of China's communist rulers, affirming this legitimacy entails regularly making China seem more respected all over the world and successfully protecting China's growing interests around the globe.

China's belief in the potency of principle in the Lesser Middle East is evident in recent pronouncements and gestures. Beijing has taken public positions on the Israel-Palestine issue and the Syrian civil war. But these policies are virtually meaningless, because China does not back up these words with deeds. Moreover, Beijing's appointment of a Middle East envoy in 2002 was all about symbolism rather than substance. Although the PRC makes more public pronouncements about "national interests," continued reference to "principles" provides justification for little or no Chinese action in defense of those interests. In the Greater Middle East, promoting the "One Belt, One Road" strategy on the basis of "mutual benefit and win-win" depicts China as a powerful but benevolent and generous benefactor focused on common economic development.[75] But the question of how to protect Chinese interests presents a dilemma.

Economy of effort plus the power of symbolism together would logically lead China to explore greater cooperation with other states in an effort to secure China's expanding interests in the Greater Middle East. Beijing's approaches in this regard are shaped by positive and negative lessons of international cooperation.

The lessons of cooperation

China is used to acting unilaterally or with one other country, but only for limited periods to protect interests closest to home. Prime examples are the de facto brothers-in-arms military alliances with North Korea (1950–58) and North Vietnam (1965–9). The years in parentheses are those in which Chinese troops were actually on the ground in these countries, either in combat or stationed on foreign soil. In both cases, China military assistance began before troops were dispatched and continued after the troops returned home.[76]

Greater cooperation with other states up to and including formal alliances is one way for China to respond to threats. Indeed, China has demonstrated a greater willingness to cooperate both bilaterally and multilaterally in the post-Cold War era. This is evident from the growing number of partnerships that China has established with more than seventy countries around the world and their great participation in multilateral fora.[77]

Negative learning

But the PRC is officially opposed to alliances, which it argues are detrimental to global peace and harmony. Beijing has long been critical of the United States for its network of alliances in the Asia-Pacific and around the world. However, China does have one formal alliance (with North Korea since 1961) and a number of enduring partnerships, some of which seem to approximate to alliances. Moreover, Beijing has long insisted that "it does not station any troops abroad nor occupy one inch of foreign soil," and yet it is interesting to note that the 2015 defense white paper omits any mention of this standard line. *China's Military Strategy* stresses that the PLA will "faithfully fulfill ... China's international obligations [and] ... engage in extensive regional and international security affairs."[78] I do not mean to suggest that China's armed forces are preparing to engage in military conquest or foreign adventurism. Rather, it appears that there has been a sea-change in Chinese thinking about the deployment and employment of military forces beyond existing PRC borders and disputed territories claimed by Beijing. Such efforts are no longer completely out of the question.

China also has very modest experience of working cooperatively in security matters with other states, and the extent of PRC cooperation with other states since 1949 has been remarkably limited and short-lived, with only a handful of exceptions. This trifling record hampers China's ability and willingness to cooperate. This has led the scholar Harry Harding to remark on the "volatility of China's international relationships."[79] "Over time," most of China's cooperative relationships, especially those "with its clients, have experienced either a falling out or a fading away," according to Harding.[80] Moreover, the PRC possesses a low trust political culture and outsiders are distrusted even more. This suspicion seriously hampers China's potential to cooperate with other states unless trust can be built, and this process takes time.[81]

Positive learning

China has gleaned positive lessons from international cooperation: stick with states that you have learned you can trust and restrict these cooperative relationships to limited partnerships. These trustworthy states are few in number—Iran and Saudi Arabia in the core region and Pakistan in the Greater Middle East.

PRC leaders are fundamentally distrustful of other states. "Chinese leaders," observes Harding, "have traditionally been highly ambivalent about the desirability of extensive and durable cooperative relationships with foreign societies." This feeling persists today in Beijing as PRC leaders have a deep "mistrust of foreign contacts." According to this scholar, "Chinese leaders ... have ... been afraid that international cooperative relations would lead to strategic dependence and economic exploitation [by China's foreign partner]."[82]

Of course entrapment is a familiar dynamic to students of alliance politics. But in the Chinese case there is a heightened level of distrust reinforced by Beijing's troubled history of alliance relationships with three brother communist party-states and the United States.[83] China has been the junior partner in one major alliance: that with the Soviet Union between 1950 and 1960. Beijing believes that this was a bad experience in which Moscow never lived up to its promises and dumped the overwhelming burden of the conflict in Korea on Chinese shoulders. Moreover, China also believes that it was exploited by its junior allies, North Korea and North Vietnam. Both states dragged China into conflicts that were costly to Beijing, both in blood and treasure.[84]

And since the 1960s, China has had a quasi-alliance with Pakistan. While this relationship has stood the test of time and is arguably China's most enduring cooperative partner, from Beijing's perspective the danger of entrapment has been and continues to be significant. Since Pakistan views itself as bereft of true friends—the United States is perceived as being a fickle and untrustworthy ally—China looms very large for Islamabad. Beijing was fearful of becoming embroiled in the Indo-Pakistan wars of 1965, 1971, and the 1999 Kargil conflict, and the periodic crises between Islamabad and New Delhi. And yet China persists in the relationship and is committed to deepening it economically. The reason why Beijing remains committed is that, over the decades, Chinese leaders have learned that Islamabad can be trusted. China has a dearth of reliable friends in the Greater Middle East, notably on the vulnerable geostrategic fault line between Central and South Asia. Since the 1960s, India has been considered a threat and China's alignment with Pakistan serves as a valuable counterweight. In addition, Pakistan is a key player in managing the Afghanistan problem and the threat of Islamic radicalism to Central Asia and China.[85] Indeed, according to one Chinese analyst, "if China decides to develop formal alliances Pakistan would be the first place we would turn. It may be the only place we could turn."[86]

Conclusion

China's involvement in the Lesser Middle East—with the exception of economic activities—appears to be minimalist. Thus, while China is an economic heavyweight, it continues to be a diplomatic lightweight and military featherweight. This is despite the fact that the core Middle East holds a prominent place in China's economic, foreign, and security policies. The region is an important source for China's growing energy needs, is considered of key geostrategic significance, and in the twenty-first century Beijing seems to view the Middle East as "greater": inexorably linked to the PRC's internal security, national unity, and stability around its continental periphery.

For all the hype surrounding Beijing's growing economic heft, military power, and diplomatic clout, fundamentally China remains an Asia-Pacific power, albeit one with an expanding global presence. Nevertheless, China's overseas interests outside of its immediate neighborhood are nowhere more important than in the Lesser Middle East. However, these greater interests and the PRC's higher profile in the core region belie Beijing's underwhelming efforts to secure China's interests in the Lesser Middle East.

Realist analysis—both offensive and defensive variants—would anticipate China to be much more engaged in diplomatic and military domains through activities such as forming alliances and establishing bases, to outright conquest and occupation of key areas (most likely in coordination with key regional allies). But this is not happening. So why the glaring interest-effort mismatch? A composite answer of geostrategy and constructivism provides the strongest explanatory power.

Geostrategically, China has tended to perceive the Middle East as being in the outer fourth ring of security. And yet, this thinking appears to be evolving as Chinese leaders increasingly see the Middle East as more closely intertwined to the first, second, and third rings in both positive and negative ways. The growing geostrategic salience of this region to China is underscored by PRC analysts embracing the term "Greater Middle East." This term refers not just to the rump Middle East, but also to at least portions of Central and South Asia. Behind this geostrategic reconceptualization is greater awareness of the ethno-religious bonds extending from inland China across the mountain ranges and steppes of Central Asia to the shores of the Persian Gulf and Mediterranean Sea. Rising Chinese fears about terrorism spring from the radicalization of the Uyghur minority within China in the context of a supportive Uyghur global diaspora and sympathetic wider Islamic world. More recently, President Xi's "One Belt, One Road" initiative aims to strengthen China's links to the Greater Middle East through trade routes, railroads, and pipelines.

Constructivism underscores how China is on a steep learning curve where the Greater Middle East is concerned. In sum, China's minimalist efforts in the Middle East can be explained with reference to socialization. China is socialized to economize on its level of effort and to value symbolism and gestures over substantive actions. In addition, China does have limited resources to apply to the Lesser Middle East. To compensate for this, one might expect Beijing to seek help from states in the region. However, the very modest effort to work with friendly countries is constrained by Beijing's negative lessons of cooperation: China is reluctant to form alliance-like relationships. There are also positive lessons of cooperation, and Beijing has learned to stick with capitals it has learned it can trust, but restrict these ties to limited partnerships.

In Beijing's eyes, the Middle East seems to straddle all four of China's rings of insecurity. While the Lesser Middle East is clearly located in the fourth ring, the Greater Middle East spills across into the third (e.g. Central and South Asia) and second rings (countries immediately adjacent to China such as Afghanistan and Pakistan) and thence penetrates the first ring (inside the PRC). In both the Greater and Lesser Middle East, China confronts the challenge of how to protect considerable interests from an array of threats and potential threats. Most of them are non-traditional security threats, especially terrorism, but traditional security threats, such as interstate war, are also present. Only time will tell whether Chinese learning will result in greater diplomatic and military presences or, possibly, in enhanced partnerships with other states. Certainly, there is a lively ongoing debate within China about how best to protect China's overseas interests in the Middle East.[87]

2

CHINA, THE UNITED STATES, AND THE MIDDLE EAST

Jon B. Alterman

As China's global footprint expands, it finds itself relying more and more on parts of the world where it has little influence and seeking to flourish in a system largely developed by others. As China's global interests broaden, the country constantly finds itself in contact with the United States, which is neither a clear rival nor a clear adversary, but is clearly the world's leading global power. While China faces many challenges in its foreign policy, one of the most fundamental is how to manage its own rise without either clashing with the United States or creating undue burdens for itself as the largest Asian power. This challenge manifests itself especially in the space between East Asia and the Middle East, a space that, from a US perspective, is truly the other side of the world.

The challenge is particularly acute because conditions in Asia are in flux. While some observers take the enduring US presence in this space to be a given, the United States in fact retains an array of options there. It can occupy that space in ways that complement China's ambitions, or in ways that confront them. It can seek a strong imprint on the region, or it can decide that its vital interests lie elsewhere. China, too, has choices about how it will move in this space. It can seek to shape the space to advance its interests, or it can accept the contours as they are. It can develop its economic, diplomatic, and military capacities in this space simultaneously, or it can focus principally on economic matters. It can work to establish broad multilateral frameworks for international interaction, or it can stress bilateral relations.

What is certain is this: how the United States and China handle their mutual interests in the Middle East, and in the Asian space leading to it, will not only be an important indicator of how they relate to each other globally, but it will also strongly affect their broader ties. The geopolitics of this area will have a profound effect on the future of geopolitics more broadly.

This chapter begins by considering the ways in which the US and Chinese governments have approached the Middle East in the past, and then describes China's rising interests there. It next analyzes the countries' shared objectives and the contrasting ways in which they have pursued them. It considers the appeal of China to regional governments and the limits of Chinese influence, and then analyzes China's more immediate task, which is securing the space between its Middle East interests and China itself. This analysis partly involves understanding the role of the United States in Asia, and how the US military presence on the maritime route pushes China to pursue terrestrial alternatives. The chapter then considers how a shift in the US approach to the maritime space could have a profound effect on China's security and could push China to articulate more aggressively a "Chinese order" in Asia—one that could be well accepted and serve Chinese interests. It concludes by analyzing some of the new realities that China will have to confront as its global interests deepen.

The United States in global affairs

The United States has long had an idiosyncratic approach to global power. Unlike Europe, it never tried to assemble a collection of far-flung colonies or lock in advantages for its investors abroad. In the nineteenth century, while European powers competed for the world, the United States government was largely preoccupied with settling a continent and was far removed from most of the European-based battles for wealth and influence. When the United States rose on the global scene in the mid-twentieth century, its strategy was not so much to exert control as to set universal standards by which all nations competed, including the United States. Europeans had sought to grow national power through establishing direct control, but the United States approach was indirect. Embedded in the US strategy—even in its robust anti-communism—was an interest in promoting stability, predictability, and transparency abroad. This interest had both military and economic components, involving soldiers and businesspeople alike. While much of the resultant structure and many of the resultant rules naturally favored US interests and conduct, benefits were not reserved to the United States alone. Allies flourished under the aegis of *Pax Americana*, which was, in the end, a set of evolving common rules rather than a fixed outcome that insisted on US primacy. The approach helped cement an acquiescence to US global leadership out of a belief that it was in broad common interest.

When the United States swept into the Middle East after World War II, it did so under a clear Cold War framework. That is, US efforts had a clear military component that was supplemented with economics. US and allied forces sought to advance Western interests by securing oil fields, ensuring the safe passage of shipping, and inoculating formerly feudal and colonial societies against the attractions of communism. Israeli security was an important concern, but not an overwhelming one; peace was pursued as much to prevent the Soviets from gaining a foothold among antagonists as to advance discrete US commercial interests. The strategy went through different emphases for half a century—sometimes more state-centric in its approach, sometimes more grass-roots; sometimes more economic, and sometimes more military. But it was always predicated on seeing the Middle East as a strategic prize.

After the Cold War ended, the Middle East remained strategically important to the United States, which feared not that an outside power would sweep in, but that the region would succumb to its own demons and damage US interests. The United States rushed to defend Saudi oil fields after Saddam Hussein invaded Kuwait in 1990, and it assembled a broad international coalition to push Saddam back. The US objective was order, not control. Similarly, the United States' confrontation with Iran since 1979 has reflected its desire to maintain regional stability and defeat Iranian efforts to pick apart the US-led status quo (though for its part the Islamic Republic sees the US strategy as part of an attempt to isolate and weaken it).

For the last half century, the United States has occupied an increasingly confounding role in the Middle East. Intraregional actors wishing to change the status quo pushed many governments to seek protection from the United States. At the same time, close US relations with authoritarian allies, a commitment to secular liberalism, and support for Israel have often made the

United States come across as an arrogant and immoral power, one that presents an easy demon in public debate. The US view of itself in the Middle East, as a pro-democracy force supporting public demands for a voice and greater accountability from authoritarian governments, does not prevail. The broad view is more negative. Most governments see the United States as a naïve but necessary partner, and publics broadly tend to see the United States as a sometimes admirable society with a despicable government.

China in global affairs

China's general approach to global affairs has been thoroughly different from that of the United States. Even at its zenith of power, what is today modern China was a regional power and not a global one. It never sought far-flung possessions or devised rules governing international affairs. When Zheng He set out on his fifteenth-century voyages to the Persian Gulf and the Red Sea, he did not seek land for the monarch as did his European counterparts. For centuries, the various Chinese dynasties conquered contiguous territory and demanded—and received—tribute from their near neighbors, but they never showed a thirst for a global role. Rather, those with such a thirst thrust themselves into China's consciousness when the Qing dynasty, which would eventually become modern-day China, was at its nadir. European powers established colonies in East Asia throughout the nineteenth century and (along with the United States) wrung concessions from the Qing imperial leadership after the Opium Wars. China suffered further under Japanese expansion in the early twentieth century, and was almost wholly inner-directed for decades, while it sorted out the consequences of the Communist Revolution of 1949. By the time China began to shed its isolation in the late 1970s, a whole set of global post-war rules had been set. China's dizzying rise in the years since has been driven not by challenging those rules but by capitalizing on them. China's rise has not involved the creation of NATO-like military alliances, and China maintains a deep aversion to overseas military bases. China's articulated strategies are light on security concerns and full of concern for mutual benefit.

China's spectacular rise has engendered widespread speculation on the country's ultimate strategy. A generation of American strategic thinkers has absorbed the writings of classical Chinese military theoreticians, and many view the present Chinese quietism as a sign of patience rather than benign intent. As they read Chinese history, the common thread in Chinese thinking is not peaceful accommodation but well-timed confrontation.[1] In this view, the modesty of China's announced ambitions on the global stage signals a shrewd reserve rather than modest aspirations.

Even for close analysts of China, though, it is hard to know what the Chinese leadership genuinely seeks, if indeed it has a plan at all. So much is evolving so quickly in so many places, and the Chinese government is so large and complex—and opaque—that separating intent, reality, and illusion might be impossible. And even if China does have a long-term strategy, there is no way of knowing whether that strategy would be successful in an extended time of peace, let alone whether it could survive the contact of war.

China's interests in the Middle East

When it comes to the Middle East, China's interests are relatively more recent than those of the United States, and they are narrower. The territory of modern-day China has had a modest cultural connection to the Middle East, largely through Islam, for centuries. The Silk Route long pre-dated Islam, but Chinese travelers themselves rarely traversed it. By the medieval period, Muslim traders had established enclaves in Chinese ports, but there were no Chinatowns in the Middle East. China today has several distinct Muslim communities—not only the Turkic Uyghurs, but also the Hui, who are in most respects indistinguishable from Han Chinese. A few of those Chinese Muslims made their pilgrimage to Mecca over the centuries, but before regular air travel, such trips were rare. Chinese students in the Qing imperial period began to study regularly in Cairo's al-Azhar University only in the twentieth century, and in relatively small numbers. Furthermore, governmentally, there was little connection.

Politically, the People's Republic of China has felt an emotional connection to anti-colonial movements in the Middle East, especially when they held sway in the 1950s and 1960s, but it was mostly engaged in the politics of symbolism. Egypt's Gamal Abdel Nasser extended official diplomatic recognition to China in 1956, precipitating the withdrawal of Western support for the High Dam at Aswan and the subsequent nationalization of the Suez Canal Company. In so doing, Abdel Nasser was making a political point that had little practical effect on Egyptian-Chinese relations. Similarly, it is little coincidence that the Chinese embassy in Algiers is in Charles de Gaulle's former residence—a location no doubt intended as a slight for Algeria's former colonial masters in France. China extended relatively little in exchange for Arab support, which one could also argue was not especially valuable to China.

With China's growth on the world stage in the last two decades, the stakes have changed, and China has become increasingly involved in the Middle East. The country's direct engagement has been overwhelmingly economic, through three avenues. By far the most important is energy. China became a net oil importer only in 1993, but the Middle East has consistently been the source of more than 50 percent of China's imported oil. China's growing demand for oil has frustrated efforts to diversify Chinese supply, as incremental increases in supply from non-Middle East sources have disappeared into a rapidly growing basket of imports. China's oil imports increased 9 percent between 2013 and 2014 alone,[2] and that increase in Chinese oil demand accounted for 43 percent of total global demand growth.[3] That year, it is worth noting, was a somewhat modest one for growth in Chinese GDP, clocking in at less than 8 percent compared to the many years of double-digit growth that preceded it.[4]

The second avenue is trade in manufactured goods. The Gulf Cooperation Council (GCC) is among China's fastest-growing trading partners, but not only because of rising energy imports. China sells a broad range of manufactured goods to the GCC, and that trade is increasing rapidly. The Economist Intelligence Unit estimated that by 2020, China would become the dominant global exporter to the GCC, doubling its 2013 volume and accounting for $135 billion a year.[5] Dragon Mart, a vast mall on the outskirts of Dubai that acts as a showroom for myriad Chinese manufacturers and wholesalers, recently tripled its floor space to more than 2 million square feet, or 46 acres of retail space.[6] Some 250,000 Chinese now live in Dubai, although some serve the clientele from Africa and Europe who prefer to do business with China there rather than traveling to China itself.

The third avenue is contracts for infrastructure and other construction. China has applied its expertise—gained from its own rapid building and engineering—to the needs of the boom cities of the Middle East. Chinese construction companies have a reputation for being both cheap and fast, qualities that allow local leaders to take credit for quick progress. China's investments and contracts in the Middle East between 2010 and 2016 totaled more than $60 billion and included such high-profile projects as a light rail line in Mecca, an oil pipeline in the United Arab Emirates that allowed direct access to the Indian Ocean, and 40,000 housing units in Bahrain.[7] As Middle Eastern governments consider the role of material deprivation in generating the Arab Spring protests, the prospect of rapidly erected housing and infrastructure at attractive prices, often backed by Chinese state financing, has been enticing.

China's approach to the Middle East in the last two decades has been almost entirely state-centered. The Chinese government is comfortable with the large public sectors in Middle Eastern states, and it is comfortable striking trade agreements with state institutions. When operating anywhere overseas, the United States government generally seeks to reach beyond state-to-state relationships in order to establish direct ties with business elites, academics, and other members of civil society. China, by contrast, has contented itself to accept the Middle East as it is. While there is some Chinese concern that the region lacks the requisite resilience to cope with its domestic social, economic, and political challenges, the Chinese government seems to distrust opposition groups and to see government forces as the only powers able to contain terrorism and other kinds of disorder. Caught off-step by the Arab uprisings of 2011 and the rise of populists who blamed the Chinese for giving succor to overthrown dictators, Chinese officials have appeared relieved to see powerful regional strongmen return, while being careful not to close the door completely on opposition groups.

China and the United States in the Middle East

Fundamentally, at least theoretically, there should be no natural conflict between the United States and China in the Middle East. Both share an interest in stability, and both are deeply invested in the status quo. This is in part because of the US commitment to open markets in the Middle East; and it is worth noting here that Chinese firms have invested more than $16 billion in Iraq,[8] making China one of the country's largest foreign investors.[9] China benefits from a system in which the United States invests billions of dollars in helping to secure the region. But China does not benefit only by avoiding similar investments in security; it also benefits by avoiding the hostility that such investments arouse in those who oppose the status quo. Some Chinese officials privately express a certain satisfaction with the US involvement in the Middle East, because US forces deployed to the Middle East are US forces that cannot be deployed to China. The US Navy, for example, generally has three carrier strike groups on station at any one time, and a commitment to keep one in the Middle East makes it difficult for more than one to be on station in the Pacific at any given time.[10]

The Chinese strategy toward power in the Middle East appears quite different from the country's attitude toward power in its near vicinity. While China is comfortable operating under the penumbra of US power far from home, it is increasingly wary of US power in East Asia. China's caution toward the US presence seems to have at least two explanations: China believes that East Asia is rightly its own proper area of influence, and it fears that the United States seeks to use China's near neighbors to contain China. China's sparring with the United States over its assertions of sovereignty in the South China Sea are a reminder that China's acquiescence to US naval power is highly situational. A third explanation for China's caution is also likely. China does not feel that it needs the United States to maintain order in East Asia, which is well within the range of the Chinese Navy and where China is the overwhelming local military and economic power. The same does not hold for the Middle East, where potential threats are rampant, local politics are complex and often opaque, and the application of Chinese military force so far afield is a much more tenuous operation.

Differing approaches to the Middle East

Even where US and Chinese interests overlap—on security, stability, and trade—the two countries have profound differences in approach. Many of these differences stem from a professed US commitment to process, and a Chinese focus on outcomes. The US focus on process has not been a consistent thread in US foreign policy, but it has become increasingly consistent over time. In the early years of the Cold War, US officials pushed land reform and economic development projects as ways of immunizing populations in the developing world from the appeal of communism. If feudalism made communism more attractive, the logic went, then the United States and its allies had a strategic interest in eradicating feudalism. A host of US agencies labored by various means to improve economic and political conditions overseas, from the global technical assistance promised by President Harry Truman's "Point IV Program" in 1949 to the massive reorganization of aid in the Foreign Assistance Act of 1961.[11] Even so, the United States pursued close ties with authoritarian governments across Asia, the Middle East, and Latin America, in part to keep communism at bay.

The agonizing US defeat in Vietnam and public criticism of the Central Intelligence Agency's Cold War exigencies in the mid-1970s not only created a demand for a "moral" US foreign policy, but also sharpened the critique that realpolitik approaches were damaging to US interests in the longer term. The end of the Cold War had two impacts on the debate. First, the common narrative emerged that the West won the Cold War because its system was superior. Spreading liberal systems became a security imperative because democracies were understood not to fight wars against each other, or more colloquially, "no two countries that both have a McDonald's have ever fought a war against each other."[12]

Second, the absence of an existential security threat for the first time in a half century freed the United States and its allies from the perceived necessity of supporting thuggish leaders. As new strategic frameworks for the post-Cold War world emerged, some in the United States proposed that the United States should seek to become a persistent force for good in the world—even at the expense of US short-term interests. This view of the US role partly reached back to a history of American exceptionalism. It also derived from the fact that the US encounter with the world in the nineteenth century was dominated by missionaries and not by generals. Bonaparte had his "*mission civilisatrice*" as a governmental task with a clear connection to state power. In the United States, evangelization was a public enthusiasm, and it continues to have deep roots.[13]

As a consequence of these two strands of thought, democratization and governance have been a major part of US foreign assistance for decades. Linking governance to security has played an important role in every presidential National Security Strategy since 1990.[14] The Obama administration ran more than 350 projects in 64 countries under the "Democracy, Human Rights and Governance" rubric,[15] and boasted in September 2015 that "the United States is the largest supporter of civil society in the world, with more than \$3.2 billion invested in strengthening civil society since 2010."[16] The 2010 National Security Strategy was clear:

> The United States supports the expansion of democracy and human rights abroad because governments that respect these values are more just, peaceful, and legitimate. We also do so because their success abroad fosters an environment that supports America's national interests. Political systems that protect universal rights are ultimately more stable, successful, and secure.[17]

China does not appear to have any global evangelization streak and seems to have no desire to persuade the world of the superiority of China's ideology or culture. Further, China's population does not seek to transcend state power to be a positive force in the world. Chinese government actions in the foreign policy space are wholly limited to state interests, and the state sees its interests furthered by close relations with other governments. China's "Five Principles of Peaceful Coexistence," articulated more than a half century ago, insist not only on respect for sovereignty and territorial integrity, but also on non-interference in the domestic affairs of other states.[18] In pursuing cooperative relationships on development-related issues with other countries, the Chinese government focuses on governmental interlocutors to a far greater extent than does the US government. China shares the sense of some governments that the NGO sector may be a hotbed of opposition and social unrest, and it does not seek to embolden or empower civil society in other states. The US approach is different. Whereas the US government certainly seeks to empower partner governments and is cautious not to support terrorist groups, it also aggressively seeks to enlist civil society actors in its programs, and it is often careful to include voices out of favor with the sitting government.

The different US and Chinese approaches to the Middle East were apparent when revolts broke out throughout the Arab world in 2011. The United States government jumped on the protests as confirmation that undemocratic governance was unsustainable. While the White House did not encourage protesters, its satisfaction with events was evident. Upon learning that the Egyptian president and long-time US ally Hosni Mubarak had stepped down in 2011, President Obama said, "There are very few moments in our lives where we have the privilege to witness history taking place. This is one of those moments. This is one of those times. The people of Egypt have spoken, their voices have been heard, and Egypt will never be the same."[19] China, by contrast, viewed the uprisings with alarm. Rather than celebrate them, the Chinese government sought to limit domestic reporting on them, fearful of spawning a copycat uprising in China itself. When the results of the Arab revolts of 2011 were far less clear, it looked as if China had a major problem brewing in the Middle East. The collapse of the status quo meant not only that China lost state partners in places like Libya and Egypt, but that it had gained the enmity of newly powerful revolutionary groups who believed China had contravened their interests.[20]

The appeal of China

The pendulum has swung back in the region, and security officials have reasserted control. Consequently, it is the United States that has lost the trust of those in power; China, prized for its indifference to domestic affairs, appears to be back in favor. In fact, we may see the different approaches of the United States and China promoting a quiet rivalry between the two in much of the world, as the United States insists on bilateral relationships with "strings attached," and China signals its disinterest in precisely the kinds of internal considerations that constrain US policy. Of course, the United States has more to offer than China in absolute terms—in the way of economic strength, technical prowess, and military sophistication—but the Chinese approach, unlike the American, makes military and economic resources accessible.

For countries that the United States has tried to freeze out—such as Iran—China represents a counterweight in global affairs. For countries that believe the United States is turning away from its old friends—such as Saudi Arabia and Egypt—China represents a competing offer against which the United States must bid, and a pathway to obtain what the United States will not sell. Almost every country in the Middle East believes it would benefit from a heightened Chinese role in the region, even if what each country wants to see from China is different.

For the Middle East, a large part of China's appeal is not so much what it is, but what it is not. This sentiment is similar to the popularity that the United States enjoyed in the Middle East in the 1920s, as the region sought to free itself from the imperial grip of the United Kingdom and France. Governments have long resented what they see as US meddling, and publics have long resented what they see as a hostile bias against their interests. To both, China is a blank canvas on which Middle Eastern countries project their aspirations for a different kind of great-power relationship. Chinese officials do not condition, and they do not moralize. They do not complain that the legislature has tied their hands, and they do not produce extensive compliance documents that require signature and verification. Western countries in general, and the United States in particular, have become more cumbersome partners, and China promises a more straightforward relationship.

It certainly helps that China is a success as a nation, and one that has made remarkable economic progress in the last several decades. Looking forward, China is likely to remain one of the world's fastest-growing markets for fossil fuels, and a growing market for materials produced with fossil fuels (for example, fertilizer, petrochemicals, plastics, and aluminum).[21] Elsewhere, the prospects for energy sales are not so good. Conservation has caused European imports to weaken, and a combination of conservation and unconventional oil production in the United States has diminished Middle Eastern exports to what was once the world's largest importer. In fact, with increased domestic production, the United States has recently resumed its status as the world's largest producer of oil and natural gas.[22]

Middle Eastern countries long believed that the US reliance on oil from the Middle East would keep the United States vitally concerned with events in the region. The end of that reliance, even if temporary, has persuaded many of those countries that the United States is eager to cuts its ties. Initial US discussions of the "pivot to Asia" sent a signal to many in the Middle East that the United States was desperately trying to pivot away from the region. China's growing reliance on Middle Eastern energy, and its growing ties to the region, persuade Middle Eastern governments and populations that China is the rising power and the United States is the diminishing power.

The limits of Chinese influence

Expectations of the future, however, tend to cloud understandings of the present. It is premature to argue that China is playing a major role in the Middle East, or that it will do so any time soon. China's boosters in the region tend to underestimate the large gap between the United States and China militarily and diplomatically. It will be decades before China's capabilities in the region match those of the United States.

A broader cultural element blunts China's impact as well. There is simply less comfort in the Middle East with China than there is with the United States, whose deep exposure to the region began more than two centuries ago. It is partly an issue of language and culture, as Mandarin-speaking atheists find it hard-going in Arabia. But in the Middle East and around the world, the United States is starting far ahead of China. Harvard is the world's gold standard for education, not Beijing University; the computers people want are Apples and not Hasee; drivers aspire to own Jeeps and not Great Wall SUVs. When it comes to prestige and the perception of innovation, the United States does the glamorous piece, while Chinese workers grind out products. Chinese products are cheap and available in the Middle East, but they are a poor man's substitute. This same phenomenon can be found in China itself, of course, whose elites aspire to Western brands (including many manufactured in China itself). This state of affairs suggests that the pro-Western tilt is likely to endure for some time to come.

Closer to home

In the face of security concerns in the Middle East and a dominant US position in the region, the Chinese government's instinct in the near-term is to avoid over-exposure to the Middle East. Instead, China seeks to grow Middle East ties slowly, as a continuation of deeper ties with China's neighbors.

Central Asia represents relatively uncontested territory and thus a sort of virgin territory for China to win over. Even more important is Asia's role as a gateway to some of China's most strategically important trading partners, not only in the Middle East but in Europe as well.

China's still somewhat hazy Belt and Road Initiative focuses initially on contiguity and patterns of trade. China is the leading trading partner of all of its close neighbors, and it is a growing trading partner for most countries in the world. China's expansion westward began more than a decade before Xi Jinping proclaimed the Belt and Road Initiative in 2013. Between 2000 and 2013, Chinese trade with the five former Soviet states in Central Asia—Kazakhstan, Kyrgyzstan, Tajikistan, Turkmenistan, and Uzbekistan—increased 28-fold, largely because of energy trade.

China surely realizes that a key variable in its ability to expand its influence is its neighbors' acquiescence to China's rise. Outside of Central Asia, many of those neighbors have close ties to the United States, in part a legacy of Cold War relationships, and in part a consequence of US economic strength. Tens of thousands of US troops are stationed in South Korea and Japan, and both countries have trade relationships well over $100 billion a year with the United States.[23] Warming US-India ties, combined with Indian uncertainty over China's regional ambitions, also represent a potential check on China's westward push, especially by sea.

The United States' Cold War history of resisting Soviet influence in Europe provides a useful reference point, in part because it differs so starkly from the issue of Chinese influence in Asia. First, the Soviet push into Europe was explicitly military, and it was an outgrowth of World War II. As such, it represented a somewhat sudden change to the status of Eastern European states struggling to recover from the war. By contrast, Chinese influence across Asia is much more subtle and much less military, and the general trend of welcoming closer ties with China seems genuinely widespread in regional states, in part because of the importance of growing trade relations. Whereas the United States' closest allies were alarmed by Soviet actions in Europe, close US allies have much more nuanced views toward China's rising influence in Asia. Indeed, China is the largest trading partner of most US allies in Asia, and many Asian countries are deeply resistant to the notion that they would have to "choose" between China and the United States. That circumstance is wholly different from the "Iron Curtain" mentality that prevailed in Western Europe in the second half of the twentieth century.

Second, Soviet moves in Europe during the Cold War were clearly offering an alternative system to that put forward by the United States and its allies, while China argues that its system is complementary. China takes pains to minimize the effects of Chinese influence, strongly arguing that it merely seeks win-win arrangements that serve the national interests of both sides. The proclaimed modesty of the efforts has the effect of minimizing the opposition to them.

Third, the United States felt intimately connected to Europe because of ethnic and cultural ties. Many Americans felt that any change in the status quo was a threat. While an increasing number of American citizens have Asian (and in many cases specifically Chinese) origins, Asia simply feels more culturally remote. Asians who reside in the United States are also less alarmed by growing Chinese influence in Asia than Europe-oriented Americans felt in the face of growing Soviet influence, creating less domestic pressure to check Chinese growth.

The United States in Asia

A question that must be central to Chinese strategists is how permissive the United States will be toward China's expansion westward, an expansion that would presumably have economic, diplomatic, and security dimensions. Thus far, the two sides have sought to build constructive relations arising out of their common interests.[24] China received US encouragement for joining anti-piracy efforts off the coast of Somalia, for example. Similarly, the United States is supportive of the Chinese commitment to global security, which China has demonstrated by sending more than 3,000 peacekeepers to ten UN missions around the world.[25] The United States has not seemed to interfere with China's efforts to build closer ties with Pakistan (including developing the port at Gwadar) and Sri Lanka, nor with China's efforts to develop naval and shipping facilities in Djibouti, where the United States has a navy base.

And yet, the United States seems to be moving to counter China's expansion, or at least retain the ability to counter it, especially in the maritime domain. The growing US bilateral relationship with India is one manifestation of this, in its military and economic dimensions. So, too, is the gentle US nudging of Japan and India to have closer naval ties. Closer military ties between the United States and Australia, which create a more durable US presence in the western Pacific, are another sign of how the United States views the geometry of the region. A new nomenclature about the US military commitment to the "Indo-Pacific" seems to be gaining some currency, although some scholars criticize it as a meaningless term.[26] On the economic front, the US sought to undermine the Asian Infrastructure Investment Bank (AIIB) before its launch, and the Trans-Pacific Partnership is an initiative to deepen US-East Asian trade relations that do not involve China.

It is clear that the United States has a far more powerful military presence in the Middle East and South Asia than China will be able to muster for decades. At the same time, China's deepening trade relations, growing economy, and rising consumption clearly make it an attractive partner for many Asian governments and businesses. There is a certain complementarity here, as it is clear that China can afford to have a relatively light military presence in the region because the United States has a heavy one. The US Navy has ensured freedom of navigation through the Indian Ocean, even as much of the trade making use of this route has been with China. It is true that regional trading systems function because of the consensus of the participant countries, but they have done so under the penumbra of US protection and with the active support of US diplomacy, which together promote robust multilateral cooperation.

China gains both security and vulnerability from the US role. In peacetime, it benefits from a secure and predictable environment for trade. One sign of just how open the present system is to Chinese benefit is the successful Chinese investment in the Iraqi oil sector—which took place in the wake of a large US military effort in which China did not participate. In extremis, however, China shares no confidence in the current system's durability. The United States will retain a significant ability to disrupt Chinese maritime operations should it wish to—certainly in the Indian Ocean, and even in the South China Sea. Similarly, the US ability to amass an array of allies in Asia dwarfs the current Chinese ability to do so. This is in part because of the US distance from the region, and in part because of regional confidence that the United States does not seek domination.[27] Current conditions help preserve Chinese interests throughout Asia, but future conditions may favor US-led containment.

To take on a heightened regional role in the near term that would serve China's interests in differing security environments, China would require the acquiescence of the United States for its expansion into the Indian Ocean, or else would need a strategy for overcoming US obstruction. It seems to be focusing thus far on winning US acquiescence, ensuring that US-Chinese naval tensions remain isolated in the South China Sea. China's ability to continue to win US acquiescence is uncertain. It is true that China has successfully boosted Sino-American economic cooperation, making the eruption of serious bilateral tensions unlikely. China has also smoothed its path by emphasizing that it is not seeking any more military role than is necessary, stressing that it seeks "win-win solutions" and is willing to invest billions to ensure that benefits flow to Chinese partners. China's suggestion is that its development is in harmony with US influence in the region rather than a challenge to it. But the "win-win" language is much less prevalent in China's near periphery, where some of the closest allies to the United States are located. The post-World War II settlement drew the United States close to Korea and Japan, and the significant US military presence built up to counter Soviet expansion in the Pacific now stands as a bulwark against Chinese adventurousness.

The appeal of land routes

In contrast to rising tensions in the maritime domain, China finds much less resistance to developing terrestrial routes, for several reasons. First, rising tensions between the United States and Russia preclude the two cooperating to isolate China and make Russia especially eager for positive relations in the East. The balance in the Sino-Russian bilateral relationship tips toward China, as Russia's economic and demographic weakness undermines national strength. Second, the Soviet experience left Central Asia relatively underdeveloped and ambivalent toward Russians. The need for infrastructure and trade is deep, and China can deliver both better than the Russians can. China can also play off the Central Asian states and Russia against each other, as both provide China with routes to Europe. Russia's rail lines run on a unique gauge, creating incentives for China to develop rail routes that bypass Russia or force Russia to haul Chinese goods at concessionary rates.

China's uncertain plans in the terrestrial space play significantly to the country's advantage. There is no map of where the Belt and Road Initiative will run, and no list of participating countries. Combined with confidence in the future success of Chinese plans, the uncertainty leads many governments and businesses along the potential route to believe that they have an opportunity to be part of something great, even if none has a clear idea of exactly what it is. The explicit way in which Chinese officials have touted the "win-win" character of China's expansion, combined with the promise of resources from the growing economic powerhouse, increases the likelihood that target states will welcome Chinese influence.

Even so, the economic superiority of the maritime route is striking. Shipping costs to Europe are a third to a half of land trade costs, and volumes are almost thirty times greater.[28] The United States has weaker ties to the countries on China's land borders than with its maritime neighbors in

Southeast Asia, but the logic of China's economic growth requires an emphasis on maritime trade.

Potential shifts in the US maritime role

What would happen if the United States took a less active role in protecting the sea lines of communication between the Strait of Hormuz and the Straits of Malacca? Currently, the US Navy has a unique role in this space, although many of the littoral powers have some naval presence in the area. While the US Navy does not have a large permanent presence in that space, almost half of the troop movements to Afghanistan and the Gulf went westward out of San Diego, California, rather than eastward from Norfolk, Virginia.

Barry Posen has argued that the unique power of the United States is its uncontested "command of the commons"—that is, its unique ability to deploy swiftly to defend interests anywhere.[29] Yet one might argue that the United States could afford to spend much less defending the so-called "global commons." In part, malign actors' reach is quite limited. For example, while piracy has been a problem in the Horn of Africa and the Indonesian archipelago, it has been a problem in areas relatively close to shore and within the reach of national coast guards and navies. Where there was an enduring piracy threat off the coast of Somalia, a concerted international effort (which included China) proved quite effective, and no large merchant vessel has been hijacked since May 2012.[30] When it comes to preserving free navigation on the high seas, there are few national navies that could even contemplate blocking the sea lanes, and the ones that could have deep trade relations with each other that would make hostile actions unlikely, if not unthinkable. While US government officials are often quick to insist that the United States is committed to allies across Asia, and while it has begun describing something called the "Indo-Pacific" to encompass a US commitment across the region, there are still some determined voices suggesting that the level of US commitment to Asia is folly.[31]

Two other aspects of US global primacy are worth considering. The first is the unique US ability to deploy large military forces swiftly anywhere in the world, as discussed above. While that ability certainly exists, the rather mixed results from the last half-century of global deployments raise reasonable questions about its utility. As the tools of asymmetrical warfare grow in strength, the US government's, or any government's, ability to deliver swift and decisive political outcomes through military action becomes more constrained.

The other aspect is the US role in maintaining a broad global order in all its facets—military, diplomatic, and economic. The United States becomes the senior partner in all its global endeavors, one bearing a disproportionate share of the burden while being careful to distribute benefits broadly. In the face of what many Americans see as welcome insulation from global energy markets and migrant flows—and with looming budget challenges brought on by aging demographics, rising entitlement spending, and a persistent resistance to tax increases—calls for the United States to spend less blood and treasure on sustaining order for a seemingly ungrateful world are likely to rise.

A Chinese order?

In a time of growing Chinese interest in regions like the Middle East, one important question to answer is how different a Chinese-led order in Asia might be from one guided by the United States and its allies, as this offers perspectives on what such a China-led order might look like in other regions. On one level, the difference would likely be less than during the Cold War, when the world was divided into communist and capitalist spheres. Capitalism has all but won the economic argument. While there are still differences over the proper scope for state-owned enterprises, the economic basis for judging the utility of activities is widely accepted, and we see startling overlaps between free-market systems and "socialism with Chinese characteristics." But on another level, disparities emerge. The United States has invested a tremendous amount in negotiating multilateral trade regimes that promise the equal treatment of goods. It has also invested in good governance, and in global institutions that promote good governance. Central to the US approach has been a sort of economic evangelism, which is predicated on the confidence that the US model offers developing societies a route to prosperity. Especially during the Cold War, the United States understood itself as the promoter and defender of a free world that stood in contrast to a world first of tyranny, and then of communism.

China's approach, by contrast, has been to live alongside something extant rather than to displace it. Like the United States in the late 1940s, it does not seek formal empire. Unlike the United States in the post-war period, China does not seek ideological hegemony, either. Instead, its thrust has been to emphasize bilateral business arrangements of mutual benefit—where increasingly China is the stronger party. Skeptical of broad schemes of mutual obligation, China has striven for simpler "win-win" arrangements, often directly between governments. China has not prioritized the growth of an independent business class abroad, nor has it sought to constrain the role of governments in the economy. China has also not emphasized eradicating corruption (although it has an active anti-corruption effort underway at home). China is simply seeking to pursue its national economic interests, and it perceives other states as willing partners.

Some China-watchers make the argument that China has acceded to US norms as it has grown its economy and increased its share of global trade. In this view, China is not a disruptor of the status quo but a party to it. Seen from the perspective of the Cold War, when capitalist and communist systems battled for primacy, this is true. There is no grand ideological principal at stake. Yet the US system is about much more than a profit motive. The US system is predicated on a desire to foster competition, transparency, and opportunity. The Chinese system, by contrast, stresses the importance of winning; whispers of corruption and cronyism are rarely far from discussions of Chinese contracting. In its most recent survey of bribery around the world, for example, Transparency International judged that Chinese companies were the second most likely to bribe in their overseas operations after Russian companies, and the difference between them was so slight as to be well within the margin of error.[32] Writing in 2013, two years after China passed legislation making overseas bribery a crime, one critic noted that China appeared to have launched no investigations of overseas bribery at all and suggested that the government had little interest in pursuing the problem.[33] As China reaches out more vigorously to the world, and as Chinese funds play a larger role in global economic development, a question is looming: will China seek to use its rising profile on the international stage to protect its institutions from international standards, or will it use its rising international engagement to bring Chinese institutions up to international standards?

In this regard, the Asian Infrastructure Investment Bank represents an unusual Chinese investment in a multilateral institution that China does not itself control. Whereas China may have initially believed that the AIIB could be an instrument of Chinese policy, the bank's startling success in attracting sixty initial stakeholders—sixteen of them from Europe—means that China's ability to direct the bank's actions will be limited. In fact, such a large multilateral bank may have the paradoxical effect of actually constraining Chinese conduct rather than projecting Chinese values abroad. The AIIB can help advertise China's arrival as a global power, but as a multilateral institution beyond Chinese control it is unlikely to be the principal instrument through which China invests in Asia. For that, China is likely to rely more on institutions such as the Silk Road Fund and the China Development Bank for investments that are intended to advance state interests.

As the United States government has talked openly of the need to make China a "responsible stakeholder" in global affairs, China has made a great show of its effort to define a "new type of great power relations." The components are 1) no conflict or confrontation, 2) mutual respect, and 3) mutually beneficial cooperation.[34] What is most striking, however, especially in a Middle East context, is China's effort to articulate what it means to be a "new type of great power." In the nineteenth century, status as a great power was a reflection of how much territory an individual country could control. In the mid- and late-twentieth century, power was often measured by how much a country could influence and shape others, largely through institutional arrangements. What China is seeking to do in the Middle East context is add to its power through emphasizing economic diplomacy and the prospect of mutual gains, while limiting the contributions it makes to hard security or to strengthening institutions of economic governance. The bet on the Chinese side is that others will continue to contribute sufficiently to sustain the value of Chinese investments, while China will reap the benefits without expending resources. Diplomatically, China's desire seems to be to have positive relations with a wide variety of antagonists, while powers such as the United States provoke animosity by choosing sides.

While China gives up some agency through pursuing this strategy, it has benefits beyond merely saving on expenditures. By not projecting itself into the Middle East, it helps avoid a confrontation that it cannot win with the United States and its allies. Many would read any Chinese effort to move in aggressively with its forces as an effort to displace the United States. Further, China is decades away from being able to begin to match the US ability to defend positions far from its shores. Similarly, the global economic institutions that the United States has helped establish—not only in the Middle East—enjoy a perception of global ownership, and any Chinese effort to subvert them would be read as a sign of Chinese aggression and ambition. Just as the United States has benefited from a perception that the systems it has established leave ample room for others to benefit as well, so too does China profit from a perception that it is not being as assertive as it might be in amassing national power.

But at the same time, China does need to amass more national power. The country is confronting concerns that its traditional approach to regions far from

China is no longer adequate. Large-scale citizen evacuations from Libya and Yemen, the Islamic State group's execution of a Chinese hostage in Syria, and persistent security concerns for Chinese nationals in Iraq are a reminder that perhaps a million Chinese citizens abroad represent a growing consular responsibility for China that the country is still struggling to meet.[35] With a limited diplomatic corps, no overseas bases, and ties with foreign intelligence services and law enforcement organs that are still in their infancy, China's ability to protect a growing number of overseas Chinese citizens is hardly adequate.[36]

New realities

China's need to adjust to global realities comes at a time when those realities themselves are in rapid transition. The world's interest in the Middle East for the last century has been intimately tied to fossil fuels, and Middle Eastern oil has fed much of Asia's economic growth since World War II. Changing global patterns of trade for fossil fuels, and growing concern about fossil fuels' environmental impact, create uncertainty. For China in particular, this cuts two ways. China's reliance on domestic coal for electricity generation has fouled the air of Chinese cities, but shifting to gas would make China more reliant on imported fuel. Similarly, the growing transportation infrastructure in China drives greater fuel growth, but much of China's transportation fuel must be imported—and much of it from the Middle East. The United States, by contrast, has diminishing reliance on imported fuels now, although the durability of the unconventional oil and gas revolution is in question. Technological advances could enhance every country's ability to develop its own domestic energy resources and diminish global trade. By contrast, a failure to develop new technologies could put the United States back at the center of the global trade in gas and oil in twenty years.

China, then, has increased its presence on the world stage at an unusual inflection point. Whereas many of the previous shifts in global power have occurred in the wake of warfare, today's shift is advancing in peacetime among the prevailing powers. Yet the Middle East is at one of its greatest periods of instability, and that has a profound effect on the world's great powers as well. While we have grown used to talking about instability in the Middle East, the Middle East of the 1970s and 1980s, which seemed so unstable at the time, in retrospect seems like a bastion of certainty. Enfeebled states, rising non-state actors, and Iran's potential re-entry into global politics all create profound uncertainty. Even so, it is hard to imagine that, in the next twenty years, China and its Asian neighbors will not be heavily reliant on the Middle East for energy. Less clear are the ways in which the United States will still feel a commitment to sustaining its global role.

China's efforts to secure its growing ties to the Middle East provide an important window into how China sees its global role. China's Middle East strategy not only provides insight into how the Chinese government views its security interests, but it also forces China to make choices about its ties to the United States and the post-World War II environment that the United States helped to construct. What is often forgotten is how many choices both China and the United States have to make about security in this part of the world, and how many of those choices have not yet been made. Which patterns of behavior change over the next decade, and how, will be among the most important indicators of Chinese intent, US intent, and the structure of great-power relations around the globe.

3

THE CHINA MODEL AND THE MIDDLE EAST

Mehran Kamrava

Developing countries are increasingly having to opt for one of two patterns of development: one advocated by the United States, known as the "Washington Consensus", and the other represented by China, generally referred to as the "Beijing Consensus" or the "China model" (*zhongguo moshi*). Given their traditions of statist activism in the economy and the development process, Middle Eastern countries almost uniformly have come closer to adopting the China model. In fact, across the world and especially in the Middle East, today's China "offers a seductive model" to states that "have not yet settled into a democratic structure."[1] This is despite the fact that in rhetoric, many have sought to identify themselves as being closer to the Washington Consensus. This inconsistency between appearance and reality suggests deeper structural incongruities in the political economies found in the Middle East and North Africa (MENA) region that undermine their ability to adopt and implement effectively China's largely successful pattern of development. Reinforced by expansive trade, commercial, and political linkages between China and the Middle East, the China model may hold great allure and appeal in the MENA region. But its transferability as a viable pattern of organizing economic and political arrangements is far from certain.

This chapter examines the applicability, or lack thereof, of the China model to the Middle East. As we shall see presently, the China model has three intertwined and mutually reinforcing ingredients. They include state capitalism, featuring state control of the economy's commanding heights alongside a vibrant market capitalism; authoritarian state mechanisms and a tightly controlled political arena; and a measure of meritocracy derived from merit-based promotions through the communist party. Two of these features, namely state capitalism and authoritarian political control, also characterize a majority of political systems in the Middle East and North Africa. At a time when the allure of the Washington Consensus has steadily declined across the Middle East because of its perceived ideological and diplomatic baggage, the appeal of the China model has inversely increased. This appeal has not, however, translated into success. Middle Eastern political systems have by and large failed in their efforts to foster rapid and extensive economic development and industrialization, especially as compared to their Latin American and East Asian counterparts.

Essentially, this chapter argues, despite its ideological appeal among most policy and many intellectual circles, and the commonality of its objectives of promoting economic growth and development by a centralized and non-democratic state, the China model has not had, and is unlikely to have, much transferability to the Middle East. The key variable is state capacity, defined broadly as the state's ability to mobilize resources in its society and economy toward its own objectives, in this case fostering economic development. The essence of the China model is developmentalism, the necessary ingredients for which are conspicuously absent in the Middle East. But an absence of ingredients and preconditions does little to lessen the model's luster and appeal. As an ideal path for organizing political economies, the allure of the China model is likely to resonate for some time to come.

More specifically, whereas the Chinese state has been able to marshal societal, economic, and political resources for purposes of national development, most states in the Middle East have failed to do so. This failure is the result of a number of overlapping, mutually reinforcing developments. These include, most importantly, the continued underdevelopment or at best uneven development of the institutions of the state; the emergence of crony capitalism within a narrow, politically connected group of economic elite actors whose primary preoccupation is safeguarding clientelist links; and the state's inability or unwillingness to articulate a clear developmental agenda.

The chapter begins with a broad examination of the context within which China-Middle East relations have unfolded over the last couple of decades. Anchored in economic and commercial concerns, the expansion of China-Middle East connections has facilitated the transmission of not just materiel but more importantly ideas, and the ideal of economic miracle specifically. This ideal has been encapsulated in an overall blueprint that combines elements of political centralization, consumerism, and nationalism for purposes of policy-making to promote economic growth and development.

After examining the contours of the China model, the chapter focuses on patterns of political and economic management in the Middle East, highlighting the essential absence of political, institutional, and economic preconditions for the replication of the China model in the region. The institutional requisites needed for the implementation of the China model are conspicuously absent in the Middle East. But as an ideal, whereby a highly centralized, authoritarian state fosters rapid economic development, the model continues to hold great appeal across the region. This appeal rests less in it being a model per se than in its representation of power. China matters in the Middle East—and elsewhere for that matter—because its model represents a guide to development, and development means power. The attraction of the China model is in its soft power, and the China model has fostered both hard power and economic development, and then brought about the popularity of the China model as a source of soft power.

As the following pages demonstrate, the very idea of a "China model" is contested both inside and outside China. However, regardless of its actual existence as a blueprint for the management of politics and economy, what China represents—a seemingly successful mixture of economic liberalization and political authoritarianism—is what the states of the Middle East aspire to. For now, the chapter concludes, most states of the Middle East lack the institutional mechanisms and resources to turn their aspirations into reality.

China and the Middle East

In some ways, the Middle East appears to pull Chinese policy-makers in different directions. On the one hand, the close connection between the two both challenges the dominance of the Western liberal order and highlights China's rise as a global power. But it also presents multiple challenges, such as the potential contagion of religious extremism and political instability. Seeing itself as a "responsible but dissatisfied developing power that seeks to reform the norms underlying the global order from within," China sees MENA as a region that is organically tied to the West.[2] It has therefore sought to avoid direct confrontation and competition with Washington in the Middle East. For the time being at least, it appears that besides pursuing economic interests, China is not prepared to take on a leading political and strategic role in the region just yet.[3] Not surprisingly, China has generally approached the MENA region with high levels of economic pragmatism, reserving its proactive involvement in geostrategic competition to developments and issues closer to home, in East and Southeast Asia.[4]

Its geostrategic apprehensions notwithstanding, recent decades have seen an exponential rise in the depth and breadth of China's relationships with and presence in the countries of the Middle East and North Africa. Some observers have gone so far as to suggest that "the entire Middle East is fast becoming a region where China's shadow of activity and influence looms large."[5] While this engagement has revolved around the five broad dimensions of energy, trade, arms sales, cultural relations, and political cooperation,[6] the economics of the relationship by far outweigh all other aspects of China's connections with the region.

The economics of China's engagement with the Middle East pivots on the twin pillars of Chinese investments: in infrastructural projects on the one hand, and China's purchase of oil and gas from Middle Eastern suppliers on the other. Energy relations in particular have been at the heart of China's relationship with, and interests in, the Middle East and an important driver of China's strategic posture toward the region.[7] In 2011, for example, China imported 51 percent of its oil needs from the Middle East.[8] This figure is expected to rise to 70 percent by 2020.[9] Similarly important and extensive are Chinese investments across the region, especially in large-scale infrastructural projects in the energy sector and in mining, railways, and construction. China's investments in the Middle East nearly doubled, from approximately $4.19 billion in 2005–6 to an estimated $8.55 billion in 2015–16, totaling more than $143 billion between 2005 and 2016.[10] The China Development Bank and the Export-Import Bank also provide low-interest loans to the countries of the Middle East and North Africa, thereby deepening China's economic engagement with the region.[11]

Driven primarily by economic interests, China's foreign policy has remained pragmatic and adaptable, enabling the country to maintain close and cordial relations with multiple and often conflicting actors, including Israel, Iran, and Saudi Arabia, especially the latter two.[12] Saudi Arabia is one of China's most important trading partners and one of its major suppliers of oil. Equally important is Iran, which is a key player in China's geopolitical interests in the region. While keen not to appear to court and further empower Iran's anti-American stance in the Middle East and beyond, China has steadily deepened its strategic and economic ties with the Islamic Republic.[13] Not surprisingly, Iran-China trade rose from $400 million in 1994 to $11 billion in 2008 and $50 billion in 2012, and it is expected to rise exponentially after the easing of international trade sanctions on Iran.[14] By 2015, China had risen to become Iran's largest trading partner, constituting the biggest foreign investor in the country and the number one purchaser of Iranian oil.[15]

For their part, many in the Middle East look to China to play a greater role in the region.[16] China's biggest asset in the Middle East, in fact, is its appeal as an alternative to the heavy-handed, and historically fraught, involvement of Europe and the US in the region.[17] How long China's appeal and soft power will last, however, is an open question. For now, largely because China does not promote a preferred normative basis for international order or domestic political and economic governance, its recent involvement in the MENA region is welcomed by many regional actors.[18] This is particularly the case with policymakers in countries such as Iran, Syria, and Iraq (as demonstrated in Chapter 7 by Joseph Sassoon), who see in China a potential strategic and diplomatic counterweight to the United States, and also those in post-2011 Egypt, who are eager to attract Chinese investments in the country's infrastructure.

China's appeal among Middle Eastern intellectual circles is more difficult to discern, though anecdotal evidence suggests that it is somewhat limited. Given East Asia's apathy toward the Middle East because of the latter's chronic political instability, economic underdevelopment, and frequent bouts of religious extremism in recent decades, so far East Asia and especially China have for the most part failed to capture the imagination of intellectuals in the Middle East.[19] Nevertheless, there have been isolated calls by a few intellectuals that "it is time for Middle Eastern and East Asian countries to develop full-spectrum relations and build the institutions that can sustain them." The academic Cemil Aydin, for example, claims that the Middle East may reap "many benefits to strengthen intellectual and political ties between the eastern and western parts of Asia, to complement the economic exchanges."[20]

The 2011 Arab uprisings added a layer of complexity to China's relationship with the Middle East. Following the uprisings, some studies went so far as to suggest that China's would be the next regime to fall as part of a wave of mass protests against authoritarian regimes.[21] While in hindsight this conclusion turned out to be wildly off the mark, the Arab Spring initially did appear to have somewhat dented the legitimacy of the China model.[22] Chinese leaders themselves greeted the Arab Spring with fear and apprehension.[23] China's official media referred to the uprisings negatively, often implying that China is not MENA and that in China the government is the solution and not the problem.[24] This apprehension was not altogether misplaced as the Arab Spring contagion did in fact inspire small and localized protests in the village of Wukan and in parts of Beijing.[25] Nevertheless, the disquiet settled down before too long and a Chinese Spring did not materialize.

The China model

The astounding transformation and growth of the Chinese economy over the past three decades has prompted observers and scholars in China and elsewhere to speculate on whether or not there is a distinctively Chinese model for the political management of the economy. This discussion has been equally robust both inside and outside China, focusing on whether or not Chinese policy-makers have indeed articulated a "model" of economic growth and political management, and if so what this model looks like, and whether or not it can be replicated elsewhere.

Within China, most scholarly discussion of the China model revolves not so much around its existence; the fact that the Chinese state has pursued a clearly identifiable path for political decision-making and the management of the economy cannot be denied. It is clear that a new model is emerging in which the state controls a partially liberalized economy and the citizens give up much of their political freedom in return for rising quality of life.[26] Much of the debate in China instead revolves around whether such a model can be sustainable in the long run.[27] There is also debate regarding the replicability of the model, with most Chinese scholars pointing to the uniqueness of the Chinese historical experience, features within Chinese culture, especially Confucianism, and institutions such as the Chinese communist party.[28] Scholarly discussions of the China model in China are often imbued with a strong sense of nationalism.[29] For their part, some Chinese dissidents view talk of a China model with skepticism, seeing it as little other than ploys by the state to legitimize the current political arrangement.[30] Interestingly, Chinese political leaders themselves tend to eschew use of the terms "China model" and "Beijing Consensus".[31]

Skepticism about the China model (or the Beijing Consensus) abounds in the US intellectual and policy-making circles as well. Scott Kennedy, for example, claims that while "interpretations of the China model vary far and wide ... none stand up well as a rigorous summary of a distinctive Chinese developmental experience."[32] In dismissing the Beijing Consensus's viability as an alternative to the Washington Consensus, Kennedy maintains that "the original conception of the [Beijing Consensus] is not up to the task of being a worthwhile competitor to the alternative model from which its name was coined" because of its "misguided and inaccurate summary of China's actual reform experience."[33] Kennedy also maintains that the various components of the Chinese state "have not acted in concert with each other" and do not pursue well-defined goals, and that China's economic performance has not been necessarily a product of the pursuit of clearly-articulated objectives.[34]

Barry Naughton similarly dismisses the term Beijing Consensus as "an oxy-moron" since, he claims, there is no consensus among Chinese economists and also because of the built-in flexibility of China's economic policies.[35] Minglu Chen and David Goodman also see "distinct limits to the conceptualization of China's development in terms of a model."[36] They see the China model as "a twenty-first century version of the East Asian developmental states," comprising the key elements of economic pragmatism and agency, developmental state behavior, and the state's control of ideas.[37] Nevertheless, Chen and Goodman do concede that regardless of its actual existence or fictive nature, there is "a fairly widespread assumption" that this is indeed a replicable model.[38]

In much of the non-Western world, in fact, the China model's combination of economic freedom and political repression offers a compelling alternative to the Washington Consensus.[39] Since the 1980s, the belief that markets rather than governments drive progress and that democracy is the optimal way of organizing society is no longer universally accepted outside the West. This trend has been strengthened especially in the 2000s, when there emerged new centers of wealth beyond the West and capitalism without democracy.[40] These new centers of wealth are giving rise to new levels of confidence in alternative models.[41] Economic autonomy from the West and the appeal of illiberal capitalism have become "dual engines for the diffusion of power away from the West" and "a force multiplier in the global rise of China."[42]

Ideas travel along the arteries of commerce and power. And, in recent years, China has emerged as "a beacon of ideas and management capitalism."[43] Conversely, in much of the world apart from the West, especially in the Middle East, the Western model of free market democracy has failed to take root.[44] One of the reasons for this failure of the Washington Consensus in non-Western lands is its emphasis on procedural interpretations of accountability, rather than viewing accountability in terms of substantive outcomes. As Francis Fukuyama reminds us, in Confucian China, historically "moral accountability was central to the functioning of the system."[45] Both before and after 1949, Confucianism served as a moral and ethical doctrine whose institutionalization in China's vast and complex bureaucracy served as a moderating force on state behavior.[46] At a time when Western-dictated structural adjustment programs result in widespread economic dislocations in much of the developing world, the appeal of an alternative economic framework that emphasizes state commitment to raising income levels and increasing consumption is hard to deny.[47]

At its core, the China model rests on the simple premise of "market authoritarianism."[48] The Chinese state has replaced ideology with economic growth, has rekindled a sense of nationalism, and has employed a fair amount of pragmatic flexibility.[49] Broadly, the China model contains a number of key components. These include a highly centralized and restrictive state that is proactively involved in the management and orchestration of a high-growth market economy. The interaction between the state and the economy, specifically state efforts aimed at fostering rapid economic growth, are formulated within a highly nationalistic context. In this context, the China model is much more nuanced and complex than a merely upgraded version of the bureaucratic authoritarianism of the 1970s.[50] The model accounts for subtle but substantive differentiations in China's economy and its political system, and the intersection between the two. Economically, there is a mixed economy, with market capitalism at the bottom, mixed state-private joint ownership in the middle, and state-owned enterprises at the top. There is a nuanced approach to political governance as well, with democracy at the bottom, experimentation in the middle, and centralized meritocracy at the top.[51] Instead of creating a host of new institutions from scratch, the Chinese leadership has worked within existing economic and political institutions in order to reform them for purposes of fostering rapid modernization and development. At the same time, the Chinese state has remained strong, pro-development, and capable of shaping national consensus, all while ensuring stability and pursuing reforms at the same time.[52]

The political components of the China model include the following: institutions of policy-making and intra-party democracy; efforts designed to make the state more accountable to an increasingly pluralistic society; constitutional reform; and reform of the communist party.[53] Insofar as constitutional reforms are concerned, there have been a number of changes to the 1982 constitution designed to improve the rights of citizens. And, in terms of reforms to the CCP itself, concerted efforts have been made to make the party less intrusive and more inclusive.[54] Accountability in the system runs upward rather than downward, directed at progressively higher echelons of the CCP rather than at a democratically empowered electorate. Nevertheless, the state does provide its citizens with much of what they want—jobs, security, rising living standards—far more effectively than most other authoritarian regimes.[55]

Critically, characterizing the Chinese state as simply oppressive is overly simplistic and inaccurate. Chinese intellectuals and policy-makers often hotly debate the transition to democracy and the compatibility of restrictive politics with open economics.[56] In fact, internal reports by the communist party in 2004 and 2007, the latter known as "Storming the Fortress," warned that unless governance was improved and corruption eradicated, the CCP ran the risk of widespread social strife and political instability.[57] These and other similar internal analyses have spurred the CCP to try to update the China model in three respects: 1) creating "national champions" so that Chinese brands can become competitive in the global market; 2) encouraging the growth of the middle class in order to spur consumption; and 3) trying to improve the quality of local governance in addition to maintaining high levels of investment in infrastructure.[58] This updating reflects the priorities of the current leadership, which, motivated by the imperative of political stability and regime continuity, sees the updating of the model as a pre-emptive move meant to meet some of the popular demands that could lead to protests.[59]

Another feature of the Chinese state that simultaneously embeds it within Chinese society and also aids in the efficacy of policy-making is the emergence of three broad, interrelated planks within it. The first plank involves democracy at the bottom, enabling the state to remain socially grounded and, as much as possible, aware of and responsive to local needs and demands. The second plank involves experimentation in the middle tiers of the state bureaucracy, whereby the central government tries to assess which policies work at the sub-central level before spreading them to the rest of the country.[60] At the very top, the third plank operates based on meritocracy.

Since the early 1990s, the Chinese communist party has steadily developed a rather sophisticated system of meritocratic recruitment and promotion within its ranks. The mechanisms for meritocratic promotion extend from leadership positions at the local county/division level (*xianchu ji*) all the way to the highest positions within the CCP.[61] While corruption and nepotism continue to be pervasive, or what the Chinese call *guanxi* (informal influence), "there are highly meritocratic features to the system, beginning with recruitment into the party and state bureaucracy and promotion within these hierarchies."[62] Meritocratic promotions, especially at the very top, have become common features of the Chinese system.

The Chinese political system, to be certain, is fundamentally authoritarian. As such, on rare occasions it provokes outbursts of political opposition by politically aggrieved actors. But these outbursts remain largely localized in scope and magnitude.

As "the world's most decentralized autocracy," the Chinese state does not provide a ready target for "mobilizing national level contention." At most, it creates "opportunities for localized, parochial forms of contention."[63] Consequently, "high profile outbreaks of protest" in China "have diffused across regions."[64] This feature endows the state with a built-in flexibility that enhances its endurance and its ability to deflect or to absorb societal pressures. Reinforced by its penchant for accountability and its emphasis on the promotion of meritorious leaders within its ranks, the Chinese state enjoys a level of stability that is the envy of authoritarian systems the world over. This stability is further strengthened by the state's successful management of the economy and its promotion of policies that foster high rates of economic growth.

Another pillar of the China model is the promotion of state capitalism. In the Chinese context this has resulted in opening doors (*kai fang*) to foreign investment, technology, and management skills. Both the flow of foreign investments and the continued economic well-being of the middle classes are ensured, among other means, through the state's continued control of the currency exchange rate and other key economic policy levers. In fact, the state retains ultimate control over the strategic sectors of the economy.[65] After nearly thirty years of *kai fang*, the Chinese economy remains only selectively open, and most strategic industries remain under government control.[66]

It is usually some of the more strategically important state-owned enterprises that are targeted for becoming "national champions." Policy-makers have emphasized economic growth as an overall national goal and political stability as a precondition for modernization.[67] The reinforcing means of a powerful developmental state and world class infrastructure are represented by the rise of a number of global cities across China.[68] Over the last thirty years, the marriage of economic and political liberalism has been replaced steadily in China by a state-sponsored and supported capitalism that confers on the state greater control domestically and more influence internationally. Private enterprise exists side by side with state ownership of strategic industries like banks, steel and aluminum plants, transport, and communication. Equally prominent are the development of large, state-owned investment funds, along with the emergence of close ties between political elites and wealthy economic actors.[69] The owners and bosses of large energy corporations and national champion companies are often closely connected with influential policy-makers and key political elites.

One view of the China model sees a centralized and decisive national leadership as both necessary and beneficial for economic growth.[70] Unlike traditional authoritarianism, however, the China model has actually produced economic growth, therefore reducing the potential for political tensions.[71] In fact, the China model has accomplished what the growth-oriented, bureaucratic-authoritarian states of the 1970s in Latin America failed to do, namely to compensate for authoritarian politics by providing economic growth and opportunities. This is largely due to the Chinese state's approach to the management of the economy. As one scholar has observed, "economic management is pragmatic ... while political management is stern but increasingly collegiate, the personality cult having been jettisoned after Mao and factions having faded together with ideology."[72]

Over the last several years, Chinese leaders have promoted efforts aimed at fostering "indigenous innovation" (*zizhu chuangxini*) in order to create champion and global brands. But so far much of this innovation, especially in the field of technology, has not had its intended success.[73] China has undertaken a sustained process of organizational innovation within a highly developed institutional context, in which institutions are modified, abandoned, or, as the need might be, strengthened. In China, institutional innovation has resulted from compromises between the desire to reward productive behavior while still maintaining control over resources. In other words, institutional innovation has resulted from political control over resources.[74] Both the mechanisms for the innovation and the outcome have been highly specific to the Chinese context; they cannot be easily replicated. However, the *process* of institutional innovation in China can indeed provide valuable lessons about the nature of institutions and the interaction between institutions and the development process.[75]

Many international admirers of the China model agree that the opening of the economy has fostered consumption, while the state remains strong enough to silence "troublemakers." This has fostered a political system that is "half liberal and international, half authoritarian and insular."[76] Old-style communist values are being replaced by a combination of nationalism and Confucianism that echo the "Asian values" espoused by leaders elsewhere in Southeast Asia.[77] In the process, class warfare has been abandoned for consumerism and a concomitant expansion of economic opportunities.[78]

Such astoundingly rapid rates of economic growth cannot help but create tectonic dislocations and tremendous unevenness. The CCP's legitimacy has necessarily come to depend on its ability to continue very high rates of economic growth.[79] But the Chinese economic miracle has generated some of the very symptoms that are endemic to neo-liberal economies, namely levels of income inequality comparable to those in the United States and the world's highest urban-rural income gap.[80] It is through fostering sustained growth and appealing to the nationalist sensibilities of the Chinese that the state seeks to maintain social cohesion in the face of great change.[81] But most observers agree that today's China is an "index of contradictions." To stay in power and to continue the course, Chinese leaders have had to become adept at bending to avoid breaking, "adapting to change and constantly adjusting to strategy to maintain the seemingly impossible balance of governing a fragmented and colossal polity."[82]

Earlier I raised the question of whether the China model is replicable. As the doctrinal underpinnings of market economics and the Washington Consensus have been tarnished, there has been a rise in the appeal of the China model or the Beijing Consensus. The global emergence of new centers of wealth is diminishing the traditional appeal of Western economic power and adversely increasing the appeal of state capitalism. Unlike the world from 1919 until the 1990s, today's China is the principal international creditor.[83] Significantly, China's loans and its infrastructural investments are unconditional.[84] Moreover, the Beijing Consensus offers alternatives to some of the core assumptions that underlie the Washington Consensus in such fundamental areas as: the ideal political economy, the types of institutions needed for managing and regulating economic and political arrangements in society, which growth models to follow, how to manage information, how to dispense with international aid, and assumptions as to whether or not each is exportable. The Washington Consensus, incidentally, assumes its global applicability; the Beijing Consensus does not.[85]

This allure has been magnified by what some have called the "China effect," when a global network of Chinese trade and economic relationships chip away at the liberal agenda of Washington and the West.[86] China's success in places like Africa has much to do with the West's failures there, where, by and large, China's approach has not been patronizing but instead respectful and free of conditions.[87]

Also adding to the appeal of the China model is its "non-ideological, pragmatic, and experimental approach to spur social stability and economic growth."[88] This appeal rests on three key developments. First, China's rapid economic development captures the imagination of policy-makers and intellectuals, and even many in the urban middle classes, across the developing world. Second, compound failures in foreign policy, economics, and politics on the part of the United States have only enhanced the seeming legitimacy of the China model. And finally, China's value-free diplomacy toward developing countries only serves to enhance its appeal compared to the seemingly patronizing tenor of Western aid donors and financial institutions.[89]

To assess the China model's relationship with or applicability to the Middle East, first it would be helpful to ascertain whether or not there is any sort of a model to patterns of political management and economic growth in the Middle East. It is to this question that the following section turns.

A Middle East model?

Given the rich diversity in the political economies, access to resources, and the institutional make-up of states across the Middle East, scholars of the region have devised different typologies for their categorizations into "most alike" clusters. The most common of these typologies have divided Middle East states into republican versus monarchical states, or resource-rich versus resource-poor states, or some combination thereof.[90] For our purposes here, I have divided the states of the Middle East into the two broad categories of authoritarian republics and monarchies.[91] While both categories are broadly authoritarian, most of the monarchies that remain in the Middle East are located in the Arabian Peninsula, tend to have much smaller populations compared to the region's other countries, and are endowed with much greater wealth derived from natural resources. This combination of massive rent revenues and smaller, more manageable populations makes these monarchies less reliant on coercion and instead more dependent on redistributive clientelism for staying in power. With clientelism systematized and permeating all aspects of political life uniformly, these states are generally perceived by their populations to be more observant of the rule of law, more effective in governance, less corrupt, and less repressive as compared to how the authoritarian republics are viewed by their populations.[92] Conversely, the authoritarian republics, which were increasingly unable from the 1970s onward to live up to their end of the ruling bargains they had imposed on their populations, are seen by their subjects as more repressive, more corrupt, less effective, and less law-abiding.[93]

These popular perceptions, of course, are not without merit, and are conditioned by actual structural characteristics inherent in these states' institutional make-up. Bereft of meaningful electoral legitimacy, authoritarian republics across the Middle East rely essentially on their coercive apparatus to stay in power, whether in the form of direct military rule (as in Sisi's Egypt) or, more commonly, on the intelligence machinery to entice fear and enforce political compliance. At the apex of such systems is usually a highly centralized, insular executive, surrounded by coteries of politically dependent enforcers and crony capitalists. The bureaucracy over which they preside, meanwhile, is seldom efficient or even effective, a source not so much for implementing the state's developmental agendas but more for secure, and politically dependent, employment for the middle classes. In addition to pervasive corruption and nepotism across the bureaucracy, state agencies often suffer from structural incoherence, thus further undermining the effective formulation and implementation of state policies.[94] Inefficient and ineffective though it may be, the state still retains unchallenged control over the commanding heights of the economy, further choking off developmental possibilities.

Reinforced by structural weaknesses of civil society, these systems remain robustly authoritarian and unchallenged from within, so long as their fiscal health and international support remain uninterrupted.[95] The strength of the coercive apparatus of the state is further reinforced by the pervasiveness of extensive patrimonial linkages between its various institutions, especially among the armed forces and the other organs, further enmeshing them into each other.[96] Privatization of state assets provides Middle Eastern rulers with additional sources of patronage.[97] As Eva Bellin has observed, where patrimonial institutions are wedded to coercive capacity, authoritarianism is likely to endure.[98] As the 2011 uprisings were at their zenith and it appeared as if the tentacles of authoritarianism in the Middle East might be crumbling, Bellin reaffirmed her earlier conclusion that "the component of the coercive apparatus is pivotal to determining the durability of authoritarian regimes in the Arab world (and beyond)."[99]

Critically, political parties, especially ones with the robust procedures and extensive bureaucracy of the CCP, simply do not exist in the Middle East. And if they do, they are either bureaucratic appendages of the state (the Ba'ath in Syria and Iraq, the National Liberation Front in Algeria, the National

Democratic Party in Egypt), or exist in the form of illegal or at best semi-legal entities under state surveillance and are subject to its harassment (the Egyptian Muslim Brotherhood being a prime example). Whatever their status, political parties in the Middle East have failed to function as meaningful forums for recruiting and promoting qualified cadres of policy-makers and state agents, mediating elite disputes, and preventing defection to the opposition.[100] This absence of meaningful political parties, therefore, has not only seriously impeded the emergence of elite consensus and cohesion but has further reinforced the insularity and inefficacy of the ruling inner circle.

By the time the 2011 uprisings engulfed much of North Africa and the Middle East, hybrid forms of authoritarian systems had mushroomed all over the region.[101] In MENA, single-party organizational structures and patronage-based economic liberalization had ushered in what one scholar labeled as "new authoritarianism."[102] But even these newer varieties of authoritarianism could not mask the inherent fragility of many of these systems, a number of which succumbed to mass uprisings in what has become known as the Arab Spring. The uprisings wrought havoc across the region. So far, however, with the possible exception of Tunisia, they have failed to effect a fundamental alteration of the nature of state-society relations in the Middle East.[103] As if the forces of institutional resilience are far too powerful to be overthrown and reconstituted anew, older patterns of political and economic management are re-emerging throughout the region.

It should come as no surprise that these states have been consistently unable to meet their own developmental goals. These "patron states" are at once providers and entrepreneurs, propelled to such a position by "assuming greater economic initiative and by acts of compulsion" on the one hand, and by resorting to mass mobilization and the incorporation of the popular classes into their orbit on the other.[104] But the patron state has failed; it is rotting in a vicious cycle in which it is unable to generate sufficient funds for its ambitious developmental objectives, and is also unable to foster greater productivity due to a lack of sufficient funds. Before long, as early as the 1970s, even the populist republics could not meet their redistributive commitments.[105]

To compensate, many states launched ambitious liberalization campaigns beginning in the 1970s and the 1980s, selling off state assets to private concerns and trying to attract foreign investments under the rubric of *infitah* (open door) policies. But the break with socialism was at best partial and half-hearted.[106] In states where there existed a politically connected and protected economic elite, as was the case in Iraq and Saudi Arabia, for example, they reaped considerable benefits from the wave of economic liberalization and the sales of state assets that occurred in the 1980s.[107] Continued fiscal crises and economic difficulties into the 1990s prompted many states to engage in further rent-seeking behavior—through, for example, the sale of licenses for mobile-phone networks—further undermining potential for economic growth and development. Market reform and privatization also generated new forms of rent, further encouraging patronage and clientelist practices. Patronage politics and crony capitalism thus became pervasive and "a central feature of politics" across the Middle East.[108] Steffen Hertog has pointed to the emergence of what he calls "segmented clientelism," in which clientelism characterizes "unequal, exclusive, diffuse, and relatively stable relationships of exchange within and around the state apparatus."[109] Although Hertog's analysis focuses on Saudi Arabia, his observations apply to most other regional political economies as well. According to Hertog, clientelist relationships are segmented in that they exist in parallel and separate institutions throughout the system that are, at best, linked together through crosscutting, small-scale networks. What ultimately results is a system whose economic performance is somewhat compromised.

What does the foregoing analysis of patterns of political and economic management in the Middle East tell us about the applicability of the China model to the region? What are some of the key elements that the two overall patterns—if not necessarily "models"—have in common, or in which they fundamentally differ? In the Chinese case, the state has been able to mount policies that have successfully fostered high rates of economic growth and development. Whereas the Chinese state has been a "developmental" one, the states of the Middle East have been singular failures insofar as meaningful development is concerned. The Middle East has lacked the China model's most crucial element, namely developmentalism.

Developmentalism

The critical difference between the Chinese state and the states found in the Middle East is the capacity of state institutions to devise and implement developmental goals and agendas. In this respect, China shares a number of characteristics with some of the other core countries of East Asia, especially Japan and South Korea. All three states have had long and relatively continuous traditions of high quality, centralized bureaucratic states. These states have been able to consolidate uniform national identities among ethnically homogenous populations before those societies had a chance to develop countervailing institutions of law and accountability that could check and balance the powers of the state.[110] Historically, the evolution of all of these states, the Chinese included, was interrupted with the West's insertion of itself into East Asia. Nevertheless, despite being "undermined, altered, and replaced" in their encounter and confrontation with the West, a "powerful and highly institutionalized executive branch re-emerged" in all of them in the second half of the twentieth century.[111] Significantly, while East Asian states were able to retain much of their capacity, their societies lacked a coherent and well-organized social group that could effectively resist state power, mount legitimate protests against political rule, and engage in adversarial politics. These comparatively high levels of capacity enabled the East Asian states to institute industrial policies that successfully promoted economic development. Not surprisingly, it was in East Asia rather than in other parts of the world where a cluster of successful authoritarian modernizers emerged.[112]

This pattern of state formation was not replicated in the Middle East. Throughout the Middle East and North Africa, state formation occurred under the auspices and in conjunction with the popular mobilization of highly charged groups of political aspirants. The fledgling states that were born across the region in the 1950s and the 1960s had no option but to cater to the demands of the popular classes. An implicit bargain between the state and society emerged in which the state demanded political compliance in return for the delivery of state services such as national defense and security, social services, and economic growth. In the process, rational economic policy-making and developmental goals often fell victim to the needs of continued popular mobilization, concessions to allies, and the necessity to placate the middle classes with immediate economic gratification through shortcuts such as subsidized imports and innovative forms of rent. Seldom did these bargains hold on their own, thus requiring the state to resort to systemic use of coercion as an integral component of rule.

When state formation occurs simultaneously with the incorporation of the popular classes, economic outcomes are usually less than positive. When state-building precedes the political incorporation of popular classes, the state has a relatively freer hand and can perform better economically.[113] In the Middle East, in order to hold on to power, states frequently had to incorporate the popular classes into their governing apparatus, either through populist gimmicks, or clientelist networks, or both. This undermined their ability to pursue developmental goals. In East Asia, including China, the state consolidated itself first and then sought to incorporate the popular classes into its orbit through—rather than simultaneously with—the pursuit of developmental goals.

In addition to diverging patterns of state formation, a number of other factors specific to the Chinese and Middle Eastern states are also important in terms of explaining different developmental outcomes. In his analysis of the success of the Chinese model, Francis Fukuyama looks at three measures for the analysis of China's authoritarian government: institutionalization, recruitment, and responsiveness.[114] As the earlier analysis of the Middle Eastern states' management of the economy demonstrated, none of these three ingredients feature prominently in the conduct or make-up of MENA states. If we accept Samuel Huntington's definition of institutions as "stable, valued, recurring patterns of behavior," then the Chinese state is not only highly institutionalized but is also "far more rule-bound" than many of the authoritarian states of the Middle East, including those of Zein Al-Abidene Ben Ali in Tunisia and Hosni Mubarak in Egypt.[115] China's policy-makers have also shown "remarkable competence" in the management of macroeconomic policy, and, especially compared to their counterparts in the United States and Europe, "can make large, complex decisions quickly."[116]

Another critical difference appears to be the overall acceptability of the state's developmental agenda among the urban middle classes in China and the absence of such an acceptance in the Middle East. This is not to imply that the Chinese state in general and the China model in particular enjoy high levels of legitimacy among the country's citizens. As we saw earlier, when the opportunity has presented itself, there have been "parochial forms of contention" in China.[117] And, by some accounts, the Arab Spring somewhat dented the legitimacy of the China model inside China itself.[118] But the same level of system-wide resentment and repulsion that drove throngs of Middle Easterners to city squares to overthrow their rulers in 2011 does not appear to be present in China. On the contrary, in fact, there appears to be general buy-in from urban Chinese regarding the state's goals of spreading consumerism, raising living standards, and fostering economic development. The middle classes, after all, do not necessarily support democracy in principle. They are mostly self-interested and are motivated by the protection of their property and position against the redistributive demands of the state. They therefore are inclined to support an authoritarian state that protects and promotes their interests.[119]

There are, nevertheless, two cases in the Middle East in which the China model has either been openly discussed as a viable developmental option or, more substantively, has come close to being followed. The two cases are Iran and the GCC states respectively, the former having discussed the China model and the latter actually coming close to implementing it. As mentioned earlier, the small oil monarchies of the Persian Gulf region tend to have highly centralized leaderships, inordinate resources, and comparatively small demographies. These states have created and nurtured a powerful entrepreneurial class, one whose fortunes are tied directly to those of the state and its massive investments in infrastructure and its proactive courting of investments from aboard. Giacomo Luciani has called this "the Gulf Consensus," comprising "an original blend of openness in areas where other countries are frequently closed (e.g., capital movements but also controlled labor inflow) and protectionism where others are frequently open (e.g., the treatment of foreign direct investors)."[120] The results—particularly for the cases of Qatar, the United Arab Emirates, and Kuwait—have been higher levels of state capacity and impressive levels of infrastructural growth.

If there is a Gulf model, it depends almost entirely on unearned income from rent. This begs the question of how much state capacity will be left when and if rent sources dry up. For now at least, flushed with rent revenues, these small states can act as if they are "developmental."

In Iran, meanwhile, the idea of the China model was introduced by the more conservative factions within the Islamic Republic state, who assumed that a combination of economic growth, jobs, consumerism, and limited social freedom would be enough to entice Iranians to give up demands for political pluralism and a loosening of restrictions on political space.[121] The state's so-called "hardliners" see the China model as a means to forestall reforms, and to engage in redistributive and patronage politics by using oil wealth strategically, doling out subsidies to the population, and opening up the private sector in a very limited way.[122] These regime actors prefer not so much economic reform but a form of crony capitalism that spends state resources on the political patronage of key constituents, including the secret services. This model closely reflects similar patterns in places such as Saudi Arabia, Egypt, and Syria.[123] More pragmatist actors within the Iranian state similarly view the China model as a useful safety valve, but they also envision more opportunities for the private sector as spurred by more extensive foreign investments.[124]

Slogans and political maneuvers aside—and of these the Iranian polity features plenty—profound structural shortcomings in the Iranian economy are likely to impede the ability of the country's leaders to implement the China model even if they had the political will to do so.[125] Cut off from the rest of the world for nearly a decade because of crippling international sanctions, Iran's market economy remains underdeveloped and state-dependent. The country's business sector often features crony capitalism, government-linked and government-owned businesses, insider dealings, and predatory practices meant to crush large competitors.[126] Additionally, the country's fractious leadership appears to lack the political wherewithal to emulate the China model. State bureaucracy is used as a patronage network instead of a collection of technocratic agencies, fostering mass, system-wide inefficiencies in the public sector. And Iran's confrontation with the United States has cost it both economic sanctions as well as friends and allies abroad.[127] One observer has emphatically noted that "the China model will fail in Iran."[128]

For Iran, a more modest version of the China model, what Afshin Molavi calls "China model lite," might work well as a sort of crisis management strategy to get over bumpy periods. The country's political hardliners, however, tend to understand and embrace the model's repressive impulses more readily than its reformist aspects.[129] But even then, as Molavi notes, it is not clear whether the politically savvy Iranians will "accept the crude authoritarian bargain of the China model."[130]

To sum up, the China model does not appear to have either replicability or applicability to much of the Middle East. As a pattern of political and economic management, it is "highly contingent upon the situation it is in, certainly not an all-conquering winning strategy."[131] As such, it is "unlikely to ever become a serious alternative ... in regions outside East Asia," because it is culturally specific and applies only readily to states that are "already within the Chinese cultural zone."[132] The most important benefit of the China model to developing countries, including those in the Middle East, may lie not so much in its wholesale adoption and replicability, but in "imitating some of the institutional entrepreneurship that underpins the Chinese transition process."[133] For now, oil states such as Iran and Saudi Arabia are "developmental dead ends."[134]

For economies like those of Iran, Egypt, Algeria, and even in the GCC, successfully adapting to the China model would require large infusions of foreign investment into the economy.[135] But even more important is the development of viable institutions for the recruitment and promotion of qualified policy-makers, the establishment of system-wide mechanisms for policy formulation and innovation, and agile yet accountable leadership. In a number of Middle East countries, the Arab Spring overthrew unresponsive, unaccountable regimes while putting many others on notice. But so far the region-wide response has been authoritarian retrenchment and counter-revolution, rather than greater responsiveness, accountability, or developmentalism. Thus, for the time being, the future of the China model in the Middle East appears bleak.

Conclusion

What is certain is that the future of the China model itself is far from certain. In some ways, China faces many of the same problems that the Arab Spring countries did before the uprisings erupted: youth unemployment, underemployment, and rises in income inequality being the most notable ones.[136] And, similar to pre-uprising Egypt and Tunisia, for example, there are also high levels of corruption and "decentralized predation" among state agents in China.[137] The model itself is in some respects problematic. It "lacks moral appeal" and is "guided entirely by pragmatism"; it has not been effective in dealing with many dimensions of human development; and it has only been around for a relatively short period and so has yet to prove its resilience.[138] But by themselves these cracks in the veneer of the China model are unlikely to lessen its luster and its appeal to aspiring developmental states in the foreseeable future. The essential question of the twenty-first century is whether it will be an American or a Chinese century. It is in this century when China's "story," the most potent source of soft power, confronts that of the West.[139] Daniel Bell put it succinctly: "now the world flirts with another shift in philosophy and the rules of global commerce."[140] And it is here, in its appeal and allure, where the enduring appeal of the China model, regardless of its applicability to borders far and near, resides.

Despite efforts at emulating China's success, "there is little chance that much of the world will look like today's China 50 years down the road."[141] But China's primary source of power is more ideational than anything else. More specifically, China is exporting the idea of "market authoritarianism," whose appeal rests largely in its simplicity, as well as its challenge to the basic tenets of the Washington Consensus.[142] As a region where China has extensive economic interests, and as the region within which the liberal democratic model is seriously challenged, the Middle East can potentially emerge as a future testing ground for China's global weight and influence.[143] Be that as it may, it is more the idea of the China model and the replication of its economic miracle that is likely to hold the imagination of future generations of Middle Easterners.

PART II

CASE STUDIES

4

CHINA'S MILITARY RELATIONS WITH THE MIDDLE EAST

Degang Sun[1]

China basically perceives the Middle East as a "market". Its military force has therefore kept a low profile in the Middle East to safeguard its geo-economic interests, such as energy, investments, and trade; and such a military tactic is the outcome of its development-oriented geo-economic strategy. So far, China does not need hard military bases in the Middle East so as to influence local governments. Bilateral economic relations and military dependencies provide a channel of influence more powerful than hard military bases. The forms of China's military ties with the Middle East include long-term and ad hoc military presence. The former includes the Chinese naval fleet in Somali waters, the logistical site of Djibouti, and peacekeeping forces in the Middle East. The latter includes military exchanges and arms sales, the deployment of security contractors, joint military rehearsals, evacuating overseas nationals, and participating in other UN Security Council missions temporarily aimed at protecting Beijing's practical interests. Such a soft military presence is unlikely to be transformed into hard military bases in the foreseeable future, although China has already built a logistical site in Djibouti in 2017.

At the beginning of its reform and opening-up policy in the late 1970s, China identified itself as a "bystander" and "free rider" in the Middle East, and China's Middle East policy was characterized by "business first" tactics of "reaping economic benefits while shelving political entanglement."[2] Since the outbreak of the global financial crisis in 2008, however, China's interaction with the Middle East has become more intensive. In 2014, for instance, China was the largest trading partner of the Arab League and Iran, and the major economic partner of Turkey and Israel as well. Beijing's increasingly major economic presence in the Middle East has exerted a far-reaching effect on its traditional diplomatic policies, represented by the "Four Nos": non-interference in others' internal affairs, non-alignment, no political conditions attached, and no foreign military bases abroad. As Andrew Scobell explains, the Chinese prefer low-cost security arrangements with surrounding states, as alliances and other forms of partnership do not work in China's favor. China's military footprint in the Middle East, albeit relatively weak compared with its economic presence, seems set to become more tangible in the years to come.

The current research on China's military relations with the Middle East is sparse. The first school, represented by foreign scholars, perceives China's soft military footprint in the region as being the so-called "string of pearls," describing China's military footprint in the Middle East as the natural extension of its military presence in Thailand (Songkhla), Myanmar (Port Sittwe), Pakistan (Gwadar Port), Bangladesh (Chittagong), Sri Lanka (Hambantota), Maldives (Gan Island), Seychelles (Mahe Island), Republic of Sudan (Port Sudan), and Djibouti (Port Djibouti): a military string stretching from the South China Sea to the Red Sea.[3] These scholars stress that China's initiative of the "Maritime Silk Road in the 21st Century," raised by Chinese President Xi Jinping in Indonesia in October 2013, is by nature a snake-shaped military "string of pearls" in the name of economic and commercial exchanges.[4] As Daniel J. Kostecka puts it, with China's expanding economic and political interests, Beijing is increasingly flexible in its overseas military deployment, such as dispatching convoy fleets to combat Somali pirates.[5]

The second school, mostly Chinese scholars, probes the legitimacy of China's military presence in the Middle East. Some researchers, particularly Chinese right-wing scholars, argue that Japan opened its first overseas military base in Djibouti with the pretext of anti-piracy in 2011; India opened its first overseas military base in Tajikistan as early as 2003; and therefore China should not "bind its own hands" or waste its precious time building overseas military bases to protect its legitimate overseas interests.[6] Since the outbreak of the Libyan civil war in 2011, China took great pains to withdraw thousands of its overseas nationals; and when the Malaysia Airlines Flight 370 went missing in 2014, China sent out military forces from its home ports to search for the missing airplane and passengers. Due to its lack of military forces deployed abroad, China had to rely on its military might at home in such a case of emergency. Given the vicissitudes of the Middle East situation, China's overseas interests are vulnerable, and it has an innate duty to protect its legitimate interests by all means, including military means.[7] Therefore, this school argues that since Beijing's overseas interests are expanding, its traditional diplomatic principles such as no foreign military bases can be superseded.

The third school, dominated by Chinese scholars and military experts, investigates the feasibility of China building overseas military bases in the new era. Some scholars highlight the urgency for the People's Liberation Army (PLA) to go global, while Zhang Deshun, the Deputy Commander of the PLA Navy, suggests that Chinese and American troops are totally different in essence, and the former does not need overseas military bases because China does not seek hegemony.[8] Professor Li Guoqiang of the Air Force Command College stresses that there is little possibility for China to build overseas military bases because China is an inward-looking and strategically defensive power. Geographically and politically, China's establishment of overseas military bases is contrary to its national conditions of being a socialist and developing country.[9]

The above research findings touch upon quite an interesting and thought-provoking question, i.e. whether or not China should or will establish military bases abroad,[10] but they lack any in-depth analysis on the different forms of China's existing soft military footprint in the Middle East since the outbreak of the global financial crisis in 2008. Unlike the US, French, British, and Russian military bases in the region, China's military footprint is non-traditional: it is soft and less visible; it does not aim to seek long-term geopolitical rivalry with other powers, but to protect its practical commercial interests and to project a positive image to the world.

Great powers' hard military bases versus China's soft military footprint in the Middle East

Foreign military presence can include either hard military bases or soft military footprints. The former refers to the existence of overseas military powers as the international commons, mandated territories, and territories of other countries, reserving the right to undertake specific military activities. The key elements are as follows. First, the owner of the military bases has the right to free access to their bases; this is normally based on status of force agreements. Second, the military bases are built on other countries' territory. Third, the military bases mainly have military objectives of combating, detecting, deterring, commanding, and collecting intelligence, rather than civil objectives. Fourth, the military bases enhance the containment and deterrence capabilities of the user nation. However, they may incur friction between the user and host nations, and also the economic cost of renting the base.

The Middle East hosts many foreign military bases. At present, the United States has deployed approximately 50,000 personnel and dozens of military bases in the Gulf Cooperation Council member states of Kuwait, Qatar, Bahrain, the United Arab Emirates (UAE), and Oman, as well as Turkey, Djibouti, and Afghanistan; the US military influence is unparalleled, dominating other foreign powers in the area. Britain deploys about 3,000 personnel in Cyprus and Bahrain, and France deploys about 3,000 troops in UAE and Djibouti, both powers owning several military bases; their influence ranks at secondary level. Russia and Japan each deploy about 200–1,000 personnel in Syria and Djibouti, and each has one military base in the host countries; Russia and Japan rank third in military influence. China, like India and South Korea, has not yet established military bases in the Middle East, but it has sent out convoy fleets, peacekeeping forces, and has left a military presence in the Middle East as well as in the waters off Somalia; these three countries rank fourth in influence.

When examining the West's strategic position in the Middle East, scholars may start from a geopolitical point of view. The definition of their national interests is usually considered to derive from the perception of their national security threat, especially in the forms of anti-terrorism, non-proliferation of weapons of mass destruction, promoting democracy, defending allies and, preventing other great powers from seeking political and military dominance in the Middle East. Such traditional powers are usually concerned more about the regional military balance and their relative position in the region, instead of starting from a pragmatic strategy of safeguarding their economic, trade, and energy interests, which are perceived as a secondary focus.

With the rise of China's comprehensive national strength, China's frontiers are expanding with twofold implications: one is the natural frontier of its 9.6 million sq km territory and sovereignty; the other is the boundary of its overseas interests. China's military relations with the Middle East countries

Table 4.1: Foreign powers' military presence in the Middle East: a comparison

User nations	Host nations	Number of troops	Main military bases
USA	Turkey	1,780	Incirlik AB; Izmir
USA	Kuwait	14,000	Camp Buehring; Camp Arifjan; Ali Al Salem
USA	Qatar	10,000	Al-Saliyah; al-Udeid; Umm Said
USA	Bahrain	1,496	Sheikh Isa; Port Bahrain
USA	UAE	546	Port Jabel Ali; Fujayrah
USA	Oman	200	Seeb; Al Thumrait
USA	Afghanistan[11]	11,000	Bagram; Shindand
USA	Djibouti	2,000–3,000	Camp Lemonier; Ambouli
UK	Cyprus	3,000	Akrotiri and Dikelya
UK	Bahrain	Unknown	Bahrain
France	UAE	500	Zayed; Al-Dhafra
France	Djibouti	2,900	Camp Lemonier; Arta
Russia	Syria	500	Tartus
Japan	Djibouti	180	Port Djibouti, Ambouli International Airport
China	Djibouti	Soft military footprint	The supporting site of Djibouti; peacekeeping forces; security contractors; naval convoy fleets; military training sites; joint military rehearsals; arms sales

Source: Donna Cassata, "US Plans Significant Military footprints in Kuwait," *Times of Israel*, 19 June 2012; Kenneth Katzman, "Oman: Reform, Security, and U.S. Policy," Congressional Research Service, 29 June 2009, p. 9, http://fas.org/sgp/crs/mideast/RS21534.pdf, accessed 5 July 2015; US Department of Defense, *Report on Progress Toward Security and Stability in Afghanistan*, Report to Congress (November 2013), pp. 11–13, www.defense.gov/pubs/October_1230_Report_Master_Nov7.pdf, accessed 5 July 2015; Joint Force Command, *British Forces Cyprus Pre-arrivals Guide* (London: Military of Defence, 2011), https://www.gov.uk/government/uploads/system/uploads/attachment_data/file/319700/BFC_PRE_ARRIVALS_GUIDE_V9_6_NOV_2013.pdf; Andrew E. Kramer, "Russian War Vessels Said to be Going to Naval Base in Syria," *New York Times*, 18 June 2012; Alex Martin, "First Overseas Military Base since WWII to Open in Djibouti," *Japanese Times*, 2 July 2011.

constitute an important way of protecting Beijing's practical commercial interests and providing public goods for the international community at large. In the Middle East, for instance, China's major interest is oil: Saudi Arabia, Iran, Oman, Iraq, Kuwait, and Sudan are major oil exporters to China, according to the International Energy Agency (IEA).

The main differences between the soft military footprint and the hard military bases could be listed as below. First, as to the former, the user country does not have the extra-territoriality of there being "a state within a state" or "special military zone."[12] Second, the user nation does not seek institutionalized foreign military arrangements. Third, the overseas military forces have to carry out civil as well as military missions, such as evacuation of nationals, humanitarian relief, search and rescue, protecting expatriates, escorting, logistics supply, peacekeeping, conflict prevention and so on, meaning the "soft use of hard power." Fourth, the soft military footprint is not for geopolitical rivalry, but for mission-oriented tasks; its objective is problem resolution, and results in both more flexibility and lower cost.

The necessity of China's soft military footprint overseas could be further expanded on three levels: the political dimension, the interest dimension, and the technical dimension.

The political dimension is about the diplomatic principle of China's soft military footprint overseas. A soft military footprint is less aggressive than hard military bases. Beijing is able to adhere to the principles of traditional diplomacy and peace, namely non-alignment, non-interference in other countries' internal affairs, non-violation of others' sovereignty, no sphere of influence, and no hegemony or power politics. Therefore, a soft military footprint is compatible with traditional Chinese diplomatic principles. In December 2015, China confirmed that it would build its first overseas logistic base in Djibouti, which is actually a supportive site for its convoy fleets in Somali waters, not intending geopolitical rivalry with the Western powers. That is why US Army General David Rodriguez, the head of the US Africa Command, did not perceive such a support site as a threat.[13]

The interest dimension is about China's need to maintain a soft military footprint to protect its overseas interests. Projects such as the Gwadar seaport in Pakistan under construction by China, the China-Myanmar energy transport lines, the high-speed railway construction projects between China and its neighbors, China's increasing energy projects overseas, etc., require necessary military forces to ensure their operational security. In the volatile Middle East, particularly in Iraq, Yemen, Afghanistan, Libya, Egypt, Somalia, Sudan, and South Sudan, China's overseas investment projects are particularly fragile. In 2013, Sino-Arab trade reached a new high of US$ 240 billion, so China's efforts to protect its energy, investment, and trade interests in the region are quite formidable. On 26 July 2015, China was greatly shocked by the suicide attack on Jazeera Palace Hotel in Mogadishu, which killed more than a dozen people and injured others. In the Chinese embassy, a Chinese security guard was killed and three embassy staff wounded.[14]

The technical dimension is about the feasibility of building a soft military presence: where, for what purpose, and in what forms the military force is deployed. A soft military footprint is the functional extension of the user nation's domestic military bases. In terms of China's soft military footprint in the Middle East, it has to solve the problem of where to station troops, and how to provide logistical supplies to the military personnel in the region, etc.

China justifies its incremental deployment of a soft military presence abroad with the excuse of "meeting its domestic need." Since the end of the Cold War, the Chinese government continues to make "economic construction their priority"; such a development strategy indicates that China strives to impress others that its peaceful rise will not challenge the existing international power structure, relying on the contemporary international order to achieve national rejuvenation instead of challenging the US predominance in the world. Through the deployment of soft military forces, China wants to confirm to the international community that it has no "foreign military bases," and that China's diplomatic principles are against the "sphere of influence" mentality; but Chinese diplomatic principles do not ban the deployment of China's soft military footprint when their interests are under threat. China's soft military presence is the reflection of its power projection within its surrounding areas, Beijing claims. Also the military forces serve the purposes of international peacekeeping, rescuing, combating piracy, safeguarding the security of marine channels, maintaining maritime rights and shouldering other military and civilian missions: for the public good.

Nowadays, the conditions for China to establish a soft military footprint in the Middle East are increasingly mature. First, now that the Liaoning aircraft carrier has been built and put into use, China's military power projection can not only reach the South China Sea and the western Pacific, but also the Indian Ocean. It is able to provide technical support for China to achieve flexible functionality and to recharge its docking between domestic bases and its military footprint in the Middle East.

Second, Beijing highlights its difference from Western colonial powers by claiming that modern China was, like its Middle East counterparts, a victim of Western colonial rule and suppression. The Soviet Union, Germany, Japan, the United States, and Britain all deployed military bases in China during the twentieth century. China seeks an indirect way to affect the military situation in the Middle East, without active participation. Under the banner of peace and development, the non-military functions of the Navy forces continue to expand. Naval diplomacy, combating piracy, maritime implementations, disaster relief, and ocean rescue have all become crucial functions of the PLA Navy. Historically, the journey of Zheng He's peace voyages overseas used several logistical bases on the way, which did not stop the journey from being a peaceful one.[15] That being said, China's military presence along the Maritime Silk Road does raise grave concerns not only for Western powers, but also for Japan and India.

Third, military exchange continues to expand between China and Thailand, Myanmar, Cambodia, Pakistan, Maldives, Sudan, Seychelles, Saudi Arabia, Iran, Israel, Turkey, and other countries. It has laid the foundation for a future establishment of military presence in the western Indian Ocean and the Persian Gulf.

Fourth, since the Chinese convoy fleet was dispatched to Somali waters in 2008, China has been launching a series of military diplomacy missions to neighboring countries and regions, such as joint anti-piracy exercises and warship visits. It has also built interim technical stops in Port Djibouti, Sultan Qaboos in Oman, Jeddah in Saudi Arabia, and Port Sudan. This creates the conditions for establishing further Chinese military footprints overseas.[16]

Fifth, currently both established and emerging powers have built military bases overseas, including Japan's anti-piracy base in Djibouti. China conforms to international law in maintaining a soft military footprint to safeguard its legitimate rights and interests in the Middle East.

Therefore, as a developing country with a chief concern for expanding domestic economic growth, China regards its primary objective as being to meet domestic demand. The Chinese consider that solving domestic problems is more urgent, so that they can have an upper hand in the world economic competition, which is a so-called "soft control." In this way, they could erase the conflict within their domestic economy and society that is caused by over-population and scarcity of resources. The implementation of geo-economy-oriented strategy mainly relies on the strength of the Chinese government to expand its overseas investment and foster energy and trade cooperation. By increasing Chinese people's well-being and developing the domestic economy, they hope to maintain stability and reshape the world economic order. The geo-economy-oriented countries take their own interests as the main pursuit, and their overseas interests are essentially practical: a soft military footprint meets their needs.

Since the end of the Cold War, the overseas trade routes of China have seldom been threatened directly. Although China's sea power is facing challenges in the west Pacific, this has never stopped China from expanding its interests globally. The geo-economy-oriented strategy has always been the cornerstone of China's diplomacy. In 2013, the "21st-Century Maritime Silk Road" invented by President Xi became the priority from the logic of geo-economic development. In June 2014, at the sixth ministerial conference of Chinese-Arab cooperation, Chairman Xi highlighted the "1+2+3" cooperation pattern between China and the twenty-two Arab states: China proposed to take energy cooperation as the principal axis, infrastructure construction and trade investment as two wings, nuclear power, the aerospace satellite and new energy areas as breakthroughs, all of which are based on the geo-economic strategy.[17] China's military presence is prepared to protect such commercial interests in the Middle East.

China's long-term soft military presence in the Middle East

In 2015, China issued its first National Military Strategy (white paper), which defined the major missions of its troops: to tackle all kinds of contingencies and military threats, and to defend national territorial integrity, space, and maritime sovereignty; resolutely to defend national reunification; to maintain China's new forms of security and interests and safety of overseas interests; to keep strategic deterrence and prepare for nuclear counterstrike; to participate in regional and international security cooperation for regional and world peace; to strengthen anti-penetration, anti-secession and anti-terror struggles; to safeguard national political security and social stability; to participate in disaster relief; to safeguard the rights and interests of Chinese people; to support national economic and social development.[18]

The Chinese military footprint in the Middle East can be classified in two categories: the long-term and the ad hoc military deployment. The former seeks relatively stable and long-term objectives, such as counter-piracy endeavors, the use of logistical military bases, and UN peacekeeping operations in the Middle East; while the latter aims to pursue relatively short-term and dynamic objectives. These two forms of military deployments aim to protect Beijing's commercial rather than geopolitical interests, as mentioned above.

At present, the soft military footprint is an important part of Chinese military diplomacy. The main forms are listed below.

First, the Chinese convoy fleet in the Gulf of Aden. According to the International Cooperation Department of the Ministry of Transportation, in October 2008 China's Ministry of Transportation lobbied the Foreign Ministry, requesting the Chinese government to dispatch convoy fleets to protect commercial vessels belonging to China and other countries as they passed through areas adjacent to Somali waters. By analyzing the overall situation at home and abroad, China's Foreign Ministry and Ministry of Defense jointly submitted a scenario to the central government, facilitating Chinese deployment of convoy fleets near the Gulf of Aden.[19]

In the early twenty-first century, a dozen ports in Pakistan, Singapore, Oman, Yemen, Djibouti, Sri Lanka, Bangladesh, the Seychelles, and Tanzania were visited by the PLA Navy, in order for Beijing to select "places" or "far ocean footholds" to be used as informal bases to support forces deployed for non-traditional security missions like the counter-piracy patrols in the Gulf of Aden.[20] From 2009 to 2015, China dispatched twenty convoy fleets to the Gulf of Aden and Somali waters at large. They visited Port Djibouti, Mombasa in Kenya, Port Sultan, Qaboos in Oman, Jeddah in Saudi Arabia, Abbas in Iran, Karachi in Pakistan and other seaports near the Red Sea and the western Indian Ocean, as part of China's military diplomacy.

For a long time, the US has been concerned about Beijing's possible ambition to grab and even monopolize Middle East oil; China's congenial relations with all Middle East oil exporters including Iran has enhanced its advantage in rivalry with the US.[21] China's convoy fleets in Somali waters are perceived as their exploration of a foreign military presence in the near future. Nevertheless, China so far is reluctant to build a permanent hard military base in the Middle East. The floating convoy fleets have offered a golden opportunity for China to interact with other great powers. According to China's 2013 Defense White Paper, released in December 2012, China had dispatched 34 convoy fleets, 28 helicopters, 910 special forces, and had completed 532 convoy missions for 4,984 commercial vessels in four years, including 1,510 vessels from Mainland China, 74 from Taiwan, and one ship from Macao; they rescued two Chinese commercial vessels under pirate attacks, and 22 vessels chased by pirates.[22] With intensive multilateral cooperation and improvement of international regimes, China is bound to expand its area of military presence.

Second, we shall deal with the Chinese Navy's logistical bases in the Middle East. In March 2014, one of China's nuclear submarines entered the Indian

Table 4.2: China's convoy fleets dispatched to the Gulf of Aden, 2008–16

Missions	Main Fleet A	Main Fleet B	Comprehensive supply fleet	Affiliations	Starting date of missions
1	Wuhan 169	Haikou 171	Weishanhu 887	South China Sea Fleet	26 December 2008
2	Shenzhen 167	Huangshan 570	Weishanhu 887	South China Sea Fleet	2 April 2009
3	Zhoushan 529	Xuzhou 530	Qiandaohu 886	East China Sea Fleet	16 July 2009
4	Ma'anshan 525	Wenzhou 526	Qiandaohu 886	East China Sea Fleet	30 October 2009
5	Guangzhou 168	Hengyang 568	Weishanhu 887	South China Sea Fleet	4 March 2010
6	Kunlunshan 998	Lanzhou 170	Weishanhu 887	South China Sea Fleet	30 June 2010
7	Zhoushan 529	Xuzhou 530	Qiandaohu 886	East China Sea Fleet	2 November 2010
8	Ma'anshan 525	Wenzhou 526	Qiandaohu 886	East China Sea Fleet	21 February 2011
9	Wuhan 169	Yulin 569	Qinghaihu 885	South China Sea Fleet	2 July 2011
10	Haikou 171	Yuncheng 571	Qinghaihu 885	South China Sea Fleet	2 November 2011
11	Qingdao 113	Yantai 538	Weishanhu 887	North China Sea Fleet	27 February 2012
12	Yiyang 548	Changzhou 549	Qiandaohu 886	East China Sea Fleet	3 July 2012
13	Hengyang 568	Huangshan 570	Qinghaihu 885	South China Sea Fleet	9 November 2012
14	Harbin 112	Mianyang 528	Weishanhu 887	North China Sea Fleet	16 February 2013
15	Jingganshan 999	Hengshui572	Taihu 889	South China Sea Fleet	8 August 2013
16	Yancheng 546	Luoyang 527	Taihu 889	North China Sea Fleet	30 November 2013
17	Changchun 150	Changzhou 549	Chaohu 890	East China Sea Fleet	24 March 2014
18	Changbaishan 989	Yuncheng 571	Chaohu 890	South China Sea Fleet	1 August 2014
19	Weifang 550	Linyi 547	Weishanhu 887	North China Sea Fleet	2 December 2014
20	Jinan152	Yiyang 548	Qiandaohu 886	East China Sea Fleet	3 April 2015
21	Liuzhou 573	Sanya 574	Qinghaihu 885	South China Sea Fleet	4 August 2015
22	Qingdao 113	Daqing 576	Taihu 889	North China Sea Fleet	6 December 2015
23	Xiangtan 531	Zhoushan 529	Chaohu 890	East China Sea Fleet	7 April 2016

Source: "China's Navy Convoy Fleets," http://baike.baidu.com/link?url=9EdNnSkAH_hesazsPS_Aq1YddF9t_p4vDzeUKDAQERYkNfMXQDfmqgT5xU5GJz-ZAyywpe0WN0R0LznA0jAnjtK, accessed 21 July 2016.

Ocean on patrol, indicating that China was exploring its military "going global strategy," which caused grave concern from India and the US. China relies on logistical bases (technical stops) in the Middle East and the Indian Ocean at large, which can be categorized into three types.

One is usually shipping fuel and material supply points, such as Port Djibouti, Aden in Yemen, Jeddah in Saudi Arabia, Mombasa in Kenya, Salalah in Oman, etc. In August 2010, Chinese naval hospital ship *Peace Ark* visited Port Djibouti. In May 2015, Djibouti's President Ismail Omar Guelleh announced that China was in talks about building a military base in northern Obock region in the country, implying that it would overlook the US military installations there. The base's installation would also bring in $100 million, slightly more than the US' annual $63 million.[23]

The second category is for relatively fixed supply ship berthing, and fixed-wing reconnaissance aircraft taking off and landing points, such as the Seychelles. This is based on a short-term agreement. The governments of the Seychelles and Djibouti both offered China technical stops and even military bases to support Beijing's military maneuvers in the Middle East and Black Africa,[24] but the Chinese government declined, arguing that the current logistical bases near the Red Sea, Gulf of Aden and the West Indian Ocean were sufficient to support China's convoy fleets and expatriate evacuation operations.

The third category is for more complete recharge, resting weaponry, and large ship repair centers, such as Gwadar Port in Pakistan, which is backed by a long-term agreement.[25] Should a crisis erupt in the western Indian Ocean, Gwadar Port might be transformed from a commercial seaport to a cooperative security site between China and Pakistan, which would offer an ideal foothold for Beijing. In 2016, India, Afghanistan, and Iran agreed the joint construction of Port Chabahar in Iran, and India decided to reconstruct a 600-meter-long container handling facility at the port. Chabahar will provide an alternative for trade between India and Afghanistan, and will be competitive with Gwadar Port under Chinese construction.[26]

Third, we consider China's peacekeeping forces in the Middle East. As of October 2015, China's peacekeeping forces number a total of 3,040 personnel, including 173 police, 29 military experts, and 2,838 troops.[27] In the Middle East, China has participated in the following UN peacekeeping missions: (1) in Jerusalem, "the United Nations Truce Supervision Organization" (2 observers); (2) "United Nations Interim Force in Lebanon" (343 soldiers);[28] (3) "the United Nations Mission in the Sudan" located in South Sudan (444 soldiers, 18 police, and 12 military observers); (4) "The United Nations: African

Union Hybrid Operation in Darfur" (321 soldiers); (5) "The United Nations Mission in Western Sahara referendum" (12 military observers).[29]

Before 2012, China's peacekeeping forces were mainly engineering corps, as well as a certain number of military observers, police, doctors, nurses, and logistics personnel. In January 2012, China dispatched combat troops for the first time, aiming to provide a security guarantee to Chinese peacekeeping forces and medical personnel. These combat troops are affiliated to No. 162 Motorized Infantry Division of No. 54 Group Army of Jinan Military Area.[30] No. 162 Motorized Infantry Division is China's first emergency maneuvering combat unit of rapid deployment forces. Chinese peacekeeping forces in South Sudan, for instance, have expanded their service, conducive not only to China building its image as a responsible power, but also to building a "new model of great-power relations" to strengthen partnerships with US, EU, Russia, among others. In October 2014, China dispatched 700 infantry battalion troops to the South Sudan for the first time in history within the UN peacekeeping missions.

Table 4.3: Ranking of military and police contributions to UN operations

Country	Male	Female	Totals	Ranking
Ethiopia	7781	545	8326	1
India	7658	42	7700	2
Pakistan	7154	21	7175	3
Bangladesh	6662	202	6864	4
Rwanda	5876	256	6132	5
Nepal	4951	165	5116	6
Senegal	3634	81	3715	7
Egypt	3055	0	3055	8
Burkina Faso	2904	128	3032	9
Ghana	2648	326	2974	10
Indonesia	2818	48	2866	11
China	2578	67	2645	12

Source: United Nations Peacekeeping, "Ranking of Military and Police Contributions to UN Operations," Month of Report, 30 June 2016, http://www.un.org/en/peacekeeping/contributors/2015/sep15_2.pdf, accessed 21 July 2016.

China's soft ad hoc military presence in the Middle East

Different from the aforementioned long-term military presence with its relatively stable objectives, China's ad hoc military presence in the Middle East has more multi-dimensional functions, such as arms sales and military training programs, the deployment of security contractors, joint military rehearsals, evacuating overseas nationals, and participating in other temporary UN Security Council missions, etc.

First, China's military exchanges and arms sales are increasingly extensive in the Middle East. In recent years, with its expansion of arms sales to developing countries, China has intensified its military exchanges with over 150 countries and established over 100 military representatives either independently or inside Chinese embassies. From 2009 to 2011, the PLA dispatched high-level delegations to over forty countries, and received about sixty Defense Ministers and Chiefs of General Staff, including those from the Middle East.[31]

According to SIPRI's statistics, the Middle East reports the fastest growing military budget. As early as the 1980s, China was one of the major weapon suppliers to both Iran and Iraq, including selling Type 69/WZ-121 Main Battle Tanks to Iraq and Silkworm missiles to Iran. In return, China obtained MG-23 Floggers from Iraq and F-14 Tomcats from Iran. In 2012, the Middle East defense budget reached US$ 100 billion, an increase of 8.4 percent since 2011. Compared with the US, EU, and Russia, China's arms sales to the Middle East are insignificant. In 2012, for instance, China's arms sales to the region were worth only US$ 753 million, while the Obama administration's were as high as US$ 28.5 billion, according to SIPRI.[32]

In 1988 China sold DF-3 strategic ballistic missiles to Saudi Arabia, and in this century China reportedly sold MBT-2000 tanks to the Kingdom. According to another report, China signed an arms sale contract with the Kingdom to supply "Pterosaurs-1" Unmanned Aerial Vehicles (UAV) in April 2014, after PLA Deputy Chief of Staff Wang Guanzhong visited Riyadh.[33] In September 2014, Annwa Majid, a consultant of the Saudi Joint Military Commission, confirmed that the Kingdom of Saudi Arabia had bought DF-21 missiles from China to protect Mecca and Medina and the lesser Arabian monarchies of the GCC. Beijing justified its arms trade with Riyadh, and the spokesperson for its Defense Ministry highlighted that China adheres to three principles in exporting its arms: that they be conducive to strengthening the defensive capabilities of the importers; that they would not harm world and regional peace, security, and stability; and that they would not interfere in others' internal affairs.[34]

Turkey, the only NATO member in the Middle East and the Islamic world, abruptly declared that it would purchase China's FD-2000 missile defense system in September 2013, which defeated the US PAC-3, EU SAMP-30, and Russian S-300 bids, with a sale price of only US$ 4 billion. Although the system is incompatible with NATO's, Turkey is quite interested. Besides, in recent years the Gulf countries, such as the UAE, are quite interested in China's "Pterosaurs-1" unmanned aerial vehicle (UAV), which is able to carry BA-7 and YZ-212 missiles.[35] Although researchers have limited knowledge about the inside stories of China's arms sales to the Middle East, the number of arms sales to the region will undoubtedly surge in the years to come.

Second, China has sent out security contractors to the war-torn states in the Middle East. In recent years, there have been about one million Chinese expatriates in West Asia and North Africa. In 2014, for instance, there were about 15,000 Chinese employees and staff in war-torn Iraq, and Chinese contracted projects in the country reached US$ 5.25 billion.[36] Yet, according to Chinese Security Service Management Regulations, Chinese officials at all levels, as well as its public servants, are prohibited from establishing government-run security service companies, compelling Chinese enterprises to seek US and British security contractors and Chinese private security contractors for protection. Blackwater, the notorious US security company, was an influential security service in the Middle East. It hired over 100,000 retired soldiers from the US Defense Ministry in 2011–13, with contracted projects totalling over US$ 1 billion.[37]

For a long time, China lacked any security service companies like Blackwater. Moreover, according to Chinese law, China's nationals are banned from carrying weapons while abroad; but Chinese expatriates are suffering all sorts of harassment and assault in the target countries of investment. In June 2004, eleven Chinese workers were shot and slaughtered at midnight in Afghanistan; in early 2012, twenty-five Chinese workers were kidnapped in Egypt; several months later, twenty-nine Chinese employees were kidnapped in Sudan;[38] on 24 August 2014, one of the Chinese working sites bordering Turkey and Iraq was attacked, and three Chinese engineers went missing; on 26 July 2015, the Jazeera Hotel in Mogadishu, Somalia was attacked and at least fifteen people were killed and several others injured; a security guard at the Chinese embassy was killed and three embassy staff wounded;[39] a similar tragedy happened in Mali and South Sudan, where three Chinese were killed in the Mali terrorist attacks in 2015 and two peacekeeping officials the civil conflict of South Sudan in 2016. Usually Chinese workers are geographically dispersed across different regions and working sites, making it hard to protect them in case of armed attacks from local rebels or terrorist groups.

There are three layers of "firewall" in the protection of Chinese workers in the Middle East. The outer layer is US, UN, or other great powers' troops deployed in the countries or regions; the second layer is the host nation's oil police or armed police; and the third layer is the security contractors employed by Chinese companies, such as Huawei Security Group. Unlike the US troops and the Middle East oil police or armed police, Chinese security contractors are not allowed to carry guns on foreign soil. There are two reasons behind this: first, as mentioned above, according to current Chinese law, Chinese citizens are not allowed to travel abroad with guns; second, China prefers to avoid political ventures with the host nations, and portable weapons are politically sensitive. In Iraq, for instance, China has made substantial investments in the country. The SINOPEC, SINO Petroleum (such as its oil investment at the CPF, OQDOS and WSN sites), Lvzhou and Daqing Petroleum have created a presence in the war-torn state and also dispatched a group of retired special troops for the protection of the workers. The special forces have served in several military areas of China, such as the "Sirius" Assault Team of PLA, the "Snow Leopard" Commando affiliated to China's armed police, the Tibet Armed Police Corps, etc. They are mostly senior non-commissioned officers who can boast rich combat experience and have received special training on the target country's culture, religion, and customs, and have proved they can get on with people from different backgrounds.[40]

For example, Chinese security company Tianjiao Tewei (GSA) was founded in 2008, composed of retired PLA soldiers. The security service is one of the most experienced and professional organizations of "very important people protection operatives" (VPOs). Through partnership with the Israeli International Security College, GSA has established the first training institute for the protection of international VPOs in Ningbo of Zhejiang province, China.[41] Huaxing Zhong'An Security Service Ltd is another case in point, which is constantly expanding its overseas business in the Middle East.

Third, China has participated in joint military rehearsals with the pivotal states of the Middle East. In April 2009, then Air Force Commander Ma Xiaotian paid a visit to Turkey and reached an agreement with his counterpart, Hassan Aksayi, Turkish Air Force Commander. From 20 September to 4 October 2009, the two sides set up a two-week joint military training in Turkey.[42] On 4 February 2012, China joined with Russia to veto UNSC draft resolution S/2012/77, tabled by Morocco. In addition to these diplomatic efforts, China was also more assertive militarily by sending Chinese warships to the Mediterranean Sea in a "show of flags" along with the Russian naval presence near Syria.[43] During its stay in the Mediterranean Sea, on 25 January 2015 China's Yangcheng missile frigate carried out a joint drill with the Russian nuclear-powered cruiser *Pyotr Veliky*, "to raise the level of operative compatibility between the Russian and Chinese warships."[44] In May 2015, Chinese convoy fleets consisting of the Linyi missile frigate, Weifang missile frigate, and the comprehensive logistic missile frigate launched joint military rehearsals with their Russian counterpart. The three missile frigates entered the Mediterranean Sea for the joint military exercise, named China-Russia Joint Maritime 2015, after their joint commemoration of the WWII triumph in the Black Sea.[45]

In addition, the PLA Navy convoy fleets have held two joint anti-piracy drills with the US, in 2012 and 2013, and one with EU NAVFOR in 2014.[46] In September 2014, Chinese convoy fleets of the Changchun missile frigate and Changzhou missile frigate (Mission 17) paid a visit to the Abbas Port of Iran, and the two naval forces initiated joint military rehearsals near the Persian Gulf on counter-piracy and joint rescue.[47]

Fourth, China's military forces are used to support the evacuation of Chinese citizens from the Middle East. From 2008 to 2015, due to local emergency issues such as civil wars, terrorist attacks, anti-government riots, uprisings, and other armed conflicts, China was compelled to withdraw over 50,000 Chinese expatriates from Libya, Sudan, Yemen, Egypt, Afghanistan, Iraq, among others. The evacuations from Libya and Egypt were conducted without adequate logistics, forcing China to rely on foreign shipping companies, and the operation was run by the Foreign Ministry instead of the Ministry of Defense, but such a situation can hardly be sustained in the longer run. On 12 April 2015, Zhai Leiming, Deputy Director of the Department of Consular Affairs, China's Foreign Ministry and Director of Consular Protection Center told reporters that China's consular protection is faced with an overwhelming task. Each official needs to protect 200,000 workers abroad, while the US proportion is 1:5,000 and the Japanese proportion 1:12,000.[48] In 2012, for instance, with the worsening of the North-South Sudan conflict, over 200 Chinese workers were pulled out from the oil sites of South Sudan, with the direct economic loss of at least US$ 3 billion.[49]

Apart from Djibouti and the Republic of Seychelles, China has taken advantage of its military presence in the Somali waters and Port Sudan by pulling out 35,860 overseas nationals in 2012 from war-torn Libya to security regions.[50] Beijing made the best use of the Ministries of National Defense, Foreign Affairs, Commerce, Civil Administration under the combined leadership of a government task force led by vice premier Zhang Dejiang (currently chairman of the National People's Congress Standing Committee) and state councillor Dai Bingguo. The objective of the task force was to manage and coordinate efforts to evacuate Chinese citizens from Libya.[51]

Since the eruption of the Yemen crisis in early 2015, China had been ready to pull out expatriates from the country. In four operations after 29 March, a total of 629 Chinese nationals and 279 foreign citizens were successfully evacuated from Yemen aboard Chinese vessels (including the Linyi missile frigate). Lending a helping hand to its nationals as well as citizens of fifteen other countries in need, China played its role as a major responsible country and demonstrated the spirit of humanitarianism.[52]

Finally, China has engaged in other ad hoc UN Security Council operations in recent years. For instance, taking into account the decision of the Syrian government to accede to the Chemical Weapons Convention and the commitment of the Syrian authorities to apply the convention provisionally prior to its being enforced, the United States and the Russian Federation expressed their joint determination to ensure the destruction of the Syrian chemical weapons program in the soonest and safest manner.[53] China worked with Russia, Denmark, and Norway on the shipment of Syria's chemical weapons for destruction, known as "returning chemical weapons for peace."[54] The day after the Organization for the Prohibition of Chemical Weapons' (OPCW) Director General, Ahmet Üzümcü, submitted a plan for the destruction of Syrian chemical weapons to the organization's Executive Council, Chinese Foreign Minister Wang Yi announced that a PLA Navy missile frigate would join the Danish, Norwegian, and Russian frigates to escort the weapons from the Syrian port of Latakia to Italy. On 31 December 2013, the Yancheng, a Type-054 frigate, part of the 16th counter-piracy task force, was re-routed to the Mediterranean Sea and docked at Limassol, Cyprus, on 4 January 2014.[55]

Implications and conclusion

Since the early twenty-first century, the traditional powers, such as the US, UK, France, Russia, and Japan, generally perceive the Middle East as a "battle zone," and they have deployed hard military bases in the Middle East to further their interests, including maintaining the political predominance of the region, carrying out anti-terrorist and non-proliferation tactics, popularizing Western-style democracy and values, defending allies, and preventing anti-

Western radicals from challenging the regional order. All of these have been under the guise of security-oriented geopolitical strategies.

Apparently, Japan, India, and the US are still suspicious of Beijing's real motive, and are concerned that their soft military presence will sooner or later be transformed into real and substantial military bases for geopolitical purposes. To avoid being demonized as a "China threat," Beijing stresses that it is a responsible rising power, and its soft military footprint is different from the hard military bases of the Western powers, because theirs is a contribution of "security public goods" to the international community, compatible with the Western hard military bases in the Middle East. The "21st Century Maritime Silk Road" is the consideration of Beijing's geo-economics, and its soft military footprint has no intention of putting the "string of pearls" strategy into effect, as Chinese top leadership repeats time and again.

First, through the growth of wealth, the Chinese are convinced that they will achieve a peaceful transfer of global power structure in a progressive way. The Middle East is the traditional sphere of influence for the Western powers. The United States, Britain, and France have important military and political influence in the Middle East. China has a strong intention to strengthen its economic and trade exchanges and expand its economic presence in the Middle East with a soft military footprint as its guardian. China's soft military footprint in the Middle East is located around the relatively concentrated areas of China's overseas interests. In Saudi Arabia, currently seventy Chinese-funded enterprises employ 16,000 Chinese workers engaged in commercial activities. In Dubai, "China-Middle East Investment and Trade Promotion Center" covers an area of 150,000 square meters. There are 3,000 Chinese enterprises and representative offices, and a total of 200,000 Chinese expatriates living in Dubai—the largest non-permanent-resident overseas Chinese community. Chinese permanent and ad hoc military deployment is concentrated in the Gulf, Sudan, and the East Mediterranean Sea.

Second, the Chinese convoy fleet in the Gulf of Aden and Somali waters and other soft military footprints will play a "bridgehead" role in case of crisis, such as disaster relief, expatriate evacuation, etc. It looks after up to 5,000 km of routes of maritime trade and transport lines' safety, and the security of investment projects from the South China Sea to the Persian Gulf. The Middle East is not only about trade relations between China and the Middle East; it is also a transit market for Chinese expansion of its trade with Africa and Europe. It became a transit site for the saturated domestic industries and commodities, and a middle ground connecting China with its European and African economic presence.

Third, China's soft military footprint in the Middle East is compatible with traditional Chinese diplomatic principles: no overseas military base deployment, no hegemony or power politics. It also fulfills the practical needs of protecting its interests in the Middle East. It is the foundation for building up the new model of great power relations. In the twenty-first century, the United States, Europe, and Japan have formed a "traditional core area," while China, India, and Brazil have forged a "new core area," as the author of *The Pentagon's New Map*, Thomas Barnett, put it. These two core regions have a higher degree of globalization, becoming the two engines of human development. In contrast, the Middle East, Central, Asia and Africa are marginalized. They pose a direct or indirect threat to the core areas and bring challenges, becoming key areas of global governance.

Fourth, the connotation of Chinese overseas interests is increasingly rich, and the forms of soft military footprint that protect Chinese overseas interests are becoming diversified. Nowadays China is still a developing country. It faces the formidable task of promoting domestic reform and development while maintaining social stability. Economic construction remains the fundamental policy of China in the near future. This means that whether in Asia-Pacific regions or in the Middle East, the geo-economic strategy will be the long-term strategy of Beijing. As the outcome of the strategy, China will rely on its soft military footprint to build a Maritime Silk Road from the South China Sea to the Mediterranean Sea in the twenty-first century.

5

CHINA AND TURKEY

SAILING THROUGH ROUGH WATERS

Altay Atlı

The relationship between China and Turkey is best described as one of ebb and flow, with economic initiatives aimed at mutual benefit being welcomed by both sides, peppered with much rhetoric on both countries' "rise" in the global system and their "importance" to each other, certain steps being taken, only to be eventually put on hold or totally derailed due to political issues and miscalculations, as is recurrently the case. The relationship between China and Turkey is developing, starting from 1971 when the two countries officially recognized each other; but the nature of this development is better described as oscillating, rather than following a linear progress.

Events during the second half of 2015 and early 2016 clearly illustrate the magnitude of volatility in the Sino-Turkish relationship. Anti-Chinese demonstrations erupted in Turkish cities in reaction to speculative reports of an alleged Chinese ban on Ramadan fasting in the Xinjiang Uyghur Autonomous Region,[1] which caused significant tension between the two sides; but these incidents were soon followed by an official visit by Turkey's President Recep

Tayyip Erdoğan to China, which went remarkably well.[2] In the background to these developments, China was accusing Turkish diplomats stationed in Asian countries of providing fake passports to members of the Uyghur minority attempting to flee China for Turkey. The accusations followed the forced deportation to China of 109 asylum-seeking Uyghurs from camps in Thailand to which they had fled. More than 400 Uyghurs had ended up in Thailand, and Turkey agreed to take 173 of the Uyghurs, many of them women and children. Ankara officially protested Thailand's decision, on the grounds that the individuals repatriated to China would be facing persecution and punishment, while China claimed that the Uyghurs seeking to leave the country were trying to join jihadist groups overseas, especially in Syria. In the meantime, China's Ministry of Public Security declared that Turkish diplomats were providing Uyghurs, who are in fact citizens of the People's Republic of China, with Turkish travel documents in order to make their transit to Turkey possible.[3] After a few months, the Turkish government decided to annul a major missile defense system tender, which was initially awarded to a Chinese company, to great dismay by the Chinese side.[4] Two days later, China's President Xi Jinping was in the Turkish Mediterranean town of Antalya for the annual G20 summit, and during the event the two sides signed a number of agreements focusing on large-scale industrial cooperation and infrastructure projects.[5] This positive development was followed only a few weeks later by the Chinese government's decision to tighten visa requirements for Turkish passport holders.[6]

These developments that took place over a period of a couple of months do not actually reflect a drastic change in the nature of the relationship. On the contrary, there have been similar volatilities before. For instance, observers of Turkish foreign policy can easily recall the summer of 2009 when the then prime minister Erdoğan reacted to the riots in Xinjiang's capital Urumqi: they were harshly suppressed by Chinese security forces and around two hundred people lost their lives, which Erdoğan described as "almost genocide." The riots and hence Erdoğan's reaction took place only a few days after the then president Abdullah Gül's successful visit to Xinjiang. After the incident, despite a brief coolness in the relations between Ankara and Beijing, a conciliatory tone was eventually adopted, and the Chinese government invited Turkish business representatives to visit Xinjiang to explore the investment opportunities there. Only a few months after the incident of Urumqi, the then Chinese premier Wen Jiabao was in Turkey to announce—together with his counterpart—the Turkish-Chinese strategic cooperation.[7] However, even the fact that the two governments had elevated their relationship to the status of strategic cooperation back in 2010 has so far failed to bring about greater stability to the relationship.

China and Turkey are strategic cooperation partners, and both sides subscribe to the discourse that there should be greater collaboration between two G20-member countries located at both ends of the Asian continent. Initiatives like China's "One Belt, One Road" (OBOR) project, which is welcomed by Turkey with great enthusiasm, serve to nurture this idea, and studies inquiring into the dynamics of the relationship between China and Turkey offer much optimism for the future. For example, Zhou Zhiqiang argues that these two countries "share similar ambitious goals and development targets" and that "bright prospects can be predicted in bilateral cooperation in aspects including trade, investment, finance and global economic governance."[8] Whereas Xiao Xian assures that "neither party regards this strategic partnership as mere diplomatic rhetoric. Rather, they view it as inclusive and substantial."[9] On the Turkish side, Selçuk Çolakoğlu defines the relationship as a "rising partnership."[10] Later he characterized it as "deepening economic and political cooperation between the two countries which has also made Turkish-Chinese relations more important from a global standpoint."[11] International pundits seem to agree. For Vali Nasr, "Asia is getting smaller as Turkey moves east and China moves west. The two booming emerging markets now bracket the continent, and as economic integration takes root the vast expanse between the Mediterranean and the Yellow Sea will shrink into one geostrategic space."[12] Whereas Johan Galtung declares that he "would watch out for this—for Ankara-Beijing cooperation" as "the whole area will be managed by some cooperation between Turkey and China and the countries in between, the countries in between being Iran, Pakistan, Afghanistan."[13]

Despite this positive outlook and profound optimism, which is not only nurtured by politicians but also subscribed to by several academics, China and Turkey appear to be rather reluctant when it comes to practical progress in the relationship. Intentions easily fall prey to political concerns, perceptions, miscalculations; barriers are erected against progress in the relationship. The Sino-Turkish relationship is one of "great expectations,"[14] as Yitzhak Shichor puts it, but whether and to what extent expectations translate into concrete outcomes is a different question.

This chapter offers a critical perspective on the Sino-Turkish relationship. The inquiry starts from the widely-accepted premise that it is the economic dimension of the relationship that both sides are emphasizing, and argues that the level of economic interaction between the two countries does not produce an incentive that is strong enough to ensure stable and uninterrupted progress between them. As will be shown below, despite the appearance, there is no significant economic dependence between China and Turkey, which contrasts with most of the other dyadic cases between China and the countries of the Middle East, where China depends profoundly on the region's hydrocarbons and the countries of the region similarly depend on Chinese capital and infrastructure, as discussed in the chapters of this composite volume. The absence of a certain level of economic interdependence leads to greater vulnerability of the relationship against non-economic factors.

In order to test this hypothesis, this chapter will employ four different paradigms from the literature on international relations that inquire into the impact of economic dependence on overall dyadic relations, namely liberalism, realism, trade expectations theory, and constructivism. Guided by insights from these paradigms, the chapter shows that the lack of economic dependence between the two countries makes them more prone to political conflicts and miscalculations, and despite the officially declared strategic nature of their relationship, China and Turkey are far from acting in political alignment on several issues, as developments such as disagreement over Syria, cancellation of the missile system deal, and tension over the Uyghur issue reveal. The chapter makes the point that this would not have been the case if there had been greater economic interdependence linking the two countries' interests.

Following the introductory section, this chapter will first provide a brief historical background of the relationship between China and Turkey. Second, a theoretical framework employing insights from liberalism, realism, trade expectations theory, and constructivism will be established with the purpose of explaining the relationship between economic dependence between countries and the extent of political alignment and conflict between them. Third, the chapter will investigate empirical data from the Sino-Turkish relationship through the perspectives established in the previous part, hence explaining how economic dependence between the two countries, or the lack/insufficiency of it, impacts on the overall relationship. The chapter's conclusion will summarize the main findings.

Historical background

The Chinese and the Turks like to trace back the roots of their relationship to the exchanges between the two peoples in the Central Asian steppes centuries ago, when Turkic merchants traded goods between their own territories and the Chinese realm, subject to the tributary conditions dictated by the Chinese imperial administration.[15] This trade through the Silk Road went on for centuries, and it was not only products that were carried and traded; commerce made the exchange of ideas, world views, and cultural goods also possible. During the age of empires, individuals continued to travel between the Ottoman Empire and Imperial China for commercial and religious purposes, forming linkages between these two different worlds, which eventually led to attempts to establish diplomatic relations in the late nineteenth century.[16]

Following the First World War and the Turkish War of Liberation, the modern Republic of Turkey was founded in 1923, a time when China was going through a period of chaos and uncertainty in the aftermath of the dissolution of the Qing dynasty and the proclamation of the Republic of China in 1911. Efforts were made in this period to establish an official relationship between the two countries, culminating in the opening of a Turkish consulate in Nanjing in 1934.[17]

The Second World War and the seismic shifts in the international order in the war's aftermath had a profound effect on the relationship between Turkey and China. Ceren Ergenç accurately claims that the two countries spent the first half of the twentieth century focusing on their state-building process, but the beginning of the Cold War pushed the two countries into opposite camps.[18] Turkey, as a member of the Western camp in the bipolar setting of the Cold War, indeed refused to recognize the communist People's Republic of China when it was founded in 1949, and preferred to maintain its relations with the Nationalist government on the island of Taiwan as the legitimate representative of the Chinese people. Turkey sent troops to fight in the Korean War of 1950–53, became a member of NATO, and refrained from having dialogue of any form with the communist government in Beijing.

While the ideological polarization in the international order kept Turkey and China politically isolated from each other in the early Cold War period, it did not take long for the two countries to start exploring opportunities for economic interaction. Early steps were taken in the late 1960s when small-scale trade began to be carried out through third-party intermediaries. This period was also marked by indications that the United States and China were considering rapprochement. Turkey, as a staunch ally of the United States, considered the Beijing-Washington rapprochement as an opportunity and embarked on its own normalization process with China, consequently recognizing the People's Republic with an agreement signed in Paris on 5 August 1971. This recognition was followed in 1974 by a trade agreement.

During the 1970s, neither of the two countries attempted to invest much energy in their relationship. Turkey in this period was suffering from internal political polarization, which frequently turned violent, as well as from economic malaise as the import substitution industrialization model failed to reach its objectives, instead crating serious deficits and shortages. China meanwhile was going through the last stages of the Mao Zedong era, and it was only in 1978, after the death of Mao and under a new leadership, that China began to open up to the world. Political debates within Turkey in this period reveal serious concerns about the threat of ideological infiltration from China and doubts about expected economic benefits from this country.[19] As Selçuk Çolakoğlu writes, Turkey saw East Asia as a new frontier for economic expansion as early as the 1970s, but "its unstable governments and the economic crises of the 1970s prevented Turkey from establishing more rooted economic relations with China."[20]

With the 1980s, however, a new era began in the relationship. Both China and Turkey began to liberalize their economies, while diplomatic and commercial traffic between the two countries gained momentum. Presidents, prime ministers, bureaucrats, and businesspeople began to exchange visits and explore opportunities with each other, and the mood in this period was generally positive as both sides made efforts to understand each other and establish the foundations of a longer-term relationship.[21]

The end of the Cold War and the dissolution of the Soviet Union in 1991 brought new constraints on China's relationship with Turkey, and the positive environment of the 1980s marked by attempts to explore opportunities was replaced by a confrontational setting shaped by shifts in the regional and international order. Turkey's foreign policy was active toward the newly independent republics of Central Asia and the Caucasus, emphasizing the common Turkic heritage, common religion, and shared cultural and historic roots between Turkey and these countries. This troubled China, which worried that Turkey's interest might spill over into its own sovereign territory, the Xinjiang Uyghur Autonomous Region, through this discourse of common ethnicity.[22] In the meantime, both transnational activism by the Uyghur diaspora based in Turkey and Turkish politicians' contacts with and support for the Uyghur diaspora leaders led to serious deterioration in the relationship. As a result, Beijing began to pressurize Turkey to curb the Uyghur community's anti-Chinese actions which "Ankara earlier disregarded, tolerated, approved, or even supported, if not explicitly, then at least implicitly."[23]

During the second half of the 1990s, Turkey's foreign policy took another turn, this time opting to act in coordination with Russia and China in the

Central Asian region, instead of competing against them in order to establish an area of influence of its own. Russia was the dominant actor in the post-Soviet realm, both economically and politically, and China was the rising economic power, becoming increasingly influential not only in this region but worldwide. For Ankara, cooperating with both these powers was the rational choice; and in the Chinese case, with a more assertive and self-confident Beijing increasing its pressure on the Turkish government to curtail Uyghur activities, Turkey chose to cease its support for Uyghur nationalist movements and adopted a new policy of supporting the Uyghurs economically and culturally while rejecting any attempt that would jeopardize China's territorial integrity.

In November 2002 Turkey entered a new era, with the Justice and Development Party (AKP) emerging victorious from the parliamentary elections and entering office as a single-party government with a parliamentary majority. The foreign policy of the AKP government prioritized economic considerations, and aimed to engage proactively with regions that were hitherto ignored or superficially engaged, such as Asian, African, and Latin American countries; this brought a renewed momentum to Turkey's efforts to improve relations with China.[24] With greater mutual understanding on the Uyghur issue between the two governments, there was now a favorable environment to extend business with each other.

In the 2000s, trade between China and Turkey did indeed increase, and new forms of economic linkages were established such as cooperation in the defense industry, large-scale infrastructure improvement projects, and efforts at technology transfer, as will be discussed below. Increased business has been a key factor in the two governments' decision to upgrade the status of their relationship to strategic cooperation, and future expectations such as the prospective benefits of China's OBOR project add fresh motivation to this partnership. In the meantime, there was greater cooperation in multilateral institutions such as the G20 and the Conference on Interaction and Confidence-Building Measures in Asia (CICA).[25] Mutual people-to-people exchange also increased through activities such as the opening of Confucius Institutes in Turkey.[26] Then 2012 was Chinese Culture Year in Turkey, and 2013 was Year of Turkish Culture in China, both of which aimed, as stated on the website of the Ministry of Foreign Affairs of Turkey, "to enhance friendly relations, promote cultural exchange and further improve mutual understanding between Turkey and China."[27] However, despite all these developments, the relationship between China and Turkey is subject to strong volatility, and the relationship is easily derailed. Recent events discussed in the introductory part of this chapter, such as the anti-Chinese demonstrations in Turkey; accusations of fake Turkish passports supplied for Uyghurs trying to flee China; summoning the Chinese ambassador to the Turkish Ministry of Foreign Affairs, followed by Erdoğan's successful visit to Beijing, which in turn was followed by the almost simultaneous acts of Turkey cancelling the missile defense system tender awarded to China and the two governments signing new cooperation projects; and the Chinese decision to tighten visa requirements for Turkish citizens, are only a few examples of the increasing magnitude and frequency of ups and downs in the bilateral relationship between China and Turkey.

In addition to these developments, the rapidly changing political landscape in the Middle East in the aftermath of the Arab uprisings, with civil war in Syria and the terrorist threat of the self-proclaimed Islamic State (IS), is creating another source of friction between China and Turkey, adding further volatility to the relationship. The two governments' stance towards the turmoil in Syria offers a clear illustration of how the two sides diverge on the issue. China has, together with Russia, repeatedly vetoed a draft United Nations (UN) resolution that would have referred the conflict in Syria to the International Criminal Court, which has drawn Turkey's criticism. China and Russia have in fact vetoed four UN Security Council draft resolutions between 2011 and 2014. In each case, the rationale behind the decision to veto as stated by the Chinese representative at the UN was that the conflict in Syria had to be solved through dialogue between the relevant parties inside the country and not through outside intervention. In every instance, Turkey criticized China and Russia's decision to veto, and after the second case in February 2012, the reaction was especially harsh when the then prime minister Recep Tayyip Erdoğan called the veto "a fiasco for the civilized world" as the "UN Security Council failed to fulfill its duty of protecting peace and security," and said that it is "unacceptable for any country, whatever its interests for doing so are, to give the license to kill to the hands of a tyrant."[28] As civil war continues to devastate Syria, Turkey maintains that the removal of the Bashar al-Assad regime is an absolute condition for lasting peace in the country, whereas China believes that Assad's government is the sole legitimate authority in Syria. China refrains, at least at the time of writing, from getting directly involved in the Syrian conflict, and prioritizes its economic interest in the greater Middle East region. However, Turkey's perception of China being pro-Assad and overall aligned with Russian preferences in the region is problematic, especially since the relations between Turkey and Russia are at an all-time low after the shooting down of a Russian jet by a Turkish fighter plane over a violation of Turkish airspace in November 2015. While China refrained from taking sides on this issue, it has not made any efforts to ease the tensions between Turkey and Russia either.[29] It was clear to many that "China was not happy with Turkey's Syria policy."[30] Reports about Chinese citizens of Uyghur origin using Turkey as a gateway into Syria where they joined jihadists only served to complicate the situation further.[31]

In sum, the current state of the relationship between China and Turkey is defined on the one hand by increasing trade and investment as well as hopes for even bigger business in the future through projects like OBOR; and on the other hand escalating disagreement and political conflict. Not only are these two countries strategic cooperation partners, but their leaders also frequently make statements like "bilateral relations have gained progress in recent years thanks to the mutual trust established between two states" or "we have maintained close high-level exchanges, our mutual political trust has been growing and our cooperation and exchanges in economic, technological, cultural and other arenas have been expanding."[32] However, at the same it is observed, with increasing frequency, that politics can pull the relationship to the opposite direction. Raffaello Pantucci calls it an "awkward relationship," which "they wouldn't want to complicate further."[33] Yet despite all the rhetoric about the importance of their relationship and expressions of interest on having more economic interaction with each other, a diverse range of issues continues to complicate the relationship.

The question is, if it is really the economic interests that the two countries are after, as suggested by several scholars, why are the relations between China and Turkey so easily overshadowed by issues such as those discussed above? Both China and Turkey declare their intent of building stronger ties with each other, and economics is key to this task. Why this reluctance then? In order to answer these questions, the link between economic considerations and political relations will be investigated, using insight from the relevant perspectives in the international relations literature.

Analytical framework

The argument put forward in this chapter is that the level of economic interaction between China and Turkey does not produce an incentive strong enough to ensure stable and uninterrupted progress between them, nor a significant degree of economic dependence between them, in contrast with China's dependence on many Middle Eastern economies, especially the hydrocarbon-producing ones. This factor causes reluctance on both sides to further the relationship. In the absence of strong mutual economic dependence, even "strategic cooperation" can easily be undermined by political factors. The scholarly literature in international relations provides a number of perspectives that can be helpful toward explaining this linkage.

The liberal paradigm of international relations asserts that cooperation can be possible between states depending on the distribution of state preferences. Economic interdependence, which is the defining feature of globalization, can lead to greater cooperation between states. Cross-border economic exchange creates more cooperative foreign policy interests, as economic flows between countries leads to a dependence on maintaining the mutually beneficial relationship. According to the liberal theory, countries seek to maximize the utility they derive from trade, and any country that is dependent on trade makes efforts to avoid war, since peaceful trade gives countries all the benefits without the risks associated with war. Economic interdependence between countries increases the cost of conflict, and countries that depend on each other economically tend to have harmonious relations, as they do not want to face the risk of trade interruption.

Realism asserts that international politics is a struggle for wealth and power among independent actors in a state of anarchy. It assumes that economic wealth is vital to the states' ability to wage war and ensure their survival, and for this reason states keep a positive trade balance by protecting against competing imports and maximizing exports. In this view, economic interdependence is an asymmetrical situation, as in every case one country in the dyad depends on the other country more than the other way around. While the more dependent state has greater incentive to avoid conflict due to the high opportunity costs it is facing, the less dependent state can force it into making concessions through the use or threat of force. This is why one can argue that the greater the magnitude of asymmetry in the relationship, the greater the likelihood of conflict; and economic dependence between the two parties can be expected to have a peaceful effect only if the dependence of the two countries is to a large extent symmetrically balanced.

When discussing the effects of economic relations on political alignment or conflict between countries, one is faced with two shortcomings of the current literature. The first is related to the tendency to take the use of force and military conflict as the common measure when discussing whether economic interdependence leads to conflict. There are, however, other types and levels of political conflict that fall short of inter-state war. Tansa G. Massoud and Christopher S. Magee have undertaken an empirical study into how trade is related to other forms of political conflict between states, and found that while trade significantly raises net cooperation on political and economic issues, it does not lead to cooperation in military issues; and while trade leads to more economic cooperation, it does not affect the amount of conflict over economic issues.[34] While Massoud and Magee shed light on the impact of trade on overall political and economic relations between countries, the bulk of literature from liberal and realist international relations perspectives is not useless either. Using these paradigms' corollaries, by replacing the "likelihood of military conflict" with lower level forms of conflict such as "likelihood of having conflictual issues in the political realm," and the "likelihood of peaceful relations" with "likelihood of greater political alignment," it is possible to hypothesize, from the liberal view, that greater economic interdependence between the two countries will lead to greater political alignment and less political conflict. From the realist perspective, then, the greater the asymmetry in the economic relationship, the higher is the likelihood of having more political conflict. Solomon W. Wolachek's study confirms these corollaries, as he finds that "conflict occurs when gains from trade are not as high as one party deems possible or when parties fight over economic rents. Cooperation occurs when parties work together to protect gains from trade."[35]

The other weakness in the liberal and realist literatures on the relationship between economic linkages and the likelihood of conflict between countries is that bilateral trade, and particularly trade in goods, is taken as a common measure of the level of the economic relationship and dependence between the country dyad. The globalized world of today is defined by complex and multidimensional interdependence, and economic interaction in this respect comprises not only trade in goods, but also financial flows, transnational production, and trade in services such as construction services, education, tourism, etc.[36] This is why, when investigating the link between economic dependence and political alignment or conflict, the entire set of economic interactions rather than only the trade in goods needs to be taken into consideration.

It has also to be noted that the paradigms discussed above consider the economic relations at a given point in time, as they stand at the current time. Dale C. Copeland argues that it is not only the current state of economic interactions between the states, but also these states' expectations from future trade and investment that play a crucial role in shaping the political relations between them. According to his trade expectations theory, the positive expectation of future trade can impact a country's foreign policy behavior when current levels of economic exchange are low, because the country anticipates future benefits and wants the other country in the dyad to carry out its commitments to increase overall trade and investment levels. In contrast, if the less dependent country in the dyad decides to deny the more dependent country what it needs in the future, it can choose to exacerbate current conflicts.[37] As a corollary to Copeland's trade expectations theory, one can hypothesize that the more countries expect benefits from their economic exchange in the future, the more political alignment and the less conflict they will have at the current time; and in contrast, negative future expectations are likely to lead to greater conflict and hostility, even if current trade levels are high.

Constructivism argues that while material factors are important, ideas matter as well, as the world is socially constructed, and international relations do not result from an objective social reality, but reflect the actors' ideas, perceptions, assumptions, and the norms to which they adhere. Foreign policy goals are defined not only by material parameters such as trade patterns, access to raw materials, defense budgets, and so on; they reflect immaterial, shared and collective beliefs and identities as well.[38] In the relationship between economic exchange and political alignment or conflict, therefore, it matters profoundly how the actors "construct" each other, how the two countries in the dyad perceive each other, and how their ideas about each other are shaped. Even at high levels of trade and investment, domination of negative ideas and perceptions can lead to deterioration in the relationship.

In the light of these perspectives, it is possible to investigate the relationship between China and Turkey and examine the dynamics behind its volatilities.

Analysis of the Sino-Turkish economic relationship

A first look at the bilateral economic data between China and Turkey actually offers a bright picture. In 2015, the trade value between these two countries was $27.3 billion—a remarkable number, particularly considering that there is no large-scale trading of hydrocarbons involved, as opposed to China's trade with several Middle East countries. Investment figures are also on the rise, and the OBOR project brings much promise for future cooperation.

In order to find out whether this picture represents a certain level of economic dependence between the two countries, one has to delve deeper into the details of the statistics. Firstly, it has to be noted that there is significant imbalance in the trade: Turkey is running a large trade deficit with China. In

2015, Turkey's exports to China amounted to $2.4 billion, whereas imports from China totaled a massive $24.9 billion. This deficit is a major concern for Turkish economic policy-makers, especially because Turkey is suffering from a chronic current account problem. In 2015, Turkey's overall export/import ratio was 69.4 percent, while its export-to-import ratio with China was only 9.7 percent, revealing the seriousness of the situation.[39]

The structure of Turkish exports to China also paints a picture that is hardly sustainable. According to latest annual data, Turkey's major export item to China is marble, corresponding to 28.8 percent of total exports. Marble is followed by chromium ore at 9.5 percent, copper ore at 7.5 percent, precious metal ores at 4.7 percent, and natural borate at 4.1 percent.[40] While these figures reveal a lack of diversity in Turkish exports, with the top five export items making up 54.8 percent of all exports, it is also possible to argue that Turkey is largely dependent on China as an export market for these products. For instance, China's share of Turkish export products is 84.5 percent for marble, 80 percent for iron ore, 79.7 percent for chromium ore, 68.4 percent for lead ore, 63.8 percent for wool and fleece, 58.4 percent for copper ore, and 44.2 percent for natural borate. In all these items, all of them primary products without much value-added, Turkey depends on the Chinese market.

Whether China depends on Turkey for the same products is a different question. With marble, Turkey sells 84.5 percent of its export to China, but China buys only 48.1 percent of its marble needs from Turkey. The opposite picture emerges for natural borate: Turkey exports 44.2 percent of its natural borate to China, which buys 74.9 percent of its borate needs from Turkey. So there is a variable picture of trade dependence.

It is in raw materials such as marble and natural borate that there is significant mutual dependence between the two countries, rather than in oil and gas. This dependence, however, makes both sides concerned, as the realist paradigm would claim. The rapidly growing construction sector has created an insatiable appetite for marble and other construction materials. But in order to reduce its dependence on Turkey for marble, China is now buying up the marble quarries in Turkey, instead of importing the marble from locally owned companies.[41] Turkey, on the other hand, is concerned about the fact that China is buying the marble in raw form and processing it when it arrives in China. Turkish industry representatives have repeatedly claimed that this is not a sustainable position for them, and Turkey would gain more if the marble were processed at home before being shipped.[42]

In 2015, China was Turkey's largest import partner. Turkey imported $24.9 billion worth of goods from China, while imports from Germany and Russia totaled $21.3 billion and $20.4 billion respectively. This fact, however, does not create a significant degree of dependence for Turkey on Russia either. One reason is that the import structure is highly diversified in terms of products. Turkey's main imports from China are telephone equipment amounting to 10.6 percent of all Turkish imports from China, followed by IT equipment at 7.2 percent, monitors and projectors at 2.3 percent, man-made filaments at 1.9 percent, and lighting equipment at 1.7 percent. The first items in Turkey's top imports from China make up only 29.9 percent of total imports. This situation contrasts with Turkey's imports from Russia, wherein one single item, i.e. oil and gas, corresponds to 63.4 percent of total Turkish imports, thus creating a real dependence for Turkey in this respect.

It is true that in several areas Chinese products have a large share in Turkish markets. For instance, 91.7 percent of all toys imported by Turkey are Chinese-made, as are 97.6 percent of artificial flowers, 92.2 percent of shoes, and 95.2 percent of umbrellas. This situation, however, does not create a significant degree of dependence on China for Turkey, as the products in question are low value, unsophisticated consumption goods. They are bought from China purely because of their low cost, and do not amount to crucial inputs for the Turkish economy, as do Russian oil and gas.

Turkey's economy depends profoundly on imports of raw materials and intermediate products, which are then assembled into final products and eventually exported to other markets. In this sense, China can be seen as a source of cheap intermediary goods for Turkish producers, providing them with a competitive advantage in their own export markets, thanks to low input costs. A recent study by the Turkish-China Business Council operating under the Foreign Economic Relations Board of Turkey (DEİK) reveals that in fact Turkish producers rely to a significant extent on intermediary products from China. For instance, the Turkish textile and clothing industry buys 20.6 percent of its raw materials from abroad. The share of Chinese products in Turkey's total imports of these products is 41.8 percent.[43] There is a certain level of dependence for Turkey on China in this respect, but it should be viewed with caution as the motivation behind the tendency to source from China is because of low costs rather than securing higher value for the Turkish economy. Moreover, it is not about sourcing strategic raw materials either, which is another reason why one cannot talk about real dependence on China in this area.

China depends on Turkish marble and to some extent on Turkish borate as well, but that is all. This shows the asymmetric nature of Sino-Turkish relations. According to the International Monetary Fund (IMF), China had the second largest economy in the world after the United States, with a total nominal GDP of $11.0 trillion; whereas Turkey ranked eighteenth, at $733.6 billion.[44] Similarly, China is the world's largest exporter with $2.15 trillion worth of exports per year, while Turkey comes twenty-seventh at $143 billion. But neither is reliant on the other for exports. Chinese exports to Turkey make up only 1.1 percent of China's total exports, while exports to China make up only 1.7 percent of Turkey's total export volume. In other words, China does not really depend on Turkey as an export market, and Turkey's dependence on China as an export market is minimal as well.

Forms of economic interaction other than trade in goods offer a similar picture. Cross-border investment relations between China and Turkey have so far remained limited. According to data released by the Turkish Under-secretariat of the Treasury, the total stock of Turkish direct investment in China was $104 million as of 30 June 2015.[45] Turkish direct investments are scattered around the country in various sectors, such as shopping centers, the retail trade in general, food and beverages, household appliances, textiles, and clothing.

China's total direct investment in Turkey, on the other hand, is reported by the Ministry of Commerce of China to amount to $642 million, more than six times larger than Turkish investment in China, but still only a tiny slice of China's total outward investment, which totals $107.8 billion. In other words, Turkey receives only a fraction of China's total investment around the world. According to Turkey's Ministry of Economy, there were 46,756 companies with foreign capital registered in Turkey as of 1 January 2016, out of which only 739 were Chinese companies; 338 of these companies were involved in wholesale trade, 103 in retail trade, and 35 in hospitality (hotels and restaurants).[46] An overwhelming majority of these companies are small- and medium-scale enterprises, in many cases even one-person companies, whereas large-scale Chinese direct investment is yet to enter the Turkish market.[47]

In the services trade, Turkey is a surplus country, while China is a deficit country. In 2014, Turkey's service exports totaled $51.1 billion, of which tourism services amounted to $29.6 billion. In the same period, China's total service imports were $223.5 billion, of which tourism amounted to $128.7 billion. In other words, tourism is the major item in the services trade for both countries, but while Turkey is a net recipient of tourists, China is a supplier of them. Despite this seeming complementarity, there are no significant tourism flows between the two countries. This situation is particularly a concern for

Turkey, which relies on tourism revenues to cover, albeit partially, its current account deficit. According to data released by Turkish National Police, 36.2 million foreign nationals entered Turkey in 2015, out of which only 314,000 were Chinese citizens, meaning the share of Chinese passport holders within all foreigners entering Turkey was 8.7 percent, compared with 15.4 percent Germans and 10.1 percent Russians.[48] Turkey depends more on Germany and Russia for tourism income than on China. Meanwhile, the number of Turkish tourists visiting China is difficult to identify, but from observation one would expect that the revenue they generate has minimal effect, if any, for the Chinese economy.

The liberal perspective on the relationship between economic dealings and political alignment or conflict between countries implies, in a nutshell, that the more the two countries depend on each other economically, the lower is the likelihood that they will have conflict, and the greater are the chances that there will be political alignment between them. Countries that are economically dependent on each other solve their differences through peaceful means, through dialogue. As the investigation above suggests, there is no real dependence between China and Turkey in the economic realm, except maybe in the marble industry where China depends on marble bought from Turkey, and Turkey needs China as a market to sell it. However, even this single industry is problematic when viewed from the angle of dependence, because first of all marble is rather a luxury product, and secondly, as discussed above, while China is making attempts to reduce the vulnerability caused by this dependence, Turkey is not happy with the way the marble is traded. Larger volumes of crucial raw materials and/or technological products, greater tourism exchange, more direct investment especially in heavy industry and infrastructure could have made these two countries more dependent on each other economically, but this does not exist so far. In the meantime, the realist paradigm asserts that in asymmetrical relationships of dependence, greater asymmetry can lead to higher likelihood of conflict.

According to trade expectations theory, anticipation of future trade and investment can bring countries closer together, reducing the likelihood of conflict and making political alignment more likely. Expectations from future trade and investment between China and Turkey are very high at the discourse level. For instance, in 2010 the two governments announced that they would increase the bilateral trade volume to $50 billion by 2015 and to $100 billion by 2020.[49] The target for 2015 reached just over a half of that figure, with the actual trade volume for 2015 at $27.3 billion. If the objective for

2020 is achieved, and the current export-to-import ratio remains unchanged, this will place an additional burden of more than $90 billion annually on Turkey's already problematic current account deficit.

While trade volume targets boasted by politicians do not usually come with detailed roadmaps, Turkey and China can be more specific with respect to their expectations in other areas. For instance, Turkey officially expects more investment from China, and as Turkey's Ministry of Economy stated in a report: "In order to contribute to the efforts of partially making up for the growing trade deficit between the two countries, China is expected to initiate greater overtures into Turkey in the form of investments, construction services, projects in transportation, tourism and energy sectors. The deepening of our relations in the field of investment constitutes a vital process with respect to the establishment of stable and lasting cooperation."[50] Turkey's business community is also very explicit when expressing its expectations. An unpublished study prepared by DEİK's Turkish-China Business Council provides a list of products of which the Turkish producers are expected to export more to China, a similar list of import products from China that are deemed to have the potential to add greater value to the Turkish economy, and makes the point that "Turkey should encourage investments with high technology component from China in a way that these would serve Turkey's development requirements."[51]

The OBOR project is opening up new opportunities for Turkey to receive more Chinese investment, and Turkey has high expectations from this initiative. In the meantime, China also expects to make Turkey a part of this project. Railroads, as OBOR's backbone, hold a key position with regard to these mutual expectations. China is implementing what international pundits call "high-speed rail diplomacy" in order to promote its technology expertise, which is welcomed by Turkey.[52] In November 2015, China and Turkey signed a number of inter-governmental agreements, two of which were related to joint investment in railroads. The memorandum of understanding for the "harmonization of the Silk Road Economic Belt and the 21st Century Maritime Silk Road with the Middle Corridor Initiative" and the "railroad cooperation agreement," which is about building a high-speed railway link between Kars and Edirne, in other words between the easternmost and westernmost points of Turkey, will make Turkey officially a part of OBOR, fulfilling both sides' expectations.[53] Turkey will in this way modernize its domestic rail network through new high-speed rail lines, and improve its ability to reach export markets in Central Asia and beyond, while China will consolidate OBOR through the Turkish route. These agreements are welcomed by both sides, but a note of caution is required at this point in case of a gap between deals concluded on paper and outcomes achieved on the ground. For instance, the recent railroad cooperation agreement is in fact a renewal and extension of a framework agreement reached five years ago, which expired due to inactivity. In conclusion, trade and investment expectations have a more positive effect on the relationship between China and Turkey than the actual levels of trade and investment between the two countries. Nonetheless, if these expectations are not at least partially met, there is doubt that China and Turkey will be able to build a stronger connection.

Finally, how the Chinese and the Turks perceive and—borrowing from the terminology of constructivist literature—"construct" each other also plays a role in determining the shape of the relationship between the two countries. Public opinion surveys do not paint a favorable picture here. A Pew Research Center Global Attitudes survey shows that in 2015 only 18 percent of the Turkish respondents answered the question of whether they have a favorable view on China in the positive (compared with 40 percent in 2005), while 59 percent expressed an unfavorable view.[54] These findings are confirmed by Liu Zuokui's survey, which found that 22 percent of the Turkish respondents had "very unfavorable" views of the Chinese, whereas 45.5 percent had "somewhat unfavorable" views.[55] The situation is similar in China with respect to attitudes toward Turkey and the Turks. Kutay Karaca's study reveals that only 17.7 percent of the respondents in China have a favorable view of Turkey, with the main reason for the unfavorable attitude being the Uyghur issue and Turkey's perceived role in it.[56] In an environment dominated by negative mutual perceptions, it is only natural that the relationship between the two countries is easily derailed, despite ongoing economic interaction.

Conclusion

This chapter has offered a critical take on Sino-Turkish relations. Turkey and China have declared that they engage in strategic cooperation, they take steps to improve their relationship particularly in the economic realm, and there is often a positive outlook on the development of the relationship, which does not remain restricted to politicians' rhetoric but is also raised by members of the business community and academics. Despite this seemingly favorable picture, the relationship can easily go off the rails, and there are strong ups and downs in the relationship, as witnessed during the second half of 2015 and early 2016. If both China and Turkey pursue their economic interests, and if there is a positive mood shared by all the stakeholders, why do the relations deteriorate so rapidly? If these countries are cooperating strategically, why this reluctance in furthering their partnership?

This chapter has attempted to answer these questions by investigating the relationship between economic interaction and the prospects of political conflict or political alignment. Despite the appearance, and relatively high trade figures, only minimal economic dependence is found between China and Turkey, which makes the relationship vulnerable to effects such as developments in the Uyghur issue. In the meantime, the asymmetry in the relationship caused by China being the economically more influential partner in the dyad makes the relationship even more prone to conflict. Expectations from future trade and investment are shared by both sides, but the positive effect of these expectations on the overall relationship is likely to remain limited if not enough concrete steps are taken to turn expectations into outcomes. In addition, mutual perceptions between Turks and Chinese citizens are distinctly negative, inflicting an adverse effect on the development of relations between the two countries.

There is, however, still considerable room for growth in the relationship between the two countries. The reluctance between the two partners will continue as long as economic dependence on each other remains low and perceptions do not change for the better. However, things can and do change. Through projects like OBOR, Turkey and China can do more business with each other, and in this way they can grow more interdependent. Greater interaction can also replace misperceptions. If this can be the case, and there is no reason to suggest otherwise, a more stable relationship with fewer ups and downs will be the case between China and Turkey. Such a strong partnership will surely have major implications for the region and the global order.

6

CHINA AND THE IRAN NUCLEAR NEGOTIATIONS

BEIJING'S MEDIATION EFFORT

John W. Garver

The problem and the thesis

This chapter analyzes China's policies toward the negotiations over Iran's nuclear activities between Iran, the five permanent members of the Security Council, plus Germany (P5+1) (hereafter the "Seven Party talks") from the inauguration of Barack Obama as president in January 2009 to the signature of the Joint Comprehensive Plan of Action on 14 July 2015. The chapter seeks to identify the contours and evolution of Chinese policy toward those negotiations, plus the calculations underlying those Chinese policies.

The thesis developed by this chapter is that China's policies underwent a significant shift early in Obama's second term that started in January 2013, with China playing a much more active and substantive role in the talks. Earlier, including during Obama's first term but following an approach tracing all the way back to the 1979 hostage crisis, Beijing was content to remain a bystander to big power diplomacy involving Iran; follow the lead of the United States, Moscow, and European capitals; and garner the status rewards of being deemed a responsible power willing to work in tandem with other leading powers to address important security concerns. Simultaneously, Beijing sought to protect China's commercial/energy interests with the Islamic Republic of Iran (IRI). Prior to early 2013, Beijing sought to keep both sides (Washington and Tehran) minimally happy, and took the initiative only when China's commercial interests with Iran were threatened by Western-driven sanctions. In essence, Beijing sought to balance the relationship between Washington and Tehran.[1]

Early in 2013, however, following Obama's re-election the previous November, China shifted gear. It began using its good offices to ease tension and facilitate communication between the bitterly hostile US and Iranian negotiators. It began advancing its own suggestions, with a "basket proposal" accommodating the core concerns of both sides. Namely, these concerns were Iran's non-pursuit and non-possession of nuclear weapons; recognition of its "right" under the NPT to non-military research and utilization of nuclear energy; and the lifting of sanctions imposed on Iran since 2006, when Security Council sanctions began. China's top leaders, including Xi Jinping, began openly lobbying Tehran about the need to address international concerns satisfactorily about possible military dimensions of Iranian nuclear programs. Foreign Minister Wang Yi "actively mediated" (*jiji woxuan*) the dispute between Tehran, the United States, and Europe, encouraging the two sides to compromise and meet each other half way (*xiang xiang er xing*).[2] As part of this effort, authoritative Chinese representatives made clear to Iranian leaders that China was prepared to participate largely and generously in Iran's development effort, but that the premise of such participation was a satisfactory resolution of the Iran nuclear issue. Given the political and economic importance of China to the IRI, it seems likely that Beijing's more active approach played a significant role in bringing about the agreement of 14 July 2015.

The activist shift in Chinese policy toward the Iran nuclear talks seems to have grown out of five main factors. These are:

1. A long-pending proposal by one of China's top Iran hands, Ambassador Hua Liming, that China's traditional policy of balancing from the side lines was sub-optimal and should be modified by a Chinese effort to mediate the Iran-US conflict. This proposal seems to have been "in the filing cabinet" of the Ministry of Foreign Affairs (MFA) for several years, before it was drawn out of the cabinet and put into practice in early 2013.

2. A pattern of low-level Chinese mediation between the US and Iran during 2009–10, behavior welcomed by both Tehran and Washington as it provided concrete examples of what China might do. In a sense, China experimented with mediation of Iran-US relations at a lower and confidential level before publicly putting the imprimatur of China's top leaders on that effort in 2013–15.

3. New fluidity in Iran's internal and foreign policies that made successful mediation more likely.

4. Xi Jinping's accession to paramount power in November 2012 led to a determination that China's greater power and global interests mandated a more active diplomacy in many regions, including the Middle East. The resulting higher-profile diplomacy was expected to mobilize popular support for China's communist party regime, and Xi's helmsmanship of that regime. The Iran mediation effort seems to have been one component of this more activist approach to China's diplomacy.

5. A rethinking of the consequences of an Iran-US war for China's interests, especially as focused by mounting apprehensions over Xinjiang's internal stability.

Evolution of China's handling of the Iran nuclear issue

Hua Liming, born in Shanghai in 1939 and educated in a Christian mission school, was one of the first college students in the PRC to be trained in Farsi at Beijing University. Premier Zhou Enlai directed in the mid-1950s that a cohort of young people already fluent in English be selected to train in other major languages, and Hua chose to study Farsi. After mastering that language, Hua entered China's diplomatic service. He served six years in Afghanistan, acted as interpreter for the flurry of Sino-Iranian interactions in the early 1970s, then in 1977 was posted to Tehran. There he watched the mounting uprising against the Shah in 1978–9, and then witnessed Iran's new Islamic regime excoriate China for its firm support of the Shah. Hua returned to Tehran as China's ambassador, 1991–5, then further as ambassador to the UAE and the Netherlands. Hua retired from China's diplomatic service in the early 2000s to become a Distinguished Research Fellow at the Ministry of Foreign Affairs' think tank, the China Institute for International Studies, a position he occupied when he wrote the items discussed in the following paragraphs. Hua Liming is one of China's top Iran hands. He also had good relations with American diplomats in Tehran during the Shah's reign and, after the revolution, had many discussions with Iranians about Iran's relations with the US. These interactions influenced Hua's later views about the likelihood of eventual US-Iran rapprochement, and about how China might best navigate that process to its advantage.[3]

In early 2015, Hua published a concise history of China's policy toward the Iran nuclear issue.[4] That study identified three stages of China's handling of the Iran nuclear issue: 1991–2002; 2003–12; and 2013 through early 2015. Hua dates the beginning of China's involvement in the Iran nuclear issue to 1991 when, after the end of the Iran-Iraq war, Russia and the IRI began discussing possible Russian cooperation in the construction and operation of a large nuclear electrical power plant at Bushehr, on Iran's Persian Gulf coast. That project had been planned with projected German assistance prior to the 1979 revolution, after which Germany withdrew from the project, leaving the way open for Moscow. This immediately roused US opposition and made Iran's nuclear programs an issue in Sino-US relations. During the mid-1980s, China had emerged as Iran's major partner in the nuclear area. By the end of 1991, according to Hua's account, Washington condemned China's nuclear cooperation with Iran, calling that cooperation "unacceptable" and demanding that Beijing end such ties. In Washington's eyes, it presented to China "strong and convincing evidence" that Iran was developing nuclear weapons in violation of the NPT, and insisted that China act responsibly to uphold the nuclear non-proliferation regime. Beijing fended off US demands and/or linked them to the Taiwan arms sales issue. Then in negotiations with the US in 1995–6 over twin summit visits to mark re-normalization of Sino-US relations, Beijing agreed to disengage from Iran's nuclear programs.

Ambassador Hua dates the onset of the second stage of Chinese policy to the revelation in October 2002 of a secret enrichment plant at Ferdow near Nantanz, and a plutonium-producing heavy water reactor at Arak. These discoveries led to US efforts to sanction Iran, first via the IAEA and then via the UN Security Council. US pressure on China to support strong sanctions against Iran became more intense, making the PRC-US relations "exceedingly complex," according to Hua.[5] Three principles guided China's approach during the second stage, once again according to Hua Liming. They were: 1) Iran should not have nuclear weapons; 2) China's economic interests in Iran should not be injured; and 3) the Iran nuclear issue should not be handled in a way that could lead to war. The US was deeply suspicious of the China-Iran relations, according to Hua, and sought sanctions against Iran that would impair Sino-Iranian economic cooperation; the US used China's ties with Iran as a "test of whether China was a responsible country." All this rendered the Iran nuclear issue a "negative factor" in Sino-US relations.[6]

China-Iran economic ties, including energy imports, expanded rapidly during the 2000s, and those ties were important to China. Yet, Beijing's core principle was that the Iran nuclear issue should not become an obstacle in development of Sino-US relations. Thus, China voted "yes" on all four sets of US-backed Security Council resolutions, but only after negotiating with the US to minimize damage to Sino-Iranian economic cooperation. Yet even then, China's policies eroded Sino-US relations. "The US thought that [China's] economic cooperation [with Iran] goes beyond economic interests and reflects sympathy for Iran" against the United States, Hua concluded in his account.[7] Washington was "extremely dissatisfied" with China's economic cooperation with Iran, seeing the advance of PRC companies to fill the void left by the exit of European, Japanese, and Korean energy firms as manifestations not as mere profit seeking, but as calculated strategic advance.[8] The corrosive effect on Sino-American relations of Beijing's traditional policy of balancing between Washington and Tehran in their chronic struggle was a major reason why Hua urged a Chinese effort to end that struggle.

In the first 2007 issue of *Guoji wenti yanjiu* (studies in international affairs), a publication bearing the imprimatur of the MFA, retired Ambassador Hua Liming laid out the logic of a Chinese effort to mediate the increasingly intense Iranian-US conflict.[9] Hua's article argued that China's traditional policy of balancing between Tehran and Washington was eroding its relations with both. The United States suspected that China was supporting Iran as part of a master strategy of tying down the US in the Middle East. China's constant support for Tehran against the United States—as equivocal as that support might be—was taken by many in the United States as evidence of a Chinese effort to undermine the US position in the Middle East. Tehran, for its part, saw China as a paper tiger because of Beijing's constant capitulation to US demands over Iran, and as an insincere opportunist because of Beijing's unwillingness to antagonize Washington even while professing solidarity with developing countries struggling against its hegemony. Moreover, there were convergent interests between Iran and the United States (e.g. regarding ousting Saddam Hussein, majority [Shiite] rule in Iraq, and stabilizing post-Taliban Afghanistan) that made some sort of eventual reconciliation between Tehran and Washington likely, and when that happened, Iranian and American dissatisfaction with China's earlier policy could leave it out in the cold. The souring of the important Iran-China relations might be the result.

On the one hand, China enjoyed good ties with both Washington and Tehran at both the personal and political levels. Both Washington and Tehran saw China as playing a balanced role in the nuclear dispute. These were assets that might be used on behalf of a Chinese effort to mediate the Iran-US conflict. Reduction of Iran-US tension would serve China's interests. China would be better able to expand economic cooperation with Iran without antagonizing the United States. China's vital relations with the United States would be relieved of constant corrosion by conflict over China's links with Iran. If successful, Chinese mediation might win Iranian and American gratitude and world recognition of China as a responsible and peace-loving rising great power. On the other hand, unmitigated Iran-US conflict could lead to yet another Middle East war that would be as disastrous for China's economic relations with Iran.

Hua's proposal lay dormant for several years, but meanwhile mid-level Chinese representatives were already engaged in de facto and secret mediation.

China's initial de facto, low-level mediation effort

Documents leaked in early 2010 by US Army specialist Bradley Manning to WikiLeaks boss Julian Assange offer a fascinating insight into PRC practical diplomacy in the period immediately preceding Beijing's decision to mediate the US-IRI conflict.[10] Two main points emerge from this rich data. First, China was under sharp US pressure to stand with Washington against Iran on the nuclear issue. WikiLeaks documents offered many examples of this US pressure. In September 2009, for example, Deputy Secretary of State James Steinberg briefed Foreign Minister Yang Jiechi and other MFA officials on key themes of President Obama's upcoming visit to China. Steinberg stressed the importance of the recent P5+1 foreign minister statement in the UN General Assembly on the Iran nuclear issue, adding that the US valued China's role in creating this statement. The P5 + 1 had to continue to present a united front to Iran, Steinberg said. Yang replied that Presidents Obama and Hu Jintao had discussed Iran at their recent meeting, and that China understood the importance of the issue to the United States.[11]

Under Secretary of State for Political Affairs William J. Burns made a follow-up visit to Beijing a week after the end of Obama's visit to China, during which it was made clear that for the US, Iran was a core national security issue, and that the US saw China's willingness to agree to apply more pressure to a recalcitrant Tehran as "an important test of China's willingness to stand with us." Washington expected full Chinese support for mounting US pressure on Iran, as a litmus test of China's sincerity in partnering with the US; whereas continued Chinese equivocation could injure China's vital relations with the US. Yet siding with the US would undermine China-Iran economic ties or, even more, Beijing's long-term effort to build an all-weather cooperative partnership with Iran. Settlement of the Iran-US conflict offered a way out of this conundrum.

Chinese leaders had long concluded that China's interest in good relations with the United States far outweighed China's interests with Iran, and therefore cooperated with the US on Iranian issues. At the same time, however, commercial transactions between China-based or China-owned firms and Iran were a constant irritant in Sino-US relations. US queries and protests over these interactions were a major theme of the WikiLeaks documents. Chinese leaders feared that, one way or another, China would be identified by US Congressional opinion as a covert sponsor of Iran's nuclear efforts. Beijing's ties with Iran might lead to anti-China economic legislation by Congress, possibly resulting in a "trade war" which would be the "worst outcome" for China. In short, Beijing's traditional policy of balancing interests threatened to erode China's ties with Washington.

The second point to emerge from the WikiLeaks documents is that for several years before Beijing's decision to mediate US-IRI conflict openly and at the highest level, mid-level Chinese representatives were already passing messages between Tehran and Washington under the protection of presumed diplomatic secrecy. In the process, China's representatives were broaching their own proposals, urging both Tehran and Washington to be calm and patient, to respect one another's interests and ego, and seek a comprehensive settlement of the nuclear issue with compromises from both sides. It seems that to some extent the policy decision of late 2012 to mediate US-IRI conflict over Iran's nuclear programs was a repackaging and endorsement at a high level of practices that had already been underway in a more piecemeal and secret fashion for several years. High policy apparently grew out of more mundane diplomatic interactions. Earlier interactions welcomed by both Washington and Tehran perhaps provided reason to believe that a more high-profile effort would succeed, or at least not lead to diplomatic embarrassment. If successful, Chinese mediation might offer a way out of the ongoing erosion of both Sino-Iranian and Sino-American ties.

Here are some examples of this early, low-level Chinese mediation. In February 2010, the deputy director of the Iran Division of the West Asian

Department of China's MFA, Ni Ruchi, advised a US Embassy Political Minister Counselor about how to handle negotiations with Iran.[12] Ni urged the US to be patient. The last year of Obama's term in office showed that a new and open-handed approach toward Iran was not enough to overcome accumulated mistrust, Ni said. At the same time, increased Western sanctions would not help coerce Iran. Instead, they would only cause Tehran to react negatively. China sought a "thorough solution" of the Iran nuclear issue, Ni said, as he reprised for the American diplomat China's recent lobbying in Tehran. China had urged Iran to be flexible. Iran had said they were willing to discuss with the P5+1 ideas about processing low-enriched uranium outside Iran, as well as parameters for processing uranium. This led Ni to suggest that the Seven Parties pursue these themes in their negotiations. PRC diplomats had stressed to Iran, Ni reported, the importance of increased transparency by the Iranians regarding their intentions in developing nuclear technology. Iran's recent open display of its progress in the nuclear field should not be taken as evidence of intent to weaponize, Ni urged. If Iran were interested in weaponizing its nuclear technology, it would do so in secret, not through public displays. Iran could not be expected to capitulate to Western demands, Ni warned, but a compromise might be attainable.

Another example: a discussion on 20 October 2009 with Li Guofu of the China Institute for International Studies (CIIS)—"a senior Middle East specialist at a well-connected [i.e. MFA] think tank," according to the US embassy report to Washington—urged the US Deputy Political Minister Counselor that in negotiating with Tehran the multilateral channel should be used to present accomplishments in public, but the bilateral rack was the only forum in which real compromise was possible. Li Guofu also informed the American diplomat that Supreme Leader Ali Khamenei was personally driving the negotiating process and was prepared to improve relations with the United States.[13]

Chinese thinking about the great quandaries facing the quest for better US-Iranian relations, as well as some of the difficulties the demands of both Washington and Tehran for China's support could cause Beijing, was conveyed to Washington by Ambassador Jon Huntsman in February 2010. Drawn from *Huanqiu shibao*, it is worth quoting at length since it elucidates both attitudes described above:

> Because Iran and the West have been hostile to each other for decades, they have lost each other's trust. For many years the West has easily and continuously threatened Iran using sanctions, which have not solved the problem but only intensified

rancor and speculation [of war] between the two. This is a problem that the West must seriously consider. They [the US and Iran] both believe that if they are tough, the other will eventually give in. Impractically, they both believe that if they apply enough pressure to China, that in this confrontation China will choose their side. China does not deny the existence of its interests in Iran. Meanwhile, China advocates the balance between the ... countries' interests concerning regional issues. Therefore, no one can kidnap China ... They should be clear that China's own national interests outweigh the interests of any other country. Whoever forces China in a more coercive way will be more likely to be refused by China. Both sides should compromise to further avoid escalating this confrontation.[14]

Beijing's mounting concern over a possible US-IRI war needs to be seen in the context of US and Israeli movement toward a pre-emptive military strike to destroy the enrichment complex at Ferdow.[15] Soon after Obama took office in January 2009, he ordered the Pentagon to develop options for a strike on Ferdow. He also approved an ongoing campaign of Israeli-US cyber attacks on Iran's enrichment program. The US Air Force analyzed the operational requirement of a successful strike, while Israeli forces practiced strike missions, probed Iranian air defenses, and pushed for US transfer of massive bunker-busting munitions. In March 2012 Obama publicly reiterated his willingness to use force to prevent Iran from acquiring an atomic bomb. But parallel to this push toward war, efforts for a diplomatic solution advanced. In December 2011 Obama sounded out Omani leaders about opening a secret back channel to Iran's leaders. The first secret US-IRI meeting in Oman followed in July 2012, but went nowhere. Diplomatic efforts persisted. Then, in October 2013, the Seven Party Talks began. Throughout this process, Israel pushed hard for US and/or Israeli military action against Ferdow.

In this context, Beijing decided to add China's weight to the search for a diplomatic solution and avoid another potentially big war in the Gulf. It did this with the approval of Washington, and probably Tehran. As will be shown later, China's "positive contribution" to the diplomatic search for peace was lauded by IRI leaders.

In sum, Iran-US confrontation posed difficult and potentially costly choices on Beijing. War could force China to choose between Tehran and Washington, and the inevitable "choice" in favor of Washington could spoil China's valued partnership with Tehran. On the other hand, Beijing's ties with both countries were not burdened by years of distrust and rancor. Mediation offered a way out. The same article in *Huanqiu shibao* quoted above made the point that by working with the US on such issues as the Iran nuclear issue, China could improve its global image: "the US relies on China on global issues such as ... Iran and North Korea .... China should take the opportunity to showcase China's positive image to the world ... [and] transform US influence into positive rather than negative factors."

New developments in Iran make success more likely

New movement in Iran on the nuclear issue also contributed to China's decision to attempt mediation by making success in that effort more likely. US Treasury Department sanctions, combined with a January 2012 EU embargo on the purchase of Iranian oil, and the exclusion of Iranian banks from the SWIFT system two months later all produced a sharp deterioration in Iran's economic situation. According to scholar Alex Vatanka, Supreme Leader Khamenei concluded that economic relief was vital to prevent revolt, and that some sort of deal with the Western powers on the nuclear issue was essential to achieving that end.[16] Khamenei also understood that a seeming moderate like Hassan Rouhani was necessary to achieve an accommodation with the West, and to this end he engineered his election as president in June 2013. Khamenei also reigned in the Revolutionary Guard Corps, ordering them not to undermine Rouhani's vital effort to ease economic pressure on Iran. The author does not know how much information about these or similar developments was picked up by Chinese intelligence agencies. In any case, to the extent that Chinese leaders were aware of these developments when deciding to attempt mediation, prospects for success would have seemed greater and risks of embarrassing failure less.

Launching of China's formal mediation effort

Hua Liming dates the third stage of China's policy toward the Iranian nuclear issue—defined by China's effort to mediate the Iran-US conflict via the Seven Party talks—to 2013. Hua identifies several factors underlying the shift in policy. The rise of Sunni extremists such as the Islamic State in Syria and Iraq, along with the potential for a Taliban return to power in Afghanistan following the planned withdrawal of US forces in late 2014 (later deferred to the end of 2016), enlarged the scope of common Iranian and American interests. Tehran accelerated its nuclear activities during the last several years of Mahmoud Ahmadinejad's presidency (2005–June 2013) in an effort to consolidate and expand its increasingly dominant position in the region, according to Hua. Washington responded to Iran's steadily stronger position and accelerated nuclear programs with tighter economic sanctions. By mid-2012 the US had put in place financial sanctions that, in effect, constituted a global embargo on normal trade with Iran.[17] US-Iranian relations were at a turning point: continued escalation of the conflict between those two countries could lead to war, a prospect that both sides feared. Both sides were willing to talk in hopes of finding a non-violent way out of their confrontation, but those talks—for example, the first round of the Seven Party talks, held in Istanbul in April 2012—were without result. The atmosphere of the talks was tense and hostile. Suspicion was high between all parties. Obama insisted on "keeping all options on the table," meaning a military strike against Iranian nuclear facilities if necessary. However, he also clearly recognized that this would encounter many difficulties, including further encouragement to extremist movements across the Middle East. All of this is according to Hua Liming.

In these circumstances, China was posed to play an "irreplaceable role" and a "critical function" in the Iran nuclear talks. The question for the United States, as posed by Ambassador Hua Liming, was whether the US could escape its old policy of hostility to the IRI and "achieve rapprochement with an independent regional power like Iran. Could the United States concede a degree of hegemony in the Middle East for the sake of its global strategy? Faced with a situation of great change in the Middle East and the world, the U.S. needed to answer these questions."[18]

It must be noted that a premise of Hua's case for Chinese mediation is that reconciliation between Iran and the United States would require US acceptance of Iran as independent regional power, not Iranian subordination to the United States. In other words, China was not helping the US achieve hegemony over the Persian Gulf, but helping a more modest, realistic and less ambitious United States cede a degree of strategic independence and autonomy to the Islamic Republic of Iran, rather as the Nixon administration had done with China in 1972. As will be discussed later, this is an important point in defense of China's mediation effort against Chinese critics. The United States' capacity to influence events in the Middle East was diminishing, Hua explained. Repeated wars with Iraq and in Afghanistan had eroded US strength, and regional powers—Israel, Saudi Arabia, Turkey, as well as Iran— were increasingly attempting to fill the growing void left by US, Iraqi, and Egyptian decline. China's own interests in the Middle East were growing rapidly: energy imports, trade, labor and engineering services, and the security of sea lines of communication. China's own comprehensive national power was growing rapidly, and in this situation, it behooved China to use its steadily greater influence to nudge developments along lines compatible with China's interests, primarily by maintaining peace and stability in the region as a vital precondition for an expanding Chinese economic role.

During the 1980s and 1990s, when China's power and Middle Eastern interests had been much less, it had been appropriate for China to follow Deng Xiaoping's prescription of *tao guang yang hui*, low-profile approach. But that traditional approach of "plugging away at its own modest task" (*du shan qi shen*, a humble and homely self-deprecatory expression occasionally used by Deng to define his self-restrained approach to China's diplomacy) no longer served well a more powerful and interested China.[19] This call for a more pro-active diplomacy comporting with China's greater power was in line with Xi Jinping's call for a new style of Chinese diplomacy.

Defense of peace and stability in the Middle East via mediation of the Iran-US conflict would not only serve China's material interests, Hua explained, but would identify China as a peace-loving and responsible rising great power, thereby enhancing China's soft power. The countries of the Middle East already universally esteemed the "hidden strength" of China's economic development, Hua continued, and looked on a rising China as expanding their "international space" by balancing traditional big powers (i.e. the US and its European allies) in the region. If China added to this impressive resumé an effort at peace-making via mediation of the Iran-US dispute, it would further strengthen China's regional appeal. Working in tandem with the West to persuade Iran to reassure the international community adequately that it was not pursuing nuclear weapons would, Hua continued, would help offset US displeasure over China's policies in the East and South China Seas.

The internal Chinese politics of the mediation effort

China's effort to mediate the Iran-US conflict and comprehensively settle the nuclear dispute between those two countries contradicted important and widely held verities of contemporary Chinese political culture: to wit, that the United States is engaged in a vast campaign to injure China in various ways, and that a good way to counter malevolent US anti-Chinese efforts is to keep it mired in strife in the Middle East. Many objections of this sort to the MFA's mediatory effort were aired on the website/radio broadcast *Qiang Guo Luntan* (Great Power Forum) in December 2012 in the run-up to its launch and at about the same time as Hua Liming and Yao Kuangyi would have been composing their explanations of China's new policy.[20] All these efforts were an ideological preparation of Chinese public opinion for the upcoming bold new departure for China's Iran diplomacy. The redoubtable Hua Liming was the key explainer and defender of the *Qiang Guo Luntan* program of the MFA's mediatory effort.[21] The second caller to the forum got right to the point: "If the United States goes to war with Iran, what injury would this do to our [China's] interests?" Hua was equally direct in his response:

> If the United States, Israel and Iran touch off a war over the nuclear issue it will be a disaster for the Middle East region. Not only will Iran suffer a potentially lethal (*zhiming*) attack, but the entire region will be consumed by the flames of war because once Iran is attacked it will definitely respond with counter attack. Then, US military bases and forces in the Persian Gulf, Iraq and Afghanistan will become targets of Iranian attack and the entire Middle East will be consumed by the flames of war. The Middle East is a major supplier of oil. Sixty percent of the world's oil comes from the Middle East and the Middle East has the world's most important oil transport lines. Once war breaks out in this area, sixty percent of world oil supply will stop. The world economy will be severely injured. The world economy that is just beginning to recover will suffer an even bigger disaster. China will be the first to suffer. Therefore, China does not want to see war break out in this region, but hopes for peace.

The next caller asked why China should help the United States when the US was sanctioning Chinese companies over economic transactions with Iran. Hua Liming responded by pointing out that China had endorsed four rounds of UN Security Council sanctions and had "sincerely implemented" the resulting obligations. But China did not participate in any sanctions outside the Security Council framework, Hua explained, and China recognized and struggled against the "serious injury" to China's economic ties with Iran done by extra-Security Council sanctions. Addressing the implication of the caller's question that China had somehow become a junior partner in US hegemonic enterprises. Hua continued:

> China's economic interests [with Iran] cannot be "kidnapped" [*bangjia*] by US hegemony, so the matter of China helping the US steal the riches of Iran (*fen dan bao fu*) does not exist. The reason why China advances diplomatic talks is because it desires a peaceful solution to the Iran nuclear issue, and not war. This is in line with China's interests, and also those of the US, as well as the rest of the world's interests.

The Forum moderator then interjected: "But if the Iran nuclear talks succeed, the American bastards [*meilao*] will be better able to confront us. Therefore is it not best to let the US and Iran fight each other?"[22] Hua responded: "In fact a US-Iran war would be a disaster for the whole world.

Once war breaks out, China would be the first to suffer; it would not be in China's interests." Another caller raised the issue of US arms sales to Taiwan and suggested that the proper response to these would be for China to form a "military alliance" with Iran along with Cuba and North Korea. Hua condemned US weapons sales to Taiwan and pledged a "strong response" to any such sales. At the same time, the notion of forming a military alliance to confront the United States was an out-of-date cold war mentality, Hua said. If countries such as China, Iran, and others wanted to become strong enough to oppose US hegemony, the most effective method was to "take good care of [zuohao] their own countries."

Still, another caller asserted that in a world dominated by a US quest for global hegemony via war, possession of nuclear weapons was a "miraculous sword" [makelijian] able to deter the United States and protect a state. Thus, China should support Iran's acquisition of nuclear weapons, the caller said. Hua responded that China had signed the Nuclear Non-proliferation Treaty and would sincerely uphold its obligations under that treaty. North Korean possession of nuclear weapons had not enhanced stability in that region, and neither would nuclear proliferation in the Middle East. It would exacerbate regional conflicts and bode absolute disaster if such weapons were ever used. Another caller returned to the same point: if Iran were pulled into the US sphere of influence because of US pressure and denuclearization, there would be no power in the Middle East able to balance the United States. This would be unfavorable to China. For China to "break out of encirclement" by the US, it should resolutely support Iran's "technological [i.e. nuclear] advance."

Scholar Zhu Xuhui, Hua Liming's co-respondent on the forum, gave considerable insight into what seems to be a key premise of Beijing's mediation effort: the proud and nationalist Persian people would not allow themselves to be controlled by the United States, and China should not worry about such a possibility. The Iranian people dream of Iran being a great power, Zhu Xuhui said. They hope to be recognized as a regional great power. To a considerable extent, Iran's desire to possess nuclear capability was a matter of internal politics, of satisfying the nationalist pride and longings of the Iranian people. No matter who ruled Iran, they would not be able to compromise on the principle of Iranian greatness; "If they did, they would lose the support of the people."

Extrapolating a bit from Hua's and Zhu's comments, one premise underlying Beijing's mediatory effort seems to be a degree of confidence that improved Iran-US relations; even a genuine strategic rapprochement between the two countries to confront the Islamic State and stabilize Syria, Iraq, and

Afghanistan would not leave China out in the cold. During the 1970s Iran under the Shah had close relations with both the United States and China precisely in order to secure the support of each for Iranian regional pre-eminence. Chinese commentators, including Hua and Zhu in the December 2012 *Qiang Guo Luntan*, expressed the belief that Iran's quest for nuclear capability was not to destroy Israel, but to influence Iran's regional rivals Saudi Arabia, Turkey, and Israel, while securing from the United States recognition of Iran's interests in the Persian Gulf region. If China helped Iran secure that American recognition via mediating a compromise settlement between Tehran and Washington, China could win a degree of Iranian gratitude and trust, constituting a significant element in the edifice of all-weather Sino-Iranian strategic partnership and mutual trust that Beijing aspires to build.

The callers to the MFA's *Qiang Guo Luntan* almost certainly were not members of China's foreign policy elite. Yet the views they expressed touched on high politics in two ways. First, the views expressed by callers probably do reflect the views of some high-ranking officials in the military, state security, and propaganda and ideology agencies of the PRC party state, and the views of those officials do figure in high-level elite politics. Second, the anti-US views expressed by *Qiang Guo Luntan* callers probably represent a wide swathe of Chinese public opinion, and this popular opinion may be mobilized by one elite group to undermine another group. This means that embarrassments or failures, especially those resulting in injury to China's reputation or interests, could become a potent criticism of the MFA's bold mediatory effort and of the top leaders who authorized this approach.

Xi Jinping and the decision to mediate

The decision to attempt mediation of the US-IRI conflict was linked to Xi Jinping's selection as Secretary General of the Chinese Communist Party and China's paramount leader on 15 November 2012. Xi took office convinced that China needed a more active, assertive foreign policy reflecting a stronger, rejuvenated China. China's relative standing in the world was vastly increased over the era several decades earlier, when Deng Xiaoping had mandated a low-profile approach for China's diplomacy. A new era with new horizons for China's diplomacy was necessary, Xi believed. A number of bold moves followed in quick succession: ratcheting down tension with Japan, free trade agreements with South Korea and Australia, the Asian Infrastructure Investment Bank, and the "One Belt, One Road" project.[23] The decision to mediate US-IRI ties has the hallmarks of Xi's bold initiatives. It sought to grow a larger regional and global role for China over the longer run, while turning down the temperature of regional conflicts in China's periphery over the short term. It sought to maintain constructive relations with the West, and it sought to uphold domestic stability by upholding China's periphery. The linkage between external and internal stability was primary.[24] As Andrew Scobell's Chapter 1 and Andrew Small's Chapter 9 in this volume explain, wars involving Iran, Pakistan, or Afghanistan could pose profound challenges to Xinjiang's stability.

China's mediatory effort

Figure 6.1 shows a flowchart of China's decision to undertake mediation of US-IRI relations.

In March 2013, in the waning months of the Ahmadinejad presidency, China's deputy ambassador to the UN Security Council, Wang Min, outlined key strands of China's position following a report by the UN Iran sanctions committee.[25] China respected the work of the Iran sanctions committee and would continue to implement measures in common with other Security Council members. The Iran nuclear issue was linked to the authority of NPT institutions, and China encouraged Iran to advance and strengthen its cooperation with the IAEA. But China did not approve of the threatened use of force (by Washington against Iran) and to unilateral promulgation of sanctions by "big powers" to expand arbitrarily (i.e. without Security Council approval) the scope of sanctions, thereby injuring the legitimate interests of other countries (i.e. China). China strongly objected to this arbitrary injury to its legitimate economic interests. According to the MFA's Yao Kuangyi,

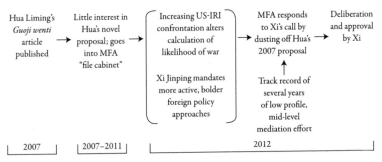

Figure 6.1: Evolution of mediation policy

throughout the negotiations over the Iran nuclear issue, China conducted "necessary struggle" against implementation of US unilateral sanctions that injured China's economic interests. This included compelling the United States to extend several exemptions on China's purchase of Iranian oil.[26]

In early June 2013, shortly before Hassan Rouhani's victory in Iran's presidential election on a platform of improving relations with the West, China's ambassador to the IAEA again laid out China's views.[27] China welcomed plans for talks between Iran and the IAEA about possible previous Iranian conduct of military-related nuclear research and development. China urged Iran to be more flexible in these negotiations, and to strengthen its cooperation with the IAEA.

During the twenty-six months between June 2013 and July 2015, Chinese representatives urged Iranian leaders to bring the Seven Party talks to a successful conclusion on at least seventeen occasions. These episodes of Chinese lobbying are summarized in Figure 6.2. These exhortations included some at the highest level (paramount leader, Politburo Standing Committee members, and foreign minister) and were openly reported by China's media. China, in other words, put its prestige on the line.

Xi Jinping kicked off China's effort in mid-September 2013 during his initial meeting with newly elected President Rouhani on the sidelines of a Shanghai cooperation organization summit in Bishkek, Kirgizstan. This was three months after Rouhani's election and a month before Seven Party talks were scheduled to resume. Xi welcomed the positive attitude of Iran's new government regarding the resolution of the Iran nuclear issue.[28] Resolution of the nuclear issue was tied to Iran's "substantial interests" as well as to regional stability. China hoped, Xi said, that all parties would focus on advancing practical dialogue. China respected Iran's legitimate rights and resolution of the issue via negotiations. China was willing to continue constructive efforts to promote the peace talks, Xi told Rouhani. Iran's new president replied that Iran's ties with China were very important, and that cooperation in all areas should be expanded. Rouhani reiterated Iran's contention that its nuclear programs were entirely peaceful and for such purposes as generation of electrical power. Rouhani also said that Iran was ready to accept IAEA inspection within the provisions of the Nuclear Non-proliferation Treaty, and in this way eliminate international concerns. The Iranian leader also expressed the hope that China would continue to play a "constructive" role in deliberations over the Iran nuclear issue.

Figure 6.2: High Level Chinese Lobbying of Tehran to Settle Nuclear Issue

Date	Event	Gist of discussion
Jul. 2012	Secret meeting US & IRI envoys in Oman	
Jun. 2013	China ambassador meets Rouhani	China welcomes new approach of IRI & talks w/IAEA
Sep. 2013	Xi Jinping & Rouhani meet in Bishkek	Xi Jinping welcomes positive attitude Rouhani re nuclear issue & urges settlement
Oct. 2013	IRI-P6 talks begin	
Nov. 2013	Interim agreement IRI & P6	
May. 2014	President Rouhani state visit to China	Xi Jinping and Rouhani agree on future expanded cooperation in all areas
Jul. 2014	VFM Li Baodong talks w/ FM Javad Zarif in Luzanne	"deep exchange" of views on on-going nuclear negotiations
Jul. 2014	Secretary General MFA disarmament section Wang Qun meets Iran Deputy Prime Minister Abbas Araghchi in Vienna	"deep exchange" of nuclear issue and discussed possible modalities for addressing issues. Wang conveys China's hope all parties show greater flexibility, narrow differences, and reach comprehensive settlement
Aug. 2014	VFM Zhang Ming meets deputy FM Ebrahim Rahimpour in Beijing	Zhang reprises increased mutual trust arising from recent summit meeting. Xi Jinping and Rouhani and China's willingness further increase cooperation "in appropriate ways"
Oct. 2014	Wang Qun visits Tehran. Talks w/Supreme Leader Khameni and Iran VFM	"deep and comprehensive exchange of views" on nuclear issue. Wang urges Iran accept "basket" deal and focus on reducing disagreements step by step
Nov. 2014	CCP internal security chief Meng Jianzhu visits Iran. Talks with Iran Interior Minister	discuss expanded law enforcement cooperation with focus on Xinjing
Nov. 2014	FM Wang Yi telephone call w/ Javad Zarif	Wang urges Iran to show greater flexibility & seek balanced comprehensive agreement

Dec. 2014	VFM Zhang Ming to Tehran for talks	"deep exchange of views" and "political consultations" regarding nuclear issue
Feb. 2015	FM Wang Yi to Tehran. Talks w/Rouhani & FM Javad Zarif	Discuss Iranian participation in "One Belt" project, Iranian development, and nuclear issue. Urge Tehran to establish trust with Six Parties & reach agreement.
Feb. 2015	IRI legislative leader to China, talks w/FM	Wang Yi reiterates support for resolution of nuclear issue via negotiations
Mar. 2015	Wang Yi telephones Javad Zarif	urges "political decision" to close gap and reach settlement
Mar. 2015	Wang Yi meets Zarif in Lausanne	express China's hope all parties seize the opportunity to reach settlement
Apr. 2015	Xi Jinping meets Rouhani in Jakarta	Xi Jinping reprises "One Belt" program and hopes for early and durable nuclear settlement
May. 2015	Wang Qun to IRI; talks w/ IRI atomic chief	discuss matters related to comprehensive settlement of nuclear issue
Jun. 2015	Wang Yi meets w/ Zarif in Moscow	Wang calls for "political will" to overcome "hardships" in reaching settlement
	FM = Foreign Minister	VFM = Vice Foreign Minister

When the Seven Party talks resumed in October 2013, China advanced several principles intended to guide the talks. According to Yao Kuangyi, this was the first time that China had advanced its own position on a comprehensive solution to the Iran nuclear issue.[29] China's principles were as follows. First, the Seven Party talks were the proper venue for the search for a settlement. Implicitly: neither party should walk away from those talks out of frustration or resort to some framework that excluded an important interested party. Second, the talks should seek a comprehensive, fair, reasonable and long-term solution. Third, the parties should strive to create an advantageous atmosphere and advance step by step toward a solution.[30]

A Xinhua commentary of November 2013, when the Interim Agreement was signed, outlined the "two hands" of China's mediatory effort.[31] One "hand" entailed "lubricating" interactions between long-estranged and deeply hostile parties, the US and the IRI. China had good relations and long familiarity with both parties and used those good offices to reduce hostility and "uphold justice." The latter formulation presumably meant recognizing the core concerns of both sides. China's second "hand" entailed advance of "constructive proposals" (*jinshexing de fangan*) at critical junctures. Shortly after the Seven Party talks began in October 2013, for instance, China proposed that "first of all," Iran should not possess nuclear weapons. Development of nuclear weapons (by Iran) was not advantageous to world peace, security, and stability, or even Iran's own real security. Secondly, Iran's security and economic concerns should be adequately addressed, and Iran's "right" to the peaceful use of nuclear energy should be upheld. Third, force should not be used. War would not "solve the problem" and would cause great instability across the Middle East.

Another "constructive proposal" by China came in February 2014, issued by Vice Foreign Minister Li Baodong.[32] After lauding the progress achieved in talks up to that point, Li called on all parties to seek a complete, fair, reasonable, and long-term solution to the problem. This could only be done on a "balanced" basis addressing the concerns of both sides. This was China's "basket" (*lanzi*) proposal. Iran should comprehensively resolve the concerns of international society regarding its nuclear activities, and fulfill its obligations under provisions of the NPT. At the same time, Iran's use of nuclear science for civilian purposes should be guaranteed by international society. As this was done, all multilateral and unilateral sanctions imposed on Iran should be "gradually" (*zubu*) lifted and international society should broadly develop various forms of cooperation with Iran. China hoped, Vice Foreign Minister Li Baodong said, that Iran would show greater flexibility regarding measures to limit its nuclear programs, and that the six powers would reciprocate appropriately by easing sanctions. All sides should demonstrate good faith and sincerity, and seek above all to maintain an atmosphere of dialogue. China was opposed to any type of pressure. The latter was an implicit reference to US threats of sterner sanctions or use of military force.

Wang Qun, director general of the arms control department of China's foreign ministry, met in Vienna with Iran's deputy foreign minister, Abbas Araghchi, for yet another "deep exchange" of views in July 2014. Wang Qun expressed the hope that Iran and its six negotiating partners would show greater flexibility, narrow their differences, and seek an early and mutually beneficial win-win comprehensive settlement of the nuclear issue.[33]

In November 2014 Meng Jianzhu, CCP Politburo member and head of the CCP's Politics and Law Committee, visited Iran as special representative of

Xi Jinping.[34] Meng met with Interior Minister Abdolreza Rahmani and Vice President Eshaq Jahangir to discuss increased cooperation in law enforcement and internal security with a focus on Xinjiang.[35] An MFA spokesperson said of Meng's talks in Tehran that China was willing "to play a positive role in maintaining both countries' security interests and promote regional peace and stability."[36] Meng apparently explained to IRI leaders China's concerns that war in the Gulf would undermine Xinjiang's internal security.

The same month that Meng Jianzhu was in Tehran, Foreign Minister Wang Yi arrived in Vienna with a new set of "modalities" (*silu*) intended to address "outstanding questions."[37] China also hoped to "mediate" (*woxuan*), especially between Iran and the United States, hoping to reduce differences and increase mutual understanding, Wang told the media. An early and comprehensive settlement would be advantageous to the "normal lives of the Iranian people," Wang said, and also to the maintenance of the NPT and to peace and stability in the entire Middle East region.

Wang Yi travelled again to Tehran in mid-February 2015 for talks with Rouhani to present China's ideas about cooperation in the ambitious "One Belt, One Road" project.[38] Wang Yi made clear the broad scope of China's projected infrastructure development, along with the reality that resolution of the nuclear issue is a precondition for realization of those infrastructure plans. China had excess production capacity that it hoped to turn toward an infrastructure expansion project along with participation in Iranian industrialization, Wang Yi said. China was also prepared to increase cooperation with Iran in efforts to advance the "democratization of international affairs." Implicit in this concept was resolution of the nuclear issue on the basis of recognition of Iran's "right" under the NPT to civilian use of nuclear power. The nuclear talks had entered their final stage, Wang Yi said. He continued: "China lauds President Rouhani's emphasis that Iran does not seek to develop nuclear weapons. We hope Iran will seize the opportunity of the Seven Party talks to establish trust [i.e. between Iran and the international community], overcome difficulties, and reach an early and mutual comprehensive agreement."[39]

When the Seven Party talks resumed in Lausanne in November 2014, Wang brought with him a set of four Chinese viewpoints (*zhuzhang*).[40] Firstly, all sides should increase political leadership and make political decisions. If the talks remained mired in technical details, settlement would be difficult. Secondly, the two sides should make compromises, meeting each other halfway. Third, the two sides should proceed step by step, and not return to ground already covered. Finally, a settlement should be a "basket" or package agreement, addressing the core concerns of both sides. Such a settlement should also utilize the important role of the United Nations.

China also donated RMB 1.5 million (about US$ 250,000) to support the IAEA's first phase of inspection of Iran's nuclear facilities under the emerging accord.[41] Modification of the heavy water reactor at Arak was one concrete area in which China played a significant role. The configuration of the reactor then under construction would produce considerable amounts of fissile plutonium, and the two sides reached an agreement to redesign the reactor so as to produce considerably less plutonium. China had experience with design and construction of the requisite lower-plutonium reactor, and agreed to assist Iran in modifying the Arak facility.[42] Chinese personnel in this role were more acceptable to Iran than would be European or American.

How significant was China's lobbying of Tehran to make compromises adequate to "settle" the nuclear issue? Two considerations address this question: first, Iranian expressions of gratitude for China's efforts; second, China's ability to render substantial assistance to Iran's national development efforts—if the nuclear issue reached a comprehensive and durable settlement.

Regarding the first factor, a few examples of the many Iranian expressions of gratitude to China will suffice:

In July 2014, Deputy Foreign Minister Araghchi thanked Wang Qun for China's active and important role in the negotiations.[43]

In August 2014, Deputy Foreign Minister Ebrahim Rahimpour praised Vice Foreign Minister Zhang Ming for China's constructive role in the talks.[44]

During a November 2014 telephone discussion with Wang Yi, Javad Zarif thanked China for its fair and important role in the talks.[45]

In March 2015, Zarif praised the "important role" that China's proposals had played in negotiations, and hoped that China would continue to exercise its influence in the ongoing negotiations.[46]

It is possible that these Iranian expressions of gratitude were merely cheap ways of giving China face. But it is equally possible that Iran's leaders were grateful for China's assistance in escaping sanctions, preventing war with the United States, and securing recognition of Iran's "right" to full scope nuclear fuel cycle, albeit one restricted to non-military parameters. If Iranian expressions of gratitude are genuine, China's mediatory effort may have been a significant stone in the edifice of a Sino-Iranian partnership that Beijing aspires to build in the long run.

China had apparently applied important economic leverage with Tehran. With Western economies mired in deep recession, financial crises, sovereign debt crises, and ballooning governmental deficits, China alone among Iran's Seven Party counterparts was in a position to offer substantial assistance to Iran's national development efforts. However, China had to do this without spoiling its vital relations with the United States via entanglement in a US-IRI confrontation. China's ambassador to Iran, Pang Lin, laid out very clearly and to an Iranian audience the link between resolution of the Iran nuclear issue and large-scale Chinese participation in Iran's development.[47] Speaking in March 2015 to a public forum jointly presided over by Iran's deputy foreign minister and head of the Sino-Iranian Friendship Association, Ambassador Pang began by reprising the long histories and "glittering civilizations" of Persia and China which gave them "much common language." Pang turned next to review the expanding exchanges of all sorts between the two counties and a "blueprint" for expanded cooperation recently agreed to by presidents Xi Jinping and Rouhani at their May 2014 meeting in Beijing. The "One Belt, One Road" program would become a major driver of greatly expanded cooperation, Pang said. Ambassador Pang then turned to the crux of the issue:

> Ladies and gentlemen, friends. Just now the Iran nuclear talks have reached a historic favorable opportunity. If a timely and comprehensive agreement can be achieved, this will create a more relaxed external environment and more investment opportunities. China has from start to finish taken an objective and fair position regarding the Iran nuclear issue and is happy if Iran and the Six Powers reach an early comprehensive agreement. China will continue to play a constructive role, urge all parties to move toward one another, and reach an early and comprehensive agreement.[48]

It is not necessary to weigh which prospect offered greater incentive to Tehran to come to terms with the international community on the nuclear issue: the re-opening of trade and investment ties with Europe; re-entry into the global financial system via lifting of US unilateral sanctions; or the prospect of expanded cooperation with China via "One Belt, One Road" and Chinese participation in Iranian industrialization. All three are important for Iran's development. But the large size of China's foreign currency reserves, its massive industrial capacity (even over-capacity), the extremely impressive record of development achieved by China over the last forty years, and the important role China has played in Iranian development since the 1988 end of the Iran-Iraq war suggests to this author that the China factor weighed heavily.

Clarification by Chinese representatives of the lesser level of Chinese assistance to Iran that would be forthcoming from China if the nuclear issue remained unresolved should not be taken as some sort of coercion—although it may fairly be construed as a type of indirect pressure. China's representatives were stating the facts of life: if Chinese firms had to choose between the US and global economies or Iran's economy, most would choose the former. China's interests with the United States far outweighed its interests with Iran; Chinese representatives had made this point clear to IRI representatives half a dozen times since 1979. China would not confront the United States on behalf of Iranian interests in a region of secondary importance to China and thereby risk spoiling the generally supportive attitude of the United States toward China's development effort. And new railways, highways, pipelines, and industrial development zones would not be built in zones of war and instability. By making clear to Iran these economic-political facts of life, China created potent incentives supporting its mediatory effort in the Seven Party talks. It may not be going too far to say that China's role in achieving the July 2015 deal was second only to the roles of the United States and Iran itself.

Beijing welcomed the agreement signed on 14 July 2015. The most important aspect of that agreement, according to Foreign Minister Wang Yi was that it safeguarded the nuclear non-proliferation system while giving Iran the legitimate right to utilize nuclear science peacefully for civilian purposes. Iran had made a political commitment not to develop nuclear weapons and that commitment was cemented with broad international agreement by all powers.[49] Wang also suggested that negotiated, peaceful settlement of the complex and difficult Iranian nuclear issue might serve as a "positive reference" for the Korean nuclear issue. Wang also highlighted China's mediatory role. Quoting directly from the MFA media statement:

> As a permanent member of the UN Security Council, China is aware of its responsibilities and obligations to international peace and security and [has taken] a constructive part in the whole negotiation process. China is not a focus of the contradiction and that enables it to carry out active mediation ... Especially at some important points when the negotiations met with difficulties and reached the deadlocks, China actively explored ideas and approaches to resolve the problem and put forward its own solution from a perspective ... of the common interests of all parties.[50]

Wang also expressed the hope that the 14 July agreement would open the way to expanded China-Iran cooperation.[51]

Summing up

The main Chinese interest served by China's effort to mediate Iran-US conflict was avoiding a war that would injure a series of major Chinese interests:

disrupting China's energy supply from the Gulf; precipitating a global recession disastrous for China's exports; disrupting projected Western-oriented infrastructure links; and most important of all, exacerbation of internal security concerns regarding Xinjiang arising from refugees and extremism.

A second-order Chinese objective was burnishing China's reputation as a responsible and important great power: as a power sincerely upholding the Nuclear Non-proliferation Treaty and the right of independent-minded non-Western countries to use civilian nuclear energy; as a peace-maker not a trouble-maker, and as a country of considerable influence on major issues of war and peace. There were several relevant audiences: the US Congress; Europe, which Beijing hoped to attract; and Third World opinion. Not least, a prominent display of Chinese diplomacy on an important issue would impress Chinese public opinion.

There was an unspoken but probably high-ranking geopolitical objective underlying China's peace-making diplomacy: preventing the collapse of Iran as a balancer of the United States in the Gulf. The simple reality was that a war between Iran and the United States could leave Iran in ruins. Drawing on the experience of Iraq, which was transformed from a major regional power in the 1980s to a failed and fragmented state, due largely to two lost wars with the United States (i.e. 1991 and 2003), Chinese strategists certainly realized that war with the US would inflict immense injury on Iran, perhaps eviscerating its comprehensive national power for decades. China's own development strategy since 1978 had been premised on avoidance of confrontation with the United States to give China a decades-long period in which to develop and become strong. China's study of the Soviet collapse and of the rise of great powers over history had also led to the conclusion that prudent rising powers avoided premature confrontations with the incumbent hegemonic power. Application of this concept to Iran suggests that Iran would be wise to avoid a possibly catastrophic conflict with the United States, making such compromises as necessary to avoid this and gain time for self-strengthening. Sharing this strategic insight in private with Iranian leaders may well be a key component of the "deep exchange of views" between China and Iran on "international issues of common concern."

China had a unique set of assets that positioned it to mediate US-Iran relations. It had good relations with both the United States and Iran. It was a valued strategic partner and interlocutor of both. It made sense to China's leaders to use those unique assets to protect China's own interests, to demonstrate to China's people the growing power and influence of their country, and to make a contribution to world peace.

China's effort to mediate US-Iran conflict via the Seven Party talks offers an example of China's use of its growing power to promote peace or—stated more explicitly—to avert war between the IRI and the United States. China's diplomacy at this juncture offers a statesman-like effort to promote reconciliation between major powers, even when such reconciliation might result in loss of certain strategic advantages for China. It offers an example of sincere Chinese effort to uphold the global non-nuclear weapons proliferation regime. It offers a clear example of an acute Chinese sensitivity to the probable destabilizing effect of war; and it offers a reassuring example to other countries that China will use its ever greater power to uphold peace and international stability. The success of parallel Chinese and US policies toward the Iran nuclear issues at this juncture also offers an example of how the two countries may work in tandem to address first-order security issues, even when they have serious differences in approach and geostrategic interests.

7

CHINA AND IRAQ

Joseph Sassoon

Relations between China and Iraq give an interesting insight to how China maintains strong and cordial relations with developing countries such as Iraq throughout decades of turbulence, and manages to benefit from dramatic changes such as the invasion of Iraq in 2003. From Iraq's point of view, China represents a very different model compared to relations with ex-colonial powers or new superpowers such as the US. As Mehran Kamrava argues in Chapter 3, the "China model" definitely appeals to countries such as Iraq: rapid growth under authoritarianism or what is known now as competitive authoritarianism,[1] without the complexities that an "American model" brings with it. This is enforced by the disillusionment among many Arab countries with the US's lack of long-term commitment to the region. This chapter will argue that China-Iraq relations could be an important litmus test for the new Chinese leadership in dealing with unstable countries which are abundantly rich in resources that are essential for China's long-term growth.

This chapter will examine the relations between China and Iraq, with the first part concentrating on a historical review of the relations between the two countries, going back to the 1950s. The chapter will then highlight the reaction to the 2003 invasion of Iraq, while the third part will analyze how relations between the two countries have developed in the last twelve years since the invasion. An assessment of three facets that has made Iraq a strategic partner to China in the decade since the invasion will be undertaken: trade and economic dealings; oil; and arms supplies. These three factors are critical to understanding how China perceives Iraq in its overall trade and global strategy. The final section of the chapter will highlight the risks and challenges that China faces in its bilateral relations with Iraq.

Historical review: 1958–2003

Addressing the history of relations between the two countries is instrumental to appreciating how relations between China and Iraq developed during the more than four decades that preceded the invasion. For instance, the 1970s shed light on how China managed to maintain some influence with Iraq in spite of the Soviet Union's pressure on the then Iraqi regime to reduce its dealings with the Chinese, given the competition between the two communist powers. The 1980s, dominated by the eight-year war between Iraq and Iran, typify how the Chinese adeptly managed to juggle between two friends who were at war, and yet both sides were purchasing huge quantities of arms, and the Chinese did not want to miss out on being part of this lucrative trade. Finally, the decade preceding the invasion, characterized by the harsh international sanctions imposed against the Ba'th regime, informs us how the Chinese government, even under such dire circumstances, succeeded in maintaining a dialogue with the Iraqi leadership. The tremendous inroads that China achieved after 2003 cannot be understood without looking at the three decades from the early 1970s until the invasion of Iraq, which clearly underline the long-term investment on the part of China in building, developing, and maintaining relations with a pariah regime.

Soon after the revolution of 14 July 1958 in Iraq that toppled the monarchy, the People's Republic of China (PRC) established diplomatic relations with Iraq, having previously perceived Baghdad as the "cradle for neo-colonialism" as it was considered to be the center of the Baghdad Pact created in 1955 to counter the spread of communism by the Soviet bloc.[2] The prominence of the communist party in Iraq in the first couple of years after the revolution inspired optimism in both the Soviet Union and China. All monarchies in the region were anti-communist, and so-called progressive regimes such as the United Arab Republic (created as a result of the union between Egypt and

Syria) under Gamal Abdel Nasser were persecuting local communists in both countries. By early 1960s, things began to change: first the local communists were losing power, and then Iraq's leader, 'Abd al-Karim Qasim, announced in 1961 that Kuwait would revert to Iraq after the British troops pulled out of Kuwait. This was the first instance of China having to deal with the uncertainties of the region. After some hesitation, China became the first communist state to recognize Kuwait since its independence, but was caught in a dilemma: China's closest Arab ally, Iraq, was threatening military action against Kuwait, the newly independent country. Although Qasim never proceeded with his threats to invade Kuwait, China was vehement against any new British military presence in Kuwait to thwart the Iraqi threats.[3]

The Ba'th Party in Iraq came to power for the first time in February 1963, and immediately launched arrests and massacres of local communists. The Chinese leadership perceived the Ba'th takeover as a "CIA-inspired coup," and harshly criticized the new regime for suppressing and persecuting the "patriotic and anti-imperialist forces."[4] Iraq became an interesting scene for the Sino-Soviet feud, and after the Ba'th regime was toppled in November 1963, China recognized the new government. As relations began to improve, China supported the arrest of the pro-Soviet local leader in Baghdad and claimed that he was responsible for the "deaths of many revolutionaries." This irked the Soviet leadership, which accused China of "trying to sow discontent among the revolutionary movements and for attempting to consolidate its influence in Iraq."[5]

The period before and after the 1967 War brought new changes: three of China's so-called friends and allies (Egypt, Syria, and Iraq) were defeated, which forced those countries to tilt more toward the Soviet Union, at the peak of the confrontation between the two communist countries. However, the Chinese took advantage of the dismay among Arab leaders with the Soviet conciliatory diplomacy toward the US, and the poor performance of Soviet military equipment during the war. The Chinese leadership increased its support to revolutionary movements such as the Palestinian Liberation Organization, and insisted that the Arabs would liberate their land from occupation.

The Ba'th rise to power in 1968 (which lasted 35 years until the 2003 invasion) ushered in a new era for the relationship between the two countries. With oil prices quadrupling after the 1973 war, Iraq's economy expanded significantly and Iraq became an influential country in the region. The Soviet Union was unhappy with Iraq under Saddam Hussein, as they believed that Iraq veered politically toward France and other Western countries during the

1970s; and even more threatening to the Soviet Union was Iraq's strengthening of its economic ties with China. This coincided with the death of Chairman Mao and Deng Xiaoping's rise to power. Economic modernization became the "center piece of China's domestic and foreign policy."[6] The 1970s witnessed China's change of policy, from promoting revolutionary models to emphasis "on government-to-government ties and increased willingness to play by the international diplomatic rules."[7]

The next dilemma for China in the region came with the outbreak of the eight-year Iraq-Iran War (1980–88). Initially, China was neutral in the conflict and urged both sides to resolve their differences peacefully. However, as the arms race between the two warring countries intensified, China decided to enter the lucrative market and began arming both sides. It supplied Iraq with tanks, artillery, and anti-ship missiles estimated by one source at $2.8 billion during the period 1984–88.[8] A much bigger predicament for the Chinese was Iraq's invasion of Kuwait in August 1990. Once again, the first reaction was maintaining neutrality, insisting that the Arab countries should resolve their problems by themselves, and disapproving of US efforts to create an international coalition to liberate Kuwait. However, under intense US pressure and promises of large economic loans, China abstained from vetoing two UN Security Council Resolutions: 660 that called for an immediate and unconditional withdrawal of Iraqi troops from Kuwait, and 661 that imposed economic sanctions against Iraq. Three weeks after the invasion, the official China policy was outlined: opposition to Iraq's invasion of Kuwait and the call for immediate withdrawal of its troops, while opposing any international intervention.[9] China's policy in this conflict underlined the adroitness of its policy-makers in international conflicts: on the one hand, it criticized the US-led military intervention in the conflict; on the other hand, it supplied arms to Saudi Arabia and, by abstaining from vetoing the UN Security Council Resolutions, it strengthened its ties to the West. Simultaneously, China maintained its friendship with the Gulf States and other Arab countries, which opposed the Iraqi invasion.[10] Furthermore, this policy enabled China to develop strong economic ties with Kuwait after its liberation. One hurdle that China had to overcome was the evacuation of 5,000 Chinese laborers from Kuwait after the invasion and Iraq's decision to prevent another 4,000 Chinese workers from leaving Iraq, as part of its policy to block the departure of many foreign workers after the invasion to create pressure on their respective governments.[11]

During the 1990s and until the collapse of the Ba'th regime in 2003, Iraq was under severe sanctions that the Chinese opposed, as they constrained any economic relations between the two countries. Once the Oil-for-Food Program was launched in the mid-1990s, the doors opened for some trade relations with Iraq, but on a relatively limited scale and with no arms exports. By the end of the twentieth century, China achieved most of its aims in the Middle East: it managed to maintain friendly relations with most Arab countries in spite of its dramatic policy switch with regard to recognizing Israel, having been in the past one of the most adherent supporters of the PLO. While China's economic relations with countries such as Iraq were hampered by the numerous inter-regional conflicts, it still succeeded in building robust bridges to the country and its leadership.

The 2003 invasion of Iraq

There is no doubt that the 2003 invasion of Iraq represented a key juncture in China's international relations. Already in November 2002, China voted in favor of the Security Council Resolution 1441 that authorized the use of force if Iraq failed to comply with a UN Resolution calling for the disarmament of Iraq. While officially, and similar to France and Russia, China opposed the invasion of Iraq, it took no steps to prevent it. For China's significant change in its usual modus operandi of abstaining in critical votes concerning other countries by voting in favor of Resolution 1441, the United States rewarded the Chinese, first by honoring the oil agreements that existed during the Ba'th era, and, more importantly, it was allowed to participate in the huge reconstruction of Iraq once the Saddam Hussein regime collapsed.[12]

In the perspective of twelve years after the war, China's gamble of shifting its priorities paid off, and it emerged as one of the main beneficiaries of the US invasion and the toppling of Saddam Hussein's regime (the other one being Iran). China, which had condemned the invasion, called for the halt of all military action, expressed its disapproval of the "flagrant abuses of human rights" by the US forces, and insisted on the need for returning the sovereignty of Iraq to its people.[13] While the invasion is seen as one of the greatest strategic blunders of the United States that led to the death of more than 4,500 soldiers, injury to approximately 30,000 others, and cost the taxpayers more than US$ 1 trillion, the occupation of Iraq can be seen as one of the big strategic wins for China, which managed to position itself advantageously. By representing itself as neutral, opposed to military actions by foreign forces, respectful of sovereignty, a middle-income country, and at the same time an economic power that could make a dramatic change in the socio-economic development of countries around the world, China became a key global player.[14] A case in point is Iraq, which found in China a significant energy and trading partner, including in arms. China, for its part, saw Iraq as an important component in its global strategy, particularly its oil potential. Beijing perceived a stable and prosperous Iraq as good for the whole region and for its core economic interests in the Arab world.

Immediately after the end of the war, Iraqi senior politicians and officials were invited to Beijing to discuss the relations between the two countries.[15] By participating in the reconstruction of Iraq after two devastating wars and thirteen years of harsh sanctions, China realized that this would open the doors for gaining a strong foothold in the country. As part of these efforts, China wrote off 80 percent of Iraq's $8.5 billion debt, as part of a deal orchestrated by the US with the Paris Club.[16] China's policy with regard to the reconstruction of Iraq was expressed by emphasizing three principles: "independence, sovereignty and territorial integrity."[17] Even after China became involved in the booming economic relations with Iraq, it continued throughout the period post-2003 to call for the withdrawal of US-led forces from Iraq and an increased role for the United Nations in the country. The next section, detailing the meteoric rise in trade and bilateral cooperation, will underline how successful China's policy toward Iraq has been from the beginning of the twenty-first century.

Relations between China and Iraq, 2003–2015

Trading relations

In coming to assess these relations, we shall first examine how trade relations developed in the twelve years since the invasion. As Table 7.1 shows, there was an exponential increase in Chinese exports to Iraq in the decade following the invasion.

Table 7.1: Annual value of Chinese exports, 2003–13

Year	Annual value of Chinese exports to Iraq in US$
2003	55,844,935
2004	148,945,230
2005	390,382,072
2006	479,236,822
2007	714,359,081

2008	1,257,305,498
2009	1,826,843,519
2010	3,581,583,986
2011	3,814,459,398
2012	4,862,313,932
2013	6,872,507,447

Source: OEC MIT data, http://atlas.media.mit.edu/en/

Chinese exports spanned a wide variety of products that Iraq desperately needed after decades of deprivation. As Table 7.2 shows, the value of these exports changed dramatically in percentage terms between 2005 and 2013.

Table 7.2: Chinese products as a percentage of total exports

Main Chinese exports to Iraq	% of total value of Chinese exports to Iraq, 2006	% of total value of Chinese exports to Iraq, 2013
Telephones	16.6%	No data*
Automotive parts	15.4%	0.9%
Men's cotton clothing	0.9%	2.6%
Air conditioning	1.3%	5.1%
Color television sets	2.1%	2.3%
Pneumatic rubber tyres	0.3%	2.3%

Source: OEC MIT data, http://atlas.media.mit.edu/en/
* Last reported data for telephones listed them as 1.8% of total Chinese exports to Iraq in 2011.

What is interesting in Table 7.2 is how China is truly a supplier of almost all products needed by Iraq, and that Chinese exports are not restricted to a dozen products but cover a wide array of exports. Furthermore, these exports substantially altered as Iraq's needs changed. For instance, during Saddam Hussein's era, mobile telephones were a luxury for government officials only; after the end of the regime, China began supplying vast quantities of telephones and mobile telephones to meet the popular demand. The public sector in Iraq is still the largest employer in the country, and immediately after the invasion, salaries were substantially raised allowing families to spend on "luxury" products such as modern color televisions and air-conditioning units.

In addition to the items mentioned in Table 7.2, Chinese exports spanned a wide variety such as containers, pipes, saloon cars, generators, pumps, etc.[18] More than forty items exported to Iraq had each a total value of over $18 million, underlining China's ability to meet the increasing demands of the Iraqi population. Hence, it is no surprise that by 2011 China was the second most important trading partner with Iraq after the European Union; 15 percent of Iraq's total imports were derived from China, ahead of the United States, which represented only 11 percent of total imports.[19] China also became involved in the construction sector, building roads, hospitals, and housing projects. Another important area where China is playing a dominant role is in the cement industry; the China National Materials Group Corporation (Sinoma) was involved in building seven cement production plants in Iraq to meet the insatiable demand for cement.[20]

The auto industry is another aspect of the growing trade between the two countries; the popular Chinese manufacturer, Chery, has a car assembly line and a very large showroom in Iraq. Telecommunications is another sector where there is huge demand: Huawei, a Chinese multinational networking and telecommunications equipment and services company, is providing training and equipment in Iraq, given the dire state of communications after decades of neglect. Iraq, for its part, has made efforts to attract foreign investment. For example, investments are tax-exempt for ten years; companies have the ability to repatriate investments and profits; and for China, an important offer was the right to employ foreign workers when needed.[21]

A comparison of Chinese exports to Iraq with other countries underscores the importance of the Iraqi market. By 2013, Chinese exports to Algeria were on the same scale as its exports to Iraq, in spite of the fact that Chinese exports to Algeria have been continuous without interruption since the mid-1990s. Along those lines, by 2010, Chinese exports to Syria were only $2 billion, and even Egypt, with a much larger population, received only $7.7 billion of Chinese exports.[22]

In sharp contrast to the extensively diverse list of Chinese exports to Iraq, China's imports from Iraq, while also increasing substantially in the decade after the invasion (see Table 7.3), were restricted to oil and gas. Oil probably represents about 98–99 percent of total Iraqi exports to China since 2009; and before that, oil constituted roughly about 95 percent of total Iraqi exports.[23]

Table 7.3 underscores how important Iraq has become to China post-2003 as it moved from being an insignificant trading partner to a major supplier of energy, as will be seen in the next section. The balance of trade was in favor of Iraq as overall Iraqi exports to China for the period under review totaled about $48 billion, while Chinese exports to Iraq for the same ten years (2003–13) reached $24 billion. Thus, Iraq has become an important source of energy for China, allowing it to diversify its imports as it becomes more dependent on that commodity. This expansion should be seen in the context of China's fast economic growth in the first decade of the twenty-first century, its rapid increase in demand for energy resources, and the need to find new markets for its expanding exports. Thus trade between China and Arab countries was boosted from $36.7 billion in 2004 to $107.4 billion in 2009,[24] although, without doubt, this trade expanded as a result of the insatiable demand for energy resources.

Table 7.3: Iraq's exports to China, 2003–13

Year	Annual value of Iraqi exports to China in US$
2003	317,633
2004	283,384,054
2005	369,361,591
2006	585,073,586
2007	684,345,115
2008	1,230,837,692
2009	2,907,673,794
2010	5,578,503,062
2011	9,219,248,694
2012	11,091,157,643
2013	16,086,105,483

Source: OEC MIT data, http://atlas.media.mit.edu/en/

Oil investments and exports to China

In 2006, China imported less than 1 percent of its oil from Iraq; by 2013, the number had jumped to over 8 percent, exceeding Algeria and Iran (the latter represented about 7.6 percent of Chinese oil imports), and slightly less than Oman (9 percent). Saudi Arabia is the only country with significantly more oil exports (about 19 percent of China's imports).[25] This was due to the increasing demand for energy by China: by 2013 it was the largest energy consumer in the world, with its share rising to 22.4 percent.[26] Beijing had changed its focus on the Middle East as a source of energy by 1993, when it realized that China's own oil production would not be sufficient for its growing demand as a result of the vast economic growth it was witnessing. Not having a colonial past in the region facilitated China's entry into the region's energy markets. The increase was nothing short of phenomenal: China's oil imports rose from 8.42 million barrels per year in 1990 to more than 270 million barrels per year in 2000, and by 2009 imports were averaging 2 million barrels per day.[27] Currently about 50 percent of China's oil imports are derived from the Middle East and about 25 percent from Africa. As a result of this increased dependence on the Middle East, China has avoided any provocation or direct confrontation with the United States related to the region. A case in point is its relationship with Iran; while China has become the largest trading partner of Iran, it has attempted not to provoke the United States and damage its Sino-US relations.[28] Energy policy is a central challenge for Beijing, and securing oil supplies to feed the continuing economic growth is now a fundamental Chinese national security issue.[29]

Iraq has the world's fourth largest proven reserves, with estimates of 115 billion barrels, and hence it is considered by China as "the wild card." Iraq's infrastructure was, and is, in a dire condition after two major wars and a prolonged period of severe sanctions.[30] What is truly remarkable is that in spite of the immense investment (almost a trillion dollars) by the United States in Iraq, the Iraqi government chose China over the US as its partner to develop its oil fields. In August 2008, Iraq signed a $3 billion agreement with the China National Petroleum Corporation (CNPC). Under the contract, CNPC will provide technical advisors, equipment, and workers to develop Al-Ahdab field south-east of Baghdad. CNPC will be paid for its services, but will not share in the profits of the oil field. The contract duration is twenty-two years, and CNPC was the first international oil company to sign a contract with Iraq since the 2003 invasion. The contract was a renegotiated version of a 1997 agreement between China and Iraq signed under the Ba'th regime.[31] Indeed, some observers ascribe the signing of the deal to the mutual interests that have developed between the two countries from the mid-1990s onward. Soon after the United Nations approved the Oil-for-Food Program, China explored the possibility of oil exploration deals, and the 1997 deal was signed soon after, as a reward for its opposition to the sanctions that gained China a lot of favor among the Iraqi regime. According to that deal, China would invest $1.3 billion to develop the Al-Ahdab field once sanctions were lifted. As a result, CNPC limited its activities to surveying the oil field.[32] The 2008 contract was a boon for Iraq: "The two sides have agreed on the only [sic] service contracts, under which Iraqi state firms keep all the oil while paying [the] Chinese company for its work, China would receive a service charge of $6 per barrel of oil produced at Al-Ahdab, which will be gradually reduced to $3 per barrel."[33]

In 2009, CNPC added to its achievements by signing a deal jointly with British Petroleum (BP) to expand Rumaila's daily production by investing $300 million to develop the field. In this contract with a duration of twenty years, CNPC has 37 percent, BP 38 percent, and Iraqi South Oil 25 percent. A few years later both BP and CNPC increased their holdings (47.6 percent and 46.4 percent respectively) as Iraq's stake was reduced to 6 percent. Rumaila's field is a very important one for Iraq's oil prospects; it has estimated reserves of 17 billion barrels, and produces around 1.3 million to 1.4 million barrels per day (bpd), almost half of Iraq's output of around 3.2 million in 2014.[34]

More deals followed: in 2010 CNPC, together with a consortium that included the French company Total, the Malaysian Petronas, and Iraq's Missan Oil, signed a service contract for the Halfaya oil field whereby CNPC has the majority of 37.5 percent and also acts as the operator for the production.[35] An analysis of Iraq's oil deals shows that Chinese companies are the leaders in terms of developing Iraq's oil fields, ports, and refineries. Of Iraq's (central government) capacity of 4,025,000 bpd, CNPC and China National Offshore Oil Corporation (CNOOC) are involved in 2,365,000 bpd, i.e. almost 59 percent of Iraq's total capacity. The next foreign company that has a significant participation is Shell with 750,000 bpd (about 18.5 percent), and the remaining oil contracts are scattered over a wide variety of European and Asian companies. The only American company that has any operation in Iraq is ExxonMobil, which together with Petrochina is involved in West Qurna oil field, which has a production capacity of about half a million bpd.[36] In order not to miss out on the potential in the north controlled by Kurdistan Regional Government (KRG), China Petrochemical Corporation (SINOPEC) is active in one of the large fields that represent about 30 percent of KRG's total capacity of 427,000 bpd. This means that SINOPEC will encounter serious hurdles in developing oil fields in other parts of Iraq, given the central government commitment that it would not deal with any international oil company that signs contracts without the approval of the Oil Ministry. But, in essence, Chinese companies have safeguarded their interests in all major locations in Iraq by having different companies explore in different regions of the country. As China's investments become more established and extensive in Iraq, the question that arises is whether China will be more involved in the long term in aiding Iraq's stability. Having invested billions of dollars, the question is: how would China react to a scenario where Iraq becomes a "political liability," and would China abandon its "offend no one policy" to protect its investments?[37] Apart from the political obstacles, China faces challenges and opportunities in helping Iraq confront some of the major constraints facing the energy sector. Most critical is the shortage of electricity, since the oil and gas industry is the major consumer of electricity at a time when the country is still struggling to meet the increasing demand by consumers, together with the challenge of having inadequate storage and pipeline capacity after years of neglect. From an economic point of view, Iraq also has its worries: China's slower growth means lower imports at a time when oil prices have collapsed to below $40. During 2015, Chinese oil firms kept the amount of crude they purchased from Iraq unchanged for the first time in a decade.[38]

Currently political obstacles seem more serious and threatening to Chinese oil interests. The Islamic State of Iraq and the Levant's (ISIL) occupation of Mosul affected production from northern Iraq, but had no impact on southern production and exports, which accounted for about 95 percent of Iraq's exports in 2014. ISIL has stolen oil from storage tanks and pumping stations, but the biggest blow to Iraq's production was the attack on Baiji, Iraq's largest oil refinery, causing the refinery to come to a halt.[39] CNPC's investments in Iraq make China the largest investor in the oil industry, and in a worst-case scenario, if Iraq were to break up along ethnic lines, CNPC's investments are all in Shi'i areas, which make it unlikely to fall into the hands of Sunni rebels or ISIL. The threat of ISIL will continue in the near future and will be further discussed in the fourth section of this chapter. SINOPEC had to withdraw some of its workers from northern Iraq when ISIL's attacks began, but a spokeswoman for the Chinese Foreign Ministry announced that there were more than 10,000 people working for Chinese companies in Iraq and the vast majority were outside conflict zones.[40] China had to evacuate most of its workers from Libya, following the collapse of the country, but it is doubtful that China will have to do the same in Iraq.

Given Iraq's increasing importance as a supplier of energy to China, it was natural that the relationship between the two countries expanded to another realm: providing arms and increasing military cooperation.

Arms sales and military relations

Unlike the US or Europe, China has no history of military bases or access agreements with countries in the region. In fact, only in late 2015, China announced that it would establish its first overseas military base in Djibouti, breaking a long-standing policy against building military outposts in other countries.[41] From the 1980s, China's strategy toward the region changed and it began to see it as an important market for its arms industry. As mentioned before, the Iraq-Iran War was a boon for Chinese arms sales, with sales estimated between $2.8 billion to $5 billion during the years 1982 to 1989.[42] Once the war ended in 1988, sales dropped dramatically; China, unlike the US, did not benefit from the First Gulf War, which boosted US arms sales significantly.[43] During the years 1998 to 2001, China's arms sales hovered around only 2 to 3.5 percent of the total arms sales to the region.[44] Given the strict sanctions imposed on Iraq from 1991 until 2003, there were no arms sales from China.

Although sanctions were lifted in 2004, the two countries first signed a deal only in 2007, when Iraq purchased $100 million of small arms for use by its police force. Iraq attributed the purchase to the slow pace of delivery of US arms. US officials were unhappy about the deal, as US intelligence concluded that some Chinese weapons such as rocket-propelled grenades and surface-to-air missiles were used against coalition forces and civilian targets. Some analysts believed that actually those arms were sold to Iran and Afghanistan and later were diverted to the insurgents.[45] Even prior to this deal, the US had been alarmed that as many as 190,000 weapons supplied by the US "disappeared" and found their way into the hands of Sunni and Shi'i militias.[46]

From the Iraqi point of view, Chinese arms are attractive on two levels: first they are cheaper than US, British, or French arms; and second, receiving military training in China is an added benefit, as some Iraqi officials perceive it as a hedge against the possibility that the US might cut its arms supplies to Iraq for one reason or another. But any discussion of Iraq's arms purchases cannot be complete without understanding the pervasive corruption surrounding the topic of training and supplying arms to the Iraqi army. There is no doubt that dubious arms contracts were one major factor behind the collapse of the Iraqi army. Tackling the extensive corruption that is impacting every facet of military and civil administration has become one, if not the most, serious challenge facing the country. The eight-year rule of Nuri al-Maliki will be remembered as a period when ministers and senior officials led the way in embezzling the country and creating a system where graft and bribery became the cornerstone of managing affairs in the country.

Statistics about arms exports to Iraq are scant, but reports indicate that China might have provided Iraq with armored vehicles, anti-ship missiles, and drones. In 2014 there took place the historic first visit by a high-ranking Chinese official since 2003; it was also the first by a foreign minister for twenty-three years. China's Foreign Minister Wang Yi told journalists that

China supported the sovereignty and territorial integrity of Iraq and its national stability, and added that he believed his visit would open new possibilities for cooperation. The Iraqi Foreign Minister Hoshyar Zebari mentioned that among the topics discussed was the purchase of Chinese arms, but he did not elaborate.[47]

In October 2015, a video released by Iraq's military showed a Chinese Caihong-4 (CH-4) drone with its own specific laser-guided missile being inspected in an Iraqi base.[48] In early December 2015, another video showed one of those drones destroying an ISIL position in Ramadi. According to a media report, "Iraq is the only known export user of the drone," and this was the first time it had been used in real combat. It is thought that Iraq bought six to twelve of these drones and received them in March 2015, in order to be able to conduct operations efficiently.[49] The sale of drones underscores the two reasons mentioned earlier in this section about the attractiveness of Chinese arms for Iraq: the lower price of Chinese drones compared to the US ones, and the ability to acquire sophisticated arms outside the influence and restrictions of the US. From China's point of view, the success of these drones in real combat situations could open huge opportunities for exporting them to many countries around the world who aspire to acquire these relatively cheap but sophisticated machines.

Other forms of military assistance have come in the shape of training Iraqi forces. Although an official Chinese spokesperson simply reiterated that "China has provided Iraq with help of various forms to the best of its capabilities," there was no elaboration as to the form of assistance. However, Iraq's foreign minister "divulged that training of Iraqi personnel is happening, but did not disclose how and to what extent."[50] Although China has declined to join the US-led efforts in fighting ISIL, it has declared its public support for coalition strikes against ISIL in Iraq.[51] Needless to say, dealing with ISIL or with terrorism threatening Chinese interests is one of the major challenges facing China in Iraq.

Risks and challenges for China in Iraq

China is facing a series of challenges in Iraq: strategic, political, and economic. Strategically, the biggest question looming is whether China will continue to adhere to its historical non-intervention policy in the domestic affairs of other countries. The policy has served China well in the last three decades, in stark contrast to the US and Europe with its long colonial history. However, China is not the same country as it was three or four decades ago, and the stakes have dramatically changed. Since 2008, China has become more assertive, given its increased capabilities and the reduced influence of the US after the bitter experience in Iraq and Afghanistan. Once the US announced its intention to withdraw its troops from Iraq, both the Chinese and Iraqi leadership realized that the US influence will begin to decrease and new opportunities would open for other powers.

China's energy security, as highlighted above, has become a core principle of China's foreign policy, given the reliance of the country's economic growth, technological advance, and human development on securing its oil supplies. "Beijing is ready to accept additional costs to ensure access to energy supplies from the region."[52] So far these have been restricted to the realm of oil investments, such as constructing a pipeline from Iran to Pakistan, without ever sending troops to protect those investments. An important feature that could lead to a change in the long term is that most of the oil and gas projects that Chinese national oil companies "have invested in since 2000 were in politically fragile countries" such as Sudan, South Sudan, Venezuela, and, since 2005, Iraq.[53] China has adopted a long-term outlook in its investments in the oil sector in Iraq, but given the almost unending state of instability, Chinese companies cannot ensure that the oil and gas they are helping to produce will reach its final destination in China. As some observers opined, the more deeply China becomes "embedded in the economies of the region, it will be harder to walk away from any supplier without causing itself severe energy and economic hardship."[54] This raises the issue of Beijing's non-intervention to protect its colossal investments if one of the suppliers, say Iraq, disintegrates politically, threatening both energy supplies and China's billions of investments. There is a further complication: the safety of Chinese workers in a country such as Iraq would carry internal political risks if many workers were to be harmed either by infighting between different groups or by acts of terrorism.

A principal constraint facing China's strategy in Iraq is its lack of political influence over the government and its public declarations that it would not send any troops to support Iraqi authorities. Frequently, Chinese analysts argue that there is not much political involvement in Iraqi politics or its military affairs, and "none of the chaos there has anything to do with us."[55] Of course this is quite a simplification, but it does abet the Chinese "no-offend" policy that has served them very well in the region since the 1980s.

Another topic is the competition between China and the United States in the region. As Dorraj and English argue, China has so far managed to exploit local tensions between the United States and major oil producers, and by its willing-ness to invest large amounts, it succeeds in securing access to vast resources of oil and gas. Their conclusion is: "The present competition between China and the United States over oil and gas resources in the Middle East is pregnant with opportunities for great power cooperation as well as conflict."[56]

Away from the global and strategic challenges, instability due to sectarian rift between Sunni and Shi'i militias, ISIL's encroachment on certain parts of Iraq, and potential terrorist attacks on Chinese workers or oil installations are all issues that Beijing will have to tackle in the coming years. As Simone van Nieuwenhuizen of Peking University wrote in *The Diplomat*:

> We shouldn't assume that China's only interest in Iraq is keeping the oil flowing. Indeed, China's security concerns are more and more tied up with stemming the growing influence of terrorist groups. Beijing sees a connection between global terror networks and domestic terrorism by Xinjiang militants, and thus China is invested in global anti-terrorism efforts.[57]

In fact, a Chinese newspaper, *Global Times*, reported that there were over 300 Chinese nationals fighting for ISIL by the end of 2014, and that the government is deeply concerned about the safety of its citizens at home and abroad.[58]

Dealing with Iraqi politics is no easy matter. Apart from the sectarian divide that has torn the country apart since 2003 and led to a civil war in 2005–7, Iraq is suffering from pervasive corruption that is impacting all economic and mili-tary decisions by the government. Al-Maliki and his ministers concocted end-less schemes to extract more money. For instance in 2011, when oil prices were hovering over $120 and Iraq received more than $72 billion from oil revenues, al-Maliki asked China to set up a fund to "help with the reconstruction of the war-battered county."[59] Unlike the Koreans or Germans who agreed to set up such funds, the Chinese wisely declined. Another key element in the relation-ship between the two countries is the fact that Iraq suffers from a debilitated infrastructure that could open the door to more opportunities to Chinese firms. However, Iraq is also suffering from high unemployment, given its utter reliance on oil, which employs about 1 percent of total labor. This raises the question whether Chinese workers, similar to what takes place in many African states, would carry out these large construction projects, thus preventing Iraqi labor from gaining employment or new skills.

Finally, there is the thorny subject of the relationship between Iraq's central government and the KRG. China has been consistent about its support of Iraq's geographical integrity, but as with many other countries, it realized that northern Iraq provides lucrative opportunities in a better and more stable political environment than the rest of the country. As mentioned, only SINOPEC invested in Kurdistan, and hence any conflict between the central government and the company would not necessarily impact Beijing's other vital interests in the country.

Conclusions

There is no doubt that, apart from Iran, China was the other country that reaped the biggest benefits from the 2003 invasion that toppled Saddam Hussein's regime. Iraq's rich resources in oil and gas opened up new possibilities for China to diversify its supplies and be less dependent on Saudi Arabia in the region. At the same time, Iraq, after decades of deprivation, wars, and sanctions, desperately needed a wide variety of cheap imports. Thus a symbiosis developed between the two countries, aided by the fact that China has no historical "baggage" in the region. It was fundamentally a bilateral relationship based on mutual benefits. Once the US administration announced its intention to pull out all American soldiers from Iraq, US influence began to wither. For instance, the Iraqis ignored the numerous calls by senior American officials not to allow Iranian planes to land in Iraq on their way to Syria carrying arms and ammunition to Bashar al-Assad's regime. The feeling within the Iraqi leadership, and in many quarters in the Arab world, is that the US is not as interested in the region as it used to be, and that its focus is more on Asia. This definitely left a vacuum of power that China from 2008 onward used to its advantage. Thus Chinese investments in building relations with Iraq over many decades, a dramatic change in Iraq's needs after the invasion, and the power vacuum mentioned above, all led to a structural enhancement of the relationship between Iraq and China. Iraqis perceive China as a positive force that will bring economic prosperity without a huge political cost, as the Chinese would not intervene in Iraq's internal affairs or "lecture" the Iraqis on how to run their institutions in a more open and free way. Another critical factor that is bolstering the relations between the two countries is China's willingness to take a long-term view on its investments, a luxury that Western companies cannot afford.

Unfortunately for both countries, Iraq has not enjoyed much political stability since the fall of the Ba'th. A bloody civil war raged for two years, and the sectarian rift, encouraged by the eight-year rule of Nuri al-Maliki, only exacerbated the situation. In 2014, the attacks of ISIL on Mosul and other parts of the country ushered in new elements of instability. Iraq, more than in any period before or after the 2003 invasion, was in 2016 most at risk of disintegrating into three parts.

Finally, economic factors might impact the bilateral relations: on China's side, the slowdown in economic growth will lead to a significant reduction in energy consumption; on Iraq's side, the collapse of oil prices in the world markets is having calamitous implications for the country after it wasted the years of oil boom in graft and mismanagement. Yet, the relationship is essential for both countries on many levels, and one could expect China to be more politically and economically involved in Iraq in the coming decade, in spite of the challenges it is now facing.

Chart 7.1

Value of Chinese exports to Iraq in millions of US$

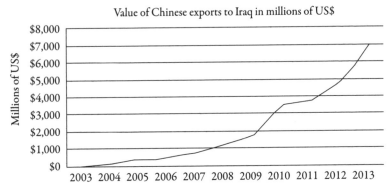

Chart 7.2

Main Chienese exports to Iraq as % of total exports

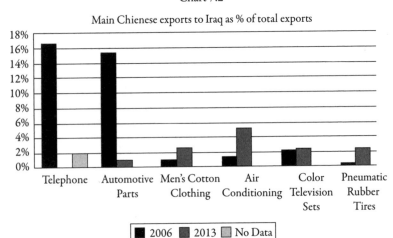

CHINA AND IRAQ

Chart 7.3

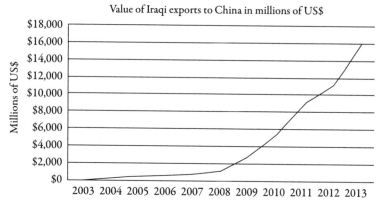

Value of Iraqi exports to China in millions of US$

Source: Observatory of Economic Complexity (OEC), MIT, http://atlas.media. mit.edu/. Data originally sourced from UN Comtrade statistics database.

PART III

"ONE BELT, ONE ROAD"

8

SILK ROADS AND GLOBAL STRATEGY

CHINA'S QUEST

Stephen Blank

Transcontinental trade and infrastructural investment plans are generally not sexy subjects in world politics or in the study of international relations. Nevertheless, the newest manifestations of globalization of international economics from the Arctic to the Indian Ocean revolve around such plans. Indeed, such projects and plans are vital for many smaller states. Thus, Elmar Mammadyarov, foreign minister of Azerbaijan, has written:

> Infrastructure has been at the core of international economic development. The global economy is based on a modern and integrated infrastructure system that allows easy transfers of goods, people, information, and financial derivatives across the world. The priority for the Caspian region is two fold. First, the infrastructure in the region needs an upgrade in order to better integrate our internal markets. Second, we need varied and secure external connections.[1]

Thus Central Asia and the entire Caspian region extending to the Caucasus sorely need such investment projects. According to one recent analysis:

Asia has an enormous demand for infrastructure that developing country governments and existing MDBs (Multilateral Development Banks) such as the World Bank and ADB (Asian Development Bank) cannot meet. According to ADB and ADBI (2009), (Asian Development Bank Institute), between 2010 and 2020 developing Asia needs to invest about $750 billion annually in energy transportation, information and communications technology (ICT), and water, and sanitation infrastructure.[2]

Likewise, Kazakh officials claim that China's projected Silk Road or "One Belt, One Road" project (OBOR) would be lucrative for every Central Asian country.[3] However, it is also the case that the profits and benefits that Central Asian governments might make from enhanced trade and investment connectivity among themselves and with Europe and China also represent to a significant degree "an offer that cannot be refused." Thus Sebastien Peyrouse and Marlene Laruelle observed in 2009:

> Contrary to widespread opinion, the ostensible Sinophilia of Central Asian states ought to be qualified. The reason that the heads of states and their foreign ministers make so much publicity about their friendly foreign relations with Beijing is precisely because they do not view their troublesome neighbor as simply a power *like the others*. Central Asia cannot afford to endorse policies that are contrary to Chinese interests.[4] [Italics in original]

And there is no reason to assume that a fundamental attitudinal change has occurred since then. Nevertheless there is, as we shall see below, no viable alternative to China's OBOR project, and Central Asian states desperately need the investments that the project has begun to implement and that are promised for the future.

Scholars have long realized that it is the construction of infrastructural projects that can overcome Central Asia's centuries-long isolation from major international trade routes and provide not just lasting economic growth but also access to new possibilities for political action and integration, and not just into regional blocs but into the wider global economy. As Robert Canfield has argued, changes in transport facilities and communication devices that began in Soviet times and have continued since then to the present are exercising a decisive influence on emerging geostrategic and economic realities in Central Asia. Specifically, the nineteenth-century vision of an integrated network of rail lines connecting the former Soviet and Tsarist empires, Iran, India, and Europe is becoming a reality. Equally importantly, market access varies inversely with transport cost. To the degree that Central Asian energy or other commodities cost more to transport to world markets, the less access they will have. But conversely, to the extent that roads and other forms of travel, transport, and communication are built through Central Asia, thus lowering the cost of transporting people, goods, and services, the more integrated it can be with the broader global economy. Surely such ideas lie behind various Russian and Chinese projects for such developments, as well as the rivalry over pipelines to send Central Asian energy to Europe and Asia.[5] Thus all so-called Silk Road projects fall squarely into that category of exemplary infrastructural projects that may serve purposes other than economic stability and global or regional integration, but which ultimately can facilitate those objectives and outcomes. These projects can, in time, also create the reality of the concept of Eurasia.[6]

Consequently, any and all "silk roads" possess as much geopolitical significance as they have economic importance for their builders and users. Indeed, by 2000 if not earlier, the expectation and construction of major infrastructural and communications developments reaching into the Trans-Caspian region, like the EU's Silk Road project, have already promoted an accelerating and deepening transformation of Trans-Caspian relationships with foreign states, and not just neighbors.[7] These transformations will probably only enhance those areas' importance as a medium through which foreign governments project power and influence into other, neighboring zones. Therefore continuing infrastructural developments will likely increase the already large number of foreign interactions with Trans-Caspian, Central Asian, and East Asian states, and add to the rivalries that dot these regions.[8]

There are many examples of these competing projects. For many years Russia has talked of plans to inaugurate a so-called "iron silk road" that would connect the Trans-Siberian Railroad to a projected Trans-Korean Railroad (TSR-TKR) and is building that network now. Indeed, the idea for this railroad goes back to Sergei Witte in the 1890s, even though it is now accompanied by a similar discussion about gas pipelines from Siberia through North Korea to South Korea.[9] However, that project as well as South Korea's corresponding vision of a transcontinental logistics grid appear to be in serious danger thanks to the newest sanctions on North Korea, because it has violated UN resolutions to make nuclear and missile tests. Russia managed to carve out for itself exemptions for Russian railway deliveries of coal to the port of Rajin in North Korea, as well as other exports to China and South Korea.[10] South Korea has had similar ideas of becoming a transcontinental hub for shipping from Asia to Europe and vice versa both by sea and by land, so its interests have to some degree overlapped with those of Russia.[11] However, for South Korea the ensuing reality is rather different, as South Korea, in protest over the DPRK's nuclear and missile tests, pulled out of a joint logistics project with North Korea and Russia:

> The Eurasia initiative is South Korean President Park Geun-hye's signature project. She wanted to create a unified logistics and energy network across the Korean peninsula, Russia, and Europe in the long term. The Rajin-Khasan project, the project just noted, was a pivotal part of the initiative introduced in October 2013. The Rajin-Khasan project would have created and secured an international sales route for Siberian coal through a railroad between Russia's border town of Khasan and North Korea's ice-free port of Rajin.[12]

Russia has also frequently raised the possibility of a north-south (Russia-India through Iran and Central Asia) trade and energy route, but that has not progressed.[13] Russia's continuing interest in such projects, despite visibly diminished capability, actually represents part of the grander design implied by President Putin in 2000–2008, as well as an effort to exploit Russia's geographic location to tie together commerce with Europe, Central, South, and East Asia.

Ultimately, these projects would also connect with Russian ambitions for north-south corridors linking together Russia, Iran, India, and Central Asia. Were this grand design to materialize, and it could only do so with massive foreign investment and support, Russia could then become the hub of a vast network of Eurasian inland trade and transportation that would materially stimulate the growth of inner Asia and Russian Asia, and greatly strengthen Russia's international political standing across the board. Certainly, if this plan could be realized efficiently, it would greatly cut the time needed for container traffic to get from Northeast Asia to European destinations.[14]

Russian officials saw its railroad net as a key link in future East-West transcontinental trade routes. Moscow's Korean project shows that it still retains this vision. They also claimed that this north-south corridor, which would link up with the East-West routes, will move export-import and transit cargo to Central and Northern Europe and Russia from the Persian Gulf and the South Asian subcontinent. These deliveries would supposedly have taken twenty days, they claim, as opposed to shipments through the Suez Canal that take forty-five days. Allegedly, the cost per container will fall by $400–500 and give the Russian government several hundred million dollars, even billions, from transit charges, taxes, and customs revenues. These projects will also effectively compete with the Suez Canal and the EU's TRACECA and Silk Road projects that bypass Russia.[15] One assessment of this corridor stated in 2000 that:

> The Russian proposal for a North-South Transport Corridor on establishing a railroad-cum-ferry link between Russia and India through several other countries

has been well received and [Indian] Transport Minister Rajnath Singh has just signed an agreement in St. Petersburg, pledging Indian cooperation in implementing the project, estimated to costs $2 Billion. It will cut delivery time from India to Russia by 10 to 15 days and save about 30 per cent in shipping costs, compared to the existing sea route all the way round Europe. It will originate in Helsinki and proceed via St. Petersburg, Moscow, Astrakhan, the Caspian Sea, Iran, the UAE, to India and could give a boost to bilateral trade between India and Russia, and open up markets for Indian goods in Eastern Europe.[16]

This project would also have exercised a strong gravitational pull on Central Asia, whose states could not afford to be left out of so large a scheme. The political motives for such projects are often quite transparent, as it is well known that an expansion of economic power and presence generally accompanies or follows a corresponding enlargement of a state's foreign political presence. In the Russo-South Korean case:

> The most immediately achievable transport project linking the TSR with the TKR would clearly provide both Russia and South Korea with the opportunity to meet their objectives to become great transit powers by maximizing their geo-strategic positioning. [The] TSR-TKR linking project explains how the realization of the railroad project would enable the two countries to diversify their commercial markets by improving resource allocation and increasing their trading volumes. Since the project envisages train shipments across North Korea, the Russian and South Korean governments also hoped that it would contribute to easing the tension in the Korean peninsula and facilitate the reunification of Korea.[17]

Indeed, Moscow remains seriously concerned to protect its interests in forging at least a TSR-TKR connection to the extent of decisively weighing in on negotiations over sanctions for North Korea due to its nuclear and missile tests to protect those equities in any new sanctions regime.[18] Since then, in addition to this project, press reports have commented that "Russia hopes to make the Arctic route a competitor to the Suez Canal and increase cargo traffic along its Siberian coast from two million tons a year now to 30 million tons annually." According to Leopold Lobkovskiy, Deputy Director for Geology at the Institute of Oceanology of the Russian Academy of Sciences, discovered reserves of hydrocarbons in the Arctic, comprising 51 billion tons of oil and 87,000 billion cubic meters (BCM) of natural gas, making it the third largest reserve in the world after the Persian Gulf and Western Siberia.[19] Moscow is therefore accelerating plans to explore the Arctic, e.g. beginning design work on Arctic carriers of LNG.[20]

However, with the exception of the Khasan-Rajin railroad line whose utility for so grandiose a transcontinental project is dubious, Russia can no longer compete against China here. Kazakh officials believe that Russia has come to terms with China's ascendancy and, as suggested below, there are good reasons for supposing this to be the case since Russia and China have agreed to coordinate Moscow's Eurasian Economic Union with the OBOR project.[21] Indeed, the evidence is mounting of a general military-cultural-political-economic, albeit slow motion, Russian retreat from Central Asia. This is not just a question of ethnic Russian out-migration or Latinization of formerly Cyrillic alphabets; Moscow simply cannot afford the burden of large-scale investment projects and possibly of military commitments to defend Central Asia. Although Russia clearly wants to monopolize the provision of military security for Central Asia, it is downsizing its military contingent (the 201st Division) in Tajikistan to a brigade. At the same time Kyrgyzstan has made clear that Russia will not and probably cannot finance the Kambarata-1 and Upper Naryn hydroelectric projects that are vital to Kyrgyzstan's future, due to sanctions and falling oil prices. Thus Kyrgyzstan, which is not amused, has had to pull out of the projects.[22] And in Kazakhstan, Moscow has already indicated that it is pulling out of even recently announced projects, including one to save the Ural River, much to Astana's discontent.[23] Moscow's devaluing ruble and economic crisis has already led it to reduce the number of Central Asian migrants it allows in to work in Russia, and those who are there see their remittances falling and are often leaving, thus reinforcing the decline of Russian economic leverage over Central Asia.[24]

India too began discussing the idea of a north-south trading corridor with Russia and Central Asian states in 2000, to connect South Asia with Europe by overland and maritime routes. And when other avenues seemed blocked for security reasons, India turned again to Russia in 2012 to reignite this project which (at the time) would bypass Pakistan, showing its clear geopolitical intention alongside the obvious economic benefits for all concerned.[25] But the obstacles to an India-initiated project of this scope in Central Asia are well known. Indeed, such a program could only emerge as part of a larger vision, e.g. Russia's earlier and now discarded one or the US' vaunted New Silk Road. Unfortunately, that project is essentially an amalgam of existing bureaucratic projects, the main one being the gas pipeline from Turkmenistan through Afghanistan to Pakistan and India (TAPI), which has not yet started. Moreover, there is hardly any serious funding for the NSR, and it looks increasingly like a legacy of the US' parallel withdrawal from Central Asia.[26] As one recent assessment observes:

The NSR (New Silk Road) vision is, at least in theory, intended to support the IP (Istanbul Process for Afghanistan), yet critics view it more as a conceptual framework than concrete plan. The US State Department has not allocated a specific budget to it nor committed diplomatic staff. Similarly the NDN (Northern Distribution Network) was meant to correlate with an increase in American investment in Central Asian economies, but this has not occurred. It has also failed to enable regional economic cooperation; the only transit is financed by international actors.[27]

Whereas in the 1990s the big push for such projects came from the European Union, the impetus for them has dramatically slowed due to economic, political, and bureaucratic difficulties. This fact has led Central Asian and East Asian governments, i.e. not only China, to show a much greater interest in picking up that baton and developing major connections to Central Asia and beyond through such institutions as the Asian Development Bank, as well as individual governments.[28] Consequently, the failure to materialize earlier versions of a silk road duly provides a backdrop and stage for China's effort to fill the ensuing vacuum with its new project.

But this is not the only factor involved here. Apart from these transcontinental visions and plans that have failed, there is a corresponding or parallel movement afoot to build regional trading and investment networks in Asia. The US' Trans-Pacific Partnership that was negotiated in 2015 not only excludes China; it is also an attempt "to use coercion to minimize the negative externality of a rising China."[29] The Regional Comprehensive Economic Partnership (RCEP) excludes the US while including China, and it aims "to maximize the positive externality of China rising."[30] But the common denominator between these programs is:

> First, multilateral institutions in Asia were initiated and promoted by countries other than China, whose choices had been limited to whether and how much to participate in these frameworks. Second, Asian regionalism has focused on economic cooperation but invariably implied political and strategic importance. Power alignment, "the China threat", and the rise of China had been among the underlying drivers of regional initiatives in Asia. Third, China was largely reactive to regional institutions offered by others, via such mechanisms as coercion and competition, at times supplemented by persuasion and socialization.[31]

The OBOR project, on the other hand, is an antidote to China's mistrust and suspicions about the TPP and skepticism about the RCEP, as it is purely China's program and initiative and represents its efforts to create a continental if not transcontinental trading and investment bloc.

China's OBOR project and its drivers

Thus China's OBOR or Silk Road project fits quite well within a comparative context of what other major Asian governments as well as the US are either trying and/or have tried to accomplish. But by 2015 it was clear that all those other programs had either failed or were failing, and that they either excluded China or subsumed it within a larger collectivity. For example, Russia has essentially surrendered with regard to competing against China's Silk Road project for Central Asia. This vision, as Russia has long known, contradicts and could eclipse Russia's rival vision of a transcontinental "iron silk road" from Europe to Asia through the Trans-Siberian Railroad and a north-south corridor to India, Iran, and Central Asia. However, as Alexandros Petersen and other analysts have said, by 2014 China already was and will remain the most consequential and pre-eminent foreign actor in Central Asia.[32]

Recognizing Russian suspicions, Xi Jinping magnanimously offered to link the Trans-Siberian Railroad to the Chinese Silk Road, an offer that Putin welcomed.[33] Putin's Chief of Staff, Sergei Ivanov, may claim in Beijing that the Silk Road will link to Russia's Baikal-Amur and Trans-Siberian railroads and have great potential if they do so by linking together East and Southeast Asia with Europe.[34] Nevertheless, there are no guarantees that Russia will play a major role here. This magnanimity cannot conceal China's victory over Russia and Russia's inability to compete in these domains with China. Russia must now resign itself to being a "junior brother" in such endeavors, even while endlessly trumpeting its Eurasian great power role. Typically, China has punctured Russia's grandiloquent Eurasian and great power pretensions, graciously but decisively. Given the expansive geostrategic benefits that will accrue to China as it realizes its Silk Road vision, the evolving Sino-Russian relationship on this issue could entail a massive and decisive Russian strategic defeat in Eurasia, rendering it here, as in energy, China's raw materials appendage.[35]

The big difference between the failed programs and the OBOR project is that unlike all those other earlier projects, the OBOR project not only appears to have real resources and commitment behind it, it also apparently is the only real manifestation of this effort to find a transcontinental trade route linking Asia to Europe. At the same time it is challenging—as the original Russian plans in the 1890s aimed to do—the primacy of the Suez Canal route for such trade, i.e. a maritime route from the Indian Ocean through the canal to Europe. And the great difference between OBOR and the TPP and RCEP is that OBOR is an exclusively Chinese initiative that China can organize to its taste. But China's OBOR project is in itself only a key part in an even grander

Chinese design, conscious or otherwise. In fact, China is developing what we might call three silk roads: the OBOR project; a maritime silk road that will go from Southern China into the South China Sea and Indian Ocean and through parts of Southeast Asia to countries like Sri Lanka, Nepal, and so on in South Asia and challenge India's strategic primacy there; and lastly China's own efforts to establish a sustained commercial presence in the Arctic, as that ocean becomes increasingly navigable.[36] Although here we are focusing almost exclusively on the OBOR project, readers should not overlook the existence of these other "silk roads" and their place in China's strategy.

The scope of this project is enormous. As a Turkish commentary observed:

This policy framework foresees the development of several corridors across the region that will be built to boost regional economies to the tune of $2.5 trillion and to the benefit of a combined population of over 4.4 billion across 65 countries. Among these corridors, the Maritime Silk Road will connect the Pacific Coast to the Baltic Sea (presumably both through the riverine network from the Black to the Baltic Sea and across the Arctic-author). With China's Guangxi Zhuang Autonomous Road and Yunnan province as starting points, The Silk Road Economic Belt will link China, Central Asia, Russia, and Europe while connecting China with the Persian Gulf, South Asia, and the Indian Ocean.[37]

These other roads parallel the OBOR project, which itself grows out of China's previous large-scale investments in Central Asia and parallels similarly large-scale trade and investment relationships with Africa, Latin America, and Southeast Asia. In some sense, as OBOR builds on the earlier foundation of past policy in Central Asia and experience in other venues, it continues the tradition by which Chinese policy in Central Asia may be seen as a kind of "laboratory" for policies that are then launched elsewhere and, in turn, provide lessons for ensuing policy stages. Certainly that laboratory analogy becomes clear when one considers Sino-Central Asian relations with regard to resolving disputed boundaries after 1991.[38]

Thus the Indian expert, Brahma Chellaney, has openly written that whereas China earlier sought to create a "string of pearls" of bases and infrastructural installations across the Indian Ocean to gain access all the way to the Middle East, the Maritime Silk Road project represents an effort to forge "win-win" projects all along the same route of strategic choke points that open the way to major infusions of Chinese trade, aid, and investment, while enhancing its favorable image and military power projection capabilities throughout this area.[39] Certainly there can be no gainsaying the audacious sweep of these Chinese projects, in both economic and strategic terms. For example, the

Chinese government has even sought North Korea's participation in the main overland Silk Road project (directly competing with Moscow as well) as a sign of the scope of the geopolitical vistas behind that project. But it would also open up opportunities to get closer to the Arctic.[40] And the sums being invested are equally enormous: $50 billion for the Asian Investment Infrastructure Bank (AIIB); $40 billion for the actual New Silk Road Fund; $100 billion for the new BRICS Development Bank that will fund many OBOR projects; and $46 billion for the China Pakistan Economic cooperation (CPEC).

OBOR's drivers

To grasp the purposes behind OBOR, we must understand, as have other scholars and observers, that the genesis of this vision lies in conditions and policies that pre-dated President Xi Jinping's major push for the project, which began in 2013. Indeed, the OBOR project, like China's overall Central Asian policies, is rooted in "intermestic" (involving both international and domestic) policy and security considerations that go back to the origin of independent Central Asian states in the 1990s and grow out of the confluence of domestic security considerations in China's policy revolving around conditions in Xinjiang since the 1990s. Thus we see that Chinese analysts and experts, in their own internal discussions, have developed an increasing appreciation of how non-traditional security threats like insurgency in Xinjiang might unhinge the territory, if not the overall Chinese political system.[41] Central Asia's rising importance for Chinese policy stems from the fact of the many new as well as traditional security problems that Chinese observers see as potential threats to regional and Chinese security, especially as great power interests there are growing in intensity.[42] Central Asia's proximity to China leads Beijing, foreign observers, and Chinese analysts to view Central Asian policy and security essentially as an outward projection of the PRC's internal security agenda.[43] Consequently, one fundamental and enduring aspect to Chinese foreign policy in Central Asia is its intermestic nature, i.e. its inextricable and continuous entanglement with some of the most primal issues in China's internal policies.

Indeed, this is still the case as the unrest in the Chinese border regions continues. As Aaron Friedberg wrote, "The party's desire to retain power shapes every aspect of national policy. When it comes to external affairs, it means that Beijing's ultimate aim is to "make the world safe for authoritarianism," or at least for continued one-party rule in China."[44] This intermestic aspect of Chinese foreign policy is particularly visible in China's approach to border issues since the 1990s. Here foreign policy aims to overcome internal security threats, either to the regime's stability or to China's integrity: especially insofar as they pertain to Central Asia, as with the well-known and ongoing threat of Uyghur disaffection and unrest in the Muslim borderlands, primarily Xinjiang, which adjoins Central Asia and where sizable Uyghur communities reside.

Therefore, Chinese analysts tend to believe that these problems and threats can be overcome through wise action by China and the other great powers.[45] In this context, wise action means providing opportunities for both China's domestic economic growth and the constriction of Western and/or Islamic military and political influence in Central Asia.[46] As Prime Minister Li Keqiang recently reminded officials, Xinjiang "is of strategic importance for the country's overall situation." Therefore local authorities need to promote development there to "consolidate the foundation of lasting stability."[47] Such consolidation is necessary because Chinese analysts believe that Muslim minority movements among the Uyghur population in Xinjiang cannot succeed except through foreign assistance, hence any possibility of such assistance must be curtailed if not suppressed.[48] Moreover, Chinese authorities have apparently internalized the Leninist belief that economic stratification and backwardness is the main fuel behind the fire of ethno-religious identification, and that economic growth mixed with tough repression and cultural discrimination against Islam and its culture will overcome the domestic causes of the ongoing violence against Chinese power, while simultaneously giving the central government in Beijing more means of leverage upon not only Xinjiang but also Central Asian governments, who might otherwise be inclined to support this unrest. Therefore, Central Asia and Xinjiang must be economically linked and developed so that the oxygen for the insurgency from within—economic and ethnic stratification—dies out, Han colonialism can police the region, and Central Asian states have too much to lose by supporting their kinsmen and must be made to know it. This logic not only stems from the Leninist tradition in nationality policy that led Moscow to undertake the massive economic development of its minority borderlands; it is also a testament to the abiding belief in the power of economic integration to subordinate peripheries to the center.

For example, Jiang Zemin reportedly observed that if Taiwan becomes economically dependent on a rising China, then "the monkey king can't get out of the grip of the [Buddha] Rulai."[49] The same reasoning underlies the decade-long effort to re-orient investment and allocational priorities to China's west, especially Xinjiang. Those policies grow out of the need to ensure central control over those provinces and that their governance remains a wholly internal one, not subject to internationalization and foreign debate. Arguably, a similar reasoning also applies to China's overall policy in Central Asia, which clearly aims to make neighboring states dependent upon China so that they will not dare support their kinsmen across the border.[50] Therefore economic development through large-scale investment, including major energy projects, entails goals that are broader than overcoming the gap between the richer coastal provinces and the interior, and the problem of mass poverty in the interior and western provinces. China's "go west" program was and remains very much a comprehensive internal and external security project.

A conjunction of conditions engendered a sizable perceived threat to China's integrity and the stability of communist rule: the fact of Soviet collapse; Central Asian independence; US military-political hegemony; the primacy of liberalizing global trends; the rhetoric of Islamic freedom and self-determination, visible in increased anti-regime violence in Xinjiang; along with domestic strife among elites and the turmoil concluding in the Tiananmen massacre. Beijing recognized this conjunction and acted to forestall it. Seen from Beijing, it was essential to prevent Central Asian states and/or Russia from embracing the Uyghurs' cause. If they received foreign backing, then the conditions outlined in the lessons cited above would become operative and generate real threats to China's territorial integrity and political stability. Accordingly, after 1991 China began to fashion a Central Asian policy which aimed to forge ties with these new Central Asian states; to deter them from intervening in Xinjiang; to fix the borders once and for all by means of a recognized treaty backed up by a strong power; and to integrate Xinjiang irrevocably into a system of central control.

Thus, China's Central Asian policies reflect many of the considerations that drive its overall foreign policy and derive from its perception of domestic security. As in China's overall foreign policy, a central motive is to forestall the possibility of internal threats to China's stability and integrity arising in its borderlands. This is particularly important given Xinjiang's history as the object of Russian and Soviet imperialism up to the end of the Sino-Soviet rift. Consequently, China's Central Asian policy possesses both external and internal functions. Since unrest in Xinjiang and Tibet are not far behind Taiwan as potential threats to either China's stability or its integrity, foreign policy must forestall those threats and create auspicious conditions for China's continuing development, the basis of its power abroad.

At the same time, the huge investment in this trade and infrastructural project also enables the government to address some pressing economic issues affecting the Chinese economy. For example, one of the key funding structures for OBOR is China's newly launched Asian Infrastructure Investment Bank (AIIB). The AIIB aims to help satisfy the aforementioned demand for infrastructure by making capital for such projects available. At the same time OBOR's huge projects will, or so it is intended, act as a magnet to sop up China's excess capacity in steel, iron, cement, etc. which is now dragging the economy down. Given sluggish global demand, exports are not a way out for these sectors, so instead foreign infrastructure projects have to step into that breach. In addition, expanding external demand rather than further depreciating the currency could help support the government's market-oriented reforms. To the degree that these projects stimulate demand in neighboring countries, they could offer export opportunities for struggling manufacturers inside China, especially given the slowdown in domestic demand and growth. Indeed, this stimulation of foreign demand to alleviate domestic bottlenecks is apparently a critical element of the government's overall strategy.[51]

Beyond those considerations, Salvatore Barbones of the University of Sydney claims that the specific projects comprising OBOR represent the government's determination to fund projects for the poorer western region that private investment cannot and will not support, and the specific projects will ultimately amount to little more than jobs programs for Chinese infrastructure companies.[52] Another contributing motive might be to create multiple new opportunities for tying this to China's consistent efforts to create a yuan bloc. Kazakhstan has just announced that it will build an offshore center for the yuan to serve all of Central Asia, in anticipation of the huge rise in trade with and investment by China. Such centers allow foreign investors to convert these foreign currencies directly into yuan and bypass the dollar, i.e. internationalizing the yuan (or renminbi) and creating a closed currency bloc, much as Nazi Germany and the USSR did. Since nobody has shown an interest from outside in stabilizing the yuan during China's current crisis, and given Kazakhstan's centrality to any Chinese vision for Central Asia, this center prospectively assumes greater importance, even as it represents another advance of Chinese power at Russia's expense in Central Asia.[53]

Geopolitical interests

Obviously, China's interests go beyond addressing pressing domestic concerns to enhancing its economic and political leverage over Central Asian states and further extending its already recognized position as the most important foreign economic presence in the region. Virtually every commentary on the OBOR project lists those goals either as obvious intentions and consequences of this project or as feared and likely designs of Beijing upon Central Asia. And undoubtedly political and military power accompanies economic power as China "marches" West. Equally obviously, the Silk Road is not an altruistic project, but one that aims to achieve well-known increasingly important security interests: pacifying Afghanistan; stabilizing Xinjiang; preventing Central Asia from exploding or supporting the insurgencies there; providing further outlets for Chinese economic power; supplanting the US in multilateral organizations where Washington is absent; and projecting power abroad.

In this context, there are two particularly striking dimensions to the OBOR project. The first dimension is how well it fits conceptually into other visible examples of China's expansive foreign investment and overall security policy. Second, it also comports very well conceptually with the practical manifestations that we see of China's reach toward the Middle East and the Mediterranean. In terms of China's ambitious foreign investment programs for the future, the overall plan to invest and finance projects in Africa over the next decade amounts to $1 trillion, while President Xi Jinping has "personally pledged investment in Latin America" of over $250 billion for the next decade.[54] Likewise, the ambitious scope and nature of the OBOR project is in complete harmony with the expansive vision of Chinese security requirements outlined in the 2015 Defense White Paper. As Andrew Erickson points out, this white paper states that China's national security plans encompass "far more subjects, extend over a greater range, and cover a longer time span than at any time in the country's history." The white paper also places "unprecedented emphasis" on safeguarding overseas investments.[55] Thus the white paper explicitly ties together security and defense perspectives with foreign investment imperatives. As Erickson writes:

> China's overseas citizens, businesses, assets, and investments are proliferating, particularly in the unstable areas to which they gravitate for lack of Western competition. Resource access abroad is essential to fueling China's rapidly growing economy, still manufacturing-focused and energy-intensive. This will be particularly challenging in an era of growing resource demands, access, and pricing instability, and even growing scarcity in some cases.[56]

Of course, although he, like the white paper, are focusing on areas where China has primarily maritime connections, every word in this paragraph applies with equal validity and force to Central Asia.

But beyond Central Asia, China is clearly embarked upon a global program of port construction that could in time lead to a far-flung network not only of ports for "port calls" but for naval bases. China is already building this kind of infrastructure in the Indian Ocean and a base in Djibouti on the Horn of Africa. Moreover, Foreign Minister Wang Yi's recent report openly confirmed that China is looking to build "some infrastructural facilities and support abilities," i.e. bases.[57] China is also now increasing its military assistance to the Afghan Army, demonstrating Afghanistan's growing security importance to China as it moves forward on OBOR.[58] China's 2015 participation with Russia in joint naval exercises in the Mediterranean also exhibits an interest in projecting power into the Middle East, if not beyond. Similarly, at a recent conference of Russia's Valdai Club on the Middle East where the need to render foreign assistance to states there was raised, an unnamed Chinese participant observed that while Beijing wants to be friends with everyone and has no intention of interfering in the Iran-Saudi rivalry, yet it will provide such assistance and investment, presumably in conjunction with the OBOR project.[59] Indeed, inasmuch as OBOR is supposed to link China through Central Asia with Europe and the Mediterranean and the Middle East, these and other projects listed below are not incomprehensible.

Apart from Iran, China is making major investments and has negotiated a currency swap with the UAE, giving it access to the very important ports and transport routes through the Emirates for the OBOR projects.[60] China has unsuccessfully sought a deep-water port on the Georgian coast of the Black Sea, in conjunction with the planned construction of overland rail and transport routes to Georgia as part of OBOR.[61] Similarly, Ukraine figures prominently in Chinese thinking now that it has a free trade agreement with the EU. In January 2016 China officially supported a freight train route from Ukraine to Kazakhstan and China (and presumably in return), which includes ferries across the Black and Caspian Seas and bypasses Russia. And traffic has started on this route as of March 2016. Chinese officials also met with Ukrainian officials to discuss a commission on the functioning of the Silk Road to increase Ukraine's transport capacity. China is also helping to build numerous railway and infrastructure projects to provide the overland dimension of OBOR to its final destination, Venice.[62] Plans also include European interest in reopening the Beskyd tunnel to connect Southern Europe with Ukraine, and in expanding the Silk Roads even into the Baltic States.[63]

Finally, given the continuing turmoil in the Middle East and the plans for OBOR to traverse parts of that region and then link up with other networks or subsidiary routes, it is clear that OBOR is connected to China's growing interest in and capacity to influence the Middle East. In January 2016 Beijing released an Arab policy white paper signifying its rising interest and presence in the Middle East. According to this white paper:

> China's proposed initiatives of jointly building the "Silk Road Economic Belt" and the "21st Century Maritime Silk Road", establishing a "1+2+3" cooperation pattern (to take energy cooperation as the core, infrastructure construction and trade and investment facilitation as the two wings, and three high and new tech fields of nuclear energy, space satellite and new energy as the three breakthroughs), and industrial capacity cooperation, are well received by Arab countries. ... Joint efforts will be made by China and Arab countries to promote the "Belt and Road" initiative under the principle of wide consultation, joint contribution and shared benefit.

China has clearly also grasped that the US is retreating from there and Russia is advancing into the breach, and while its interest in calming the area connects to its fear of Islamic terrorism, its interests also connect the region to the OBOR project because a restive Middle East that attracts Uyghurs and trains them as terrorists creates cadres for domestic unrest back home and jeopardizes these investments all along the Central Asia and Middle Eastern routes.[64]

As one analysis of Chinese strategy observes:

> China can use the One Belt One Road initiative as a tension-reduction mechanism, promoting projects that created shared Sunni-Shiite economic interests like the Iran-Pakistan gas pipeline, the port of Gwadar on the coast of the Arabian Sea, and a Silk Road high speed railway connecting Xinjiang and Tehran via the Sunni Muslim countries of Central Asia—Kazakhstan, Uzbekistan, and Turkmenistan. China is positioned to promote Iran's membership in the Shanghai Cooperation Organization, whose other members are predominantly Sunni, a shift possible now that United Nations sanctions against Iran have been removed.[65]

China could also use its new anti-terrorism law that allows for foreign counter-terrorist operations, to intervene in Middle Eastern states against terrorist operations with these countries' consent.[66] China's army has already appeared in Pakistan-occupied Kashmir.[67] In this same context, the white paper talks about expanding military exchanges, creating a regular mechanism for security cooperation and joint anti-terrorist activities, including continuing maritime operations like that in the Gulf of Aden.[68] In this context, the base at Djibouti assumes new importance as a crucial facilitator of Chinese trade and naval presence in the Indian Ocean and as the basis for rapid deployment of naval power to North Africa, the Middle East, and even South Asia, while protecting key trade routes to Africa, the Middle East, and Europe.[69]

Conclusions

The confluence of OBOR with enhanced geopolitical reach, capability and willingness to talk about "hard" security approaches apparently reflects Xi Jinping's "willingness to use every instrument of statecraft, from military assets to geo-economic intimidation, as well as economic rewards, to pursue his various geopolitical objectives."[70] Therefore the OBOR project bears watching. However, we should not assume that what is promised will be implemented. In fact, there is a great distance between what China promises and actually implements. Despite many promises of largesse and of big projects, often the money is not allocated or the project is stopped or delayed in midstream, and this has happened in many countries.[71] Neither is it clear that China's own faltering domestic economy will allow it to build all the intended projects from China to Europe. Finally, so far China has not had to deal too deeply with all the many problems and political issues that will arise in all of the intervening countries where it is building projects, and it is by no means clear how China will cope with all those problems on top of its existing agenda.

Nevertheless, this audacious project, even if only partially realized, will effect a major geo-economic and geostrategic change throughout the regions where it takes shape. Given its audacious sweep and the geo-economic and geostrategic implications inherent in the OBOR vision and projects, we ignore it at our peril. And the fact that only China is now capable of thinking on this scale, in and of itself is a marker of great significance. However much of this project is realized, it will revolutionize those areas involved and utterly transform their strategic setting. Of how many contemporary projects can this be said?

9

CHOOSING NOT TO CHOOSE

THE BELT AND ROAD INITIATIVE AND THE MIDDLE EAST

Andrew Small

The role of the Middle East in China's Belt and Road initiative (OBOR) is one of the least-clearly articulated of any of the regions that fall under the scheme. Many of OBOR's underlying objectives certainly converge there: it is a region that requires significant infrastructure; a critical energy source; a land bridge to Europe; and a major focal point for Chinese efforts to stabilize its broader neighborhood and address threats from militancy. But many of the ambiguities about the future of China's broader strategy in the Middle East apply even more forcefully to OBOR. The initiative is in its early stages, so the uncertainties surrounding it exist in many other regions too; much of the existing analysis about its ramifications are based on an assessment of the motivations, logic, and goals for the initiative, rather than a detailed look at on-the-ground developments. But in the Middle East, one of China's principal objectives has been to decouple trade and economics from the complexities of the region's politics, whereas one of OBOR's defining characteristics is the deployment of economic tools to serve strategic and political ends. In addition to examining the genesis and rationale behind OBOR, how it is being put into practice, and the challenges it faces, this chapter will look at how China might resolve the potential contradictions between OBOR and the traditional framework of Chinese policy in the Middle East. China may seek to resolve the contradictions through facing up to the political choices in the region that it had previously abjured; through a realization of OBOR that prioritizes "balance" over other political and economic objectives; or through a more modest set of activities than in other regions where political neutrality is not such an overriding concern.

The Belt and Road initiative: origins and motivations

The two components of China's Belt and Road initiative were rolled out a month apart. Xi Jinping announced the Silk Road Economic Belt (SREB) during his visit to Kazakhstan in September 2013, where his speech to Nazarbayev University was the first formal mention of the scheme.[1] The Twenty-first Century Maritime Silk Road was then announced in Jinping's speech to the Indonesian parliament in October 2013, during which China's plan to establish an Asia Infrastructure Investment Bank was also set out.[2] The combination of the two plans has been described either in its literal translation, the "One Belt, One Road" initiative, or—in what has become the preferred Chinese rendering in English—the "Belt and Road" initiative. While the two elements of the scheme are often appraised together, they are in many ways distinct, reflective of the Chinese debates that existed before the inception of the initiative.

In 2012, Wang Jisi, the Chinese foreign policy strategist, published a widely circulated article arguing that China should rebalance its strategy to the West as part of the response to the United States' pivot to East Asia.[3] His argument remains one of the clearest articulations of the economic and strategic considerations behind OBOR: that China should draw more heavily on the traditional continental orientation in its foreign policy and develop an international strategy to underpin rebalancing efforts from the coastal to the interior regions; that the westward-facing economy, running down the old Silk Road, now has the highest growth potential and should be a new focus for China's economic strategy; that addressing China's terrorist threat requires stabilizing the countries on its western periphery, which can be facilitated through economic efforts; and that unlike East Asia, in which competition between great powers is intensifying, in Eurasia there is significant scope for cooperation and an "almost non-existent risk of military confrontation" with the United States.[4] The US "pivot" would see a drawdown of its presence in the Eurasian heartland, with the diminution of the US military footprint in Afghanistan and neighboring countries that were part of the framework to support operations there. Even in the Middle East, the United States would be avowedly less willing to involve itself militarily in order to avoid continued distraction from the long-term opportunities and challenges in the Asia Pacific, described by former Assistant Secretary of State for East Asian and Pacific Affairs, Kurt Campbell, as a "a little bit of a Middle East detour over the course of the last ten years."[5] As a result, China was faced with more pressure to its east and south, and a very different context to its west, one which represented both risks and opportunities: a geostrategic "opening" as a result of reduced US security presence, but also the problematic ramifications of diminished efforts by the United States to combat threats from militancy and terrorism there. A more proactive westward strategy was hence partly a strategic choice, but in other respects a necessity if those threats were to be contained.

The argument tapped into an older, continentalist argument about China's foreign policy orientation, advanced by the likes of Lanxin Xiang, which contended that the Eurasian continent provides the best theater within which China can realize its rise, underpinned by close relations with the principal Eurasian mainland powers, Russia and Europe.[6] It had many opponents, however: strategists such as Yang Yi, and interest groups ranging from the PLA Navy to China's coastal provinces, argued that the maritime realm is where China's most important security tasks, economic opportunities, and testing grounds for its rise as a great power still lie.[7] A "westward strategy" risked China being drawn into precisely the unstable regions from which the United States was now extricating itself, just as Washington was finally placing more serious strategic attention on the East Asian maritime realm. Some in the PLA described the idea of a vacuum in Eurasia for China to fill as a "trap." But the most telling arguments that fed into OBOR came not from competing geostrategic visions but from China's commerce ministry, which laid out the case for using an external push to development infrastructure connectivity as a means to deal with China's over-capacity problems. The strategy would combine elements of Japanese industrial strategy from the 1970s, when the economy went through its transition from low- to high-value production, with nineteenth-century grand projects on the scale of the Suez and Panama canals. With the Chinese economy facing diminishing returns on domestic investment, a growth slowdown, the threat of large-scale job losses, and a weak external environment for Chinese exports, a large-scale set of infrastructure and industrial development schemes outside China would allow its industry to benefit from, effectively, an externalization of the last twenty years of Chinese domestic strategy. Infrastructure investments overseas would provide projects for Chinese firms, build new markets for Chinese products, and address many of the logistical constraints impeding Chinese exports from interior provinces through Central Asia, South Asia, and South East Asia. Industrial zones overseas would provide platforms for the global expansion of lower-value Chinese industry, retaining the strength of the manufacturing sector even as an economic transition was underway. Early connectivity initiatives of this sort after Xi Jinping took office were not framed as a grand strategy, but rather as a disconnected set of "corridors." Before Xi's announcements in late 2013, Li Keqiang was promoting a pair of schemes in India and Pakistan. The Bangladesh-China-India-Myanmar corridor (BCIM) would focus on addressing the inadequate land connections that exist between Yunnan province, in China's south-west, India's north-east, and Bangladeshi ports. The China-Pakistan Economic Corridor (CPEC) would connect Xinjiang province, in China's north-west, with the Pakistani ports of Gwadar and Karachi, with an assortment of energy projects and economic zones in between.

Many other elements of China's push for regional connectivity pre-date the initiative too. Pipelines in Central Asia, rail routes through Russia to Europe, and many other overseas Chinese investments existed well before 2013. The multi-trillion dollar infrastructure needs in Asia to which China was responding had been laid out by bodies such as the Asia Development Bank (ADB) for many years. Some strategic impulses, such as the desire to develop alternative transportation routes to the sea routes that pass through "choke points" in the Malacca Straits, are also long-standing features in Chinese foreign policy thinking. But OBOR provided an organizing concept for the disparate elements of Chinese policy. The overall framework that eventually emerged, then, was not the geopolitically coherent plan of Wang Jisi's conception but the agglomeration of two distinct strategic notions, maritime and continental, underpinned by an urgent economic impetus: support Chinese industry and stop it from hemorrhaging jobs. As a result, the initiative encompasses justifications that are at best less than wholly consistent, at worst outright contradictory. Some Chinese analysts see OBOR as a rival and counterpoint to the US "pivot to Asia" and the Trans-Pacific Partnership (TPP) agreement. Others see it precisely as the opposite: a potential area of cooperation with the United States, with no contradiction between any of the different economic initiatives, and an advocate for US membership of the Asian Investment Infrastructure Bank (AIIB) and Chinese membership of TPP. These are often matters of interpretation, depending on the broader prism through which the projects are viewed: the very same Chinese investments can be portrayed either as part of a long-term building of China's power and presence at the US expense, or as initiatives that are wholly consistent with US objectives in bringing stability and prosperity to insecure regions. In its early stages, OBOR has managed to enfold a diffuse array of goals and interest groups, functioning like a Rorschach test for its advocates and critics inside and outside China. Whether this continues will depend less on the scheme's somewhat muddy strategic intent, and more on the realization of the initiative in practice.

The Belt and Road initiative: scope and structure

The most detailed exposition of the scheme to date is an "action plan" on the "principles, framework, and cooperation priorities and mechanisms in the Belt and Road Initiative": "Vision and Actions on Jointly Building Silk Road Economic Belt and 21st-Century Maritime Silk Road," which was jointly released on 28 March 2015 by the National Development and Reform Commission (NDRC), Ministry of Foreign Affairs (MFA), and Ministry of Commerce (MOFCOM),[8] the lead government agencies involved in its implementation. This has been supplemented by a prodigious number of speeches from Chinese leaders, and official commentaries. In short form, it is described as a "trade and infrastructure network connecting Asia with Europe and Africa along the ancient Silk Road routes," encompassing "4.4 billion people in more than 60 countries, or 63 percent of the global population."[9] The action plan states that:

> The Belt and Road Initiative aims to promote the connectivity of Asian, European and African continents and their adjacent seas, establish and strengthen partnerships among the countries along the Belt and Road, set up all-dimensional, multi-tiered and composite connectivity networks, and realize diversified, independent, balanced and sustainable development in these countries. The connectivity projects of the Initiative will help align and coordinate the development strategies of the countries along the Belt and Road, tap market potential in this region, promote investment and consumption, create demands and job opportunities, enhance people-to-people and cultural exchanges, and mutual learning among the peoples of the relevant countries, and enable them to understand, trust and respect each other and live in harmony, peace and prosperity.

A series of OBOR maps have also been produced, showing a variety of different routes. Xinhua released what was assumed to be an authoritative map in May 2014, though it subsequently became clear that a number of proposed routes and corridors had not been included, while countries that had not agreed to be part of the initiative—such as India—featured prominently. Other unofficial, but widely-cited maps have been put together based on the "vision and action plan" and the schemes designated by Chinese leaders to fall under its auspices, including eight international economic corridors and eighteen Chinese provinces.[10] The impression has been one of some fluidity: while some countries and plans clearly form a part of the initiative, others have been added or downplayed depending on their enthusiasm for inclusion, while the action plan states explicitly that OBOR "is open to all countries, and international and regional organizations for engagement."[11] The process of arbitrating between the proposals and setting the agenda for the initiative falls to the "Advancing the Development of the One Belt and One Road Leading Group," which was formed in February 2015, and is headed by first Vice-Premier Zhang Gaoli, the member of the Politburo Standing Committee responsible for finance, reform and development, and the environment.[12] The rest of the leading group is composed of senior foreign and economic policy decision-makers: Wang Yang, a vice premier with responsibilities that include commerce and agriculture; Wang Huning, advisor to Xi Jinping and long-time party theoretician and speechwriter; Yang Jiechi, the state councilor with responsibility for foreign affairs; and Yang Jing, Secretary General of the State Council and Secretary of the CPC Secretariat.[13] Analysts generally agree, however, that OBOR is very much the initiative of Xi Jinping himself, who has taken an active role in overseeing, promoting, driving, and shaping it, and his personal imprimatur has been critical to the level of energy that is being arrayed behind the scheme in China.

In addition to the overall vision and decision-making structure, the financing behind the initiative has been assembled through various sources. A great deal of attention has been given to the AIIB and the Silk Road Fund, the former because of the political controversies around the bank's membership, and the international stature of the bank's president, Jin Liqun, a former Assistant Minister of Finance. Yet it is not solely an OBOR initiative, and Jin has stated that the bank will finance infrastructure in countries that do not fall under the scheme. The AIIB has its roots in the Chinese Finance Ministry, and is a specifically multilateral body, while the Silk Road Fund has its roots in the People's Bank of China, and functions on a bilateral basis.[14] In the scheme of OBOR financing, however, these two financing institutions are relatively modest: the Silk Road Fund has only $40 billion, while the AIIB has been seeded with $100 billion of capital. The other bilateral financing mechanisms are far larger. They include: the policy banks, EXIM, China Development Bank, and Agricultural Development Bank of China; the big four Chinese commercial banks, Bank of China, China Construction Bank, Agricultural Bank of China, and the Industrial and Commercial Bank of China; CITIC, the state-owned investment company; the provincial governments; the national budget, and a number of others. The Peterson Institute has estimated that as many as forty financing streams are involved, while the Chinese Academy of Social Sciences estimated that the total resources behind OBOR could add up to as much as $6 trillion; Peterson put the intended scale at $4 trillion, with $400 billion already underway.[15]

The Belt and Road initiative in practice

The political salience of OBOR has so far been greater than its economic impact. The challenges that China has faced in the first phase of the initiative have been as much about addressing strategic obstacles as they have been about project selection or delivery. A scheme with such seemingly grand ambitions and such lack of clarity around the underlying intent was inevitably going to elicit concerns from states that are disposed to some suspicion around China's motives.

The concerns have taken several forms. The first is from countries believing that OBOR will result in a loss of influence in regions of strategic interest— even areas seen as traditional spheres of influence—and will undermine their own geo-economic initiatives. In this respect, the greatest political concern for Beijing was the reaction from Moscow. Russia had already accepted a significant enlargement in the level of Chinese economic presence in Central Asia, but OBOR was seen as a step beyond that: usurping Russia's role as a Eurasian bridge, and potentially threatening Russia's own plans for a Eurasian Economic Union (EEU). Experts in China described Russian opposition to the scheme as potentially the greatest threat to its success, given Moscow's capacity to exert pressure on a number of countries critical to the scheme, and its initial reaction was one of clear hostility. Russia's subsequent confrontation with the West over its annexation of Crimea and military activities in eastern Ukraine therefore proved doubly important for China: undermining the EEU and necessitating a greater level of Russian political dependence on China as a result of Western sanctions. The agreement reached during Xi Jinping's visit to Moscow in May 2015 on the "connection" and "integration" of the SREB and the EEU[16] was seen in China as one of the most important early political achievements for the initiative.

The second concern has been that OBOR will undermine existing multi-lateral institutions. This played out most notably with the United States in the tangle over the AIIB, the Chinese-led multilateral bank that the United States not only decided not to join but discouraged other allies from doing so too. The publicly expressed concern from President Obama was that "we don't want to ... be participating in something and providing cover for an institution that does not end up doing right by its people" and that US reservations were about "[making] sure that we're running it based on best practices."[17] Privately the objections were expressed more forcefully by US officials: that "the new bank would fail to meet environmental standards, procurement requirements and other safeguards adopted by the World Bank and the Asian Development Bank."[18] China, however, was inclined to see the opposition as reflecting broader objections to a Chinese-led institution, even one that was being constructed specifically to ensure that China's overseas lending could operate to a higher standard than its usual bilateral practices. Some of these issues were addressed during Xi Jinping's visit to the United States in September 2015, when the two sides agreed on an exhaustively negotiated joint statement that "for new and future institutions to be significant contributors to the international financial architecture, these institutions ... are to be properly structured and operated in line with the principles of professionalism, transparency, efficiency, and effectiveness, and with the existing high environmental and governance standards."[19] This paved the way for a number of agreements between the AIIB and other multilateral banks on co-financing arrangements. And US opposition had never formally expanded to OBOR itself, a subject that was only tangentially addressed between the two sides during major bilateral meetings in 2015. While the United States does not yet have an evolved policy response to OBOR, China has at least been able to defuse the risk of the across-the-board opposition that the AIIB imbroglio seemed to portend.

The third concern is that the initiative will have direct military applications. This has been a particular concern for India, which has seen the development of dual-use ports under the scheme in South Asia as potential threats, and particular facets of the scheme, such as Chinese investments in Kashmir, as strategic concerns. While India has not been in a position to block a number of these plans, particularly those in Pakistan, it has had some success in pushing back in other countries, including in Sri Lanka, where it was active in opposing the re-election of President Rajapaksa, after he granted permission for Chinese nuclear submarines to dock in Colombo port, and in Bangladesh, where the contract for a major port sought by China was instead given to Japanese companies. India's opposition to the scheme is locally specific, however, and there are other aspects where it is willing to cooperate, at least tentatively, such as the BCIM corridor.

The fourth concern is a more general one: that OBOR will result in the dependency of countries on Chinese financing and investment, privileged access for Chinese firms, and the development of a Sino-centric economic order, with politico-strategic consequences. Japan is the country that—while not making such claims publicly—has acted to put in place a broader-based counterbalance to OBOR, particularly in Southeast Asia. Shinzo Abe announced a $110 billion "Partnership for Quality Infrastructure" in May 2015 and has followed a travel itinerary that closely matches Xi Jinping's OBOR tours, including in Central Asia. There are countries in which the two sides are in outright competition, for instance for a major high-speed rail contract in Indonesia. But much of the Japanese effort is intended less to prevent Chinese investments and more to provide alternative options, ensuring that countries are able to have a balanced array of investors and contractors for their infrastructure projects.

Japan's initiative matches the motivations of many of the states themselves: few countries are comfortably ready to accept tens of billions of dollars of Chinese financing unless it is paired with that of other investors. This is one of the greatest difficulties that China faces: in order to fulfill the objectives of OBOR for China's economy—mitigating the impact on Chinese jobs and Chinese companies from a serious paring back of trillions of dollars of domestic investment—Beijing needs to find projects and willing recipients at a high order of magnitude. In this respect, there are a couple of exceptions where it is possible to look in more depth at the early steps to put OBOR investments into practice on a qualitatively greater scale than has been attempted before. Kazakhstan, where the SREB was first announced, has signed memoranda of understanding with China totaling between $23 billion and $50 billion, which will integrate the SREB with its own "Bright Road" infrastructure development plans. But the case study with perhaps the greatest resonance for OBOR in the Middle East is the "China-Pakistan Economic Corridor," described as a "flagship project" for OBOR, which represents the most fully developed set of plans under the entire scheme. Chinese Foreign Minister

Wang Yi remarked in February 2015 that "If 'One Belt, One Road' is like a symphony involving and benefiting every country, then construction of the China-Pakistan Economic Corridor is the sweet melody of the symphony's first movement."

CPEC and OBOR: an early marker

Pakistan's role as a pace-setter for OBOR is in certain respects a surprise. Between 2001 and 2011, a sum of $66 billion of financial assistance was pledged by China to Pakistan, only 6 percent of which materialized, and China's economic relationship with the country had long been the weakest element in the two sides' relationship. Security threats, corruption concerns, and a lack of economic complementarity had resulted in a pattern of consistent disappointment on Pakistan's behalf at its inability to convert close political ties into economic benefit. Yet the OBOR framework has conditioned a very different mode of Chinese thinking regarding economic projects in Pakistan.

Pakistan is in many respects uniquely placed, standing virtually alone in being able to move so quickly to offer opportunities for industrial ventures on a scale that matches the scheme's ambition. It has a long list of "shovel-ready" projects, sufficient trust for the two sides to work together happily on such an ambitious plan, a unique level of comfort with the strategic factors that underpin OBOR, ports that can serve both economic and military purposes, and an economy with significant growth potential where Chinese firms have privileged access. But Beijing's other objective is to use the corridor to help build stability in Pakistan and the wider region. It is supposed to act as a force of economic attraction, an incentive for restraint, a job-creator, a source of government revenue and various other benefits. The rationale is that helping to kick-start the Pakistani economy, addressing its energy challenges, and putting on the table the prospect of tens of billions of dollars of investment will generate growth and employment while restraining Pakistan's proclivities for regional adventurism in Afghanistan and India and making it a stronger and more capable partner. More concisely, Li Keqiang is colorfully quoted in the read-out from a meeting with Narendra Modi describing CPEC as being "designed to wean the populace from fundamentalism."[20]

CPEC is often misleadingly portrayed as essentially a transit corridor, connecting Xinjiang to Gwadar via a series of different land routes. CPEC's first phase does include road-building projects and the upgrade of Gwadar into a functioning port, but the initiative is mostly composed of energy projects in an assortment of locations around Pakistan, many of them far removed from the "corridor" routes. China sees CPEC more as a package of investment than as a set of transportation connections. There are still challenges in determining a full breakdown of the CPEC projects. Figures cited have ranged from $28 billion (which is the project list that was agreed to in time for Xi's visit in April 2015) to $46 billion (a number from the Pakistani government that included many other projects under negotiation too); this is a process in flux, with many of the details of the first phase of activities still subject to rolling negotiations after the terms had been agreed upon. Some of the initiatives cited in the April 2015 list have already been frozen, while new ones have since emerged. But the composition of the list is indicative: three-quarters of the projects are focused on energy, with road, rail, mass transit, fiber optics and Gwadar forming the rest of the investments.

The details of the financing, primarily in the form of loans but also a small number of outright grants, have not been publicly released, and the terms vary considerably. The rates of return on a number of energy projects are as high as 30–40 percent, with certain other projects supposed to achieve returns of 100 percent within a year. While the timeline for CPEC as a whole runs beyond 2030, the first test of the corridor will be the early harvest phase, concluding in late 2017. Coming shortly before the next Pakistani elections, this will be the first indication of how much new energy has been added to the grid, whether Gwadar has made meaningful progress, whether the first road-building process has been completed, and the details of the twenty-five industrial zones that are also envisaged under the scheme. CPEC's opacity has already been the source of some controversy. The leaderships of Khyber-Pakhtunkhwa and Balochistan have complained that their provinces are not going to attract a due share of investment and that the Punjabi-based leadership is directing the resources to its home region. Yet despite some of the political disputes, the general expectation is that while CPEC may not deliver on its most ambitious goals, even if a modest portion of the plans are realized it will represent a significant influx of investment for an economy that has received relatively little from China in the past. China's reservations about investments in Pakistan have not gone away. It has requested an extraordinary level of protection for the projects, in the shape of a new 12,000-strong Special Security Division of the Pakistani Army, raised specifically for CPEC. But the combination of strategic and economic objectives that OBOR embodies have resulted in a set of political conditions for Beijing to push ahead with its economic plans for Pakistan, even in the face of threats, that are now far stronger than they have ever been.

CPEC points to several factors that are likely to inform China's approach to OBOR elsewhere. First, an excessive focus on transit routes is unhelpful: the scale of commerce going long distances via land routes is still going to be limited by the relative expense compared with sea travel. Although it is superficially attractive to analyze OBOR based on lines on a map, China's interest is in broad-based industrial cooperation and infrastructure investments that relate to the needs of the recipient economy, rather than solely the transportation of Chinese imports and exports. Second, when there is credible scope for Chinese investments to achieve a strategic impact that supports broader goals, China is likely to be more willing to press ahead with them despite objections that have hobbled such investments in the past. Beijing is looking to use economic tools for a wider set of purposes now, and the goals of OBOR cannot be assessed purely through a commercial prism. Third, the kinds of economy that have been the primary focus of Chinese investments in the past are not necessarily the same for this next phase of China's economic development. Countries with large populations and the scope for grand-scale industrial and infrastructure projects are now particularly appealing targets, much as resource-rich countries that could help fuel China's investment boom appealed during the previous phase. Given the special relationship that exists between the two countries, Pakistan is in many ways a *sui generis* case, but a number of the shifts in China's approach that are playing out in Pakistan are "melodies" that will almost certainly recur over the course of the "symphony."

The Belt and Road initiative in the Middle East

Xi Jinping's belated visit to the Middle East in January 2016 looked set to be the occasion on which the initiative's general goals were given greater form and focus. Trailed by China's first "Arab Policy Paper," in which OBOR receives prominent mention, Xi's three-country visit to Egypt, Saudi Arabia, and Iran was an opportunity to lay a marker for the scheme of the same sort as his trips to Southeast Asia, Russia, Pakistan, Central Asia, and Europe.[21] Yet while Xi's speech at the League of Arab States provided a general outline of how the region is supposed to fit into the initiative, his visit left many basic questions unanswered.[22] The state that arguably provides the greatest potential for an influx of Chinese financing, Iran, was the subject of an implausibly ambitious trade promotion plan, but no major investment agreements of the sort that have been seen in other strategic focal points for the initiative. The headline investment figure for the entire region, $55 billion, was comparable with the plan for Pakistan alone.[23] The plan was composed of a $20 billion joint investment fund with the UAE and Qatar, $15 billion of "special loans for industrial projects," $10 billion in commercial loans in the energy sector, and a further $10 billion of preferential loans.

Xi's speech frames OBOR as a model to "promote stability," "promote structural adjustment," and the "new cooperation model of 'oil and gas plus,'" to "facilitate industrialization in the Middle East and launch actions to dovetail production capacity," combining "China's edge of production capacity with the Middle East's human resources." It refers to OBOR in the region being based on "the establishment of the '1+2+3' cooperative pattern with energy cooperation as the principal axis, infrastructure construction and trade and investment facilitation as the two wings, and the three major high-tech fields including nuclear power, space satellite and new energy." The tone of the speech was one of evolution rather than a qualitative shift in Chinese presence. The 1+2+3 framework, which was originally proposed in 2014,[24] looks to take economic cooperation further beyond the energy sphere and the emphasis on "facilitating industrialization." But the political content was cautious, with its specific disavowal that OBOR would be "attempting to fill [a] 'vacuum.'" The visit itself was politically delicate, having been canceled once as a result of Saudi Arabia's military intervention in Yemen; featuring a careful balancing act between the trips to Iran and Saudi Arabia. Chinese experts on the region saw its primary purpose as the fact that it happened at all—the delay itself became a point of controversy—and did so without any problematic incidents. But the studious neutrality also served to ensure that the OBOR announcements were shorn of any indications of a "tilt" or any substantive political content at all.

The question is whether this consistent feature of Chinese policy in the region is likely to be reconditioned by OBOR outside the parameters of a delicate political visit. In practice, there are several reasons to expect continuity rather than a qualitative shift of the sort that OBOR represents in other regions, relating to intrinsic factors in the Middle East rather than simply due to caution on China's part about effecting a change.

First, it is less clear that the primary obstacle facing industrialization and economic development in the Middle East is lack of financing. There are exceptions: Egypt was the subject of a $15 billion investment plan of its own, and has been consistently solicitous of Chinese investment under different political leaderships in Cairo. But many of the states in the region are capital-rich and active financiers of projects in their neighborhood. As a result, the equation that China has made in its near-abroad—using money as a means to stability—does not apply in quite the same fashion. In South Asia and Central Asia, Beijing sees itself as uniquely placed to change the security equation through economic means; less so in the Middle East. A more politically directed initiative—of the sort envisaged by the periodic advocates of a "Marshall Plan for the Middle East"—would be well within China's financial capacities; but aside from Egypt, other envisaged recipients, such as Lebanon, the Palestinian territories, or war-torn states, are constrained by a combination of political obstacles, lack of viable investments, and direct security threats of a far higher order than exist in, say, Pakistan.

Second, the country most ripe for another phase of industrialization and an infusion of Chinese investment is Iran, a country with a sizable, well-educated population, the largest in the region, whose economy and industry have suffered under sanctions and would benefit from large-scale financing and economic cooperation plans. Yet despite close political ties and pressing economic needs, Iran is cautious about jumping too closely into China's embrace at precisely the juncture when it has the opportunity to attract other investors with greater technological sophistication in key sectors, such as the Western oil majors. Prior dealings with Chinese investments and financing have been complicated, particularly during the period of sanctions, with Iranian assets frozen in Chinese banks and unsatisfactory negotiations on energy investments. China has certainly been apprehensive about the fact that the EU3+3 nuclear deal—the Joint Comprehensive Plan of Action Regarding the Islamic Republic of Iran's Nuclear Program—is likely to result in a far more competitive environment for its firms; one of the reasons for Xi Jinping to pay his visit so soon after the deal came into effect. But even here, there is some near-term caution on the part of Chinese firms about continued exposure to US sanctions. While it would be a surprise if there were not a marked expansion in Chinese investment, no specific package was announced during the visit, only a trade promotion plan.

Third, the crucial OBOR country logistically is Turkey: the hub country for transportation routes that would pass through Central Asia and Iran on the way to Europe, as well as other proposed routes passing through the Caspian. Yet prior Chinese bullishness about Turkey is in abeyance. Relations with the country have been rendered increasingly difficult by its role in facilitating the arrival of Uyghurs fleeing from Xinjiang, a number of whom have gone on to join various militant groups in Syria. Coupled with concerns about the political climate in Turkey and its problematic relations with other powers, including Russia, China has become more cautious about the country's role as a critical connecting point for the region's initiatives.

None of this precludes a shift in Chinese political strategy in the region, but OBOR itself is not likely to be the catalyst for it, at least in the first phase of the initiative. The factors that may lead to a deepened Chinese military and intelligence role in the region, for instance, such as the need to take more direct action against the Turkistan Islamic Party in Syria, or further evacuations of personnel of the sort that has taken place in Libya and Yemen, are precisely those that would inhibit a significant, broad-based increase in China's economic presence. Even in the event of an end to the war in Syria, China's response is still likely to be defined by caution about exposure to the risks of being caught in the middle of region's political dynamics—in contrast to, say, Afghanistan, where China has promised large-scale investments if a peace settlement is reached.

As a result, until China is willing to make clearer strategic choices in the Middle East, OBOR is likely to take a more modest form there than in several of the regions on China's periphery: an effort to develop transportation routes through Iran and Turkey; a heightened level of involvement in the industrial sectors of relatively well-developed and stable Gulf states; investment cooperation with Gulf state financiers; expanded investments in infrastructure, particularly in Egypt and Iran; further involvement in the region's ports, including the new military base in Djibouti; and otherwise a degree of continuity in energy ties with major exporters of oil and natural gas, as well other important economic relations in the region, such as Israel. Some Chinese analysts have gone so far as to argue that China intends OBOR to "bypass" the Middle East, which is evidently too strong. This is still a substantive agenda; but it is far from being a transformative one.[25]

PART IV

DOMESTIC FACTORS
IN CHINA–MIDDLE EAST RELATIONS

10

HAJJIS, REFUGEES, SALAFI PREACHERS, AND A MYRIAD OF OTHERS

AN EXAMINATION OF ISLAMIC CONNECTIVITIES IN THE SINO-SAUDI RELATIONSHIP

Mohammed Turki Al-Sudairi

The most authoritative works dealing with the Sino-Saudi relationship have been largely fixated on analyzing its economic, political, and strategic dimensions.[1] This is naturally an outcome of the Kingdom's (eroding) status as a hydrocarbon "swing producer" and China's own global ascendancy, not to mention the ramifications that their increasingly "interdependent" engagement could entail on a whole gamut of issues: i.e. on the United States' role in the Middle East, the position and balance and power vis-à-vis Israel and Iran, and even the future structure of Gulf security. Islam—unavoidably, perhaps—also registers a presence in such discussions, albeit in a somewhat faint and cursory fashion.[2] Its inclusion stems from two inescapable factors: (i) the centrality of the religion to Saudi Arabia's national and political identity as a self-proclaimed Sunni power with custodianship over the Two Holy Mosques;

(ii) the presence of dynamic Muslim minorities within China (making up 1.6–2 percent of the total population) with complex and burgeoning ties with many parts of the Islamic world, including Saudi Arabia.[3]

Because of the dominance of politico-economic and strategic discourses, conversations on Islam are often heavily colored by a state-centered mindset, and even in works where a more nuanced attention is accorded to it.[4] That is to say, the role of Islam is appraised by how far it complicates or facilitates the advancement of strategic and politico-economic objectives defined by the two states. This mindset produces two perspectives. On the one hand, Islam is conceived (i) as a tool of the state. Its "constituent parts," in the form of symbols, organizations, institutions, and agents, are reduced to instruments that are utilized in pursuit of particular goals aimed at either courting or pressuring the other party to assume a more favorable stance as a means toward obtaining a particular objective identified by the state. On the other hand, it is identified (ii) as an external threat. That is to say, Islam is imagined to be an uncontrollable and turbulent factor that poses a challenge—security-wise, ideationally, politically, and strategically—to the development of long-term relations between the two countries. This notion also carries with it the implicit understanding that, by virtue of these states' identities, their relationship will be marred by considerable contradiction and tension, although this is not always stated.

These dual conceptualizations of Islam have in turn helped give rise to essentialist narratives about Sino-Saudi relations, thus undermining attempts at a more sober reading of their current state and future trajectory. Broadly speaking, we see two such problematic narratives, or strains, emerging as an undercurrent within the literature and media coverage, narratives which reproduce the instrumentality-threat dichotomy noted above. The first, rooted dually in China's "Peaceful Rise" and the Gulf's "Looking East" discourses, is defined by a positive rhetoric of win-win and mutual development, and is, for the most part, the operative "language" appropriated by enthusiastic officials and scholars regarding this phenomenon of Sino-Saudi engagement.[5] Herein, Islam is reduced into a neutralized "aesthetic object" or, à la Joseph Nye, a "soft power resource" enabling cultural exchange, economic development, and civilizational friendship.[6] It is often invoked in the context of the Silk Road and its modern iteration, the "One Road, One Belt" strategy (*yidaiyilu zhanlue*), as either an organic part of its romantic landscape or as a facilitating "language" of trade embodied in the form of transnational Muslim linkages.[7] This is expressed in a repertoire of imagery—ethnicized Muslim minorities, caravans laden with goods, bustling markets, Islamic Chinese architecture, and colorful "cosmopolitan" exchange—often deployed by the two states in their public engagements, and all of which serve to evoke Orientalized notions of peaceful and mutually-respectful cultural dialogue between Chinese and Islamic civilizations. Emphasis within this narrative is placed on the lack of any colonial or violent confrontations between the two parties which "share in a common eastern nature."[8] Further underlying this narrative, albeit faintly, is the possibility of building a civilizational alliance (*wenming lianmeng*), which can foster the interests of both parties as well as offer alternatives to Western hegemony and control.

The other narrative, which has gained greater currency over the past few years, paints a far more negative image as a whole. It is reinforced by China's own growing "War on Terror" in relation to Xinjiang, the ongoing instability in the Middle East, the dissemination—from various sources, including Israeli and Western ones—of anti-Islamic polemics, and the more pronounced visibility of anti-Arab and anti-Muslim sentiments within some segments of Chinese society, particularly online.[9] Islam is recast as a force of tension, violence, and antagonism that complicates if not altogether impedes civilizational dialogue. This narrative is predicated on the articulation of imagined and essentialist identities ascribed to these two states and how they relate to Islam as such. China's anti-religious stance, epitomized by its ongoing crackdowns in Xinjiang and suppression of overt markers of religiosity, can only be understood as a byproduct of its atheistic (Arabic: *illhad*) and communist (Arabic: *shuyu'iyya*) character, leaving it in a "constant state of war with Islam"—a theme one commonly encounters in the Saudi press and social media.[10] Likewise, Saudi Arabia's perceived status as an exporter of Wahhabi[11] extremism and terrorism, and its potentially malignant influence over Muslim minorities, is seen to pose a threat to China's national security (*guojia anquan*) and ethnic unity (*minzu tuanjie*). The Kingdom's ability to "activate" Muslim minorities as a means to pressure China, in ways akin to perceived Saudi influence in Chechnya and Daghestan in relation to Russia, are worth keeping in mind here. Hovering behind all this is a Huntingtonian specter of a coming "clash of civilization" (*wenming chongtu*, Arabic: *sira' al-hadarat*) that interestingly enough evokes—when considering the field of Chinese Islamology—aspects of Raphael Israeli's core arguments regarding Chinese Islam's contentious relationship with the Chinese civilization-state.[12] In all, while there can be momentary convergences in political and economic interests between the two sides, the irreconcilable nature of their identities and ideological positions ensures that there can be no long-term amity, but rather an inevitable spiral toward mistrust and even hostility.

Admittedly, such state-centered narratives are a constitutive element in how Islam is imagined and discussed among various segments involved in the relationship. They are, for better or worse, part of the story. At the same time, they offer, as interpretive prisms, a somewhat limited and impoverished picture of the actual role(s) that Islam has played. Beyond treating Islam as a reified and homogenized entity either subject to, or in opposition toward, the state, these narratives have also reduced a very complicated arena of religious, cultural, political, and social interaction in service of an overarching political-security narrative, whatever it may be. More importantly, such narratives fail to take into account the far more interesting interactions that have taken, and are taking, place outside the purview of the state. Many such interactions are not external threats to bilateral ties, and have, both directly and indirectly, contributed to its transformation, albeit not necessarily in strict accordance with the notion of instrumentality (although they may have evolved along such lines later on). This chapter seeks to propose a different framework for understanding Islam's role, and one that involves taking into account, in conjunction with state-centered understandings, the behavior of non-state actors and motivations or activities that are contrary or simply irrelevant to the relationship between the two states. By incorporating both the state and the amalgam of autonomous forces operating within and beyond its reach, with a particular focus on the latter, the chapter will be able to highlight the roles of previously unacknowledged elements (pertaining to the realm of social history) within the context of this relationship; challenge preconceptions and assumptions about how actors and spaces operate; and shed light on the dynamic interplay between the state and non-state arenas. As a result, a more granular and nuanced understanding of Islam's role should emerge.

The analysis of these various forms of engagement will be done under the rubric of "Islamic connectivities," denoting here all types of significant interactions through which Islam has been symbolically and discursively deployed, on whatever basis, and for whatever objective. These "Islamic connectivities" will be examined in this chapter along functional lines based on identifiable themes and channels, and at the backdrop of a loose chronological division of four epochs: the Late Qing and the Republic (late nineteenth-century into the 1940s), the Cold War (1950s–1970s), the Reform and Opening Up (1980s–1990s), and the Post-9/11 periods (2000s–2010s).[13] The loose approach means that particular sections, examining specific connectivities, will sometimes go beyond an identified period in favor of an analysis that covers a longer time span. As for the chronological divisions as such, the reasoning behind them is threefold: first, it situates these connectivities in their proper contexts, that is to say that it serves to shed light on the domestic and international circumstances from which they emerged. Second, such an epochal approach helps communicate the changing "mood" of Sino-Saudi relations during different time periods, not to mention changing roles and perceptions among states and other actors. Third, it allows us to trace the evolution and growing complexity of Islam's role, and the character of particular connectivities (which might be reproduced in different epochs), from the earliest beginnings of this relationship to the present. The chapter does not claim to be exhaustive of all connectivities and themes, but will try to capture the most pivotal ones in the course of its analysis.

The late Qing and Republican periods (late nineteenth century—1940s): formative links and nascent ties

Choosing this epoch as a starting point for our examination of Islamic connectivities may appear, at first glance, as somewhat unusual. Both Saudi Arabia and China were in the formative phases of their modern state-building projects. Moreover, they were caught up in different subdivisions of the Western-dominated imperial-colonial orders that prevailed in their respective regions. These circumstances as a whole inhibited any willingness to establish diplomatic ties between the two sides. And yet it is from around this period that more substantive religious and communal links also began to take form. These in turn paved the way for the inauguration of more formal political ties as well between Saudi Arabia and China. They also exercised a residual influence on later forms of interaction. The connectivities of this period can be identified as three: (i) the spread of Wahhabism (the dominant Saudi religious discourse) into China among the Hui and other minority communities, (ii) the appearance of a Uyghur or East Turkestani diaspora within Saudi Arabia, and (iii) the dispatch of the "Muslim Missions" from China to Saudi Arabia in the 1930s, which can be construed as the earliest iteration of the "Hajj diplomacy" more common to later epochs.

The spread of the Wahhabi message into China: the Yihewanis, the Salafis, and the elusiveness of an Islamic "strategic depth"

Among the three outlined connectivities, the most important one with present-day ramifications is the penetration of Wahhabi influence into China.[14]

Pre-dating even the formation of the contemporary Saudi state, this phenomenon contributed to the appearance of new ideational and spiritual communities among the Hui, such as the Yihewanis and Salafis (these two, along with the Sufi and Gedimu, constitute the four major sectarian groupings of Hui Islam). These communities, due to their orientation toward an imagined orthodoxy embodied by Saudi Arabia as well as their minority status within Chinese Islam, exhibited stronger bonds of identification with it. They accordingly became integral actors through which many subsequent connectivities later emerged. At the same time, by virtue of Saudi Arabia's association with these particular communities, and many of which reproduced its sectarian discourses and narratives and co-opted its authority, its ideational and spiritual clout over other Muslim communities in China—subject to critique and attack by these same discourses—became far more circumscribed and even antagonistic. Essentially, Saudi Arabia was incorporated into the sectarian polarizations shaping the idiosyncratic expressions of Islam there. This development eroded the country's "spiritual soft power" and helped refashion it in the popular imaginary as a partisan "Wahhabi" power—promoting alien and even dangerous foreign beliefs and practices—rather than a sympathetic "Islamic" one. This demonstrates the pivotal point that presumed Islamic solidarities are often fractured and broken by the realities of sectarianism even within ostensibly "Sunni" spaces, a fact that is often absent in analysis dealing with Islam in Sino-Saudi relations. The notion that the Kingdom has a "strategic depth" among such communities should be open to question.

The earliest transmission of the Wahhabi message into China is attributable to Ma Wanfu (1849–1934), the founder of the Yihewani reformist movement that swept through north-western China in the early twentieth century.[15] Although the Wahhabi legacy of the movement is contested, there is strong evidence to suggest that Ma Wanfu, during his four-year stay in Mecca in 1888–92, did encounter and study under a number of scholars presumably connected with the Wahhabi movement.[16] This is given further credence by the observation that the movement exhibited a puritanical and revivalist tendency—embodied by its call for "respecting scripture and reforming customs" (*zunjing gesu*)—that placed it in proximity to the ethos of the Wahhabi tradition.[17] Since Ma Wanfu's return, the Yihewani movement gained a large following in many parts of China over the following few decades. By the 1930s, and as a result of the dual impact of its leadership aligning with the Muslim warlords of the north-west and the introduction of new discourses and intellectual streams from other parts of the Muslim world, namely Turkey and

Egypt, the Yihewani movement underwent a slow metamorphosis which saw a gradual jettisoning of its Wahhabi heritage and its transformation into what Alexander Stewart has called a "patriotic scripturalism."[18]

Despite these transformations over the course of the twentieth century, the earlier intellectual and spiritual connectivities with Saudi Wahhabism have persisted up to the present. These manifest in two ways. First, there are some strains within the Yihewani movement that have sought to re-salvage aspects of this tradition and revive it once more with regard to contemporary practices and beliefs. One of the major pioneers of this among the Yihewani is the late Ma Zhixin (d. 2012), who had sought, through his highly influential school in Linxia, Gansu, to promote a more sympathetic perspective of the Wahhabi tradition.[19] Such figures and their disciples, who have extensive links with the Salafi networks, have traditionally courted and received Saudi and Gulf support since the 1980s, and have been consequently accused of being agents of the Saudi state and pseudo-Wahhabis themselves. Second, one finds a pragmatic capitalization of these connectivities by some Yihewanis in pursuit of distinct economic objectives. This takes place largely among those who operate within state-sanctioned Islamic institutions and organizations, most notably the Islamic Association of China (IAC), which is the main official conduit for religious activities and funding redistribution between China's Muslim minorities and the Islamic world at large. Yihewani-affiliated officials and scholars within the IAC are often eager to highlight the Wahhabi inheritance of their communities in front of Saudi visitors, potential patrons, dignitaries, and diplomats. They seek to position themselves as orthodox Muslims bereft of any innovational practices, and usually in contrast to other groupings like the Sufi *menhuan* (orders) or the Gedimu congregations among the Hui. They are keen, moreover, to point out that the very name of their movement—per Ma Tong's interpretation—is possibly derived from King Abdul-Aziz Al-Saud's Ikhwan forces that contributed to the unification of the desert Kingdom.[20]

At the same time, and despite these forms of cordial engagement, the Wahhabi legacy today elicits considerable anxiety and contestation among many groups within the Yihewani movement. This is especially so among those who have come to appropriate anti-Wahhabi and anti-Saudi polemics imported from other parts of the Islamic world (Turkey and Iran). Such groups—embodied by the likes of Ma Hasan and Ma Youde in Qinghai—are considered peripheral and even extreme within the larger movement.[21] This partially stems from their espousal of very problematic views rejected by the

Yihewani and Muslim mainstream, including their discouragement of Muslims from going on the pilgrimage to Mecca because the grand mosques are supposedly under "Wahhabi occupation," or forbidding their followers from praying behind Imams who had studied abroad given their possible contamination by Wahhabi influences.[22] Some of their followers have been involved in some violence, and even an assassination attempt against an Azhari-trained Imam. Notwithstanding their extreme stances, the anti-Wahhabi sentiments expressed by these groups do find resonance among the wider Yihewani and Muslim communities in China, and have been a long-standing phenomenon as the works of Long Ahong suggest.[23] The virulent opposition to Salafis—identified with the Saudis—in places like Xining, Qinghai is indicative of how this plays out in some locales.[24] Some countries, such as Iran, have sought to tap into and perhaps amplify these anti-Wahhabi sentiments, tailoring programs in its Chinese-language radio broadcasts dedicated to uncovering its dangers.[25]

The reasons behind these antagonistic sentiments among Hui Muslims are multifaceted. Genuine theological and doctrinal differences are one constitutive element in this. The Sufis and Gedimu are condemned in Wahhabi discourse as maintaining deviant and innovational practices picked up from their non-Muslim Chinese milieu. Many Yihewanis continue to profess fidelity to Ash'ari doctrine and the Hanafi legal school (both of which predominate China), affiliations which are criticized by those professing Wahhabi beliefs. These differences intersect with the issue of sectarian competition over resources and adherents, a situation very much compounded by the growth of the Salafis (to whom I will turn below) in recent years and across many parts of China, such as Yunnan, Qinghai, Ningxia, Gansu, Shaanxi, Henan, and Shandong. This expansion is usually attributed to Saudi backing—an issue that will be explored in a different section of this chapter. Beyond these, mention should also be made regarding the gaps and discrepancies between an imagined Saudi piety and the realities on the ground, a phenomenon that has a long pedigree in China. The example of the prominent Yihewani scholar Hu Songshan comes to mind, whose experiences of racial discrimination during his pilgrimage in 1924 left him deeply skeptical of pan-Islamic discourses.[26]

More recently, one finds such disillusionment among not only returning pilgrims shocked by Saudi behavior, but also graduates of Saudi universities and institutions, many of whom have found Saudi society to fall well below the ideals and values they believed it to possess.[27] All these points underline an important theme raised earlier in this section: the "strategic depth" that

Saudi Arabia supposedly enjoys among Muslim Chinese is not what it seems. More importantly, oppositional attitudes can translate into lobbying pressures mounted by various Muslim groups on the central authorities to limit the scope of Saudi activities domestically.[28] This takes place even within the venues of the IAC, where Yihewani officials at the provincial levels have been found to exhort Muslims to "to reject Salafi ideas" and therefore Saudi influence.[29]

The Saudis are not wholly bereft of constituencies of support, however, and there are certainly a few groups where Saudi "soft power" maintains its capacity for persuasion and sway. The most supportive are the Salafis, sometimes derogatively nicknamed the "Saudi sect" (*shate pai*). This is partially due to their keenness in expressing their cultural and religious fidelity toward the Kingdom and the pure doctrines it is imagined to embody through their adornment of Arab headgear, short thobes, and *niqabs* (all markers of proper religious conservatism in the Saudi context).[30] The Salafis embrace an approach to Islam more closely approximating to Saudi beliefs and practices, and constitute a small but quickly growing group within Hui Islam as of the twenty-first century. For much of the twentieth century, the connections between the Salafis and Saudi Arabia as such remained largely normative in character—the Kingdom was a source of inspiration and emulation—but a more partisan identification would arise after 1978 as new dynamics and forces reshaped the relationship between the two sides.

The Salafis first appeared in the Chinese scene in the 1930s, in part due to the expanding reach and deepening penetration of Wahhabi discourses into China. The extension of Saudi rule into the Hedjaz (western Arabia) after 1924–5, which established Wahhabism as the de facto spiritual model of authority in the holy cities, was a pivotal factor in this. Additionally, innovations in transportation technology, such as steamships and railways, allowed ever-growing numbers of Chinese pilgrims to make the Hajj since the late nineteenth century.[31] Many of these pilgrims opted to remain in Mecca or Medina and spent some time in newly-founded Saudi institutions for a few years, becoming proficient in the new interpretations of the faith prompted by the Saudi clergy. Many more returned to China carrying Wahhabi tracts and literature which became widely available.[32] Geopolitical upheavals in Central Asia also contributed, albeit indirectly, to the expansion of the Wahhabi message into inland China: individuals of various stripes fleeing, or seeking to combat, Bolshevik influences in the region were making a showing along the country's border regions (Xinjiang, Gansu, and Qinghai), preaching and spreading the word. These individuals—an amalgam of Arabs and Central

Asians—were typified by the likes of the Turkestani Sheikh Abu Ma'sum Al-Khujandi, who taught in parts of Xinjiang in the 1930s before relocating to the Hedjaz where he became part of Saudi religious establishment until his death in 1960. There were also a few Arab *mujaheddin*, associated directly with Abdul Aziz Al-Saud's court, such as Sayyid Tawfiq Bey, who flocked to Xinjiang during this time in support of the secessionist rebellions there.[33]

The experience of the Salafis' "founding father," Ma Debao (1867–1977), generally corroborates the impact of many of these developments cited above. Originally a Yihewani cleric, Ma Debao supposedly began to reassess his beliefs after encountering an "Arab" Wahhabi sheikh by the name of Said Al-Bukhari in Qinghai in the early 1930s.[34] An opportunity later on presented itself and he left for the Hajj in 1936. He then opted to stay in the Hedjaz and studied in the newly-founded Dar Al-Hadith, incidentally under the above-mentioned Al-Khujandi who found employment there as a teacher.[35] Upon his return to China a year later, Ma Debao became very critical of the Yihewani movement for what he saw as its betrayal of its revivalist roots; eventually he broke away from it. This episode elucidates somewhat the origins of Yihewani opposition to the Salafis—and by extension Saudi Arabia—although there are other factors at play driving this antagonism as alluded to above, including conflicts over resources and recruitment.

Ma Debao's new movement, much like that of Ma Wanfu, encountered considerable success in gathering followers from across China's north-west, although there were limits as to how far it could expand due to the opposition it faced from the Yihewani-aligned Muslim warlords of the region.[36] It was not until the establishment of the People's Republic in 1949 that the Salafis would enjoy the freedom, albeit briefly, to preach openly and without hindrance. This was partially due to their identification by the communist authorities as being "less feudal." This was predicated on the notion that not enough time had elapsed since their emergence in the 1930s, thus precluding them from accumulating sufficient wealth and land as the Sufis and Yihewani had done. This respite was short-lived, however, and came to an abrupt end with the launch of the 1958 "Religious Reform Campaign." It was followed only a few years later by the eruption of the Cultural Revolution (1966–76), which augured the beginning of nearly two decades of unremitted persecution and isolation from the rest of the Muslim world. The ties between Saudi Arabia and the Salafis would have to wait until the early 1980s to be revived in any meaningful sense. Nonetheless, the relatively "easy" reactivation of these ties in the post-1979 period was in many ways predicated on the earlier links forged during the late Qing and Republican eras. The process of reactivation will be examined in later sections.

The Uyghur diaspora: Immigration, agitation for the "Palestine of Asia" and Saudization

The Uyghurs who settled in Saudi Arabia throughout the twentieth century constituted a major transnational group of some importance with regard to Sino-Saudi relations, participating as they did in the construction/dissemination of images about China as well as playing other vital roles within its rubric. Since the Russian invasions of Central Asia in the mid-nineteenth century, but particularly after the Bolshevik takeover in 1917, the Hedjaz region became host to a growing community of "Western Turkestani" refugees. Similarly, throughout the 1930s and 1940s, Uyghurs ("East Turkestanis") also arrived in sizable waves, fleeing as they did the depredations of the civil war in Xinjiang. But Sino-Soviet cooperation over border controls after 1948–9 limited their influx, although refugees still succeeded in reaching Saudi Arabia well into the late 1980s. According to Dru Gladney, some 6,500 Uyghurs undertook the Hajj between 1980 and 1987, a good number of whom opted to stay in the Kingdom.[37] While exact figures are difficult to find, it appears that the Uyghurs who resided in the Hedjaz already made up a community of a few thousand by the end of the 1930s.[38] Many of them managed to obtain Saudi citizenship, usually after arduous processes extending sometimes into many decades (although many well into their third and fourth generations have not, but they do retain some privileges similar to Palestinians and Burmese Muslims residing in the Kingdom).[39] Also, as part of their process of acculturation into the Saudi environment, they adopted family names like Kashghari, Tashkandi, and Bukhari, which denoted their connections to the well-known and recognizable great cities of Central Asia.[40] They effectively became "Saudi-Uyghurs" as such.

Unsurprisingly, many members of the Saudi-Uyghur community contested—mostly in a discursive manner—the hegemony of the Chinese Han state and made strong demands for the independence of what they deemed to be their occupied homeland. Many were opposed to the Chinese state's Guomindang and communist manifestations, but greater animosity was accorded to the latter as it retained tangible control over the region. There were outliers to this overall pattern, of course: in the early 1950s there were reportedly several Chinese-affiliated Uyghur "communist missionaries" preaching during the Hajj.[41] For the most part, however, the Saudi-Uyghurs formed something of an anti-China, anti-communist lobby within Saudi Arabia, and strenuously sought to highlight the plight of their co-patriates back home to Saudi and Arab audiences.

The quality of this activism varied. In some cases, it had a professional character to it, as the example of Mohammed Amin Islami (1912–88) illustrates.[42] A native of Yarkhand's environs, Amin Islami was involved early on with the nationalist project in East Turkestan. He participated in the 1937 uprising against Sheng Shicai's forces there. Following the end of the rebellion, he traveled extensively round Asia, studying in India and Egypt, settling in Japan for a while (where he became the Imam of the Tokyo mosque), and finally moving to Saudi Arabia in 1956. During this time he published considerable amounts of literature dealing with various issues related to liberation, the communist threat, and the need to preserve Uyghur culture. Most notably, he popularized the idea of East Turkestan as the forgotten "Palestine of Asia." Amin Islami also engaged with the Saudi and Arab audiences, publishing five thousand copies of a tract (funded with the support of local Saudi-Uyghurs) entitled "A letter to the Islamic World ... facts about Muslim Turkestan" in 1963. It was distributed to many major political and religious figures across the region, and was continuously republished in the Saudi press as late as the 1980s.

Amin Islami's advocacy was significant also within the context of Saudi-dominated "global" Muslim institutions, of which the Muslim World League (MWL), founded in 1962, comes to mind. His influence was felt in many areas, including his success in connecting the nascent organization with Isa Yusuf Alpetkin's network (introducing their own publications and journal pieces into the Arabic stream), adamant opposition to allowing admission for the Republic of China into the MWL (given its claims to sovereignty over Xinjiang), and in passing a resolution that called upon Muslim states to naturalize Turkic refugees fleeing from the Soviet Union and the People's Republic of China (PRC).[43] It is interesting to note that the MWL did have something of a Saudi-Uyghur flavor to it: preliminary evidence suggests it had a sizable number of Saudi-Uyghurs among its employees, and its former general-secretary, Rahmatullah Turkestani, was himself of Uyghur descent.[44] This may explain, in addition to the activism of various individuals like Amin Islami, the attention it accorded as an organization to Xinjiang, and well before the events of 1990 (Barren), 1997 (Ghulja), or 2009 (Urumqi) ever transpired. However, it is difficult to establish whether this translated into any effective lobbying capacity vis-à-vis the Saudi state, and this feature did not appear to act as a hindrance to its later engagement with the Chinese state in the 1980s.

The professionalized forms of advocacy noted above were also joined with more populist and organic types, encompassing everything from dedicated article pieces and mass-letter campaigns to the press, more recent use of blogs and Twitter accounts in the Saudi cyberspace, and the production of Arabic-language pro-East Turkestan propaganda on YouTube and other social media outlets. In all, these various forms of advocacy served to ensure that the question of East Turkestan/Xinjiang dominated and even displaced other narratives or imaginaries regarding Islam in China among Saudis, and in ways that invisibilized other groups and communities like the Hui.[45]

Having said all this, some reservations should be noted regarding the overall effectiveness of such advocacy and its success, at least on the popular level. Although it undoubtedly "centered" Xinjiang in public discussions about China, the ongoing debates themselves had an almost peripheral character to them, and were easily subsumed under a larger anti-communist framework already prevalent in Saudi society. This may have been an outcome—at least in the 1980s and 1990s—of Xinjiang being effectively overshadowed by other conflicts that were taking place in Afghanistan, Chechnya, and Bosnia. More importantly, "China's Rise" had not yet been internalized at a global level, and its internal situation there remained largely unknown for most foreigners, let alone Saudis. This may explain why even ostensibly "transnational" groups like al-Qaeda did not express much in the way of solidarity or concern for the plight of the Uyghurs in the 1990s. During an interesting interview conducted in February 1999, Osama bin Laden appeared to be far more concerned with co-opting China in his greater struggle of fighting the United States, even if that necessitated taking the Uyghurs out of the picture (explaining thus why al-Qaeda was hesitant to cooperate with the East Turkestan Islamic Movement).[46] In his response to a Chinese journalist, he was reported to have said:

> We have good wishes for all Muslims in the world. I often hear about Chinese Muslims, but since we have no direct connection with people in China and no member of our organization comes from China, I don't have any detailed knowledge about them. The Chinese government is not fully aware of the intentions of the United States and Israel. These two countries also want to usurp the resources of China. The United States is a country which does not even refrain from destroying the human race in its own interests. It was the United States that dropped the atomic bomb on Japan. So I suggest the Chinese government be more careful of the

US and the West. China must use its force against the United States and Israel and should be friendly towards Muslims.[47]

Saudi-Uyghurs have also impacted Sino-Saudi Islamic connectivities in other ways. This can be felt for instance in the community's promotion of Wahhabism—mostly in the 1980s and 1990s—back in Xinjiang when a temporary relaxation in religious restrictions took place.[48] They did so by hosting students, offering funding for mosques and scholarly circles, and more recently, through their utilization of new modes of communication (*weixin* and other platforms of instant messaging) to spread messages and sermons. In the meantime, Saudi-Uyghur businessmen were also flocking into China by the 1980s. There, they gradually linked up with their countrymen in places like Yiwu, Guangzhou, and Shenzhen, and helped disseminate Wahhabi beliefs and practices in turn.[49] Two points should be emphasized here. First, these activities were not welcomed by all quarters within the community, and particularly among those who have continued to adhere to the Sufi and Hanafi traditions of Uyghur Islam in the Hedjaz. Such groups saw these as attempts aimed at exporting faulty understandings of the faith unto traditional environments that did not need them. Second, this promotion did not necessarily translate into support for militant jihadism. If anything, it appears that the community had exercised a moderating influence on militant elements associated with ETIM. It has, most notably, refused to extend financial support even in the 1990s, a period that coincided with the relative mobilization of Saudi society in support of the Bosnian and Chechen causes.[50]

This attitude might be attributable to various socio-economic, generational, and assimilatory dynamics that have seen the transformation of this community over the past decades into a well-integrated and affluent bourgeoisie group within Saudi society by the dawn of the twenty-first century. The Saudi-Uyghur community claims within its ranks many doctors, university professors, businessmen, journalists, as well as officials of high-standing: the former Saudi ambassador to Japan, Abdulaziz Al-Turkestani, who incidentally only obtained his citizenship three years before his assumption of that post in 2008, was purportedly of Uyghur descent.[51] These new-found class identities as bourgeois Saudis, hand in hand with their vulnerability under the existing citizenship-regime, entail necessarily the appropriation of a quietist political stance within the Saudi context. Accordingly, many segments within the Saudi-Uyghur community have become either less invested or less willing to demand an independent East Turkestan, if only to avoid attracting political complications from this. This does not mean that residual sympathy "evaporated," but there is recognition that the parameters of such activism are concretely circumscribed by the Saudi state.[52] This partially explains why societal mobilization for Bosnia and Chechnya took place and not with regard to Xinjiang: the latter simply did not benefit from state endorsement (after all, formal diplomatic ties were only established a few years before, in 1990), or for that matter why, unlike other countries, the diaspora has not endeavored to establish an organization of its own. Having said all this, it should be noted that popular advocacy can and does continue; and the Saudi state in any case cannot clamp down completely on what has been identified as an "Islamic issue" and which has some public resonance. And sometimes, as the media uproar over 2009 events showed, such advocacy can be useful toward pressuring Beijing. Nonetheless, the state will not countenance agitation that either embarrasses it or jeopardizes its fundamental interests with China.

The early Hajj missions: inaugurating a diplomatic practice

The Hajj missions of the 1930s established a pattern of diplomatic practice that would be emulated in subsequent decades by the Chinese state in its overtures toward Saudi Arabia. These missions, involving two major delegations sent to Mecca in 1938 and 1939, took place to the backdrop of the Japanese invasion of China in 1937. They were organized at the behest of Hui elites in order to counteract growing Japanese propaganda efforts in the Middle East.[53] During the interwar years, the Japanese developed a sophisticated Muslim-oriented propaganda apparatus aimed at constructing an image of Japan within colonized Asia as a Muslim-friendly—and perhaps even potentially Muslim—liberatory power that merged Pan-Islamic and Pan-Asian discourses together.[54] They tried to accomplish this through a variety of means: by hosting the Islamic World Exhibition (1939) and constructing the Tokyo mosque (1938), offering refuge for numerous oppositional groups such as the Tartars, Baskhirs, Indians and Uyghurs, and actively setting up propaganda and espionage networks through the so-called Black Dragon Society.[55]

The Hajj was naturally one arena for such Islamic-oriented outreach. In 1938, and succeeding many earlier Hajj missions led by Japanese converts, the Japanese authorities organized a Hajj delegation drawn from Manchukuo's Muslim subjects. It was tasked with alleviating negative perceptions regarding Japan's occupation of China's north-east. Reacting to this, nationalist Hui arranged two major missions to the Kingdom, both of which obtained subsequent endorsement from the Guomindang authorities.

The second mission, made up of twenty-eight Chinese Azharite students and by far the most important, managed to obtain a personal audience with King Abdul Aziz. During their stay, the mission's members participated in a number of public debates in Mecca (including some with resident Uyghurs) and distributed pamphlets and other types of propaganda. Partially due to these efforts, they succeeded in making their case and complicated Japanese efforts at making further inroads across the region (similar forms of diplomacy and public outreach were taking place in other states, such as Egypt and Turkey). More substantially, these missions resulted—on the recommendation of the delegates themselves to the Guomindang government—in the opening of the first Chinese consulate in Jeddah in 1939 (although the establishment of formal ties would have to wait until 1946, and an embassy would only be opened in 1957).[56] This experience, which began as a wholly private initiative launched by Hui elites and students, proved formative for the Chinese state and demonstrated the instrumentality of the Hajj as a diplomatic tool for effective outreach.

The Cold War period (1949–1978): ruptures and transitory shifts

The end of the Chinese civil war and the founding of the PRC in 1949 signaled a new phase with regard to the Islamic undercurrents of Sino-Saudi relations. The connectivities formed during the late Qing and Republican eras, due to both domestic and international considerations shaped by the Cold War, were ruptured and suspended, and in terms of whatever residue they retained, were "transferred" to Taiwan as a new locus of activity. This was compounded by the fact also that diplomatic ties between Saudi Arabia and the mainland authorities were non-existent, and there was no impetus—more so on the Saudi side—to make a real push for it.[57] As Norafidh bin Ismail notes, China and Saudi Arabia "between 1949 and 1977 shared an understanding that their ideological positions made official links between them impossible."[58] This in turn catalyzed a different set of dynamics and connectivities that resulted in new ways of re-conceptualizing the relationship from a "distance," as it were. Of these, the most defining one was the entrenchment of negative perceptions or imagery about China within Saudi Arabia as a communist/atheistic enemy of Islam and an oppressor of one of the main "pillars" of Islamic civilization, East Turkestan.[59] This legacy very much persists today and is often tapped into when conversations on China emerge.

The origins of these perceptions can be attributed to a number of factors, some of which have already been intimated above: (i) an international (bipolar) and regional (revolutionary) environment that forced Saudi Arabia to align itself with the West; (ii) the Saudi government's own struggles against a domestic Leftist threat throughout the 1950s and 1960s, including a few groups with Maoist influences such as the Popular Democratic Party of the Arabian Peninsula;[60] (iii) a religious and official milieu that identified the Soviet Union and the PRC as threats to the faith (symbolized by the depredations of the Cultural Revolution) and a potential existential challenge to the state (as the independence of South Yemen and the Chinese-backed Dhofari rebellion seemed to corroborate); and (iv) the ideational role played by the ROC (Taiwan) as well as that of the (already examined) Saudi-Uyghur (and Chinese) diasporas, in reinforcing the construction of negative imagery about China under communist rule.[61]

Given this duality of distance and fear, it could be argued that the dominant connectivities of this era were defined principally by (i) the ROC's relationship with the Kingdom, and mainly through the activities and advocacy of its Muslim minority/diasporic community there, and (ii) the PRC's efforts to establish diplomatic relations with the country. In both instances, the leveraging of Islamic solidarities and symbols was critical. This section will focus on two particular connectivities. The first examines the Muslim (Hui) community of the ROC, or what can be alternatively called the Chinese-Saudi diaspora (given its settlement and its undergoing of a Saudization process similar to that experienced by the Uyghurs). Its role in facilitating ROC-Saudi ties, its promotion of anti-communist anti-PRC discourses, and its later contributions to the spread of Wahhabi influences into the mainland by the 1980s will be touched upon. In all of this, we can identify overlaps and intersections with some of the earlier connectivities discussed earlier in this chapter. The second looks at the PRC's efforts at reactivating Hajj diplomacy. Although the story is one of state instrumentalization of religion, as with its 1930s antecedents, this type of outreach was in many ways an outcome of the lobbying of various Hui and other Muslim elites, who arguably sought to complete their religious rites and maintain ties with the Muslim hinterlands via such means.

The ROC-Saudi "alliance" and the Saudi-Chinese diaspora

He Fengshan, the famous "roving diplomat" of the ROC, once noted in his memoirs that Ibn Saud referred to Chiang Kai-Shek as his "brother."[62] While this might have been a diplomatic nicety of a sort extended by the King, it did reflect the nascent solidarity that was shaping ROC-Saudi relations in the early post-1949 years. This was predicated not only on some of the legacies of older connectivities between the two sides (i.e. the earlier missions, for instance), but also a shared common opposition to communism.[63] There was certainly a strategic dimension at play between the two parties. For the ROC, maintaining cordial ties with Saudi Arabia was vital given the island's growing energy needs on the one hand, and its growing diplomatic isolation across the de-colonizing world on the other.[64] For the Saudis, the ROC in Taiwan was part of what could be termed as the anti-communist "cordon sanitaire" of Asia—encompassing also South Korea and South Vietnam—and was thus a frontline in the global battle against the Soviet Union, Maoist China, and the forces of the Left. Particularly under King Faisal (who was the first and only Saudi monarch to visit Taiwan in May 1971), but well beyond that during the "Safari Club" years of the late 1970s, the Kingdom identified Taiwan as a critical space of interest, offering extensive moral and material support to it.[65] Saudi Arabia was certainly the only Arab state to vote against the PRC's admission into the UN in October 1971.[66] This mutual assistance against communism had more tangible manifestations as well: the ROC reportedly sent pilots and ground troops to support the Saudi military campaign against the Nasserite-backed republicans in Yemen in the 1960s (this was partially informed by the fact that the Saudi air force was deemed ideologically unreliable, due to pervasive pro-Egyptian sympathies among its ranks).[67]

The ROC, perhaps given its recognition of the primacy of Pan-Islamic discourses in Saudi foreign policy during the Cold War, actively leveraged its Muslim "cultural resources" to consolidate this strategic relationship. This played out in a variety of ways. For instance, the ROC prioritized Muslim officials in manning its diplomatic mission to Saudi Arabia, a practice that continues today in the Taipei Economic and Cultural Representative Office in Riyadh.[68] It has also maintained the Hajj diplomacy policies which it inherited from an earlier era, selecting individuals from the Chinese Muslim Association and subsidizing their pilgrimages so that, after completing the rites, they would travel round the Islamic world to coordinate and exhort greater opposition toward the forces of communism. Both states were eager to deploy a common language of Islamic-Chinese "traditionalist" solidarity against "destructive" ideologies.[69]

At the heart of this "Islamic outreach" strategy, however, was the ROC's utilization of the relatively small Saudi-Chinese community in the Hedjaz. Muslim Chinese (Hui) probably started trickling into the region throughout the early decades of the twentieth century, but the core diasporic community—descendants of the two to three hundred families who fled with the Qinghai warlord Ma Bufang—only arrived after the decisive defeat of the Guomindang in the north-west of China in late 1949.[70] Ma Bufang and his followers were warmly received by the Saudi court (Ibn Saud reportedly tried to gift him a car). Most settled in Taif, Mecca, and Jeddah, and considerable numbers from within this group became naturalized citizens of the Kingdom (hence Saudi-Chinese), adopting the Arabized term designating their origins, *Al-Sini*, as a family name.[71] Ma Bufang himself, who served as the ROC's ambassador in Saudi Arabia after 1957 (after a short tenure in Egypt), also picked up Saudi citizenship, supposedly because of his disillusionment with the whole project of "reconquering" the mainland. Despite their new allegiances and perhaps because of its intimate links with ROC and its own cultural-historical loyalties, the community espoused very strong anti-communist and anti-PRC views. These views needless to say (as was the case with the Saudi-Uyghurs) resonated well in a Saudi political context. Members of the community also lobbied in favor of ROC within Saudi official circles, and acted at times as intermediaries, due to their proficiency in Arabic and Chinese.[72]

In more recent years, and indicative of their adaptability in the midst of changing global and domestic circumstances, some of these Saudi-Chinese have also come to play a similar role with regard to Saudi engagement with the PRC, with a few for instance accompanying King Abdullah's delegation to China in 2005 as translators and "cultural interpreters."[73] It should be noted that, much like the Saudi-Uyghurs, the Saudi-Chinese have in many ways, due to their education and communal practices, become part of the Saudi middle class, with some of their members assuming notable positions within Saudi society, including for example Othman Al-Sini, the editor in chief of the popular newspaper *Al-Watan*, and Abdul Karim Yaqoub Habibullah who heads the Saudi-Chinese Chamber of Commerce. They have largely Saudized, and it is open to question whether, under assimilatory pressures and the like, the latter generations of Saudi-Chinese will be able, or willing, to maintain their linguistic and cultural inheritance to such a degree as to allow them to continue operating as "interlocutors" relevant to the future development of Sino-Saudi relations.

Given the community's size in comparison to that of Saudi-Uyghurs, it is rather difficult to ascertain the parameters of its influence in other spheres of significance to Sino-Saudi relations, although there is sufficient evidence to suggest that some of its members were involved in the dissemination of Wahhabism across "Greater China." In Taiwan, and in conjunction with Saudi funding for mosques and the provision of educational opportunities, Wahhabi discourses have become dominant as a result of their influence, at least within the confines of the Muslim Chinese community there.[74] In mainland China, more so in the post-1979 period when contact with their relatives back in the mainland became normalized, through the Hajj and personal "business" visitations, they also played a tangible role.[75] The Saudi-Chinese sought to promote a rectified understanding of the faith among the Hui communities, utilizing a number of channels; purportedly, even some members of the ROC embassy in Saudi, who had studied there in the 1960s and 1970s, helped organize "secret" missions to the north-west of China.[76] Besides directly evangelizing their relatives during the Hajj, the community also offered funds and literature critical of religious practices back home. In one illustrative example, a relative of a Sufi order's members who had moved to the Kingdom prior to 1949 sent several cassettes in the mid-1980s to his sister-in-law denouncing the veneration of saints and tombs. Persuaded by his call to reform the order, she participated in "tearing down many of the tombs, including the *gongbei* built for her father-in-law."[77] Even prior to the 1980s, Saudi-Chinese Wahhabis were making a showing: one individual appeared in Linxia, Gansu, preaching in favor of Wahhabism and distributing books there as early as 1948.[78] The same fellow in fact apparently returned in the 1980s and helped fund the renovation of the well-known Salafi Qianheyan mosque.[79]

The mid-century Hajj diplomacy of the PRC: presaging a future era

While most Islamic connectivities were unfolding through a ROC-Saudi nexus, those with the PRC, as noted above, were largely ruptured. The authorities in Beijing identified the establishment of diplomatic ties with Muslim countries, including Saudi Arabia, as a vital strategic interest. This was driven, as Kyle Fonda-Haddad's examination of Sino-Egyptian relations in the mid-1950s demonstrates, by two objectives: (i) allaying the fears and procuring the recognition of the governments of newly independent states as a means of overcoming the country's isolation, and (ii) mobilizing as well as gaining the loyalty of domestic Muslim constituencies within China by showcasing the country's new-found friendship with Muslim polities.[80] To attain this, the PRC, as a general policy approach toward foreign Muslim audiences, downplayed ideology while highlighting China's commonalities with the Arab and

Muslim worlds through an anti-imperial and Islamic platform. This entailed extensive use of various overtures, among which "Hajj diplomacy" constituted a key instrument. It was perhaps the only feasible tool that could be used with regard to the Kingdom at the time, given the centrality of the pilgrimage rite for Islamic practice. Much like earlier missions of the 1930s, the "Hajj diplomacy" of the Cold War was a product of Hui and Muslim elite lobbying pressures which was eventually, and as soon as its political objectives became clear, endorsed by the state.

During this era, several missions were sent out. The first, led by the much famed Imam Da Pusheng, left China in 1952.[81] It proved unsuccessful, however, as its members failed to get visas from the Saudi embassy in Pakistan, perhaps because of the continued fall-out from the 1950–51 events involving Uyghur "communist preachers" noted earlier in this chapter.[82] This failure led to the suspension of the Hajj for several years, but the Bandung Conference, held in 1955, presented a new opportunity to get out of this impasse. The Muslims accompanying the Chinese delegation, led by Zhou Enlai, repeatedly brought up the issue of obtaining Hajj visas, a concern that paved the way for a meeting between the premier and prince (later King) that resolved it, albeit perhaps not to the total satisfaction of Beijing. In any case, and from 1955 onward, missions which were arranged to include visitations to a number of Muslim countries besides Saudi Arabia were dispatched annually for Hajj.

Although none of these succeeded in transforming Sino-Saudi relations politically in any substantive sense, the second mission in 1956, which was led this time by the Tatar Burhan Shahidi, did see some highly symbolic exchanges: aside from meeting King Saud three times, Burhan was invited to participate in the washing of the *Ka'bah* and was even gifted a piece of its cloth (the *kiswah*).[83] This suggests that the Saudi state, at least under King Saud, contemplated recognizing the PRC. This coincided with a particular moment at both the domestic and regional level wherein the Saudi government found itself adopting a progressive and pan-Arab platform epitomized by its momentary alliance with Egypt and Syria in 1955 against the British-backed Baghdad Pact, and its somewhat conciliatory attitude toward the unrest among Aramco oilfield workers.[84] There was a temporary Leftist ascendancy within the context of the Saudi government which may have sought to strike an independent course in terms of the country's foreign policy, including establishing diplomatic ties with China. That being said, the structural realities of the Saudi-American security compact, the influence of the ROC-Saudi relationship, and the overall anti-communist milieu within Saudi

Arabia itself may have ensured that this was unlikely to come about. In any case, the PRC itself would suspend these missions by 1964 as the Cultural Revolution enveloped the country and isolated it from the rest of the world for well over a decade.

The reform and opening-up period (1979–2000): a religious renaissance and new-found opportunities

The reform and opening-up period signaled the reactivation of many of the Islamic connectivities that were forced into dormancy during the Cold War era. The Chinese state, now fueled by a new politico-economic reform project (*gaige kaifang*), was concerned fundamentally with three objectives related to the question of Islamic connectivities: (i) reinvigorating its legitimacy among its Muslim minorities, (ii) garnering the diplomatic recognition, and in turn the economic support of key Muslim powers such as Saudi Arabia, and (iii) consolidating a growing ring of alliances against the Soviet Union. This meant essentially revamping its "Hajj diplomacy" through an intensified strategy of Islamic outreach (encompassing everything from the transformation of Islam into an "aesthetic commodity," through the consecration/restoration of "Muslim sites" in Yinchuan, Quanzhou, and Guangzhou, to the dispatch of Muslim laborers abroad among the work teams of Chinese construction companies operating in Arab/Muslim countries) and a relaxation of religious restrictions internally as was done formally under the rubric of the new 1982 constitution.[85] This would allow for more effective showcasing of state tolerance as well as greater interaction and transnational engagement. This would result, over the long run, in changes in foreign perceptions, and in turn the accruement of critical economic and political gains to China's benefit. Dru Gladney has dubbed this strategy, most appropriately, as that of the "Islamic card."[86]

The Saudi state was willing to reciprocate these gestures, albeit first through low-key connectivities. Domestically, the Chinese utilization of Islam worked well with the Faisalian "Islamic ethos" of the Kingdom, and coincided moreover with the *Sahwa* or revivalist period of the 1980s wherein "Islamic identity" became paramount.[87] There was an inherent appeal for Saudi elites and non-elites in focusing on the lot of Muslim minorities on the periphery (and certainly, this process facilitated the "rediscovery" of Hui Islam). For the state and other actors, this presented an opportunity to position itself as their caretaker and protector. Behind all this also loomed the possibility of reengaging with the mainland at a time when the international environment was conducive to such a development. A detente between the two countries had a sound strategic basis insofar as it could help contain what was perceived at the time as an ascendant Soviet Union in Afghanistan.[88] It also offered the Kingdom an alternative arms source. There were of course challenges to this, including the ROC's relationship with Saudi Arabia and the prevalence of anti-communist sentiments within society. Engagement under the rubric of various "Islamic connectivities" constituted thus a safe conduit through which diplomatic ties could be fostered, and were undoubtedly contributing factors to the establishment of formal relations in 1990.[89]

Because of the complexity/experimental spirit characterizing this era, as well as the multiplicity of actors involved (some of whom were merely beneficiaries of a more relaxed era and did not fit neatly into the narrative of instrumentalization), it might be prudent to conceptualize the various connectivities that emerged as taking place through a formal-informal dichotomy. Denoting state-controlled mediums, formal channel connectivities can encompass (i) the Hajj and (ii) the influx of Saudi-backed organizations that conjoined both religious and political functions. Informal channel connectivities, taking place outside distinct state-supervision or interest (at least initially), include (iii) the growing involvement of "informal" Saudi non-government organizations (i.e. those operating without overt political connections with the Saudi government) and preachers, as well as (iv) the study-abroad phenomenon. No strict division between these formal-informal channels actually exists (and we shall see that all of them carry official/non-official dimensions), and one may find that actors of all stripes, ranging across established official entities like the IAC or the Ningxia or Xinjiang local government, not to mention Saudi preachers and the like, operating within all of them. Additionally, participants in a connectivity carrying a political objective might also retain other agendas and goals distinct from it, ones of an organizational or spiritual nature. More importantly, a connectivity often expresses its own dynamics either unnoticed or deemed irrelevant by the state. Nevertheless, the conceptual divide is useful insofar as it highlights the areas of interaction emphasized, and those neglected, by both states prior to the inauguration of formal ties in 1990.

The "formal" sphere: the Hajj and "state-led" Saudi organizations

At the heart of China's renewed attempts to win over Saudi Arabia was of course the Hajj, which was restored officially in 1979. As in the past and following the pattern of the older "Hajj missions," Beijing initially only dispatched IAC officials and religious leaders to the Kingdom, although by the mid and late 1980s, and as these missions assumed greater importance as venues for political interaction with Saudi religious and political elites, more prominent functionaries were sent.[90] These Hajj missions, as well as the provincial leadership missions (from Ningxia, Gansu, and Xinjiang) usually subsumed under them, constituted the main vehicles of interaction under the rubric of "people's diplomacy" (*minjian waijiao*) and could be considered as such a "pure form" of state instrumentalization of Islam.[91] They were especially pivotal in convincing Saudi elites to go forward with the process of normalizing their relationship with China.[92]

Yet to limit the Hajj phenomenon to this alone would miss other more interesting dynamics. In 1984, the Chinese state slowly began to dismantle some of the restrictions imposed on private pilgrimage.[93] This led to major thousand-fold increases in the number of pilgrims going to Saudi Arabia, and necessitating thus the opening of a China Hajj Office by the Saudi authorities in 1987.[94] By 1990, over 10,000 were making the pilgrimage annually. Unsurprisingly, many of these pilgrims were exposed to Saudi religious discourses (at times, through their Saudi-Chinese relatives). In some cases, pilgrims underwent wholesale conversions and opted to extend their stay, much like their predecessors in the 1920s and 1930s, for further study in the Kingdom.[95] Pilgrims also brought back with them considerable quantities of Wahhabi books, leaflets, fatwas (religious rulings), Qur'anic readings, and sermon tapes (later CDs), all of which became available nearly anywhere in China with high Muslim concentrations.[96]

The restoration of the Hajj was coupled with the entrance of Saudi-backed organizations like the MWL into China. These two channels were in fact closely intertwined, as the early Hajj missions could not have been possible without the IAC obtaining first the support of the MWL. In the spirit of reciprocity, and so as to showcase state tolerance of Islam effectively and contribute thus to the cultivation of a better image for China, the IAC invited the MWL to dispatch "fact-finding" delegations.[97] Several delegations were sent out over the subsequent years, with many touring Muslim-minority areas in Ningxia, Gansu, Qinghai, and Yunnan.[98] These MWL delegations extended significant aid and funding to the IAC (through the Islamic Development Bank) totaling US$ 4 to 5 million. Much of this money was earmarked for the renovation of mosques, the opening of Islamic institutes, arranging workshops to train clerics, providing scholarships for students abroad (initially for those in Pakistan), sending Arabic instructors, and in 1987 for the distribution (through IAC channels) of over one million copies of Ma Jian's translation of the Qur'an printed by the King Fahd Qur'anic Press in Medina as a royal gift from the Saudi state.[99] From what can be discerned from the writings of Nasir Al-Abudi (MWL's Deputy General-Secretary at the time), as well as the impression of his Chinese hosts, these exchanges proved to be quite successful in altering prevailing views within the Saudi religious and political establishments about China and its relationship with its Muslim minorities.[100] Additionally, they helped realize some of the Chinese state's economic goals, albeit in a circumscribed and narrow manner.

The non-formal sphere: the "private" Saudi organizations, preachers, and students

The MWL and other organizations were joined also by a number of private groups, charities, and preachers that operated outside the IAC official channels, helping to build mosques, distribute literature, and establishing contacts with local activists, networks, and private schools—largely those of a Wahhabi character associated with the above-mentioned Salafi communities among the Hui—in Gansu, Ningxia, Shanxi, Yunnan, and Qinghai.[101] Saudi preachers were making a showing throughout the 1980s. 'Adnan Al-'Ar'our, for example, the famous Saudi-Syrian Salafi scholar, discussed extensively in a TV show his experiences in 1986–7 of distributing Qur'ans and other Islamic literature to "secret schools" in China.[102] Since then, he appears to have become a regular visitor to China and has established close contact with some Salafi circles from the north-west.[103] More recently, popular Saudi preachers like Abdulaziz Al-Fawzan and A'idh Al-Qarni are increasingly incorporating Muslim Chinese into their *da'wah* efforts and coming to China on national tours. The latter for instance appears in one uploaded *youku* video where he is shown giving a sermon in a Salafi mosque, possibly in Lanzhou.[104] In addition, Al-Qarni has commissioned a translation of his famous book *La Tahzan* (Do Not Be Sad) into Chinese and has also begun to tweet in that language.[105] These preachers, such as Al-Fawzan, were sometimes connected to Saudi non-state organizations like the Al-Haramain Islamic Foundation (AIF). The organization managed to maintain a robust presence in the country throughout the 1990s, despite a 1994 law issued by the Chinese authorities banning foreign donations not processed through the IAC, funding as it did the construction of several Islamic institutes and mosques (in one instance, the AIF apparently procured money from the late Saudi grand mufti, Ibn Baz). It was only formally barred from operating in China in 2004, mostly in the wake of a US-backed United Nations Security Council ban due to its alleged affiliations with al-Qaeda.[106]

A pressing question emerges, especially in light of recent warnings issued by the Chinese state about growing foreign influence on religion and anti-Wahhabi campaigns in Yunnan and the north-west: why do these individuals and groups still manage to evade government restrictions? After all, such foreign clerics and preachers would arguably be considered catalysts of negative externalities, and there were attempts in the 1990s to control and limit their entry into the country.[107] A tentative answer to this appears to be that many of these clerics and preachers have over the years come to establish working relationships with the Chinese state, which probably deems their influence on the ground rather negligible. In some respects, the state might even consider their presence rather useful: it has benefited from famous Saudi clerics who, during state visits, exhorted local Muslims and residents to be loyal toward the state (the late King Abdullah's similar exhortation during his visit in 1998 is still appreciated today among some quarters in China's diplomatic and scholarly circles) and have helped in strengthening its public propaganda efforts abroad.[108] The above-mentioned Al-Qarni has called upon the Arabs settled in China to respect the laws of the country.[109] More recently in 2013, Saleh Al Taleb, an Imam of the Grand Mosque in Mecca, in an extended interview with Arabic CCTV, praised the Chinese government's record in dealing with Islam.[110] All this serves to show how connectivities can, and do, mutate and transform in unexpected ways: what is considered a risk and an uncontrollable externality was effectively co-opted by the state.

The study-abroad phenomenon constitutes another critical dimension of Sino-Saudi Islamic connectivities in the reform and opening-up period. Through middlemen and local contacts, or at times during the Hajj itself, various Saudi patrons and groups (in both official capacities as well as private) have helped extend scholarships to many Muslim Chinese students wishing to study Arabic and Islam over the last few decades. These students were offered seats in Saudi institutions such as Imam Saud University in Riyadh, Umm Al-Qura in Mecca, the Islamic University of Medina, and more recently Al-Qassim University, as well as other Saudi-affiliated universities in the Gulf, Pakistan, Malaysia, and even Thailand (Yala province).[111] Although it is difficult to find a sound estimate of the total number of students who came to the Kingdom during this period, one study detailing a breakdown of foreign students at the Islamic University of Medina (the most important internationalized Saudi religious institution in any case) from 1961 to 2000–2001 revealed that over 652 scholarships were granted to mainland "Chinese Students" (it does not differentiate between Uyghurs and Hui).[112] The bulk of these were offered during King Fahd's reign (1982–2005). Since these are for just one Saudi institution, we can only speculate as to the total numbers, but it is indicative nonetheless.

Interestingly, few from this sample ever completed their studies (91), a pattern that appears from anecdotal evidence to be common to other institutions as well. This is not surprising, as many students reported undergoing severe culture shocks (and in some cases revised their views about Saudi discourses/religious practices) or, for practicality's sake, chose to limit their aims to gaining Arabic proficiency and then dropping out (after which they would gravitate toward Guangzhou or Yiwu to work as translators for Saudi and Gulf businessmen).[113] Some graduates, including a few of those who had not completed their studies, did return to assume jobs as teachers in Salafi-affiliated schools, and in a few cases as Imams, at least after 2000 (when the laws were relaxed), but their influence and clout are open to question.[114] Although fears have been voiced about the impact of this study-abroad phenomenon, within both Muslim and official quarters, it has likely contributed, according to my assessment, to moderating Wahhabi discourses within China, and helped strengthen low-globalization trade between the two sides.[115]

The post-9/11 period (2000s–2010s): courtship, securitization, and the specter of terror

The developments that took place during the reform and opening-up period laid down the groundwork for the establishment of official diplomatic ties between Saudi Arabia and China in 1990. The following decades saw significant political and economic advances being made that were rooted in an emerging complementarity predicated on energy and a mutual identification of common strategic interests shared by the two parties.[116] Interestingly, Islam's role at this juncture, in terms of state-level rhetoric and behavior, approximated the instrumentality-threat dichotomy criticized earlier in this chapter: that is to say, Sino-Saudi relations were guided by the formula of enhancing positive utilizations of Islam while minimizing potential disruptions. This explains why these narratives had been popularized in the academic and journalistic conversations about them. This seemingly enhanced role of the state, however, as this chapter has sought repeatedly to highlight, does operate with the intensification of various other connectivities and linkages, augmented and amplified as they are by the spread of new technologies and means of communication.

In the context of Sino-Saudi relations, and for much of the 1990s and 2000s, a spirit of sensitivity and accommodation prevailed. This was probably informed, on the Chinese side, by the visible success of their "Islamic card" strategy on the one hand, and on the other hand the influence of the global isolation that Beijing had to contend with following the 1989 Tiananmen events.[117] There was thus an attitude of overt permissiveness: for example, the early 1990s saw the Chinese authorities turning a blind eye to the Saudi embassy's (illegal) distribution of Qur'ans and other forms of literature (although this has since changed).[118] There was even an eagerness to placate them on rather inconsequential matters: in 1993, an abridged version of the *Encyclopedia Judaica* contained a foreword written by the vice president of the Chinese Academy of Social Sciences, where he noted that Islam has its theological roots in Judaism. Following an official protest from the Saudi ambassador, as well as from other organs and groups, the foreword itself was redacted by the publishers to avoid offending the embassy.[119] Beijing has been willing to go so far as to exert pressures on even its non-Muslim citizens to conform to the needs of the Saudi state. During the uproar that emerged within Saudi society following the influx of thousands of Chinese laborers to work on the Al-Haramain project in the environs of Mecca (2009–10), the Chinese state purportedly, through the embassy and state-owned enterprises, "nudged" the workers to convert to Islam, both as a favor to Riyadh and so as to avoid jeopardizing its economic interests within the Kingdom.[120]

We see a similar accommodationist approach by Saudi officialdom toward the concerns of the Chinese state. In media outlets, for example, particularly from the late 1990s and much of the succeeding decade, the Saudi government has been keen to reproduce the narratives espoused by Beijing regarding Islam.[121] This was undoubtedly connected to the influence of the late King Abdullah, whose successful visit to China in 1998 made him a Sinophile of a sort.[122] Thus, in official conversations on Sino-Saudi relations, we find that the Saudis have developed the propensity for shedding light on Beijing's efforts to protect and promote the faith. (This is often expressed in quantitative terms: for example, "there are over 34,000 mosques, nearly 45,000 imams, and 10 Islamic colleges with more than 20,000 teachers.")[123] This also serves the purpose of alleviating any implicit criticisms toward Saudi engagement with a country that was viewed for so long as an atheistic and anti-Islamic power, and functions as a means of linking such engagement with the improvement of the situation of Muslim minorities there.[124]

Far more interesting, however, has been the deployment of the Saudi state's presumed religious and spiritual authority to buttress the legitimacy of the Chinese state: in ways that transcend how instrumentalization is conceived. This was already noted above with regard to the statements cyclically issued by visiting Saudi preachers and *ulema* to China, although the most significant exhortations toward respecting Beijing's political status have also come from the highest organs of power in Riyadh (gestures that are often well appreciated by Chinese officialdom).[125] During King Abdullah's visit in October 1998, under the shadow of the 1990s events in Xinjiang, he gave a speech to a Muslim Chinese congregation condemning terrorism and encouraging Muslims to abide by the laws of their homeland and promote their message peacefully.[126] In addition to the over-political utility of these overtures, they should be understood as being galvanized by a desire to disassociate the Saudi authorities from the specter of terrorism: a concern that has become ever more pressing since the 9/11 attacks.

This "workable" dynamic of instrumentalization and minimization of externalities has shaped the "golden age" of Sino-Saudi relations under King Abdullah (arguably extending from his days as crown prince, but more specifically covering the period 2005–15). At the same time, and as this chapter has argued from the very beginning, limiting our focus to these two approaches in examining Islam's role impoverishes our understanding of what is taking place. Various connectivities and linkages, with legacies extending back many decades into the past but now intensifying under the veritable forces of globalization, continued to exercise and shape state approaches within the rubric of this relationship. Some of these, especially those deemed as problematic externalities, have augured unanticipated state reactions, forcing us thus to rethink this paradigm altogether. To illustrate, this section will focus on two major connectivities often identified as "problematic": (i) the Xinjiang issue, and (ii) the Wahhabi question. The first connectivity—and it is called as such because it occupies a particular "imaginary"—actually approximates more closely to the "negative externality" narrative. At the same time, as that section will show, the Saudi state has chosen to ignore it completely as a potentially problematic factor in terms of its engagement with China. The second connectivity points to an increasingly complex connectivity which, while seemingly falling under the rubric of "negative externality"—with a particular rhetoric substantiating this—actually sees significant Chinese state cooperation and support, challenging thus our pre-existing assumptions about this matter.

The Xinjiang issue: the "Palestine of Asia" between popular support and official disregard

As discussed elsewhere in this chapter, East Turkestan/Xinjiang has enjoyed a long-standing presence in the Saudi imaginary about China. Nevertheless, and especially after 1990, the Saudi state has actively sought to sideline the issue from being an irritant to the development of more cordial Sino-Saudi ties. Saudi officials insist that this is an ethnic separatist issue, not a religious one, and they have held firmly to this operative principle.[127] Saudi official condemnation on the 1997 events in Ghulja, for example—aside from that of the religious establishment including prominent figures like Ibn Baz—was non-existent.[128] The authorities refused to issue a Hajj visa to Rabi'a Qadeer, the Uyghur World Congress leader, and have clamped down moreover on several attempts by Uyghur pilgrims to "politicize" the Hajj.[129] These stances in many ways stood against public, and in some instances official, sentiments regarding the question of Xinjiang, and there have been moments where Riyadh has tried to "reconcile" China's political requests and the Saudi state's role as a "guardian" Islamic power. In 2006, the Saudi embassy in Islamabad was subject to protests and demonstrations by Uyghurs who were no longer allowed to procure Hajj visas from Pakistan. This was in the wake of a Sino-Saudi agreement concluded earlier in the year which only permitted visa issuances to those vetted through IAC channels.[130] The Saudi government came under intense criticism from Muslim countries worldwide for this, and tried to address the situation by proposing an increase in the Hajji quota numbers for China as well as offering sponsorship, at the King's expense, for a few thousand "poor" pilgrims.[131] The Chinese authorities probably interpreted this gesture as interference in their domestic policies, so not only turned it down but also deliberately refused to permit any increases in the size of the pilgrim missions.

At times even these attempts at reconciliation were put under significant strain, to the point of being untenable. This was case for example following the 2009 Urumqi riots, which saw a major shift in public representations about China within the Saudi media.[132] The increasing daily count of the dead and the Chinese authorities' heavy-handed response to what were clearly identified as Muslim grievances led to an eruption of public outrage within Saudi society. The Saudi government had no option but to allow these expressions of public anger to simmer for a duration, which was serious enough in any case to force the Chinese embassy in Riyadh to issue three statements as part of its damage control strategy. Despite all this, the Saudi authorities never issued a condemnation of Chinese actions in Xinjiang, as their counterparts did in Turkey.[133] They also tried to re-assert state control over the circulating media narratives about the events.

This indicates that the Saudi authorities, regardless of mounting pressures, are simply not willing to allow Xinjiang to become an impediment to the development of Sino-Saudi relations. This approach has not been predicated simply on the continued comity of bilateral ties: it is an approach that has endured, remarkably, despite growing tensions in the relationship since 2011 over Syria, and more recently continued public anger over China's implementation of a number of problematic policies in Xinjiang (a crackdown on fasting, a "beautification campaign" to discourage the *hijab* and beards, "encouraging" shopkeepers in the southern regions of Xinjiang to sell alcohol, etc.)[134] This suggests that Xinjiang is viewed as an externality whose damage must be controlled by both sides, although it departs from the traditional narration that Saudi elites have repeatedly bypassed opportunities, and have resisted pressures, to express a more substantive form of solidarity with their "brethren" in the region. This is very interesting when we consider the extent to which the plight of the Uyghurs has gained traction across the Islamic world, to the point where various transnational jihadi organizations such as al-Qaeda and the Islamic State have "taken up their cause."[135]

The contemporary Wahhabi question: a problem on the horizon?

The Wahhabi connectivities discussed in the earlier section have increasingly assumed more complicated dimensions in the context of Sino-Saudi relations. This was especially so in a post-9/11 environment where "Wahhabism" was inescapably viewed through a security prism. This "securitization" was largely informed by three overarching dynamics: (i) global conversations that associated jihadism and extremism with the ideological influences emanating from Saudi Arabia, (ii) China's own intensifying "War on Terror" with restive Sunni Muslim populations in Xinjiang, and (iii) sectarian discourses emanating from anti-Salafi groups (noted above) on the threat posed by Wahhabism. All this contributed to the construction and vocal articulation, within official and academic circles in China, of Saudi Arabia as an ideational problem, given its status as a "Wahhabi power." This has entailed the need to "counteract" foreign influences emanating from there that may potentially threaten the integrity of the state and work to erode the "peaceful" and traditional forms of Islam indigenous to the country.

This perception of Saudi-backed Wahhabism as a threat (*weixie*) has been buttressed furthermore by two major developments originating from the 1980s. The first relates to the considerable growth that Wahhabism has enjoyed in China. Among the Hui, the Salafi congregations had not only succeeded in re-asserting themselves after 1979, but succeeded also in attracting converts across the country. There is a general consensus within the scholarship at present that they are now one of the fastest growing groups among the various strains of Hui Islam.[136] More troubling to the Chinese authorities, a similar development has taken place among the Uyghurs in Xinjiang where Wahhabism, prior to the 1980s in any case, had little in the way of a presence.[137] The Uyghur growth was in many ways tied to the atmosphere of religious toleration that prevailed during that period, as well as the permeation of various "Wahhabi" influences, of which the Saudi-Uyghurs were one source. The second development, which has been already discussed, refers mostly to the penetration of both officially sanctioned as well as "under-the-radar" Saudi organizations, groups, and preachers into the Chinese scene seeking to promote Wahhabism. Although the correlation between this influx and the accelerated growth of Wahhabism is, in my opinion, tenuous—and particularly because of the very serious cultural and linguistic issues that continue to persist—it increasingly holds true for Chinese officialdom. This provides the context for the more recent "anti-Wahhabi" campaigns launched in Yunnan and the north-west provinces targeting various Salafi institutions and schools, and to a certain extent the growing negative tone adopted in the media when discussing this issue. The recent All-National Religious Work Meeting (*quanguo zongjiao gongzuo huiyi*), held in April 2016 and well attended by high-ranking members of the Standing Politburo, saw stronger calls for the "sinifaction of religion" and also provides a broader context for these crackdowns amidst growing party-state apprehension over "foreign influences" in the religious sphere.[138]

Yet all this should have led, one would expect, to an even more visceral suppression of all the various connectivities promoting Wahhabism within China. Instead, what we see is considerable leeway still being accorded to Saudi-affiliated groups which have, as of late, begun to express overt missionizing intentions toward China, and partially in response to a perceived Shi'ification campaign being undertaken there by Iran.[139] Al-Fawzan, for example, the preacher discussed earlier in this chapter, succeeded in extending his Risalat Al-Islam broadcasting network to Ningxia under the name of Heping TV (Peace TV) in 2015.[140] Opening a Saudi-connected channel could only have come about with official endorsement, which he had succeeded in obtaining. Similarly, a self-proclaimed missionary center in Riyadh, the "China-Saudi Cultural Communication Center" (*zhongsha wenhua jiaoliu zhongxin*), which has operated under the rubric of the Saudi Religious Affairs Ministry since 2009, has begun to make more direct inroads into China. Saudi preachers moreover continue to come into the country on national tours relatively unhindered or unimpeded by the authorities, which often—as highlighted above—co-opt these visits for their own legitimation purposes.

One is thus faced by a contradictory approach embodied as it were by both a perception of an ideational threat from Saudi-inspired Wahhabism on the one hand, and an apparent toleration of its main organs of promotion on the other. This suggests that the Chinese state, while discursively opposed to Wahhabism, still sees significant utility in the maintenance of various connectivities, and is perhaps aware that they carry a limited impact on the internal situation of Islam within China. It may also trust some of these individuals and groups, insofar as many of them have worked to cultivate close ties with certain figures within the Chinese establishment, suggesting that the state does not treat these channels in a generalized or categorical way. Beyond that, it is possible that the state is simply overplaying the threat posed by Wahhabism in front of particular audiences: this is given some credence by the fact that Beijing has not deigned to discuss these issues with their counterparts in Riyadh, who remain, according to my own observations, oblivious to the changing discourses on Wahhabism within China.

Conclusion

This chapter has attempted to look at the role of Islam in Sino-Saudi relations over the span of a century. It focused on a number of "Islamic connectivities," defined by particular epochs, as spaces through which Islam's role has found expression. This examination tried to demonstrate that the narrow approach of looking at these forms of engagement through the lens of state-centered mindsets, i.e. positive instrumentality and negative externality, is insufficient and indeed impoverishes our understanding of Islam's role. This is not an attempt to dismiss necessarily centrality of the state and how it conceives of Islam's role, but the roles and activities of various non-state actors—some of which have been accorded little or no attention whatsoever in the literature— need to be emphasized for a richer overall picture to emerge. In many instances, we find that the ways in which the state comes to instrumentalize Islam are very much an outcome of the advocacy, lobbying, and pressures exerted by these non-state actors. More importantly, there is a need to transcend, when considering Islam's role in Sino-Saudi relations, our propensity toward adopting the narratives of comity and conflict. The connectivities selected for this chapter—and there are certainly many others to consider— demonstrate the complexities and multidimensional nature of these engagements, not to mention the capacity of states to co-opt and capitalize upon even the most problematic of these. Abjuring reductive narratives allows us to focus better not only on often-neglected "stories" as it were, but more significantly it enables us to put Islam's role, as an amalgam of many disparate and different interactions, within this relationship, in its proper place.

11

CHINA'S UYGHURS

A POTENTIAL TIME BOMB

James M. Dorsey

Lurking in the background of Chinese President Xi Jinping's "One Belt, One Road" vision of Eurasia as a Chinese sphere of influence undergirded by a Chinese-funded network of transport and communications infrastructure lies a potential time bomb: the long-standing refusal of north-west China's Uyghur population to be assimilated in the same way that their Muslim Hui cousins have melted into the fabric of Chinese society.

China hopes that Chinese-built infrastructure in Pakistan and Central Asia will increase interdependency and spur economic development in its troubled north-western, resource-rich province of Xinjiang or New Frontier, where harsh measures against the cultural and religious practices of the restless Uyghurs have fueled Islamist and nationalist violence. A job boom in Xinjiang, engendered by the infrastructure development, would allow the government to dilute the region's Uyghur population further, through the immigration of non-Uyghurs.

China's stakes in Xinjiang are huge. Xinjiang hosts 15 percent of China's proven oil reserves, 22 percent of its gas reserves, and 115 of the 147 raw materials found in the People's Republic.[1] With 2,800 kilometers of border with Central Asian nations, Xinjiang is China's gateway to Eurasia. Its 1.6 million square kilometers account for 16.6 percent of China's territorial landmass. Xinjiang is moreover home to some of China's most sensitive military facilities, including its nuclear arsenal.

Uyghurs, Turkic rather than Chinese speakers, currently account for 46 percent of Xinjiang's 22 million inhabitants, and together with their cousins of Central Asian and Tartar origin make up 52 percent.[2] While still the largest group in Xinjiang, Uyghurs have seen their relative numbers dwindle over the decades as the result of a government effort to marginalize them in their own homeland. Economic policy aimed at fostering growth favored the country's Han majority. Han, who once accounted for a mere 5 percent of the region's population, now constitute Xinjiang's second largest ethnic group with 40 percent.[3]

The Uyghurs' disenfranchisement is evident in statistics quoted by the Xinjiang Uyghur Autonomous Region's census office. The numbers show that the percentage of Uyghurs working in agriculture, 80.51 percent, is higher than the national average of 61.6 percent and far higher than the 36.7 percent among Han in the region. Similarly, only 5.3 percent of the Uyghur have moved into professional and technical jobs, while 11.1 percent of Han have graduated into those slots. The same is true for managerial and administrative jobs: less than 1 percent of the Uyghur workforce occupies such positions, compared to 3.9 percent of the Han labor force.[4]

Demographics matter in a region in which Xinjiang's capital of Urumqi and other major cities like Kashgar are far closer to Central Asia than they are to Beijing. Urumqi is 2,400 km from Beijing, but only 1,000 km from the Kyrgyz capital of Bishkek, and 1,800 km from Kabul. The Uyghur city of Kashgar further west is a mere 400 km from Bishkek and 800 km from Kabul. To compensate for this geostrategic weakness in what Beijing considers its soft belly, China enhanced its grip on Xinjiang in the 1980s and 1990s with the dispatch to the region of the Han paramilitary Xinjiang Construction and Production Corps. Initially focused on securing China's borders, the Corps took control of 48 percent of Xinjiang's land.[5] Since the demise of the Soviet Union and the eruption of Uyghur protests, it has expanded its focus to include the quelling of domestic unrest.[6]

CHINA'S UYGHURS

A geographical pivot of history

The ethnic and religious tensions ensuing from Chinese policy in Xinjiang go to the core of the country's national and security interests and the People's Republic's ability to project itself in Central and South Asia. While ethnic unrest in Xinjiang has a long pedigree, Chinese concern about the region has risen on Beijing's list of priorities since the demise of the Soviet Union, the gaining of independence of Central Asian nations with ethnic and cultural affinity to the Uyghurs, and the rise of Islamism in Afghanistan and Pakistan. It is likely to increase as competition with the United States, Russia, and India for influence and resources mounts in Central Asia, a region with which many associate Xinjiang; a British geographer described it already in the early twentieth century as a "geographical pivot of history."[7]

Chinese policy-makers hope that infrastructure development in Central Asia and Pakistan, coupled with hundreds of millions of dollars of investment in Xinjiang, will provide an incentive to Uyghurs to model themselves on Hui Muslims in the province of Yunnan and elsewhere in China. The Hui pride themselves on their Islam with Chinese characteristics, a blend of Islamic and Confucian principles that has encouraged them to identify as Chinese, albeit a Chinese minority. Assimilation has allowed Hui Muslims to become successful in business, and with significant interests in mining, despite a history of massacres dating back to the nineteenth century; a memorial in the city of Shadian in Yunnan Province commemorates those killed during the Cultural Revolution in 1975 by the People's Liberation Army.[8]

China hopes that its investments, particularly in an array of projects in Pakistan, including a 1,700-mile trade route to the Gulf as part of its "One Belt, One Road", will help it succeed in the South Asia nation where the United States has failed. China expects that its funding of interconnected infrastructure will persuade Pakistan to enforce its crackdown on Pakistani militants and end the way the country's intelligence service, Inter-Services Intelligence (ISI), supports radical Islamist groups. It is a gamble that would require confronting Saudi-backed ultra-conservative interpretations of Islam, which over decades have been woven into the fabric of Pakistani society as well as key branches of government; and also confronting Pakistan's long-standing use of militant Islamist groups to pursue policy goals in Afghanistan, Kashmir, and India.

Ironically, for China to pin its hopes on Pakistan runs against experience in recent history. The opening of the Karakoram highway connecting Xinjiang with Pakistan's region of Gilgit–Baltistan in 1979, the year of Iran's Islamic revolution and the Soviet invasion of Afghanistan, promoted not only increased traffic of people and goods but also of Islamic awareness and militant forms of the faith. The highway facilitated travel and communication of Uyghur militants educated in Pakistani madrasas, which often served as recruiting grounds for fighters in the Islamist resistance against the Soviets in Afghanistan as well as in the 2001 US-led invasion of the country.[9] In a further twist of irony, some of those fighters were trained by China itself as part of its desire to make life difficult for the Soviets.[10]

The Chinese approach toward Xinjiang, despite China at times playing both ends against the middle, fails to take into account the role that Islam plays in Uyghur life, identity, and social relations, as well as its importance in Uyghur history. Islam is also a key player in the Uyghurs' attitude to modernizing influences, which many Uyghurs see as alien and designed to favor the country's majority Han. Uyghur demands for independence date back to a century after China's Qing dynasty completed its annexation of what is now Xinjiang, when in 1865 Muhammad Yaqub Beg, a Tajik chieftain, led an uprising. Exploiting a Hui uprising in the region, Beg initially captured Kashgar and Yarkand. His fierce resistance grounded in religious and ethnic identity won him diplomatic recognition from the Ottomans, Russia, and Britain. Ottoman military officers moreover served as Yaqub Beg's advisors and supplied him with arms.[11] He was nonetheless defeated by China's armies twelve years after he launched the revolt.

China's refusal to acknowledge the combination of religion and ethnicity in Uyghur identity and its policy of forced assimilation produced a vicious circle, in which acculturation was identified with foreign domination and refusal to become Chinese led to cultural and economic marginalization. The vicious circle meant that areas in which Uyghurs were willing to accommodate have been narrowed. Uyghur willingness, for example, to accept Chinese control of Islam through the training and nomination of imams and the censoring of sermons, provided the religious leaders were ethnic Uyghurs, has been undermined by the government's repression of cultural and religious expression.

The result is a return to more literal interpretations of Islam that position the faith as an anchor of identity and a bastion of resistance to foreign encroachment and reinforces what China sees as the three forces of evil: ethnic separatism, religious extremism, and international terrorism. Chinese scholars Yufan Hao and Weihua Liu in a reflection of China's approach asserted that "the direct international threat to Xinjiang is Pan-Turkism along with Pan-Islamism."[12] The vicious circle further weakens Beijing's ability to capitalize on advances it has achieved, including the fact that an increasing number of Uyghurs speak Mandarin and have integrated into Chinese political and economic networks. Those advances translate into a majority of Uyghurs' desire for greater cultural and political autonomy, rather than secession.[13]

Tilting toward Iran

Xi Jinping's hopes of employing close ties with non-Arab Muslim nations, such as those in Central Asia as well as Pakistan and Iran, to nudge Uyghurs to a Hui-like position are further rooted in China's perception of Iran following the toppling of the shah in the 1979 Islamic revolution. The revolution coincided with the launch of Deng Xiaoping's reform and opening up policy that was intended to modernize China. Iran shared with China a rhetoric of revolution, defense of the oppressed, and opposition to US imperialism, as well as having modeled its elite Islamic Revolutionary Guards Corps (IGRC) on China's Red Guard, and also saw mileage in exploiting differences between Beijing and Washington over Taiwan.[14]

China's view of Iran as a nation with which it had common interests and some degree of shared values, coupled with a belief that Shiism could serve as an antidote to Sunnism, the prime anti-Chinese mobilizer in Xinjiang in Beijing's view, further paved the way for close Chinese-Iranian cooperation in areas ranging from Chinese support for the development of an Iranian missile and nuclear industry to transportation links across Central Asia.[15] These moves prompted Xi Jinping to visit the Middle East in January 2016, the first visit by a Chinese leader in seven years.[16]

Xi Jinping's tilt toward Iran during his visit arose in part from Chinese concerns that alleged funding of Islamic schools or madrasas in Xinjiang by wealthy Saudi nationals of Uyghur origin was encouraging Uyghur militancy. Saudi officials sought to assure their Chinese counterparts that they did not support militant Uyghur violence, despite the fact that the Uyghurs, some of whom had joined Islamic State (IS), were largely Sunni Muslims. Those assurances, however, did little to put Chinese concerns to rest. "Our biggest worry in the Middle East isn't oil—it's Saudi Arabia," said a Chinese analyst.[17]

Saudi Arabia began establishing links to the Uyghurs in the 1980s as relations with China, long strained over the kingdom's ties to Taiwan and condemnation of communism as atheism, began to thaw and Chinese Muslims were allowed to perform the Hajj. Official representatives of the Xinjiang autonomous regions eventually joined the Hajj and met with Saudi officials while in the kingdom.[18]

At about the same time, Chinese Muslims began to explore religious education opportunities abroad. Saudi Arabia, compared to Egypt, Pakistan, Syria, or Yemen, offered the most generous scholarships. Based on interviews in 2005 and 2006, China scholar Jackie Armijo concluded that most of the students and graduates might not have embraced the Kingdom's austere Wahhabi and Salafi interpretation of Islam, but that some had returned with a "degree of intolerance regarding some of the local practices of Islam within China."[19] They campaigned against Chinese-style mosques that featured architectural designs similar to traditional Buddhist temples, which they viewed as foreign when compared with more "authentic" Middle Eastern styles. This led to the destruction of a large number of historic mosques, replaced with allegedly more authentic ones.[20]

The notion of shared revolutionary values with Iran and Shiism's potential in offering Uyghurs an alternative perspective paved the way for a watershed visit to Xinjiang in 1992 by then Iranian President Ali Akbar Rafsanjani, during which he signed agreements to link Iran and north-west China by air and with a railway that would traverse Kazakhstan and Kyrgyzstan.[21] In Kashgar's Etgar mosque, Uyghurs and Central Asians welcomed Rafsanjani as a rock star.[22]

A visit to the region five years later by reformist Iranian president Seyyed Mohammad Khatami in the wake of a Uyghur uprising highlighted Iran's initial ability to influence Chinese policy. China at first acceded to Khatami's request to re-open mosques that had been closed because of suspicion that they were centers of radicalism. China also loosened restrictions it had placed on communal prayer, but maintained its efforts to cut links between the Uyghurs and groups in Uzbekistan's Fergana Valley, Afghanistan, and Pakistan whom it blamed for growing militancy in its north-west.[23] Fallout from the militant Uyghur presence ultimately contributed to Iranian advocacy for a more inclusive Chinese approach, which increasingly fell on deaf ears in Beijing as China reverted to a policy that aimed to restrict Uyghur religious and cultural identity and squash nationalist sentiment.

Turning a blind eye

China saw its dim view of the ability of Uyghur militants to operate near its borders affirmed when a US drone in the border regions of Pakistan in 2012 seriously wounded militant Uyghur leader Abdul Haq al-Turkistani, a member of al-Qaeda's executive council and emir of the Turkistan Islamic Party.[24] Earlier, US-led forces had captured Uyghurs fighting against coalition forces in Afghanistan, some two dozen of whom were imprisoned in Guantanamo.

Chinese fears were also reaffirmed when it emerged that twelve of the fifteen non-Afghans killed in 2008 in fierce fighting between Pakistani security forces and militant Islamists holed up in Islamabad's Lal Masjid or Red Mosque had been Uyghurs, both men and women.[25] China had earlier blamed Uyghurs for the kidnapping of seven Chinese nationals in an Islamabad massage parlor in 2007 by militants associated with Jamia Hafsa, a madrasa located in the Pakistani capital not far from the Red Mosque.[26] The incident sparked high-level Chinese pressure on Pakistan to crack down on the militants, and is widely seen as paving the way for the subsequent siege of the Red Mosque in which more than a hundred people died.

China refused to follow Iran's advice and stepped up its repression in Xinjiang in the wake of 9/11 and the ethnic tensions in 2009, the worst in the region since the establishment of the People's Republic in 1949, in which at least 180 people were reportedly killed.[27] But few Muslim governments protested, with the exception of Turkey[28] and Islamic scholars associated with them. Two Pakistani Islamist parties, Jamaat-e-Islami (JI) and Jamaat Ulema-i-Islam (JUI), whom the Chinese embassy had asked to assist in engineering the release of the Chinese hostages in Jamia Hafsa, were among those who remained silent in 2009. A year later the leaders of both parties paid separate visits to Beijing at the communist party's invitation.[29]

This silence was effectively bought by China's economic engagement, its increasingly hollowed out principle of non-interference in the domestic affairs of others, and similarities in Chinese and autocratic Muslim efforts to criminalize Islamist opposition forces; it contrasted starkly with responses to earlier riots in 1997. Then, Saudi scholars had urged their government to support the Uyghurs while the mufti of Saudi Arabia, Sheikh Abdulaziz Bin Baz, insisted that Muslims had a duty to come to the aid of their brethren in Xinjiang.[30]

China's wielding of its economic clout to stifle criticism was built on its long-standing support for causes in the Muslim world, including the Palestinian struggle for nationhood, opposition to US domination, the resistance against the Soviet occupation of Afghanistan, and the Islamic revolution in Iran that toppled the shah, an icon of US influence in the region.[31] Author Lilian Craig Harris noted that China had recognized since the birth of the People's Republic the significance of linkages between its Muslim minorities, including the Uyghurs, and the Muslim world. "Since 1949, China's ten Muslim 'nationalities' or ethnic groups have consistently been dealt with more favourably than any other religious group, not only because their treatment has international repercussions, but also because they have been...useful to Peking as links to the Islamic world," Harris wrote.[32]

Recovering occupied land

The silence did not extend to independent scholars and businessmen, however, nor jihadist groups like the Islamic State (IS) which constituted a retrograde revolutionary force. With no relation to jihadists, individual Muslim businessmen and scholars have taken on their Chinese counterparts in conferences and at private meetings for their repression of Muslims and their utilitarian view of China's relations to the Muslim world.[33]

IS's caliph, Abu Bakr Al Baghdadi, identified East Turkistan as one of the group's target areas in 2014, and listed the People's Republic at the top of his list of countries that violate Muslim rights.[34] Maps circulating at the time on Twitter purporting to highlight IS's expansion plans included substantial parts of Xinjiang.[35] Al-Qaeda expressed a similar attitude, condemning Chinese policy toward Xinjiang as "occupied Muslim land" to be "recovered [into] the shade of the Islamic Caliphate."[36]

Al-Qaeda and IS's targeting of China followed the failure of calls by ultra-conservative Muslim scholars with close links to jihadist groups to convince the People's Republic that resolving its problems in Xinjiang by making peace with the Islamic nation would allow it to reduce the global influence of the West. Hamid Al-Ali, a Kuwaiti Salafi cleric, whom the US Treasury has described as an Al Qaeda facilitator and fundraiser, said:

Today it is our duty to stand with the plight of the Uyghur Muslims against Chinese repression (a) because this is our duty with all the Muslim people, (b) to send a strong message from our nation to China that the persecution of Muslims in China will only benefit the West, which will take advantage of this racial discrimination in order to deepen the hostility between China and the Islamic world.[37]

The IS and al-Qaeda threats added to the pressure on Beijing to ensure the safety and security of China's massive overseas investments and large number of nationals overseas. Militant Uyghur groups, not all associated with the global jihadists, have over the last two decades attacked Chinese targets, including diplomatic missions, pro-Chinese activists, businessmen, and workers. Al-Qaeda moreover vowed that it would take revenge for the Uyghur deaths during the 2009 riots by attacking Chinese workers in Algeria and sub-Saharan Africa.[38]

IS has targeted Iraq's northern oil resources in a bid to secure revenue streams and to weaken both economically and strategically the government in Baghdad. China is invested heavily in Iraq's energy sector. China Petroleum and Chemical Corporation, also known as Sinopec Ltd, has stakes in oil fields in Iraqi Kurdistan, while state-owned China National Petroleum Corporation (CNPC) has interests in multiple fields in the south.[39] Two Uyghurs were sentenced in Dubai in 2010 to lengthy prison terms on charges of planning to attack the emirate's DragonMart, a popular Chinese shopping center.[40] "The stability of the Middle East, an important link on the new Silk Road, is crucial to the success of this economic structure and the cooperation between China and the region," said Li Haidong, a scholar at Beijing's China Foreign Affairs University.[41]

China hoped that changes in Pakistan, engendered by economic growth as well as some kind of resolution of conflict in Afghanistan or at least an understanding with the Taliban, might help steer the Uyghurs in Xinjiang toward the Hui model; but so far these hopes remain just wishful thinking. In March 2014, knife-wielding Uyghur militants stabbed passengers at random in Yunna's Kunming train station, killing more than thirty and injuring more than a hundred and forty, an attack suggesting opposite trends. It was one of many violent incidents in recent years, and one of the ten deadliest in China's recent history.

News that the attackers had resided for a period of time in Shadian, a largely Hui city that hosts a house of worship modeled on Medina's Nabawi mosque that was originally built by the Prophet Mohammed, prompted large numbers of the country's majority Han Chinese to portray the city as China's Islamic State. Some depicted Shadian as evidence of the risk involved in allowing too many Muslims to congregate in one place and granting them too much freedom. "Can these yellow-skinned Arabs stop disgusting us Chinese people? We know that huaxia [a Han concept of Chinese civilization] is a pile of shit in your hearts. Why are you still here?" one commentator charged. In response, the government sought to showcase its authority and project the Hui as part of China by planting flags in front of mosques, painting green roofs white, and expelling from Yunnan religious students and teachers from other provinces, as well as hundreds of Uyghurs.[42]

Sun Degang Sun, the deputy director of Shanghai International Studies University's Middle East Institute, has argued that given the example of the Hui

Muslims, China could fend off criticism in the Muslim world of their harsh attitude toward the Uyghurs and adopt an economically focused approach, in line with their insistence on non-alignment and non-interference and differences in definitions of national interest between the West and China.

Tackling the epicenter of war

Underlying the Chinese approach is the belief that rising living standards will enhance domestic stability and the security of the regime. This notion constitutes the backbone of China's "One Belt, One Road" initiative, described as "the most expansive Chinese initiative ever" by Wu Jianmin, a member of the Chinese Foreign Ministry's foreign policy advisory group, a senior research fellow with the State Council of China, and former ambassador to the United Nations and various European countries.[43] Wu argued that the initiative was needed given that "the epicentre of war and conflict is the Middle East and North Africa" and that "Iraq, Afghanistan and Libya prove that war does not solve problems."[44]

It is a view rejected by Uyghur nationalists and countered by the fact that Uyghurs have always identified themselves as Central Asians rather than Chinese, or in other words as an ethnic minority. Uyghur perceptions of their place in China contrasts starkly with that of the Hui, who have come to define themselves as Chinese and who practice Islam with what many often call Chinese characteristics. As a result, Uyghur nationalists argue that Chinese efforts to weaken their identity through repression and strict control of religious practices are backfiring. Rather than turning Uyghurs into compliant Chinese citizens, government policy is fueling political and religious radicalism, they say. In response, China's internal security budget has surpassed that of its military every year since it squashed the 2009 uprising.[45]

Dolkun Isa, secretary of the World Uyghur Congress (WUC), an exile group that opposes what it terms Chinese occupation of East Turkistan, said:

> I travelled throughout East Turkistan until I was forced to leave in 1994. There was no radicalization. I had no idea who was a Sunni, a Shia or a Sufi. Imams would go to the opera. There was dancing and singing. That started to change in the 1990s when religious schools began to be closed and the first restrictions on religious freedom were imposed. Students at the time were returning from Saudi Arabia and Pakistan with Wahhabi ideology. Those who had been in Egypt were influenced by the Muslim Brotherhood. Repression is at the root of religious conservatism and political radicalization.[46]

The returning students often saw their religious credentials enhanced by the fact that government-employed imams were often deficient in religious knowledge.[47] The repressive policy that had started in the mid-1990s saw an Uyghur executed on average every four days in Xinjiang, which contributed to radicalization.[48]

In the process, Uyghurs joined the ranks of the Taliban, some of whom are believed to be responsible for attacks in Xinjiang.[49] Militant Chinese Muslims have since expanded their international links beyond the Taliban and increased their popularity among Uyghurs as well as with some Hui Muslims who adhere to the most puritan schools of Islam, Wahhabism, Salafism, and jihadism.[50] Up to 1,000 Uyghurs are believed to have joined IS by 2015, an increase from the estimate of 300 in 2014 by *The Global Times*, a state-owned Chinese paper.[51]

A video posted on YouTube by a user who identified himself as ayahm84 featured a purported Chinese fighter in Syria brandishing a Kalashnikov. Subtitling named the fighter as Bo Wang, who speaking in Mandarin said he had been studying in Libya before joining the struggle to overthrow the Assad regime in Syria.[52] The post has since been removed. The Iraqi defense ministry posted on its Facebook page in September 2014 a picture of an Asian man with a bruised and bloodied face; it said the man was a Chinese IS fighter captured by Iraqi forces.[53]

Uyghurs reach Syria by taking a circuitous route through Central Asia or employing people-smuggling networks in Southeast Asia. They cross borders using forged Turkish passports or by claiming that they are Turkish nationals. "There are Uyghurs that have fled overseas and joined IS. The organization has a huge international influence and Xinjiang can't keep aloof from it and we have already been affected. We have also found that some who fought returned to Xinjiang to participate in terrorist plots," said the secretary of the communist party in Xinjiang, Zhang Chunxian.[54]

IS published a video in October 2014 with Chinese subtitles claiming that it portrayed "a Chinese brother before he did a martyrdom operation (suicide bomb attack) in the town of Suleiman."[55] Muhammed Amin, an eighty-year-old Uyghur-speaking cleric from Xinjiang, features in a 15-minute IS video published in July 2015, calling on Muslims to join the group and kill "Chinese infidels."[56] The video also showed a classroom filled with Uygur boys dressed in headgear bearing the black and white IS logo. One of the boys pointed to the IS flag as he pledged: "O Chinese infidels ... we will come to you and raise this flag in Turkestan."[57] In December 2015, IS's foreign language media arm,

Al-Hayat Media Center, distributed a chant in Mandarin exhorting Muslims to revolt.[58] IS greeted 2016 by hacking the website of Tsinghua University, one of China's most prestigious educational institutions, with a call to jihad.[59]

Chinese media have accused Turkey and Syria of supporting and training Xinjiang militants recruited by the East Turkistan Islamic Movement (ETIM) and the Istanbul-based East Turkistan Educational and Solidarity Association (ETESA).[60] Pictures on the Chinese website Guancha and in the *Daily Mail* suggested that Chinese nationals had also joined Kurdish Peshmerga forces fighting the Islamic State. The pictures showed what appeared to be a Chinese male holding an automatic weapon and Chinese graffiti on a wall.[61] In its first detailed listing of Xinjiang-related incidents of violence, China asserted in 2002 that ETIM was "supported and funded" by al-Qaeda.[62]

Forefathers of primordial Turkism

Concern about Turkey's role as a conduit for Uyghurs joining IS is grounded in the fact that Turkey historically offered refuge to Uyghurs fleeing Chinese rule. Turkish empathy with the Uyghurs is rooted in a belief that the group represents the forefathers of primordial Turkism.[63] As a result, Turkey has been home to Uyghur nationalists since the PLA captured Xinjiang in 1949. Secular Turkish nationalism long served as a model for the Uyghurs who sought refuge in Turkey, but in more recent years has increasingly been pushed aside by militant Islamic ideology.

The post-1949 refugees included Isa Yusuf Alptekin, who became the voice of the Uyghur diaspora during the Cold War, and maintained close relations with Turkish leaders, including former presidents and prime ministers Suleiman Demirel and Turgut Ozal. When current president Recep Tayyip Erdoğan was mayor of Istanbul, in 1995 he named a section of the city's Sultan Ahmet Park in honor of Alptekin. A memorial in the park commemorates the martyrs who lost their lives in Eastern Turkestan's struggle for independence. The martyrs include Uyghurs who were executed by the Chinese authorities. Erdoğan said at the time: "Eastern Turkestan is not only the home of the Turkic peoples but also the cradle of Turkic history, civilization and culture. To forget that would lead to the ignorance of our own history, civilization and culture... The martyrs of Eastern Turkestan are our martyrs."[64]

Chinese analysts have compared the presence of Uyghur nationalists and Islamists in Turkey to the Taliban's harboring of Osama bin Laden.[65] Chinese officials, hoping to exploit Turkey's conflict with the Kurds, have insisted in discussions with their Turkish counterparts over the last two decades that the two countries need to combat the "three evil forces of separatism, terrorism and extremism," including "East Turkestan terrorism."[66] Ultimately, China highlighting the discrepancy between Turkish support for Uyghur nationalist demands and their refusal to recognize similar rights for their Kurdish population, coupled with the gradual rise of China as an economic power, persuaded Turkey to moderate its support for Uyghur independence.

Turkey's changing attitude was enshrined in a directive issued in 1999 by Prime Minister Mesut Yilmaz recognizing Xinjiang for the first time as a part of China, and banning government officials from attending events promoting the concept of Eastern Turkestan.[67] In 2002, during a visit to Turkey by Chinese minister Zhu Rongji, Prime Minister Bulent Ecevit described the Uyghurs as a "friendship bridge" between the two countries.[68] The effect of the Chinese pressure proved to be double-edged, however. When some Uyghurs left for Europe and the United States, they spread their nationalist voice to countries that were less susceptible to China's carrot-and-stick approach.

Dolkun Isa, the exiled activist, exemplifies the consequences of their departure from Turkey. A student protest leader in Xinjiang in the 1980s, Isa left China in 1994 after he was advised by friends that authorities suspected his Uyghur restaurant in Beijing of being a cover for the dissemination of anti-Chinese information. He spent two years in Istanbul before successfully seeking asylum and later getting citizenship in Germany, from where he travels freely in Europe.[69]

Turkey's bowing to Chinese pressure has however failed to erase the legacy of Turkish support for Uyghur nationalism. Turkey, unlike Southeast Asian nations such as Thailand and Malaysia, has so far refused to compel Uyghurs who may have left the mainland illegally to return to China. As a result, China, which denounces Uyghur nationalism as a foreign conspiracy and international terrorism, continues to view Turkey as what China scholar Yitzhak Shichor termed "the political and cultural epicentre of Pan-Turkism."[70]

Chinese perceptions were reinforced by Turkey's response to the 2009 riots in Xinjiang's capital of Urumqi, days after Turkish President Abdullah Gul had visited the city, and Thailand's deportation to China of more than 100 Uyghurs in 2015, which sparked violent demonstrations in Istanbul and Ankara.[71] Then Prime Minister Erdoğan described the events in Urumqi as "almost genocide." Erdoğan's industry minister Nihat Ergun called for economic sanctions against China, saying "organizing protests is not enough."[72]

Six years later, Turkey's foreign ministry used strong language to denounce the deportation of the Uyghurs.[73]

Turkish support for the Uyghurs has meant that its doors remain open to Uyghurs who manage to flee from China. A WUC report concluded in 2016 that "increasing numbers of Uyghurs have been opting to flee their homelands to avoid the real risk that they may be unjustifiably arrested or even killed."[74] The report, based on interviews with Uyghur refugees, suggested that:

> the common motivation to escape East Turkestan for many of the interviewees originated from their sense of helplessness and an inability to continue to live a normal life according to cultural and religious traditions. With the continued regression in the ability of Uyghurs to control essential aspects of their own lives, many became unsure that they could continue to live under Chinese rule. There was a definite sense that interviewees felt more and more squeezed by the government each and every day, which led to the profoundly difficult decision to leave—a decision that was by no means taken lightly.[75]

Uyghurs estimate that some 10,000 of their compatriots have made it out of China since 2013. Many of them have found their way to Turkey, where they are allowed to settle in Istanbul and the Anatolian city of Kayseri, where Uyghurs first settled in the 1950s.[76] With Uyghurs required to have not only an identity card to travel inside China and a passport for trips abroad but also a separate official permit, many sell their homes and land to pay off Chinese officials and guards where the borders to China, Myanmar, Vietnam, and Laos meet. Uyghurs prefer the Southeast Asian route to Central Asia, because of the Central Asians' record of extraditing refugees from Xinjiang ever since they became independent after the collapse of the Soviet Union; more than a decade later they joined the Shanghai Cooperation Organization (SCO), a political, economic, and security alliance that includes China, Russia, Kazakhstan, Kyrgyzstan, and Tajikistan. From there, they make their way to Thailand and Malaysia with the help of Uyghur, Thai, and Malaysian mafias, as well as a Turkish criminal underground that has close ties to Turkey's ultra-nationalist, Pan-Turkish Milliyetçi Hareket Partisi (MHP) or Nationalist Action Party. Chinese authorities said in January 2015 that they had arrested ten Turks and a number of Uyghurs in Shanghai for smuggling Uyghurs out of the country.[77]

Uyghurs and China's nuclear arsenal go underground

China has used its assertion that IS and al-Qaeda are linked to a rising number of violent incidents in China to justify the adoption in December 2015 of controversial counter-terrorism legislation. It requires technology firms to help decrypt information and allows the military to venture overseas on counter-terror operations.[78] The legislation, said Mei Jianming, director of the Counterterrorism Research Center at the People's Public Security University of China, "took the growing influence of Islamic State into consideration after it planned to recruit Muslims from all ethnic groups in China, posing new challenges for the country."[79]

Pan Guang, director of the Shanghai Center for International Studies and Institute of European and Asian Studies at the Shanghai Academy of Social Science, added that "we are very worried about this. We are worried that young Chinese will go through Turkey to Syria and then come back to China."[80] Concern about Xinjiang, alongside the principle of non-intervention, also informs Chinese opposition to military aid to rebel groups in the Middle East and North Africa. It has further prompted China to expand its international cooperation on counter-terrorism significantly, through regional frameworks like the SCO and in its bilateral relations.

The threat to China took an alarming step in August 2014, when Chinese police scrutinizing satellite images captured by China's National Space Administration detected dozens of cross-border tunnels in Xinjiang, which could facilitate the infiltration of members of ETIM and other Uyghur groups.[81] The tunnels raised the specter of nuclear weapons being stored in tunnels under Urumqi as well as under the Lop Nur nuclear weapons testing facility, a former salt lake in the south-east of Xinjiang.[82]

Fears of IS's potential impact on Xinjiang have prompted some Chinese analysts to call on their government to join the US-led coalition in Iraq. "China lacks military capabilities to join anti-terror operations ... China can instead provide funding, equipment and goods for the allies. It can also help by providing training local army and police personnel, an area in which China is experienced," said Ma Xiaolin. He noted that China was already sharing intelligence with coalition partners.[83]

A Chinese religious leader, Adudulkrep Tumniaz, deputy director of the Xinjiang Islamic Association, warned that a lack of respected Chinese Muslim leaders puts the country at a disadvantage in its ideological battle with IS:

> If the religious leaders compete with the extremists on Islamic knowledge, I cannot guarantee that they would win. That's what worries me. The extremists often start by teaching people about the parts of the Qur'an—Islam's holy book—that have never been mentioned by their imams and then inject violent thoughts in people by misinterpreting doctrines.[84]

In a white paper on religious freedom in Xinjiang, issued in 2016 on the eve of Ramadan and in advance of the seventh anniversary of the 2009 riots, the government insisted that "respect for and protection of freedom of religious belief is a long-term basic national policy of the Chinese government." It was the second white paper on Xinjiang issued within a year. In September 2015, the government published a paper entitled "Historical Witness to Ethnic Equality, Unity and Development in Xinjiang," which focused on improving living conditions in the region, emphasized ethic equality, opposed any form of ethnic oppression or discrimination, and vowed to eliminate "ethnic misunderstandings carried over from the past."[85]

The latest paper was issued as part of a broader government effort to win hearts and minds in Xinjiang, which involved instructing the military to learn local Uyghur folk songs and dances and sending thousands of cadres to the region to befriend local villagers to "explain the party's ethnic and religious policies ... and refute rumours."[86] In a statement to the *People's Liberation Army Daily*, the communist party committee for the Xinjiang military said that "with face-to-face communication and heart-to-heart exchanges (we can) increase ethnic unity and feelings, like the closeness between fish and water."[87]

The white paper asserted that the government's approach to the region was in accordance with China's constitution. "No citizen suffers discrimination or unfair treatment for believing in, or not believing in, any religion," the paper said. It said that the government respected religious customs and did not interfere with a restaurant owner's decision on whether or not to open his establishment for business during Ramadan. The government had also allocated funds for the renovation of historic mosques and other sites as well, "to protect and edit" the Qur'an and a biography of the Prophet Mohammed, the translation of other historic religious texts, and the training of clerical personnel, the paper said.[88] It said that the government managed religious affairs in accordance with laws and regulations "protecting the legal, stopping the illegal, containing the extreme, resisting infiltration, and combating crimes." Insisting that "no Xinjiang citizen has been punished because of his or her rightful religious belief," the paper noted that individuals and organizations were banned "from splitting the country, disseminating extremist religious thoughts, inciting ethnic hatred, undermining national unity, disturbing the social order, or impairing citizens' physical and mental health in the name of religion."[89]

The paper blamed "religious extremism" in Xinjiang, which it defined as "anti-human, anti-society, anti-civilization and anti-religion," "an important ideological foundation for violent and terrorist activities," and "the common enemy of all humanity," on radical foreign influences. "The Chinese government resolutely opposes the politicization of religious matters and any other country's interference in China's internal affairs in the name of religion," the paper said.[90]

Xinjiang's "de-extremization" policy had contained the spread of religious extremism, the paper said. It said that Xinjiang's religious leaders:

> [guided] believers to master advanced technologies, participate in economic construction and improve living conditions. They encourage religious believers to become better off through diligent work, for instance, contract of land, setting up businesses, planting, animal breeding, transportation and food processing. They hold demonstrations to introduce experiences of achieving prosperity through hard work and hold up model households as examples.[91]

Uyghur activists dismissed the white paper as government propaganda. They noted that males had to be eighteen years of age before they were allowed to enter mosques and that all places of worship needed to be licensed by the government. Uyghur exiles said that despite the white paper, authorities had detained people calling for compliance with the fast. They said that sermons during Ramadan had to be vetted before being delivered in mosques.[92] Nury A. Turkel, a Washington-based lawyer and leader of the Uyghur Human Rights Project, said: "The government is not giving Uyghurs their constitutionally guaranteed rights. They are cracking down brutally and lumping Uyghurs with Islamic extremists in Xinjiang and abroad. It is a policy that radicalizes people by forcing Uyghurs to give up their way of life to be accepted as Chinese citizens. Uyghurs want to be left alone."[93]

In a riot days before the white paper was issued, five people, including a warden of Uyghur descent, were killed in a juvenile prison in Xinjiang. The incident occurred when up to sixty inmates attacked wardens in response to the harsh disciplining of a prisoner who had been praying. A notice in a police department said that ten prisoners had escaped during the riot. Many of the inmates were sentenced for endangering state security and watching religious films on cell phones.[94]

Uyghur students at Kashgar Normal University reported as early as 2014 that they had been forced to share a meal with their professors during Ramadan, to demonstrate that they were not fasting. Students who refused received official warnings and risked losing their degrees. "Most of us would like to fast. But with the current situation most of us have decided against it," one of the students said. "If you want a normal life here then you'd better not fast," said another. The students said that fasting had been banned at all universities in Xinjiang. A similar ban was imposed on civil servants. At least one government hospital obliged its staff to sign a pledge that they would not observe the daytime fast. State-run newspapers ran articles and editorials warning about the health dangers of refraining from eating and drinking.[95] At about the same time, authorities in various parts of Xinjiang banned women from wearing face-covering veils in public.[96]

Mao's Great Leap Forward lives on

Renewed Chinese repression is rooted in Mao Tze Tung's Great Leap Forward, a three-year social and economic campaign from the late 1950s and early 1960s that involved: suppression of opponents of the policy; an assimilationist cultural thrust; attacks on Uyghurs believed to have links to the short-lived, Soviet-backed East Turkestan Republic that existed in the 1940s; and an upsurge in Han immigration and settlement in north-western China.[97] The pattern repeated itself during the Cultural Revolution of the late 1960s, with the countering of alleged subversive religious activity and assimilationist policies directed at minorities. The Chinese military took direct control of Xinjiang at that time.[98] Religious leaders and intellectuals who resisted government policy were often executed. A generation of more moderate spiritual leadership was effectively decimated. The demise of the Soviet Union and the independence of Central Asian states in a region to which Uyghurs had longstanding ethnic and cultural ties raised the specter of a renewed Uyghur drive for independence and sparked a new Chinese attempt at forced assimilation.

The result is an emerging situation in Xinjiang that could over time complicate China's relations with Middle Eastern and other Muslim nations, despite their current willingness to turn a blind eye. That may become increasingly difficult as Beijing emphasizes improvement of Uyghur standards of living without addressing political and cultural grievances; seeks to eradicate Uyghur culture by restricting fasting during Ramadan and the consumption of yogurt; forbidding men to wear beards; and the marginalization of teaching the Uyghur language or using it in interactions with the government and the judiciary; and moves to ensure Han Chinese dominance in Xinjiang.

Iran's example demonstrates that Middle Eastern sensitivity to the Uyghur issue could help China resolve their problem, provided they respect Uyghur cultural rights. That willingness was already evident in the 1980s when the Kuwaitis agreed to invest in a chemical fertilizer plant in Xinjiang. The investment was in line with Kuwait and the Gulf's aid policy that was designed to buy friends in the international community, particularly among Muslim-majority countries and regions.[99]

China's refusal to address Uyghur grievances risks making it more difficult for the Muslim world to remain silent, particularly if the violence escalates. Uyghur scholar Ilham Tohti, who was arrested in 2014 by Chinese authorities, warned that China's policies:

> will likely have a positive short-term effect, but because they do not address deep-seated problems, we cannot afford to be sanguine about Xinjiang's future, nor can we be certain that violence will not erupt again. If the government is to win broad-based popular support and achieve genuine long-term peace and stability, it must promote further systemic and social adjustments.[100]

For now, Middle Eastern and North African governments, determined not to muddy relations with China, have remained largely silent about the plight of the Uyghurs. Their attitude appears to confirm Chinese scholar Zhang Xiandong's call for close Chinese political and economic cooperation with Middle Eastern nations in a bid to create a favorable environment for a crackdown in Xinjiang, should Chinese Muslims "integrated with the minority separatism" spark a development that would "be a great challenge to the social stability and economic development in Northwestern China."[101]

NOTES

1. CHINA'S SEARCH FOR SECURITY IN THE GREATER MIDDLE EAST

1. Quoted in David Schenker, "China's Middle East Footprint," *Los Angeles Times*, 26 April 2013, p. 19.
2. Quoted in Edward Wong and Chris Buckley, "China, Beckoned, Dips a Toe Into Mideast Peacemaking," *New York Times*, 9 May 2013, p. A6.
3. "The Great Well of China," *The Economist*, 20 June 2015, p. 47.
4. "Rising China, Sinking Russia," *The Economist*, 14 September 2013; Edward Wong, "China Quietly Extends Footprints into Central Asia," *New York Times*, 2 January 2011.
5. Charles Wolf, Xiao Wang, and Eric Warner, *China's Foreign Aid and Government-Sponsored Investment Activities Scale, Content, Destinations, and Implications* (Santa Monica, CA: RAND, 2013), p. 33.
6. Reliable figures on the number of Chinese citizens abroad are notoriously difficult to come by. See Niu Xinchun, "China's Interests in and Influence over the Middle East," *Contemporary International Relations*, vol. 24, no. 1 (January/February 2014), pp. 42–3; and Mathieu Duchâtel, Oliver Bräuner, and Zhou Hang, *Protecting China's Overseas Interests: The Slow Shift away from Non-interference*, Policy Paper no. 41 (Stockholm: Stockholm International Peace Research Institute, 2014), pp. 41–2.
7. See, for example, Michael D. Swaine, "Perceptions of an Assertive China," *China Leadership Monitor*, no. 32 (11 May 2010), pp. 1–19; Thomas Christensen, "The Advantages of an Assertive China," *Foreign Affairs*, vol. 90, no. 2 (March/April 2011), pp. 54–67; Andrew Scobell and Scott W. Harold, "An 'Assertive' China? Insights from Interviews," *Asian Security*, vol. 9, no. 2 (2013), pp. 111–31.
8. See, for example, Liu Zhongmin, "Zhongguo bugai zhuiqiu Zhong Dong shiwu lingdao zhe jiaose [China should not pursue a leadership role in the Middle East]," *Dongfang Zaobao* on line [Oriental Morning News], 26 August 2011. The article's title is misleading, since the author argues that China should play a greater role—

albeit not the dominant one—in the Middle East, guided by a clear strategy. See also Qian Xuewen, "Zhong Dong jubian dui Zhongguo haiwai liyi de yingxiang [Impact of Middle East turmoil on China's overseas interests]," *Alabo Shijie yanjiu* [Arab world studies], no. 6 (2012), pp. 50–51; Zhao Jingfang, "Pojie nengyuan anquan kunjing: waijiao he junshi shouduan [Solving energy difficulties: diplomatic and military methods], *Shijie Zhishi* [World affairs], no. 18 (2012), pp. 50–51. Zhao is a professor at PLA National Defense University.

9. See Andrew Scobell and Alireza Nader, *China in the Middle East: The Wary Dragon* (Santa Monica, CA: RAND, 2016), ch. 2.

10. Liberalism is omitted because it does not appear to have much utility in interpreting China's international behavior.

11. Thomas J. Christensen, "Chinese Realpolitik," *Foreign Affairs*, vol. 75 (September–October 1996), pp. 37–52.

12. Alastair I. Johnston, *Cultural Realism: Strategic Culture and Grand Strategy in Chinese History* (Princeton, NJ: Princeton University Press, 1995); and Alastair I. Johnston, "Cultural Realism and Strategy in Maoist China," in Peter J. Katzenstein, ed., *The Culture of National Security: Norms and Identity in World Politics* (New York: Columbia University Press, 1996), pp. 216–68.

13. Alastair Iain Johnston, *Social States: China and International Institutions, 1980–2000* (Princeton, NJ: Princeton University Press, 2007).

14. Andrew J. Nathan and Andrew Scobell, *China's Search for Security* (New York: Columbia University Press, 2012).

15. See the classic tome by John Mearsheimer, *The Tragedy of Great Power Politics* (New York: W. W. Norton, 2001).

16. See the quick overview by Mearsheimer, *The Tragedy of Great Power Politics*, pp. 19–20 and Table 1.1 on p. 22.

17. Stephen Walt, *The Origins of Alliances* (Ithaca, NY: Cornell University Press, 1987), p. 1, n. 1 and p. 12.

18. See Alexander Wendt, *Social Theory of International Politics* (Cambridge, Cambridge University Press, 1999).

19. See also Alexander Wendt, "Anarchy is What States Make of It: The Social Construction of Power Politics," *International Organization*, vol. 46, no. 2 (Spring 1992), pp. 391–425.

20. See the writings of Sir Halford John Mackinder (1861–1947).

21. On Korea, see Andrew Scobell, *China and North Korea: From Comrades-in-Arms to Allies at Arm's Length* (Carlisle Barracks, PA: US Army War College Strategic Studies Institute, 2004), pp. 1–2; on Vietnam, see Chen Jian, *Mao's China and the Cold War* (Chapel Hill, NC: University of North Carolina Press, 2001), pp. 221–35.

22. *China's Military Strategy*, "Part I: National Security Situation."

23. Matt Schiavenza, "What is China's Plan for the Middle East?" *The Atlantic*, 10 May

2013, http://www.theatlantic.com/china/archive/2013/05/what-is-chinas-plan-for-the-middle-east. President Xi actually invited both Mahmoud Abbas and Benjamin Netanyahu to China, and they both came but did not meet each other while there.

24. Modechai Chaziza, "China's Policy in the Middle East Peace Process After the Cold War," *China Report*, vol. 49, no. 1 (2013), pp. 161, 199.

25. "China's Arab Policy Paper, January 2016," http://www.fmprc.gov/cn/mfa_eng/wjdt_665385/2649_665393/t1331683.shtml

26. See, for example, Ting Shi, "How China is Building Bridges with the Middle East," *Bloomberg News*, 26 January 2016.

27. Mu Chunshan, "Revealed: How the Yemen Crisis Wrecked Xi Jinping's Middle East Travel Plans," *The Diplomat*, 22 April 2015, http://thediplomat.com/2015/04/revealed-how-the-yemen-crisis-wrecked-xi-jinpings-middle-east-travel-plans

28. Liu Zhongmin, "Zhongguo bugai zhuiqiu Zhong Dong shiwu lingdao zhe jiaose."

29. Weilie Zhu, "On the Strategic Relationship between China and Islamic Countries in the Middle East," *Journal of Western-Sino Communications*, vol. 3, no. 1 (July 2011), pp. 5–6.

30. Jonas Parello-Plesner and Mathieu Duchâtel, *China's Strong Arm: Protecting Citizens and Assets Abroad* (London, International Institute for Strategic Studies, 2015), p. 9.

31. Duchâtel, Bräuner, and Zhou, *Protecting China's Overseas Interests*. For a list of NEOs between 2006 and 2014, see Table 4.1 on p. 46. On the Libya NEO, see pp. 48–50.

32. On cooperation between China and Iran and China and Saudi Arabia, see Scobell and Nader, *China in the Middle East*, ch. 3 and 4, respectively.

33. Andrew Scobell and Andrew J. Nathan, "China's Overstretched Military," *Washington Quarterly*, vol. 35, no. 4 (Fall 2012), pp. 35–48.

34. See, for example, Andrew Scobell, *China's Use of Military Force: Beyond the Great Wall and the Long March* (New York: Cambridge University Press, 2003).

35. For operational details of the anti-piracy mission, see Andrew S. Erickson and Austin M. Strange, *No Substitute for Experience: Chinese Anti-Piracy Operations in the Gulf of Aden*, Naval War College CMSI China Maritime Study 10 (November 2013).

36. Scobell and Nathan, "China's Overstretched Military," pp. 135–48; and Nathan and Scobell, *China's Search for Security*, ch. 11.

37. Jane Perlez and Chris Buckley, "China Retools its Military with a First Overseas Outpost in Djibouti," *New York Times*, 26 November 2015.

38. Andrew Scobell and Mark Cozad, "China's North Korea Policy: Rethink or Recharge?" *Parameters*, vol. 44, no. 1 (Spring 2014), pp. 60–61.

39. Andrew Small, *The China-Pakistan Axis: Asia's New Geopolitics* (New York: Oxford University Press, 2015), ch. 2.

40. Nathan and Scobell, *China's Search for Security*, pp. 3–7.

41. Unlike the first effort of the post-1949 era, the campaign launched in 1978 by Deng Xiaoping, in which China opened up to the outside world and embraced the global economic system. But the current policy, unlike the earlier one, has been successful beyond the wildest dreams of CCP leaders. See Andrew Scobell, "Introduction," in Andrew Scobell and Marylena Mantas, eds, *China's Great Leap Outward: Hard and Soft Dimensions of a Rising Power* (New York: Academy of Political Science, 2014), pp. 5–6.

42. Nathan and Scobell, *China's Search for Security*, p. 35.

43. *Vision and Actions on Jointly Building Silk Road Economic Belt and 21ˢᵗ Century Maritime Silk Road*, Beijing, 28 March 2015, issued by the National Development and Reform Commission, the Ministry of Foreign Affairs, the Ministry of Commerce of the People's Republic of China with State Council authorization.

44. Another candidate region for this status is Southeast Asia. Both the Middle East and Southeast Asia are of key importance to China.

45. See, for example, an article written by a professor of international relations at Beijing University: An Weihua, "'Da Zhong Dong' xi ['Greater Middle East' analysis]," *Guoji zhengzhi yanjiu* [Studies of international politics], no. 92 (2004), pp. 81–8.

46. Liu Zhongmin, "Zhong Dong bianju yu Zhongguo waijiao de jige jiben wenti [The changing situation in the Middle East and China's foreign policy: a few fundamental issues]," *International Survey*, no. 1 (2012), p. 20.

47. See, for example, An Weihua, "'Da Zhong Dong' xi," p. 82.

48. Li Weijian, "Zhong Dong zai Zhongguo zhanlue zhong de zhongyao xingji shuangbian guanzi [Bilateral relations between China and the Middle East and the importance of the Middle East in China's strategy]," *XiYa Feizhou* [West Asia and Africa], no. 6 (2004), pp. 18–19.

49. Liu Zhongmin, "Zhong Dong bianju Zhongguo waijiap de jige jiben wenti," p. 20.

50. John B. Alterman and John W. Garver, *The Vital Triangle: China, the United States, and the Middle East* (Washington, DC: CSIS, 2008), p. 18.

51. Ibid., p. 127.

52. For an elaboration on this point, see Scobell and Nader, *China and the Middle East*, pp. 10–12.

53. For more on the SCO, see Scobell, Ratner, and Beckley, *China's Strategy in South and Central Asia*, pp. 29–36. For a list of summits and participating states, see Table 3.1 on pp. 32–3.

54. Andrew Scobell, "China Ponders Post-2014 Afghanistan: Neither 'All In' nor Bystander," *Asian Survey*, vol. 55, no. 2 (March–April 2015), pp. 325–45.

55. Scobell, Ratner, and Beckley, *China's Strategy in South and Central Asia*, pp. 36–42. For a list of exercises, see Table 3.2 on pp. 38–9.

56. Perlez and Buckley, "China Retools its Military with a First Overseas Outpost in Djibouti."

57. See Louis Ritzinger, "The China-Pakistan Economic Corridor: Regional Dynamics and China's Geopolitical Ambitions," *Commentary* (Seattle, WA: National Bureau of Asian Research, 5 August 2015).

58. Data collected by authors from various sources. For more on the topic see, Rashida Hameed, "Pakistan and China: Partnership, Prospects and the Course Ahead," Policy Perspectives, Vol. 14, No. 1, (2017), pp. 11–13.

59. General Liu Yazhou, "Xibu lun [Theory on the Western Region]," *Fenghuang Zhoukan* [Phoenix Weekly], 5 August 2010, p. 36.

60. Ibid.

61. Chris Zambelis, "Sino-Turkish Strategic Partnership: Implications of Anatolian Eagle 2010," *China Brief*, vol. 11, no. 1 (14 January 2011).

62. Burak Ege Bekdil, "Turkey Scraps $3.4B Air Defense Contract," *Defense News* (15 November 2015).

63. The greater attention to overseas interests is evident in many places, including the most recent defense white paper issued in May 2015. See *China's Military Strategy*, Beijing: State Council Information Office of the People's Republic of China, May 2015, "Part II: Missions and Strategic Tasks of China's Armed Forces."

64. Nathan and Scobell, *China's Search for Security*, pp. 9–10.

65. See, for example, the excellent treatment in Gardiner Bovingdon, *The Uyghurs: Strangers in their own Land* (New York: Columbia University Press, 2010).

66. See, for example, *China's Military Strategy*, "Part I: National Security Situation." See also Andrew Scobell, "Terrorism and Chinese Foreign Policy," in Yong Deng and Fei-ling Wang, eds, *China Rising: Power and Motivation in Chinese Foreign Policy* (Lanham, MD: Rowman and Littlefield), 2004, pp. 305–24.

67. See, for example, Scobell and Nader, *China in the Middle East*.

68. See, for example, John Calabrese, "From Flyswatters to Silkworms: The Evolution of China's Role in West Asia," *Asian Survey*, vol. 30, no. 9 (September 1990), pp. 862–76.

69. See, for example, Yitzhak Shichor, "China and the Middle East since Tiananmen," *Annals of the American Academy of Political and Social Science*, vol. 519 (January 1992), pp. 86–100.

70. On the perception of declining US commitment to the Middle East, see Scobell and Nader, *China in the Middle East*.

71. This is a variant of the principle outlined by Samuel S. Kim. See his "International Organizations in Chinese Foreign Policy," *Annals of the American Academy of Political and Social Science*, vol. 519 (January 1992), pp. 140–57.

72. See, for example, Yong Deng, *China's Struggle for Status: The Realignment of International Relations* (New York: Cambridge University Press), 2008.

73. Harding, "China's Cooperative Behavior," p. 391.

74. Peter Hayes Gries highlights what he called the "Kissinger Complex," in which Chinese political elites crave the praise of their country by prominent foreign dig-

nitaries and scholars which is then reported to the Chinese people as evidence of the wisdom of PRC leaders. Henry Kissinger is probably the most revered US citizen in China, because he is seen as a sage old friend of China who frequently makes public statements lauding China. See Gries, *China's New Nationalism: Pride, Politics, and Diplomacy* (Berkeley, CA: University of California Press, 2004), ch. 4.

75. See "China's Arab Policy Paper," Foreword.

76. On Korea, see Scobell, *China and North Korea*, pp. 1–2; on Vietnam, see Chen Jian, *Mao's China and the Cold War* (Chapel Hill, NC: University of North Carolina Press, 2001), pp. 221–35.

77. PRC Foreign Minister Wang Yi's speech to a seminar in Beijing, titled "2014 in review: a successful year for China's diplomacy," delivered on 24 December 2014.

78. *China's Military Strategy*, "Part VI: Military and Security Cooperation."

79. Harry Harding, "China's Cooperative Behavior," in Thomas W. Robinson and David Shambaugh, eds, *Chinese Foreign Policy: Theory and Practice* (Oxford: Clarendon Press, 1994), p. 370.

80. Harding, "China's Cooperative Behavior," p. 391.

81. David Shambaugh observes that in China "trust is at a minimum." See his *China Goes Global: The Partial Power* (New York: Oxford University Press, 2013), p. 154.

82. These quotes come from Harding, "China's Cooperative Behavior," pp. 398, 399, and 376, respectively.

83. On China's rocky cooperation with the United States, see Nathan and Scobell, *China's Search for Security*, ch. 4.

84. For a deft overview of all these relationships, see Chen Jian, *Mao's China and the Cold War*.

85. Scobell, "China Ponders Post-2014 Afghanistan."

86. Small, *The China-Pakistan Axis*, p. 181.

87. Author discussions with analysts and academics in Beijing and Shanghai, September 2014 and September 2015.

2. CHINA, THE UNITED STATES, AND THE MIDDLE EAST

1. See, for example, Alastair Iain Johnston, *Cultural Realism: Strategic Culture and Grand Strategy in Chinese History* (Princeton, NJ: Princeton University Press, 1995), p. 249.

2. Energy Information Administration, "China" (full report), p. 10, http://www.eia.gov/beta/international/analysis_includes/countries_long/China/china.pdf

3. Ibid., p. 1.

4. World Bank, "GDP Growth (annual %)," http://data.worldbank.org/indicator/NY.GDP.MKTP.KD.ZG

5. Economist Intelligence Unit, "GCC Trade and Investment Flows" (2014), p. 9.

6. Andrew Scott, "Nakheel Triples Retail Space in Dragon Mart with Opening of Extension," *The National*, 10 November 2015.

7. American Enterprise Institute, "China Global Investment Tracker," https://www.aei.org/china-global-investment-tracker/

8. Ibid.

9. Dexter Roberts, "Iraq Crisis Threatens Chinese Oil Investments," *Bloomberg Business*, 17 June 2014.

10. At times the United States Navy has maintained a two-carrier presence in the Pacific to make a point to its Chinese counterpart. See, for example, "Two Carrier Strike Groups Double Down in Western Pacific," http://www.navy.mil/submit/display.asp?story_id=95284

11. See Jon B. Alterman, *Egypt and American Foreign Assistance, 1952–1956: Hopes Dashed* (New York: Palgrave Macmillan, 2002), pp. 21–38; Robert A. Packenham, *Liberal America and the Third World* (Princeton, NJ: Princeton University Press, 1973).

12. For the first theory, see, for example, Bruce Russett, *Grasping the Democratic Peace: Principles for a Post–Cold War World* (Princeton, NJ: Princeton University Press, 1993). The quote is from Thomas Friedman, "Foreign Affairs Big Mac I," *New York Times*, 8 December 1996.

13. See William R. Hutchison, *Errand to the World: American Protestant Thought and Foreign Missions* (Chicago: University of Chicago Press, 1987). A more recent take on exceptionalism comes from Governor Mike Huckabee. He complained that President Obama "grew up more as a globalist than an American," and asserted that "to deny American exceptionalism is in essence to deny the heart and soul of this nation." Ben Smith and Jonathan Martin, "The New Battle: What It Means to Be an American," *Politico*, 20 August 2010, http://www.politico.com/story/2010/08/the-new-battle-what-it-means-to-be-american-041273

14. US Agency for International Development, *USAID Strategy on Democracy, Human Rights and Governance* (Washington, DC: USAID, 2013), p. 9, http://pdf.usaid.gov/pdf_docs/PDACX557.pdf

15. US Agency for International Development, "Interactive Map," http://map.usaid.gov/?s=DHRA

16. White House, Office of the Press Secretary, "Fact Sheet: U.S. Support for Civil Society," 29 September 2015, https://www.whitehouse.gov/the-press-office/2015/09/29/fact-sheet-us-support-civil-society

17. White House, "National Security Strategy of the United States," May 2010, p. 37, https://www.whitehouse.gov/sites/default/files/rss_viewer/national_security_strategy.pdf

18. Ministry of Foreign Affairs of the People's Republic of China, "China's Initiation of the Five Principles of Peaceful Co-Existence," http://www.fmprc.gov.cn/mfa_eng/ziliao_665539/3602_665543/3604_665547/t18053.shtml

19. White House, "Remarks by the President," 11 February 2011, https://www.white-house.gov/the-press-office/2011/02/11/remarks-president-egypt

20. See, for example, "China's Evolving Foreign Policy: The Libyan Dilemma," *The Economist*, 10 September 2011.

21. "Fossil Fuel Markets in China," *Research and Markets*, April 2015, http://www.researchandmarkets.com/research/wk2fch/fossil_fuel

22. Energy Information Administration, "U.S. Remained World's Largest Producer of Petroleum and Natural Gas Hydrocarbons in 2014," 7 April 2015, https://www.eia.gov/todayinenergy/detail.cfm?id=20692

23. United States Census Bureau, "Trade in Goods with Japan," https://www.census.gov/foreign-trade/balance/c5880.html; United States Census Bureau, "Trade in Goods with Korea, South," https://www.census.gov/foreign-trade/balance/c5800.html

24. See Andrew Erickson, "More Willing and Able: Charting China's International Security Activism," Center for a New American Security, May 2015, http://www.cnas.org/sites/default/files/publications-pdf/CNAS_MoreWillingAndAble_final.pdf

25. United Nations, "UN Mission's Summary Detailed by Country: Month of Report: 31-Oct-15," http://www.un.org/en/peacekeeping/contributors/2015/oct15_3.pdf

26. Chengxin Pan, "The 'Indo-Pacific' and Geopolitical Anxieties about China's Rise in the Asian Regional Order," *Australian Journal of International Affairs*, vol. 68, no. 4 (2014), pp. 453–69.

27. Richard Wike, Bruce Stokes, and Jacob Poushter, "Global Publics Back U.S. on Fighting ISIS, but are Critical of Post 9/11 Torture," *Pew Research Center*, 23 June 2015.

28. Greg Knowler, "China-Europe Rail Services Starting to Turn Shippers' Heads," 11 March 2015, JOC.com, http://www.joc.com/international-logistics/china-europe-rail-services-starting-turn-shippers'-heads_20150311.html

29. Barry R. Posen, "Command of the Commons: The Military Foundation of U.S. Hegemony," *International Security* 28, no. 1 (Summer 2003), pp. 5–46.

30. Control Risks, "Maritime Risk Forecast 2015," https://www.controlrisks.com/~/media/Public%20Site/Files/Reports/MaritimeForecastReport2015.pdf

31. See, for example, Christopher Preble, "U.S. National Security Strategy after Primacy," testimony to the Senate Armed Services Committee, 29 October 2015, p. 5.

32. Transparency International, *Bribe Payer's Index 2011*, 6, http://www.transparency.org/bpi2011/results

33. Samuel R. Gintel, "Fighting Transnational Bribery: China's Gradual Approach," *Wisconsin International Law Journal*, vol. 31, no. 1 (2013), p. 10.

34. See Cheng Li and Lucy Xu, "Chinese Enthusiasm and American Cynicism over the 'New Type of Great Power Relations,'" Brookings Institution, 4 December

2014, http://www.brookings.edu/research/opinions/2014/12/05-chinese-pessimism-american-cynicism-great-power-li-xu

35. Anjani Trivedi, "China Takes Its Debt-Driven Growth Model Overseas," *Wall Street Journal*, 6 August 2015.

36. Mathieu Duchâtel, Oliver Brauner, and Zhou Hang, "Protecting China's Overseas Interests: The Slow Shift Away from Non-interference," Stockholm International Peace Research Institute, June 2014.

3. THE CHINA MODEL AND THE MIDDLE EAST

1. Rowan Callick, "The China Model," *The American*, (November/December 2007), p. 98. Conversely, for the increasing lack of appeal of the Washington Consensus in the developing world, see Charles Gore, "The Rise and Fall of the Washington Consensus as a Paradigm for Developing Countries," *World Development*, vol. 28, no. 5 (May 2000), pp. 789–804.

2. Shuan Breslin, "China and the Arab Awakening," *ISPI Analysis*, no. 140 (October 2012), p. 2.

3. Ibid., p. 8; Mohammad Salman and Gustaaf Geeraerts, "Strategic Hedging and China's Economic Policy in the Middle East," *China Report*, vol. 41, no. 2 (2015), p. 108.

4. Breslin, "China and the Arab Awakening," p. 1. See also Chapter 8 by Stephen Blank and Chapter 9 by Andrew Small.

5. Abbas Varij Kazemi and Xiangming Chen, "China and the Middle East: More than Oil," *European Financial Review* (February–March 2014), p. 43.

6. Muhammad S. Olimat, *China and the Middle East: From Silk Road to Arab Spring* (London: Routledge, 2013), p. 34.

7. Kazemi and Chen, "China and the Middle East," *European Financial Review*, p. 40.

8. Salman and Geeraerts, "Strategic Hedging and China's Economic Policy in the Middle East," p. 103.

9. Kazemi and Chen, "China and the Middle East," p. 40.

10. Data collected from "China Global Investment Tracker," American Enterprise Institute, https://www.aei.org/china-global-investment-tracker/

11. Breslin, "China and the Arab Awakening," p. 2.

12. Kazemi and Chen, "China and the Middle East," p. 41. For more on this point, see Chapter 1 by Andrew Scobell, Chapter 2 by Jon B. Alterman, and Chapter 4 by Degang Sun.

13. Kazemi and Chen, "China and the Middle East," p. 42.

14. Ibid.

15. Salman and Geeraerts, "Strategic Hedging and China's Economic Policy in the Middle East," p. 108.

16. Breslin, "China and the Arab Awakening," p. 8.

17. Jon B. Alterman, "China's soft power in the Middle East," in Carola McGiffert, ed., *Chinese Soft Power and its Implications for the United States: Competition and Cooperation with the Developing World* (Washington, DC: Center for Strategic and International Studies, 2009), p. 71.

18. Breslin, "China and the Arab Awakening," p. 1.

19. Cemil Aydin, "Changing Modes of Political Dialogue Across the Middle East and East Asia, 1880–2010," *Middle East Report*, vol. 44 (Spring 2014), p. 19.

20. Ibid.

21. Steve Hess, "From the Arab Spring to the Chinese Winter: The institutional sources of authoritarian vulnerability and resilience in Egypt, Tunisia, and China," *International Political Science Review*, vol. 34, no. 3 (June 2013), p. 255.

22. Breslin, "China and the Arab Awakening," p. 4.

23. Olimat, *China and the Middle East*, p. 92.

24. Breslin, "China and the Arab Awakening," p. 4.

25. Ibid., p. 5.

26. Stefan Halper, *The Beijing Consensus: Legitimizing Authoritarianism in Our Time* (New York: Basic Books, 2012), p. 3.

27. Ming Won, *The China Model and Global Political Economy: Comparison, Impact, and interaction*, (London: Routledge, 2014), p. 26.

28. Ibid., p. 27.

29. Ibid., p. 33.

30. Ibid., p. 35.

31. Ibid., pp. 29–31. For a useful summary of assumptions about the China model among the different actors across the Chinese body politic—namely the state, dissidents, liberals, and the so-called New Left—see ibid., p. 30.

32. Scott Kennedy, "The Myth of the Beijing Consensus," *Journal of Contemporary China*, vol. 19, no. 65 (June 2010), p. 473.

33. Ibid., p. 462.

34. Ibid., p. 471.

35. Barry Naughton, "China's Distinctive System: can it be a model for others?" *Journal of Contemporary China*, vol. 19, no. 65 (June 2010), p. 437.

36. Minglu Chen and David S. G. Goodman, "The China Model: one country, six authors," *Journal of Contemporary China*, vol. 21, no. 73 (January 2012), p. 169.

37. Ibid., p. 177.

38. Ibid., p. 169.

39. Callick, "The China Model," p. 36.

40. Halper, *The Beijing Consensus*, p. 27.

41. Ibid., p. 28.

42. Ibid., p. 30.

43. Ibid., p. 3.

44. Ibid., p. 26.

45. Francis Fukuyama, "The Patterns of History," *Journal of Democracy*, vol. 23, no. 1 (January 2012), p. 19.

46. Ibid.

47. Stefan Halper maintains that the greatest challenge that China poses to the West is the promotion of a "Chinese brand of capitalism and a Chinese conception of the international community," one in which China is "*beating the West at its own game*" (original emphasis). Halper, *The Beijing Consensus*, p. 11.

48. Ibid., p. 32.

49. Ibid., p. 43.

50. See Mehran Kamrava, *Politics and Society in the Developing World*, 2nd edn (London: Routledge, 2000), pp. 16–19.

51. Daniel A. Bell, *The China Model: Political Meritocracy and the Limits of Democracy* (Princeton, NJ: Princeton University Press, 2015), pp. 179–80.

52. Suisheng Zhao, "The China Model: can it replace the Western model of modernization?" *Journal of Contemporary China*, vol. 19, no. 65 (June 2010), p. 423.

53. Ibid., pp. 425–30.

54. Ibid., pp. 429–30.

55. Fukuyama. "The Patterns of History," p. 23.

56. Zhao, "The China Model," p. 424.

57. Breslin, "China and the Arab Awakening," p. 3.

58. Bruce J. Dickson, "Updating the China Model," *Washington Quarterly*, vol. 34, no. 4 (Fall 2011), p. 39.

59. Ibid., p. 40.

60. Bell, *The China Model*, p. 182.

61. Ibid., pp. 185–7.

62. Fukuyama. "The Patterns of History," p. 21.

63. Hess, "From the Arab Spring to the Chinese Winter," p. 266.

64. Ibid., p. 267.

65. Callick, "The China Model," p. 37.

66. Ibid., p. 38.

67. Dickson, "Updating the China Model," p. 42.

68. Zhao, "The China Model," p. 423.

69. Halper, *The Beijing Consensus*, pp. 121–2.

70. Barry Naughton, "Singularity and Replicability in China's Developmental Experience," Paper presented at the American Economics Association, San Francisco, CA, January 2009, p. 3.

71. Callick, "The China Model," p. 37.

72. Ibid., p. 40.

73. Kennedy, "The Myth of the Beijing Consensus," p. 469.

74. Naughton, "Singularity and Replicability in China's Developmental Experience," p. 16.

75. Ibid., p. 2.

76. Callick, "The China Model," p. 96.

77. Ibid., p. 40.

78. Ibid., p. 103.

79. Halper, *The Beijing Consensus*, p. 43.

80. Yang Yao, "The End of the Beijing Consensus: Can China's Model of Authoritarian Growth Survive?" *Foreign Affairs* (2 February 2010), www.foreignaffairs.com

81. Halper, *The Beijing Consensus*, p. 154.

82. Ibid., pp. 206–7.

83. Ibid., p. 47.

84. Ibid., p. 30.

85. Won, *The China Model and Global Political Economy*, p. 50. For a succinct summary of similar differences in assumptions underlying the China model and other, non-Western models of development—the Soviet, Russian, Indian, Brazilian, and East Asian developmental state models—see ibid. pp. 88–9.

86. Halper, *The Beijing Consensus*, pp. 38–9.

87. Ibid., p. 104.

88. Zhao, "The China Model," p. 431.

89. Ibid., pp. 432–3.

90. Two of the earliest, and still most significant, studies of the state in the Middle East include Ghassan Salame, ed., *The Foundations of the Arab State* (London: Croom Helm, 1987); and Nazih N. Ayubi, *Over-Stating the Arab State: Politics and Society in the Middle East* (London: I. B. Tauris, 1995).

91. This is a much simplified typology that I developed in the late 1990s, in which I further divided authoritarian republics into populist (I. R. Iran, Qaddafi's Libya, and Saddam's Iraq) and exclusionary ones (Assad's Syria, Mubarak's Egypt, Algeria, and Tunisia), and monarchies into oil monarchies (those in the GCC) and those relying on a "civic myth" as their source of legitimacy (Jordan and Morocco). See Mehran Kamrava, "Non-Democratic States and Political Liberalization in the Middle East: A Structural Analysis," *Third World Quarterly*, vol. 19, no. 1 (Spring 1998), pp. 63–85.

92. These conclusions are based on analyses of polling and other longitudinal data by Melani Cammett, Ishac Diwan, Alan Richards, and John Waterbury in *A Political Economy of the Middle East*, 4th edn (Boulder, CO: Westview, 2015), pp. 78–86. I am only summarizing some of their main findings here.

93. For more on authoritarian ruling bargains in the Middle East, see Mehran Kamrava, "The Rise and Fall of Ruling Bargains in the Middle East," in Mehran Kamrava, ed., *Beyond the Arab Spring: The Evolving Ruling Bargain in the Middle East* (New York: Oxford University Press, 2014), pp. 17–45.

94. Steffen Hertog, *Princes, Brokers, and Bureaucrats: Oil and the State in Saudi Arabia* (Ithaca, NY: Cornell University Press, 2010), p. 31.

95. Eva Bellin, "The Robustness of Authoritarianism in the Middle East: Exceptionalism

in Comparative Perspective," *Comparative Politics*, vol. 36, no. 2 (January 2004), pp. 139–43, 147.

96. Ibid., p. 143.

97. Stephen J. King, *The New Authoritarianism in the Middle East and North Africa* (Bloomington, IN: Indiana University Press, 2009), p. 4.

98. Bellin, "The Robustness of Authoritarianism in the Middle East," p. 152.

99. Eva Bellin, "Reconsidering the Robustness of Authoritarianism in the Middle East: Lessons from the Arab Spring," *Comparative Politics*, vol. 44, no. 2 (January 2012), p. 142.

100. Jason Brownlee, *Authoritarianism in an Age of Democratization* (Cambridge: Cambridge University Press, 2007), p. 42.

101. Steven Levitsky and Lucian A. Way, *Competitive Authoritarianism: Hybrid Regimes after the Cold War* (Cambridge: Cambridge University Press, 2010).

102. King, *The New Authoritarianism in the Middle East and North Africa*, p. 4.

103. Amid much early excitement and euphoria, one of the earliest calls for sobriety came from Marc Lynch, who in 2012 wrote: "History warns us that within a few years, the Arab uprisings of 2011 are likely to result in an even more repressive, stifling regional order." Marc Lynch, *The Arab Uprisings: The Unfinished Revolutions of the New Middle East* (New York: Public Affairs, 2012), p. 65.

104. Iliya Harik, "Privatization: The Issue, the Prospects, and the Fears," in Iliya Harik and Denis J. Sullivan, eds, *Privatization and Liberalization in the Middle East* (Bloomington, IN: Indiana University Press, 1992), p. 2.

105. Cammett, Diwan, Richards, and Waterbury, *A Political Economy of the Middle East*, p. 4.

106. For the case of Algeria as an example, see Dirk Vandewalle, "Breaking with Socialism: Economic Liberalization and Privatization in Algeria," in Harik and Sullivan, eds, *Privatization and Liberalization in the Middle East*, pp. 189–209. Similarly partial liberalizations occurred in Egypt, Iraq, Jordan, and, slightly later on, in Syria.

107. Kiren Aziz Chaudhry, "Economic Liberalization in Oil-Exporting Countries: Iraq and Saudi Arabia," in Harik and Sullivan, eds, *Privatization and Liberalization in the Middle East*, p. 147.

108. King, *The New Authoritarianism in the Middle East and North Africa*, p. 29.

109. Hertog, *Princes, Brokers, and Bureaucrats: Oil and the State in Saudi Arabia*, p. 12.

110. Fukuyama. "The Patterns of History," p. 15.

111. Ibid.

112. Ibid., p. 16.

113. David Waldner, *State Building and Late Development* (Ithaca, NY: Cornell University Press, 1999), p. 2.

114. Fukuyama, "The Patterns of History," pp. 19–20.

115. Ibid., p. 20.

116. Francis Fukuyama, "The Future of History: Can Liberal Democracy Survive the Decline of the Middle Class?" *Foreign Affairs*, vol. 91, no. 1 (January/February 2012), p. 57.

117. Hess, "From the Arab Spring to the Chinese Winter," p. 267.

118. Breslin, "China and the Arab Awakening," p. 4.

119. Fukuyama, "The Future of History," p. 56.

120. Giacomo Luciani, "Linking Economic and Political Reform in the Middle East: The Role of the Bourgeoisie," in Oliver Schlumberger, ed., *Debating Arab Authoritarianism: Dynamics and Durability in Nondemocratic Regimes* (Stanford, CA: Stanford University Press, 2007), p. 167.

121. Afshin Molavi, "Buying Time in Tehran: Iran and the China Model," *Foreign Affairs*, vol. 83, no. 6 (November/December 2004), pp. 9–10.

122. Ibid., p. 12.

123. Ibid., p. 10.

124. Ibid., p. 12.

125. Elliot Hen-Tov, "Understanding Iran's New Authoritarianism," *Washington Quarterly*, vol. 30, no. 1 (Winter 2006–7), p. 163.

126. Molavi, "Buying Time in Tehran," p. 13.

127. Hen-Tov, "Understanding Iran's New Authoritarianism," p. 172.

128. Ibid., p. 173.

129. Molavi, "Buying Time in Tehran," p. 16.

130. Ibid., p. 10.

131. Won, *The China Model and Global Political Economy*, p. 177.

132. Fukuyama, "The Future of History," p. 57.

133. Naughton, "Singularity and Replicability in China's Developmental Experience," p. 17.

134. Fukuyama, "The Future of History," p. 56.

135. Molavi, "Buying Time in Tehran," p. 15.

136. Hess, "From the Arab Spring to the Chinese Winter," pp. 257–8.

137. Ibid., p. 259.

138. Zhao, "The China Model," pp. 434–5.

139. Halper, *The Beijing Consensus*, pp. xxi, xxx.

140. Ibid., p. 122.

141. Fukuyama, "The Future of History," p. 57.

142. Halper, *The Beijing Consensus*, p. xx.

143. Breslin, "China and the Arab Awakening," p. 7.

4. CHINA'S MILITARY RELATIONS WITH THE MIDDLE EAST

1. This research is jointly supported by the "Shu Guang" Project of Shanghai Municipal Education Commission and Shanghai Education Development Foundation

(15SG29), by "Shanghai Pujiang Talent Program" (14PJC092), and by the 2014 innovative research team of Shanghai International Studies University. The author is indebted to Professor James Reardon-Anderson for his invaluable evaluation and suggestions on the early version of the chapter.

2. Degang Sun and Yahia Zoubir, "China's Economic Diplomacy towards the Arab Countries: Challenges Ahead?" *Journal of Contemporary China*, vol. 25, no. 91 (2015), pp. 903–21.

3. Christopher J. Pehrson, "String of Pearls: Meeting the Challenge of China's Rising Power across the Asian Littoral," in *Carlisle Papers in Security Strategy*, ed. Strategic Studies Institute (Washington, DC: U.S. Army Strategic Studies Institute, 2006).

4. James Rogers and Luis Simon, *The Status and Location of the Military Installations of the Member States of the European Union and their Potential Role for the European Security and Defence Policy* (Brussels: European Parliament, 2009), p. 18.

5. Daniel J. Kostecka, "Places and Bases: The Chinese Navy's Emerging Support Network in the Indian Ocean," *Naval War College Review*, vol. 64, no. 1 (2011), p. 59.

6. Liu Xinhua, "The Power Site Effect, Gwadar Port and China's Interest in the Western Indian Ocean," *Forum of World Economics and Politics*, no. 5 (2013), p. 18.

7. Shi Jiangyue, "China is Debating Overseas Military Base Deployment," *World Journal*, 6 January 2010.

8. Cui Xiaohuo, "Navy Has No Plan for Overseas Bases," *China Daily*, 11 March 2010.

9. Shi Jiangyue, "China is Debating Overseas Military Base Deployment."

10. See Mohamed Bin Huwaidin, *China's Relations with Arabia and the Gulf, 1949–1999* (London: Routledge, 2002); Abdulaziz Sager and Geoffrey Kemp, eds, *China's Growing Role in the Middle East: Implications for the Region and Beyond* (Washington, DC: Nixon Center, 2010); Degang Sun and Yahia Zoubir, "China's Response to the Revolts in the Arab World: A Case of Pragmatic Diplomacy," *Mediterranean Politics*, vol. 19, no. 1 (2014), pp. 2–20; Thomas Parker, "China's Growing Interests in the Persian Gulf," *Brown Journal of World Affairs*, vol. 7, no. 1 (2000), pp. 235–43; Jon B. Alterman and John W. Garver, *The Vital Triangle: China, the United States, and the Middle East* (Washington, DC: CSIS Press, 2008).

11. As of 2017, the US has about 11,000 troops stationed in Afghanistan.

12. Robert E. Harkavy, *Bases Abroad: The Global Foreign Military Presence* (Oxford: Oxford University Press, 1989), p. 7; David S. Sorenson, *Shutting Down the Cold War: The Politics of Military Base Closures* (London: Macmillan, 1998), p. 8.

13. Sam LaGrone, "U.S. AFRICOM Commander Confirms Chinese Logistics Base in Djibouti," http://news.usni.org/2015/11/25/u-s-africom-commander-confirms-chinese-logistics-base-in-djibouti

14. "China Strongly Condemns Attack in Somalia," Xinhuanet, http://big5.xinhuanet.com/gate/big5/news.xinhuanet.com/english/2015–07/27/c_134450934.htm, accessed 21 July 2016.

15. Liu Zhongmin, "China Should Publicize its Overseas Military Base Project," *Maritime World*, no. 7 (2010), p. 10.

16. Degang Sun, "China's Soft Military Presence in the Middle East," *World Economics and Politics*, no. 8 (2014), p. 12.

17. See Xi Jinping, "Carry out the Silk Road Spirit, and Deepen China-Arab State Cooperation," *People's Daily*, 5 June 2014, p, A1.

18. Information Office of the State Council of the People's Republic of China, "The White Paper of China's Military Strategy, 2015," Ministry of Defense, PRC, http://www.mod.gov.cn/auth/2015–05/26/content_4586723.htm, accessed 23 October 2015.

19. Tom Pember-Finn, "China and the Middle East: the Emerging Security Nexus," *Greater China*, vol. 11, no. 1 (Summer 2011), p. 38.

20. Andrea Ghiselli, "The Chinese People's Liberation Army 'Post-modern' Navy," *International Spectator: Italian Journal of International Affairs*, vol. 50, no. 1 (2015), p. 126.

21. Michael Klare and Daniel Volman, "America, China and the Scramble for Africa's Oil," *Review of African Political Economy*, vol. 33, no. 108 (2006), pp. 297–309.

22. State Council Information Office, PRC, China's 2013 Defense White Paper: "The Diversified Employment of China's Armed Forces," p. 20, http://news.xinhuanet.com/politics/2013–04/16/c_115403491.htm, accessed 11 July 2015.

23. "China Building a Military Base in Djibouti?" http://sputniknews.com/africa/20150625/1023858381.html#ixzz3e9iVivWj

24. "China Considers Seychelles Military Base Plan," *Daily Telegraph*, 13 December 2011; "Why Does the Djibouti Government Offer a Military Base to China?" *International Herald Leader*, 21 May 2015.

25. "China's Overseas Military Base is Just Over the Horizon," *Wanxia*, no. 2 (2012), p. 25.

26. "India, Iran Moving Forward on Redeveloping Chabahar Port," *Journal of Commerce*, 9 May 2016.

27. United Nations Peacekeeping, "Troop and police contributors," http://www.un.org/en/peacekeeping/resources/statistics/contributors.shtml, accessed 24 October 2015.

28. Bonny Ling, "China's Peacekeeping Diplomacy," *China Rights Forum*, no. 1 (2007), p. 2, http://www.hrichina.org/sites/default/files/PDFs/CRF.1.2007/CRF-2007–1_Peacekeeping.pdf, accessed 25 July 2015.

29. Xulio Ríos, "China and the United Nations Peace Missions," *FRIDE* (October 2008), p. 1, http://www.fride.org/download/COM_China_peace_operations_ENG_oct08.pdf, accessed 25 July 2015.

30. Daniel M. Hartnett, "China's First Deployment of Combat Forces to a UN Peacekeeping Mission—South Sudan," p. 3.

31. State Council Information Office, PRC, *China's 2010 Defense White Paper* (Beijing: People's Press, 2011).

32. See Xiao Xiao, "China's Weapons Have Got Involved in the Middle East Turmoil," *Phoenix Weekly*, no. 26 (2013).

33. "China and Saudi Arabia Reportedly Signed a Contract on UAV Sales," http://m. guancha.cn/military-affairs/2014_05_05_226875, accessed 24 October 2015.

34. "There Exists Puzzles on China's Arms Sales to Saudi Arabia, and It's Different from the On-Line Report," *Global Times*, 22 September 2014.

35. "China is Opening the Middle East Market," 5 December 2013, http://www.qiye. gov.cn/news/20131205_11154.html

36. Lai Jingchao, "The Overseas Security Contractors from the Private Companies: Chinese Body-Guards Abroad," *Southern Weekly*, 17 April 2015.

37. Ibid.

38. "Overseas Chinese Companies Are Increasingly Reliant on Private Security Contractors," *Financial Times*, 26 November 2014.

39. Xinhuanet, "China Strongly Condemns Attack in Somalia," http://news.xinhuanet.com/english/2015–07/27/c_134450934.htm, accessed 24 October 2015.

40. "Disclosing Chinese Security Contractors in Iraq, who are Mostly Retired Special Forces," *Global Times*, 23 June 2014.

41. "GSA," http://baike.baidu.com/link?url=xddyeTe6jhBOPRO83QDkvBF-Prlw 4gA3DF8hnocwqlgaLeeMW5KZ1iGujkDmvuKhmcchp3fmG3S6uVPIUwpJra

42. "Does China-Turkish Joint Military Rehearsal Offend Anyone?" http://news. xinhuanet.com/world/2010–10/12/c_12648521.htm

43. C. Lin, "As ISIS Grows, China Upgrades Ties with Iran and Kurdistan," *Times of Israel*, 25 October 2014; Xinhui Jiang, "From Nonintervention to What? Analyzing the Change in China's Middle East Policy", *Middle East-Asia Project (MAP) Bulletin*, August 2015.

44. Ghiselli, "The Chinese People's Liberation Army 'Post-modern' Navy," p. 133.

45. "The West is Paying Close Attention to the China-Russia Joint Military Rehearsal," *Global Times* (China), 7 May 2015; Ghiselli, "The Chinese People's Liberation Army 'Post-modern' Navy," p. 133.

46. Ghiselli, "The Chinese People's Liberation Army 'Post-modern' Navy," p. 132.

47. "Chinese Fleet Launched the First Joint Military Rehearsal with Iranian Counterpart," *Southern Daily*, 17 April 2015.

48. Lai Jingchao, "The Overseas Security Contractors from the Private Companies: Chinese Body-Guards Abroad," *Southern Weekly*, 17 April 2015.

49. "Chinese Fleet Launched the First Joint Military Rehearsal with Iranian Counterpart," *Southern Daily*, 17 April 2015.

50. State Council Information Office, PRC, *China's 2013 Defense White Paper* ("The Diversified Employment of China's Armed Forces"), p. 20, http://news.xinhuanet.com/politics/2013–04/16/c_115403491.htm, accessed 11 July 2015.

51. Degang Sun and Yahia Zoubir, "China's Response to the Revolts in the Arab World: A Case of Pragmatic Diplomacy," *Mediterranean Politics*, vol. 19, no. 1 (2014), p. 8.

52. Gu Liping, "China Completes Evacuation from Yemen, Assisting 279 Foreigners," *Xinhua*, 7 April 2015, http://www.ecns.cn/2015/04–07/160875.shtml

53. Office of the Spokesperson, "Framework for Elimination of Syrian Chemical Weapons," Washington DC, 14 September 2013, http://www.state.gov/r/pa/prs/ps/2013/09/214247.htm

54. Zhu Ningzhu, "China Assists Shipment of Syrian Chemical Weapons: FM," 27 February 2014, http://news.xinhuanet.com/english/china/2014–02/27/c_133148158.htm

55. Ghiselli, "The Chinese People's Liberation Army 'Post-modern' Navy," p. 133.

5. CHINA AND TURKEY: SAILING THROUGH ROUGH WATERS

1. Xinjiang is an autonomous region within China in the north-west of the country. This region is home to the Uyghur minority, which is a Turkic ethnic group subscribing to the Sunni faith of Islam. Due to their common ethnic and religious roots, Turks in Turkey, policy-makers, and ordinary people alike feel a deep affinity and hence a commitment to fraternal solidarity with the Uyghurs. This is why the situation of the Uyghur minority in China has always been an important parameter defining Turkey's relationship with China. For a detailed study of the Uyghurs' role in Sino-Turkish relations, see Yitzhak Shichor, *Ethno-Diplomacy: The Uyghur Hitch in Sino-Turkish Relations* (Honolulu: East-West Center, 2009).

2. In June 2015, reports in the Turkish media referring to the Chinese government's ban on Ramadan fasting for public servants, teachers, and students in the Xinjiang Uyghur Autonomous Region caused public outrage in Turkey, which further escalated through disinformation spread on social media. A number of demonstrations were held and some of them turned violent. Turkey's Ministry of Foreign Affairs summoned the Chinese ambassador in Ankara to express concerns, and China in turn expressed its own concerns about Ankara's approach to the issue. Conciliatory remarks by President Erdoğan, who claimed that most reports about Chinese oppression against Muslims were fabricated and it was the work of provocateurs that aimed to damage Turkey's relationship with China, helped to calm down the situation. Erdoğan's visit to Beijing in late July, where economic cooperation issues topped the agenda, helped to restore confidence on both sides, which, however, did not last long. See Altay Atlı, "Turkey Caught in Quandary Over Uyghurs," *Asia Times*, 6 July 2015, http://atimes.com/2015/07/turkey-caught-in-quandary-over-uyghurs

3. See Lucy Hornby and Piotr Zalewski, "China Accuses Turkey of Aiding Uighurs," *Financial Times*, 12 July 2015, https://next.ft.com/content/93607210285c-11e5-8613-e7aedbb7bdb7

4. See Mustafa Kibaroğlu and Selim C. Sazak, "Why Turkey Chose, and Then Rejected, a Chinese Air-Defense Missile," *Defense One*, 3 February 2016, http://www.defenseone.com/ideas/2016/02/turkey-china-air-defense-missile/125648

5. According to reports in the Turkish media, representatives of the Chinese company CPMIEC were in Antalya by the time, apparently looking forward to receiving positive news about the missile defense system tender. When informed that the tender was cancelled, they left Turkey before the summit began. See "G20'de Çin ile Yedi Anlaşma İmzalandı," Aydınlık, 16 November 2015, http://www.aydinlikgazete.com/ekonomi/g20de-cin-ile-7-anlasma-imzalandi-h78950.html

6. See "Çin, Türklere Vizeleri Zorlaştırdı," Dünya, 4 February 2016, http://www.dunya.com/dunya/ulkeler/cin-turklere-vizeleri-zorlastirdi-289430h.htm

7. See Selçuk Esenbel and Altay Atlı, "Turkey's Changing Foreign Policy Stance: Getting Closer to Asia?" *Middle East Institute*, 30 September 2013, http://www.mei.edu/content/turkey's-changing-foreign-policy-stance-getting-closer-asia

8. Zhou Zhiqiang, "Sino-Turkish Strategic Economic Relationship in New Era," *Alternatives: Turkish Journal of International Relations*, vol. 14, no. 3 (2015), pp. 13–25.

9. Xiao Xian, "China and Turkey: Forging a New Strategic Partnership," *Contemporary International Relations*, vol. 22, no. 1 (2013), pp. 123–40.

10. Selçuk Çolakoğlu, "Turkey-China Relations: Rising Partnership," *Ortadoğu Analiz*, no. 52 (2013), pp. 32, 45.

11. Selçuk Çolakoğlu, "Dynamics of Sino-Turkish Relations: a Turkish Perspective," *East Asia*, vol. 32 (2015), pp. 7–23.

12. Vali Nasr, *The Dispensable Nation: American Foreign Policy in Retreat* (New York: Anchor Books, 2014), p. 227.

13. "Johan Galtung on the Wars in Iraq and Afghanistan, Mideast Peace Talks, and Why Obama Is Losing His Base," *Democracy Now!* 16 September 2010, http://www.democracynow.org/2010/9/16/johan_galtung_on_the_wars_in

14. Yitzhak Shichor is one of the few scholars who has a rather cautious approach to the prospects offered by the Sino-Turkish relationship. In a similar vein, Karen Kaya calls the two countries "unlikely strategic partners" on the grounds that there is wide divergence between their interests. See Yitzhak Shichor, "Turkey and China in the Post-Cold War World: Great Expectations," in Bruce Gilley and Andrew O'Neil, eds, *Middle Powers and the Rise of China* (Washington, DC: Georgetown University Press, 2014), pp. 192–212; Karen Kaya, "Turkey and China: Unlikely Strategic Partners," *Foreign Military Studies Office* (Fort Leavenworth, KS: Foreign Military Studies Office, 2013).

15. İsenbike Togan, "Türk-Çin İlişkilerinde Ticaretin Rolü," in Selçuk Esenbel, İsenbike Togan, and Altay Atlı, eds, *Türkiye'de Çin'i Düşünmek: Ekonomik, Siyasi ve Kültürel İlişkilere Yeni Yaklaşımlar* (Istanbul: Boğaziçi Üniversitesi Yayınevi, 2013), pp. 11–30.

16. Selda Altan, "Osmanlı'ya Doğudan Bakmak: 20. Yüzyıl Dönümünde Çin'de Osmanlı Algısı ve Milliyetçilik," in Selçuk Esenbel, İsenbike Togan, and Altay Atlı, eds, *Türkiye'de Çin'i Düşünmek: Ekonomik, Siyasi ve Kültürel İlişkilere Yeni Yaklaşımlar* (Istanbul: Boğaziçi Üniversitesi Yayınevi, 2013), pp. 90–114.

17. This mission was upgraded to an embassy in 1945.

18. Ceren Ergenç, "Can Two Ends of Asia Meet? An Overview of Contemporary Turkey-China Relations," *East Asia*, vol. 32 (2015), pp. 289–308.

19. Altay Atlı, "12 Mart Muhtırası ve Türkiye'nin Çin Halk Cumhuriyeti'ni Tanıması," in Selçuk Esenbel, İsenbike Togan, and Altay Atlı, eds, *Türkiye'de Çin'i Düşünmek: Ekonomik, Siyasi ve Kültürel İlişkilere Yeni Yaklaşımlar* (Istanbul: Boğaziçi Üniversitesi Yayınevi, 2013), pp. 147–69.

20. Çolakoğlu, "Dynamics of Sino-Turkish Relations," p. 11.

21. For a comprehensive list of high-level diplomatic visits between the two countries during the 1980s and 1990s, see Çolakoğlu, "Dynamics of Sino-Turkish Relations," pp. 11–15.

22. Ergenç, "Can Two Ends of Asia Meet?" p. 295.

23. Shichor, *Ethno-Diplomacy*, p. x.

24. For in-depth discussions of Turkey's foreign policy activism under the AKP government and its various dimensions, see Ziya Öniş, "Multiple Faces of the 'New' Turkish Foreign Policy: Underlying Dynamics and a Critique," *Insight Turkey*, vol. 13, no. 1 (2011), pp. 47–65; Ioannis N. Grigoriadis, "Turkey's Foreign Policy Activism: Vision Continuity and Reality Checks," *Southeast European and Black Sea Studies*, vol. 14, no. 2 (2014), pp. 159–73; Kemal Kirişci, "Turkey's Engagement with its Neighborhood: A 'Synthetic' and Multidimensional Look at Turkey's Foreign Policy Transformation," *Turkish Studies*, vol. 13, no. 3 (2012), pp. 319–41.

25. The chairmanship of G20 was held by Turkey in 2015, followed by China in 2016. CICA is a platform for enhancing cooperation toward peace, security, and stability in Asia. Founded in 1999, CICA has 26 member countries. Turkey was the chair in 2010–14, and China has assumed the chairmanship for the period 2014–16.

26. There are three Confucius Institutes in Turkey: two in Istanbul and one in Ankara.

27. "Comprehensive Cultural Activities Recently Organized Abroad," Republic of Turkey Ministry of Foreign Affairs website, http://www.mfa.gov.tr/years-and-seasons-of-turkey-recently-organized-in-other-countries.en.mfa

28. See "Erdoğan: Ey Beşşar, Men Dakka Dukka," Bloomberg HT, 7 February 2012, http://www.bloomberght.com/guncel-siyaset/haber/1077037-erdogan-ey-bessar-men-dakka-dukka

29. Jia Qingguo's comments in an interview with a daily newspaper offer a clear insight into China's approach to the incident: "China will urge both sides to maintain restraint and solve the disputes through negotiation, but it has no interest in

becoming a mediator and getting entangled in others' disputes. The two countries are telling different stories... What they are fighting about is far more complicated than an airspace violation." See Andrea Chen, "China to Stay on the Sidelines in Turkey-Russia Tensions," *South China Morning Newspaper*, 26 November 2015, http://www.scmp.com/news/china/diplomacy-defence/article/1883428/china-stay-sidelines-turkey-russia-tensions

30. Mehmet Söylemez, "Chinese Foreign Policy, Turkey and the Russian Jet," *TARK*, 7 December 2015, http://theturkishsun.com/chinese-foreign-policy-turkey-and-the-russian-jet-2–1701

31. According to data released by the Turkish armed forces, 909 foreign fighters were captured by Turkish security personnel along the Turkish-Syrian border during 2015, and 324 of them were Chinese citizens. See "Suriye Sınırında En Çok Çinli Yakalandı," *Radikal*, 9 December 2015, http://www.radikal.com.tr/turkiye/suriye-sinirinda-en-cok-cinli-yakalandi-1489153

32. The first quote is from President Recep Tayyip Erdoğan's speech at the Turkey-China Business Forum meeting in Beijing, 29 July 2015; see "President Erdoğan is in China," Republic of Turkey Ministry of Foreign Affairs website, http://www.mfa.gov.tr/president-erdogan-is-in-china.en.mfa. The second quote is from President Xi Jinping's speech at the China-Turkey Economic and Trade Cooperation Forum in Istanbul (then in his capacity as vice president), 22 February 2012; see "Vice President Xi Jinping's Speech at the China-Turkey Economic and Trade Cooperation Forum," Ministry of Foreign Affairs of the People's Republic of China website, http://www.fmprc.gov.cn/mfa_eng/wjb_663304/zzjg_663340/xybfs_663590/gjlb_663594/2898_663796/2900_663800/t908616.shtml

33. Quoted in Chen, "China to Stay on the Sidelines in Turkey-Russia Tensions."

34. Tansa G. Massoud and Christopher S. Magee, "Trade and Political, Military, and Economic Relations," *Peace Economics, Peace Science and Public Policy*, vol. 18, no. 1 (2012), pp. 1–37.

35. Solomon W. Polachek, "Current Research and Future Directions in Peace Economics: Trade Gone Awry," *Peace Economics, Peace Science and Public Policy*, vol. 16, no. 2 (2010), pp. 1–14.

36. Amitav Acharya, "Global International Relations (IR) and Regional Worlds: A New Agenda for International Studies," *International Studies Quarterly*, vol. 58 (2014), p. 653.

37. Dale C. Copeland, *Economic Interdependence and War* (Princeton, NJ: Princeton University Press, 2015), p. 5.

38. Alexander Wendt, *Social Theory of International Politics* (Cambridge: Cambridge University Press, 1999).

39. All the trade figures and ratios related to the bilateral trade between China and Turkey are either obtained from the Turkish Statistical Institute (TÜİK) or calculated using TÜİK data, http://tuik.gov.tr

40. Figures related to individual products are obtained from the International Trade Center database or calculated using figures from this database, http://www.trademap.org

41. More than 100 marble quarries in the Turkish provinces of Antalya, Burdur, and Isparta now belong to Chinese companies. See Fikri Cinokur, "3 Kentteki 100 Mermer Ocağı Çinlilere Geçti," *Sözcü*, 8 July 2014, http://www.sozcu.com.tr/2014/ekonomi/3-kentteki-100-mermer-ocagi-cinlilere-gecti-551164/

42. Özlem Yüzak, "Mermeri Çinliye Kaptırınca," *Cumhuriyet*, 27 August 2014, http://www.cumhuriyet.com.tr/koseyazisi/110811/Mermeri_Cinliye_Kaptirinca.html

43. *Türkiye'nin Çin Halk Cumhuriyeti ile Ekonomik İlişkileri İçin Bir Yol Haritası*, DEİK, unpublished report (2016), p. 28.

44. IMF World Economic Outlook database, April 2016, http://www.imf.org/external/pubs/ft/weo/2016/01/weodata/index.aspx

45. "Yurtdışı Doğrudan Yatırımlara İlişkin İstatistikler (Ülke Bazında)," Republic of Turkey Undersecretariat of the Treasury website, https://www.hazine.gov.tr/tr-TR/Istatistik-Sunum-Sayfasi?mid=100&cid=16&nm=36

46. "Uluslararası Doğrudan Yatırımlar İstatistikleri," Republic of Turkey Ministry of Economy website, https://www.ekonomi.gov.tr/portal/faces/home/yatirim/uluslararasiYatirim/uluslararasi-dogrudan-yatirim

47. Activities of major Chinese corporations such as Huawei and China Machinery Engineering Corporation (CMEC) are often confused as direct investments, which they are not. Huawei is a major provider of telecommunication infrastructure services for landline and GSM operators in Turkey, whereas CMEC is building mine infrastructure and power plants. Both companies are large-scale providers of services, and while both have announced plans to become direct investors as well, steps towards that end are yet to be taken.

48. Turkish National Police data do not distinguish between different purposes of visits by foreigners, hence making it impossible to find out the ratio entering for tourism. Data sourced through the Turkish Statistics Institute, http://tuik.gov.tr

49. "Turkiye Çin'le Stratejik Ortak Oluyor," *Radikal*, 9 October 2010, http://www.radikal.com.tr/yorum/turkiye_cinle_stratejik_ortak_oluyor-1022807.

50. *Çin Halk Cumhuriyeti Ülke Raporu* (Ankara: Ekonomi Bakanlığı, 2013), p. 19.

51. DEİK, p. 45.

52. *China Outlook 2015*, KPMG International (2015), p. 16.

53. Altay Atlı, "Turkey to Get Railroads from China, not Missiles," *Asia Times*, 19 November 2015, http://atimes.com/2015/11/turkey-to-get-railroads-from-china-not-missiles

54. "Opinion of China," *Pew Research Global Attitudes Project*, 2014, http://www.pewglobal.org/database/custom-analysis/indicator/24/countries/224/

55. Liu Zuokui, "Perception and Misperception Between China and Turkey," China-CEEC Think Tanks Network, 11 January 2016, http://16plus1-thinktank.com/1/20160111/1090.html

56. R. Kutay Karaca, "On the Misperceptions Between the Peoples of Turkey and China," *Journal of Middle Eastern and Islamic Studies (in Asia)*, vol. 7, no. 1 (2013), pp. 100–120.

6. CHINA AND THE IRAN NUCLEAR NEGOTIATIONS: BEIJING'S MEDIATION EFFORT

1. The author analyzes China's traditional policy of "balancing" between Washington and Tehran in "The U.S. Factor in Sino-Iranian Energy Relations," in David Zweig, ed., *Resource Diplomacy under Hegemony* (London: Routledge, 2015), pp. 205–23; "China and Iran: Cautious Friendship with America's Rival," *China Report* (New Delhi), Special Issue, no. 49 (2013), pp. 67–88.

2. *Zhongguo waijiao, 2015* (China's diplomacy, 2015) (Beijing: Shijie zhishi chubanshe), p. 16.

3. Interview, Beijing, 24 November 2015.

4. Hua Liming, "Yilang he wenti yu zhongguo zhongdong waijiao" (The Iran nuclear issue and China's Middle East diplomacy), hereafter cited as "Diplomacy", in Liu Zhongmin and Zhu Chenglie, eds, *Zhongdong dichu fazhan baogao (2014 nianjuan), jujiao zhongdong redian wenti* (Middle East Development report 2014, focus on Middle East hot problems) (Shanghai: Shanghai zhishi chubanshe, May 2015), pp. 394–411.

5. Ibid., p. 397.

6. Ibid.

7. Ibid., p. 399.

8. This author was among those raising such questions. See Garver, "Is China Playing a Dual Game in Iran?" *Washington Quarterly* (Winter 2011), pp. 75–88.

9. Hua Liming, "Yilang he wenti yu zhongguo waijiao de xuanze" (The Iran nuclear issue and China's diplomatic choices), hereafter cited as "Choices," *Guoji wenti yanjiu*, no. 1 (2007), pp. 58–62.

10. Manning was arrested in May 2010. These WikiLeaks documents regarding China-Iran interactions are available online at https://cablegatesearch.wikileaks.org/cable.php?id=09BEIJING59&q=and%20china%20iran

11. Deputy Secretary Steinberg's 29 September 2009 Conversation with Chinese Foreign Minister Yang Jiechi, 26 October 2009, Cable reference id: #09BEIJING 2963. WikiLeaks.

12. "Beijing Continues to Call for Patience," 4 February 2010. Cable reference id: #10BEIJING377. WikiLeaks.

13. "PRC/Iran: Scholars on Tehran's Views on Nuclear Negotiations," 22 October 2009, Cable reference id: #09BEIJING2924. WikiLeaks.

14. *Huan qiu shi bao*, 10 February 2010, in "Media Reaction: US-China relations, Iran, US Embassy to State Department," Cable reference id: #10BEIJING345. WikiLeaks.

15. Adam Entous, "Spy Vs. Spy: The Fraying of U.S.-Israel Ties," *Wall Street Journal* (23 October 2015), pp. 1, 10.

16. Alex Vatanka, "The Struggle over Iran's Future: Hardliners vs. The Reformers," Public presentation at World Affairs Council of Atlanta, Georgia State University, 12 November 2015.

17. Hua, "Diplomacy," p. 400.

18. Ibid., p. 402.

19. Ibid., pp. 407–9.

20. *Qiang Guo Luntan* is operated by *Renmin ribao*, the official newspaper of the CCP Central Committee. The website was launched to respond to and ease militant nationalist criticism of MFA efforts to avoid or ease tension with foreign countries, especially Japan and the United States, rather than giving those anti-China miscreants the firm rebuff they deserved in the view of China's more nationalistic voices.

21. Hua Liming (former ambassador to Iran) and Zhu Xuihui (researcher on China's National Nuclear cooperation) talk about Iran nuclear issue, 17 December 2012, http://fangtan.people.com.cn/n/2012/1217/c147550–199234569.html. The transcript of the program is in Chinese.

22. "*Lao*" used in this fashion can be translated in several ways, all derogatory. I believe "bastard" is the most honest and accurate translation here, reflecting Chinese popular political culture.

23. David M. Lampton, "Xi Jinping and the National Security Commission: policy coordination and political power," *Journal of Contemporary China*, vol. 234, no. 95 (September 2015), pp. 759–77.

24. Ibid.

25. Speech by Wang Min (vice representative to UN) in UNSC, 7 March 2013, http://news.xinhuanet.com/world/2013–03/07/c_124425268.htm

26. Yao Kuangyi, General Evaluation, p. 374.

27. Speech by Ambassador Chen Jingye in IAEA, 5 June 2013, http://news.xinhuanet.com/world/2013–06/05/c_116047735.htm

28. Xi Jinping and Rouhani meet at Bishkek, 12 September 2013, http://www.fmprc.gov.cn/mfa_chn/zyxs_602251/t1076106.shtml. Xi Jinping meets with President Hassan Rouhani of Iran, 12 September 2013, MFA website: www.fmprc.gov.cn

29. Yao Kuangyi, General Evaluation, p. 374.

30. Vice Foreign Minister Li Baodong lays out China's five principles for a comprehensive settlement of the Iran nuclear issue, http://world.people.com.cn/n/2014/0219/c1002–24407910.html

31. Xinhua News Agency: China's role on Iran nuclear issues, 25 November 2013, http://news.xinhuanet.com/world/2013–11/25/c_12574141.htm

32. China's suggestions, proposed by Li Baodong, 18 February 2014, http://news.xinhuanet.com/world/2014–02/19/c_119398221.htm

33. Wang Qun met Iran's vice foreign minister in Vienna, 16 July 2014, http://www.fmprc.gov.cn/fa_chn/wjbxw_602253/t1175900.shtml

34. Zhongguo waijiao, 2015, p. 136.

35. Reuters, 17 November 2014, "China's top domestic security chief visits Iran to push for anti-terror cooperation," news.yahoo.com/chinas-domestic-security-chief-visits-iran-push-020416130.html

36. Vasudevan Sridharan, "Iran and China in Close Cooperation Over Domestic Security and Nuclear Deal," *International Business Times*, 18 November 2014, http://www.ibt.nes.co.uk

37. "Wang Yi talked about China's new ideas in Vienna," 24 November 2014, http://www.fmprc.gov.cn/mfa_chn/zyxw_602251/t1214011.shtml

38. Wang Yi meet Rouhani in Tehran, 15 February 2015, http://www.fmprc.gov.cn/mfa_chn/zyxw_602251/t1238422.shtml

39. Ibid.

40. Wang Yi, "4 point viewpoints on Iran nuclear negotiations," 1 April 2015, http://www.fmprc.gov.cn/mfa_chn/zyxw_602251/t1257262.shtml

41. Zhongguo waijiao, 2014, p. 16.

42. Wang Yi, "China Will Play Important Role in Modification of Heavy Water Reactor in Arak," 15 July 2015, MFA website.

43. Wang Qun met Iran's vice foreign minister in Vienna, 16 July 2014, http://www.fmprc.gov.cn/fa_chn/wjbxw_602253/t1175900.shtml

44. Zhang Ming met Iran's vice foreign minister, 26 August 2014, http://www.fmprc.gov.cn/mfa_chn/wjbxw_602253/t1185769.shtml

45. Wang Yi-Zarif phone call, 16 November 2014, http://www.fmprc.gov.cn/mfa_chn/zyxw_602251/t1211508.shtml

46. Wang Yi met Zaril at Lausanne, 29 March 2015, http://www.fmprc.gov.cn/mfa_chn/zyxw_602251/t1249864.shtml

47. "Zhu yilang dashi Pang Lin zai 'Zhongguo yu yilang guanxi fazhan yantaohui'" (China's ambassador to Iran Pang Lin at seminar on prospects for China-Iran relations), March 2015, http://china.huanqiu.com/News/fmprc/2015–03/5817302.html

48. Ibid.

49. Wang Yi, "China Plays Unique and Constructive Role in Reaching Comprehensive Agreement on Iranian Nuclear Issue," 14 July 2015, MFA website.

50. Ibid.

51. Wang Yi, "Hope the Implementation of Comprehensive Agreement Will Open Up New Prospects for China-Iran Mutually Beneficial Cooperation," 15 July 2015, MFA website.

7. CHINA AND IRAQ

1. For a detailed analysis of "competitive authoritarianism," see Steven Levitsky and

Lucan A. Way, *Competitive Authoritarianism: Hybrid Regimes After the Cold War* (New York: Cambridge University Press, 2010). For a discussion of how Iraq since 2004 fits this hybrid category, see Joseph Sassoon, *Anatomy of Authoritarianism in the Arab Republics* (Cambridge: Cambridge University Press, 2016).

2. Muhamad S. Olimat, *China and the Middle East since World War II: A Bilateral Approach* (London: Lexington Books, 2014), p. 64.

3. Hasshim S. Behbehani, *China's Foreign Policy in the Arab World: 1955–1979* (London: Kegan Paul International, 1981), pp. 191–8.

4. Hafizullah Emadi, "China and Iraq: Patterns of Interaction, 1960–1992," *Economic and Political Weekly*, vol. 29, no. 53 (31 December 1994), p. 3315 [Article: pp. 3315–18].

5. Ibid., p. 3316.

6. Muhamad S. Olimat, *China and the Middle East: From Silk Road to Arab Spring* (London: Routledge, 2013), p. 27.

7. Lillian Craig Harris, "Myth and Reality in China's Relations with the Middle East," in Thomas W. Robinson and David Shambaugh, eds, *Chinese Foreign Policy: Theory and Practice* (Oxford: Oxford University Press, 1994), p. 328 [Article pp. 322–47].

8. Simon Henderson, *Instant Empire: Saddam Hussein's Ambition for Iraq* (San Francisco: Mercury, 1991), p. 175.

9. Emadi, "China and Iraq: Patterns of Interaction," p. 3317.

10. Ibid.

11. Harris, "Myth and Reality in China's Relations with the Middle East," p. 339.

12. Olimat, *China and the Middle East: From Silk Road to Arab Spring*, p. 79.

13. Matt Schiavenza, "Who Won the Iraq War? China," *The Atlantic*, 22 March 2013, http://www.theatlantic.com/china/archive/2013/03/who-won-the-iraq-war-china/274267/, accessed 24 February 2015.

14. Ibid. Schiavenza quotes a BBC poll conducted in 2012 across several countries showing that China was more popular than the United States.

15. See a list of Iraqi dignitaries visiting China in "Embassy of the People's Republic of China in the Republic of Iraq," *Bilateral Relations between China and Iraq*, 11 April 2013.

16. Paul Salem, *Iraq's Tangled Foreign Interests and Relations*, Carnegie Middle East Center (24 December 2013), p. 28.

17. Mahmoud Ghafouri, "China's Policy in the Persian Gulf," *Middle East Policy*, vol. 16, no. 2 (Summer 2009), p. 86 [Article: pp. 80–92]. Author quotes Minister of Foreign Affairs Li Zhaoxing addressing the fourth session of the Tenth Chinese National People's Congress in March 2006.

18. COSIT (Central Statistical Organization Iraq), *Imports (Non-Oil) by Commodity and Origin Country for the Year 2011*, http://www.cosit.gov.iq/en/stat-trade/foreign-trade

19. Ibid. In 2011 the European Union represented 29 percent of Iraq's total imports.

20. Olimat, *China and the Middle East since World War II*, p. 73.

21. Salem, *Iraq's Tangled Foreign Interests and Relations*, p. 14.

22. Organization of Economic Complexity, MIT, 2013, http://atlas.media.mit.edu/en/visualize/tree_map/hs92/export/chn/show/all/2013/

23. Observatory of Economic Complexity (OEC) MIT, 2013. The observatory provides access to bilateral trade data for roughly 200 countries over a period of 50 years and encompassing 1,000 products: http://atlas.media.mit.edu/en/

24. Zhu Weilie, "On the Strategic Relationship between China and the Middle East Islamic Countries," in Sun Degang and Yahia H. Zoubir, *Building a New Silk Road: China and the Middle East in the 21st Century* (Shanghai: World Affairs Press, 2014), p. 156 [Article: pp. 147–77].

25. Organization of Economic Complexity, MIT, 2013, http://atlas.media.mit.edu/en/visualize/tree_map/hs92/import/chn/show/2709/2013/

26. BP Statistical Review 2014, "China in 2013," www.bp.com/statisticalreview

27. Manochehr Dorraj and James E. English, "China's Strategy for Energy Acquisition in the Middle East: Potential for Conflict and Cooperation with the United States," *Asian Politics and Policy*, vol. 4, no. 2 (2102), p. 176 [Article: pp. 173–91].

28. Mohammad Salman and Gustaaf Geeraerts, "Strategic Hedging and China's Economic Policy in the Middle East," *China Report*, vol. 51, no. 2 (2015), p. 108 [Article: pp. 102–20].

29. Ibid., p. 109.

30. Dorraj and English, "China's Strategy for Energy Acquisition," p. 185.

31. Erica Goode and Riyadh Mohammed, "Iraq Signs Oil Deal with China Worth up to $3 Billion," *New York Times*, 28 August 2008.

32. Haider Hammod Radhi al-Shafiy, "CNPC, CNOOC and Sinopec in Iraq: Successful Start and Ambitious Cooperation Plan," *Journal of Middle Eastern and Islamic Studies (in Asia)*, vol. 9, no. 1 (2015), pp. 79–80 [Article: pp. 78–98].

33. Ibid., p. 85.

34. Reuters, "BP, CNPC raise shares in Iraq's Rumaila oil field—Iraqi official," 7 September 2014, http://uk.reuters.com/article/iraq-oil-rumaila-idUKL5N0R80AZ20140907

35. CNPC, *CNPC in Iraq*, 2015, http://www.cnpc.com.cn/en/Iraq/country_index.shtml

36. US Energy Information Administration (EIA), "Country Analysis Brief: Iraq," 30 January 2015, Table 1, p. 5, https://www.eia.gov/beta/international/analysis_includes/countries_long/Iraq/iraq.pdf

37. Dorraj and English, "China's Strategy for Energy Acquisition," p. 186.

38. Reuters, "China Ends Near Decade of Rising Iraq Crude Oil Orders-Sources," 18 December 2014, http://in.reuters.com/article/iraq-china-crude-idINL3N0U22PN20141218

39. EIA, "Country Analysis Brief: Iraq," p. 6.

40. Chen Aizhu and Ben Blanchard, "China's Oil Operations in Iraq Unaffected, Cuts Some Staff," Reuters, 18 June 2014, http://www.reuters.com/article/2014/06/18/us-iraq-security-china-idUSKBN0ET13120140618#QB20jwy20OBjCzw0.97

41. Jane Perlez and Chris Buckley, "China Retools its Military with a First Outpost in Djibouti," *New York Times*, 26 November 2015.

42. Richard Weitz, "China-Iraq Ties: Oil, Arms and Influence," *Second Line of Defense* (SLD), 25 June 2012, http://www.sldinfo.com/china-iraq-ties-oil-arms-and-influence/

43. Nazir Kamal, "China's Arms Export Policy and Responses to Multilateral Restraints," *Contemporary Southeast Asia*, vol. 14, no. 2 (September 1992), p. 132 [Article: pp. 112–41].

44. Steve A. Yetiv and Chunlong Lu, "China, Global Energy, and the Middle East," *Middle East Journal*, vol. 6, no. 2 (Spring 2007), p. 211 [Article: pp. 199–218].

45. Ibid.

46. Robin Wright and Ann Scott Tyson, "Iraqis to Pay China $100 Million for Weapons for Police," *Washington Post*, 4 October 2007.

47. Zachary Keck, "China and Iraq Expand Energy and Defense Ties," *The Diplomat*, 27 February 2014. See also Hamza Mustafa, "China Joins Race to Arm Iraq," *Asharq Al-Awsat*, 7 December 2015.

48. Jonathan Marcus, "China Helps Iraq Military Enter Drone Era," BBC, 12 October 2015, http://www.bbc.com/news/world-middle-east-34510126

49. Patrick Boehler and Gerry Doyle, "Use by Iraqi Military May be a Boon for China-Made Drones," *New York Times*, 17 December 2015.

50. Taylor Butch, "Why China Will Intervene in Iraq," *Asia Times*, 9 September 2015, http://atimes.com/2015/09/why-china-will-intervene-in-iraq/

51. Su, Reissa, "ISIS War: China Offers Military Support to Iraq but Declines Joining U.S.-led Coalition," *International Business Times*, December 16, 2014. http://www.ibtimes.com.au/isis-war-china-offers-military-support-iraq-declines-joining-us-led-coalition-1398125.

52. Salman and Geeraerts, "Strategic Hedging and China's Economic Policy," p. 110.

53. Liu Dong, "China's Resource Demand and Market Opportunities in the Middle East: Policies and Operations in Iran and Iraq," *Perspectives on Global Development and Technology*, vol. 13 (2014), p. 579 [Article: pp. 564–87].

54. Dorraj and English, "China's Strategy for Energy Acquisition," p. 186.

55. Peter Ford, "Why China Stays Quiet on Iraq, Despite Being No. 1 Oil Investor," *Christian Science Monitor*, 27 June 2014. The journalist quotes Ma Xiaolin, a Beijing-based Middle East analyst. http://www.csmonitor.com/World/Asia-Pacific/2014/0627/Why-China-stays-quiet-on-Iraq-despite-being-no.-1-oil-investor-video

56. Dorraj and English, "China's Strategy for Energy Acquisition," p. 187.

57. Simone Van Nieuwenhuizen, "China May Regret 'Free Riding' in Iraq," *The Diplomat*, 26 August 2014, website 22 March 2015, http://thediplomat.com/2014/08/china-may-regret-free-riding-in-iraq/.

58. Qiu Yongzheng, "Turkey's Ambiguous Policies Help Terrorists Join IS Jihadist Group: Analyst," *Global Times*, 15 December 2014, website 22 March 2015, http://www.globaltimes.cn/content/896765.shtml

59. "Iraq and China Strengthens Relationship," *Iraq-Business News*, 19 July 2011, http://www.iraq-businessnews.com/2011/07/19/iraq-and-china-strengthen-relationship/

8. SILK ROADS AND GLOBAL STRATEGY: CHINA'S QUEST

1. Elmar Mammadyarov, "A New Way for the Caspian Region Cooperation and Integration," http://www.esiweb.org/pdf/esi_turkey_tpq_id_104.pdf, p. 3.

2. Masahiro Kawai, "Asian Infrastructure Investment Bank in the Evolving International Financial Order," in Daniel Bob, ed., *Asian Infrastructure Investment Bank: China as Responsible Stakeholder?* (Washington, DC: Sasakawa Peace Foundation USA, 2015), p. 11.

3. Conversations with Kazakh officials, Washington, DC, March 2016.

4. Marlene Laruelle and Sebastien Peyrouse, "Central Asian Perceptions of China," *China Eurasia Forum Quarterly*, vol. 7, no. 1 (2009), p. 3.

5. Robert L. Canfield, "Restructuring in Greater Central Asia: Changing political configurations," *Asian Survey*, vol. 32, no. 10 (October 1992), pp. 875–87; Vladimir Kontorovich, "Economic Crisis in the Russian Far East Overdevelopment or Colonial Exploitation?" *Post-Soviet Geography and Economics*, vol. 42, no. 6 (2001), p. 399; Stephen Blank, "Central Asia and the Transformation of Asia's Strategic Geography," *Journal of East Asian Studies*, vol. 17, no. 2 (Fall/Winter 2003), pp. 318–51.

6. Canfield, "Restructuring in Greater Central Asia," pp. 875–87.

7. Manaz Z. Ispahani, *Roads and Rivals: The Political Uses of Access in the Borderlands of Asia* (Ithaca, NY: Cornell University Press, 1989).

8. Ibid.

9. Nodari Simoniia, "Russian East Siberia and the Far East," *Global Asia*, vol. 1, no. 1 (2006), pp. 71–9; Vladimir Ivanov, "Russia's Energy Politics: Focusing on New Markets in Asia," *Joint U.S.-Korea Academic Studies: New Paradigms for Transpacific Collaboration*, vol. 16 (Washington, DC: Korea Economic Institute, 2006), pp. 61–79; Stephen Blank, "Economics and Security in Northeast Asia: The Iron Silk Road, Its Context and Implications," *Global Economic Review*, vol. 31, no. 3 (2002), pp. 3–24.

10. "Russia Carved Out Exceptions to North Korean Sanctions," Radio Free Europe Radio Liberty, 3 March 2016, www.rferl.org

11. "Park Seeks 'Eurasia Initiative' to Build Energy, Logistics Links," *Korea Herald*, 18 October 2013, http://www.koreaherald.com/view.php?ud=20131018000620

12. "North Korea Sanctions Threaten Park's Eurasia Initiative," *Asia Times Online*, 10 March 2016, www.atimes.com

13. Stephen Blank, "Infrastructural Policy and National Strategies in Central Asia: the Russian Example," *Central Asian Survey*, vol. 23, nos. 3–4 (December 2004), pp. 225–48.

14. Moscow, *ITAR-TASS*, in English, 3 January 2001, Open Source Center, Foreign Broadcast Information Service for Central Eurasia, henceforth FBIS-SOV, 3 January 2001.

15. Moscow, *Interfax*, in English, 15 November 2000, FBIS-SOV, 15 November 2000.

16. Jammu, *Kashmir Times*, in English, 26 September 2000, FBIS-SOV, 27 September 2000.

17. Se Hyun Ahn, "Russian-South Korean Security Relations Reconsidered: The Lost Two Decades of Promise and Perils," *Korean Social Science Journal*, vol. 39, no. 2 (2012), p. 41.

18. Louis Charbonneau, "U.N. Delays Vote on Tough New North Korea Sanctions at Russia's Request," http://ca.reuters.com/article/topNews/idCAKCN0W34Q N?pageNumber=3&virtualBrandChannel=0, 1 March 2016.

19. "Russian Scientist Says Arctic has Almost as Much Oil and Gas as the Gulf," Moscow, *ITAR-TASS*, in English, 22 September 2010, FBIS-SOV, 22 September 2010; Moscow, *Interfax-AVN Online*, in English, 9 August 2010, FBIS-SOV, 9 August 2010.

20. Moscow, *Interfax*, in English, 9 September 2010, FBIS-SOV, 9 September 2010; Reykjavik, *Eyjam*, in Icelandic, 23 September 2010, FBIS-SOV, 23 September 2010; "Equatorial Guinea sings Gazprom Deals," Reuters, 28 September 2010; Moscow, *Interfax*, 31 August 2010, FBIS-SOV, 31 August 2010; "Putin Says LNG, Shelf Gas Projects a Priority," Reuters Africa, 11 October 2010.

21. Conversations with Kazakh officials, Washington, DC, March 2016; Uma Purushothaman, "China and Russia Step Up Cooperation in Central Asia," http://www.eastasiaforum.org/2015/06/09/china-and-russia-step-up-cooperation-in-central-asia/print/, 9 June 2015.

22. "Economy and Sanctions Derail Russia's Central Asian Investments," *Eurasia Insight*, 28 January 2016, www.eurasianet.org; Edward Acton Cavanaugh, "How Sanctions are Hurting Russia's Central Asian Ambitions," www.internationalpolicydigest.org, 5 September 2015; Yuri Barsukov, Yelena Chernenko, Alexander Konstantinov, "Russia Hopes to Increase Presence in Central Asia to Counter ISIS," *Russia Beyond the Headlines*, 14 January 2016, www.rbth.com; Catherine Putz, "Why is Russia Cutting Troops in Tajikistan?" www.thediplomat.com, 5 February 2016; Roger McDermott, "Russia Recalibrates 201st Base in Tajikistan," *Eurasia Daily Monitor*, 25 February 2016, www.jamestown.org; "Kyrgyzstan

Pulling Out of Hydropower Project With Russia-President," *Vechernyi Bishkek*, in Russian, 24 December 2015, from BBC Monitoring; "Kyrgyz Leader Says Russia Can't Finance Two Big Power Projects," Radio Free Europe Radio Liberty, 25 December 2015, www.rferlo.org

23. "Rossiia Otkazayvatesia Ot Proektov v Kazakhstane," www.rusazattyk.kg, 31 December 2015; Paul Goble, "Moscow's Inability to Fund Planned Investments Sparks Discontent in Central Asia," *Window on Eurasia New Series*, 2 January 2016.

24. Catherine Putz, "China's Silk Road Outpaces Russia's Economic Union," www.thediplomat.com, 10 March 2016.

25. Subhash Narayan and Timey Jalpuria, "Old Trade Corridor Plan Gets a New Life," New Delhi, *Financial Express*, in English, 23 April 2012, FBIS-SOV, 23 April 2012.

26. Putz, "China's Silk Road Outpaces Russia's Economic Union."

27. Marissa Quie, "The Istanbul Process; Prospects for Regional Connectivity in the Heart of Asia," *Asia Europe Journal*, vol. 12 (2014), p. 296.

28. Michael Emerson et al, *Synergies vs. Spheres of Influence in the Pan-European Space* (Brussels: Center for European Policy Studies, 2009), p. 42.

29. Min Ye, "China and Competing Cooperation in Asia-Pacific: TPP, RCP, and the New Silk Road," *Asian Security*, vol. 11, no. 3 (2015), p. 206.

30. Ibid.

31. Ibid., p. 209.

32. As stated by Petersen at a conference at the Central Asia Caucasus Institute of the Nitze School of Advanced International Studies, Washington, DC, November 2013.

33. Beijing, Xinhua Asia-Pacific Service, in Chinese, 6 February 2014, FBIS-SOV, 6 February 2014.

34. Moscow, *Interfax*, in English, 9 July 2014, FBIS-SOV, 9 July 2014.

35. Kent E. Calder, *The New Continentalism: Energy and Twenty-First-Century Eurasian Geopolitics* (New Haven, CT: Yale University Press, 2012).

36. Linda Jakobson, "China Prepares for an Ice-free Arctic," Stockholm International Peace Research Institute, *SIPRI Insights on Peace and Security*, nos. 2010/2, 2010.

37. Nurzhamat Ametbek, "Pakistan in China's 'One Belt, One Road' Initiative," *Turkish Weekly*, 20 May 2015, www.turkishweekly.net

38. Stephen Blank and Younkyoo Kim, "Rethinking China's Strategy for Border Disputes: Chinese Border Policy Toward Central Asia, 1991–2011, *Issues and Studies*, vol. 48, no. 2 (June 2012), pp. 35–69.

39. Brahma Chellaney, "China Reinvents 'String of Pearls' as Maritime Silk Road," Tokyo, *Nikkei Asian Review*, in English, 29 April 2015, FBIS-SOV, 29 April 2015.

40. "China Seeks N. Korea's Cooperation in Silk Road Initiative," www.thekoreaherald.com, 24 April 2015.

41. Susan L. Craig, *Chinese Perceptions of Traditional and Nontraditional Security Threats* (Carlisle Barracks, PA: Strategic Studies Institute, US Army War College, 2007); Andrew Carlson, "An Unconventional Tack: Nontraditional Security Concerns and China's Rise", *Asia Policy*, no. 10 (2010), pp. 49–64.

42. Ibid.

43. Stephen Blank, "Xinjiang and Chinese Security," *Global Economic Review*, vol. 32, no. 4 (2003), pp. 121–48; Valerie Niquet, "China and Central Asia," *China Perspectives, Perspectives Chinoises*, no. 67 (September–October 2006), pp. 2–10; Huasheng Zhao, "Central Asia in China's Diplomacy," in Eugene Rumer, Dmitri Trenin, and Huasheng Zhao, *Central Asia: Views From Washington, Moscow, and Beijing* (Armonk, NY: M. E. Sharpe Inc., 2007), pp. 137–213.

44. Aaron L. Friedberg, "Hegemony with Chinese Characteristics," *National Interest*, no. 114 (July–August 2011), p. 24.

45. Charles Hawkins and Robert R. Lowe, eds, *The New Great Game: Chinese Views on Central Asia* (Fort Leavenworth, KA, Foreign Military Studies Office, 2006).

46. Ibid.

47. Shannon Tiezzi, "What's Behind China's Offer of Military Aid to Afghanistan?" www.thediplomat.com, 11 March 2016.

48. Huasheng Zhao, "Central Asia in China's Diplomacy," pp. 141–4.

49. Chen Qimao, "China's New Approaches to a Peaceful Solution of the Taiwan Issue," *American Foreign Policy Interests*, vol. 25 (December 2003), pp. 513–25; Willy Wo-Lap Lam, "Dynamics of Sino-US Relations: The Perspective From Beijing," *Harvard Asia Quarterly*, vol. 6, no. 2 (Spring 2002), p. 19, citing his own article, "Trade Ties Taiwan to China's Leash," www.cnn.com, 29 January 2002.

50. Nicholas Becquelin, "Xinjiang in the Nineties," *China Journal*, no. 44 (July 2000), p. 70.

51. Kawai, "Asian Infrastructure Investment Bank in the Evolving International Financial Order," p. 13; Yun Sun, "China and the Evolving Asian Infrastructure Investment Bank," in Daniel Bob, ed., *Asian Infrastructure Investment Bank: China as Responsible Stakeholder?* (Washington, DC: Sasakawa Peace Foundation USA, 2015), p. 27.

52. Salvatore Barbones, "Russia and the New Silk Road," www.rethyinnkingrussia.ru, 25 February 2016.

53. John C. K. Daly, "Kazakhstan to Host Offshore Yuan Center," *Eurasia Daily Monitor*, 10 March 2016, www.jamestown.org

54. Robert Sutter, "Grading Xi Jinping's America Policy: C-," *ASAN Forum*, vol. 3, no. 5 (September–October 2015), p. 93.

55. Andrew S. Erickson, "Dreaming Big: Acting Big: Xi's Impact on China's Military Development," ibid., p. 71.

56. Ibid.

57. Gordon G. Chang, "China's Capacity to Project Power is Going Global," www.worldaffairsjournal.org, 10 March 2016.

58. Jessica Donati and Ehsanullah Amiri, "China Offers Afghanistan Army Expanded Military Aid," *Wall Street Journal*, 9 March 2016, www.wsj.com

59. Yevgeny Shestakov, "What's in Store for Middle East? Russia Seeks 'Golden Mean' in Region," *Rossiyskaya Gazeta*, 28 February 2016, reprinted from *Johnson's Russia List*, 28 February 2016.

60. April A. Herlevi, "China and the United Arab Emirates: Sustainable Silk Road Partnership?" China Brief, vol. 16, no. 2 (25 January 2016), www.jamestown.org

61. Giorgi Menabde, "China Loses Bid for Construction of Georgian Deep-Water Port on Black Sea," Eurasia Daily Monitor, 26 February 2016.

62. Dragan Pavlicevic, "China's Railway Diplomacy in the Balkans," *China Brief*, vol. 14, no. 20 (23 October 2014), www.jamestown.org

63. Olena Mykal, "Why China is Interested in Ukraine," www.thediplomat.com, 10 March 2016; "Latvia and China's Cooperation in Transport and Logistics to be Discussed Further, Baltic News Network, 18 February 2016, www.bnn-news.com

64. Gal Luft, "China's New Grand Strategy for the Middle East," www.foreignpolicy.com, 26 January 2016.

65. Ibid.

66. Ibid.; Andrea Ghiselli, "China's First Overseas Base in Djibouti, An Enabler of its Middle East Policy," *China Brief*, vol. 16, no. 2 (25 January 2016), www.jamestown.org

67. "Chinese Army Spotted Along Line of Control in Pakistan-Occupied Kashmir, Say Sources," www.timesofindia.com, 13 March 2016.

68. White Paper.

60. Liu Zhen, "China Starts Work on Horn of Africa Military Base in Djibouti, Defence Ministry Confirms," *South China Morning Post*, www.scmp.com, 26 February 2016.

70. Robert D. Blackwill and Kurt M. Campbell, *Xi Jinping on the Global Stage*, Council on Foreign Relations, International Institutions and Governance Program, www.cfr.org, 2016, p. 16.

71. Robert Sutter, "Grading Xi Jinping's America Policy: C-," pp. 94–5.

9. CHOOSING NOT TO CHOOSE: THE BELT AND ROAD INITIATIVE AND THE MIDDLE EAST

1. "President Xi Jinping Delivers Important Speech and Proposes to Build a Silk Road Economic Belt with Central Asian Countries," Press Release, Foreign Ministry of the People's Republic of China, 7 September 2009, http://www.fmprc.gov.cn/mfa_eng/topics_665678/xjpfwzysiesgjtfhshzzfh_665686/t1076334.shtml, last accessed 3 May 2016.

2. "Speech by Chinese President Xi Jinping to Indonesian Parliament," ASEAN-China Centre, 2 October 2013, http://www.asean-china-center.org/english/2013-10/03/c_133062675.htm, last accessed 3 May 2016.

3. Wang Jisi, "Westward: China's Rebalancing Geopolitical Strategy," *International and Strategic Studies Report*, vol. 73, Center for International and Strategic Studies at Peking University (2012), pp. 6–7.

4. Ibid., p. 6.

5. Ryan Lizza, "The Consequentialist," *New Yorker*, 2 May 2011, http://www.newyorker.com/reporting/2011/05/02/110502fa_fact_lizza?currentPage=all, last accessed 26 January 2014.

6. Xiang Lanxin, "China's Eurasian Experiment," *Survival*, vol. 46, no. 2 (2004), http://www.tandfonline.com/doi/abs/10.1093/survival/46.2.109, last accessed 3 May 2016. This has also been an argument long advocated by Liu Yazhou, a general in the PLA: "Central Asia is the thickest piece of cake given to the modern Chinese by the heavens" (quoted in Edward Wong, "China Quietly Extends its Footprints Deep into Central Asia," *New York Times*, 3 January 2011, http://query.nytimes.com/gst/fullpage.html?res=9802E6DF163BF930A35752C0A9679D8B63&pagewanted=all, last accessed 3 May 2016.

7. Yun Sun, "March West: China's Response to the U.S. Rebalancing," *UpFront*, Brookings Institution, 31 January 2013, http://www.brookings.edu/blogs/upfront/posts/2013/01/31-china-us-sun, last accessed 3 May 2016.

8. http://en.ndrc.gov.cn/newsrelease/201503/t20150330_669367.html, last accessed 3 May 2016.

9. "President Xi vows mutual 'Belt and Road' benefit," *Xinhua*, 30 April 2016, http://news.xinhuanet.com/english/2016–04/30/c_135325639.htm, last accessed 3 May 2016.

10. MERICS China Mapping, "One Belt, One Road: With the Silk Road Initiative, China Aims to Built a Global Infrastructure Network," 20 December 2015, http://www.merics.org/fileadmin/user_upload/pic/China-Mapping/ChinaMapping_Silk_Road_SiKo_Final_122015.pdf, last accessed 3 May 2016.

11. "Vision and Actions on Jointly Building Silk Road Economic Belt and 21st-Century Maritime Silk Road," issued jointly by the Chinese National Development and Reform Commission, the Ministry of Foreign Affairs, and the Ministry of Commerce, with authorization form the State Council, 28 March 2015, http://en.ndrc.gov.cn/newsrelease/201503/t20150330_669367.html, last accessed 3 May 2016.

12. Zhang Yunbi, "Initiative for Eurasia trade gains momentum," *China Daily*, 3 February 2015, http://usa.chinadaily.com.cn/epaper/2015–02/03/content_19476441.htm, last accessed 3 May 2016.

13. Jeremy Page, "The Wonk with the Ear of Chinese President Xi Jinping," *Wall Street Journal*, 4 June 2013, http://www.wsj.com/articles/SB10001424127887323728204578513422637924256, last accessed 3 May 2016.

14. Zhang Yuzhe, "Gov't Said to Name Three to Silk Road Fund Leadership Team," *Caixin*, 2 May 2015, http://english.caixin.com/2015–02–05/100781902.html, last accessed 3 May 2016.

15. "Investment on infrastructure projects for the 'Belt and Road' likely to reach $6 trillion: CASS report," *People's Daily Online*, 17 June 2015, http://en.people. cn/n/2015/0617/c98649–8908112.html, last accessed 3 May 2016.

16. "Xi Jinping Holds Talks with President Vladimir Putin of Russia," Ministry of Foreign Affairs of the People's Republic of China press release, 5 August 2015, http://www.fmprc.gov.cn/mfa_eng/topics_665678/xjpcxelsjnwgzzsl70znqdb-felshskstbels/t1263258.shtml, last accessed 3 May 2016.

17. "Remarks by President Obama and Prime Minister Abe of Japan in Joint Press Conference," White House, Office of the Press Secretary, 28 April 2015, https:// www.whitehouse.gov/the-press-office/2015/04/28/remarks-president-obama-and-prime-minister-abe-japan-joint-press-confere, last accessed 3 May 2016.

18. Jane Perlez, "U.S. Opposing China's Answer to World Bank," *New York Times*, 9 October 2014, http://www.nytimes.com/2014/10/10/world/asia/chinas-plan-for-regional-development-bank-runs-into-us-opposition.html, last accessed 3 May 2016.

19. "FACT SHEET: U.S.-China Economic Relations," White House, Office of the Press Secretary, 25 September 2015, https://www.whitehouse.gov/the-press-office/2015/09/25/fact-sheet-us-china-economic-relations, last accessed 3 May 2016.

20. Shishir Gupta, "Govt makes it clear: India has not forgotten Pakistan-occupied Kashmir," *Hindustan Times*, 24 May 2015, http://www.hindustantimes.com/india-news/nsa-makes-it-clear-india-has-not-forgotten-pakistan-occupied-kash-mir/article1–1350639.aspx, last accessed 3 May 2016.

21. "China's Arab Policy Paper," issued by the Chinese government and reproduced in English by *Xinhua*, 13 January 2016, http://news.xinhuanet.com/english/china/2016–01/13/c_135006619.htm, last accessed 3 May 2016.

22. "Xi Jinping Delivers Important Speech at Headquarters of the League of Arab States, Stressing to Jointly Create a Bright Future for Development of China-Arab Relations and Promote National Rejuvenation of China and Arab States to Form More Convergence," Ministry of Foreign Affairs of the People's Republic of China, Press Release, 22 January 2016, http://www.fmprc.gov.cn/mfa_eng/topics_665678/xjpdstajyljxgsfw/t1334587.shtml, last accessed 3 May 2016.

23. "China inks $55bn Middle East deals," *The National*, 21 January 2016, http://www.thenational.ae/world/east-asia/china-inks-55bn-middle-east-deals, last accessed 3 May 2016.

24. "Belt & Road Initiative shores up China-Mideast cooperation," *Xinhua*, 23 January 2016, http://www.chinadaily.com.cn/world/2016xivisitmiddleeast/2016–01/23/content_23216195.htm, last accessed 3 May 2016.

25. "One Belt, One Road will bypass the Middle East, and for good reason," *Xinhua*, 23 January 2016, http://www.newschinamag.com/magazine/one-belt-one-road-will-bypass-the-middle-east-and-for-good-reason, last accessed 3 May 2016.

10. HAJJIS, REFUGEES, SALAFI PREACHERS, AND A MYRIAD OF OTHERS: AN EXAMINATION OF ISLAMIC CONNECTIVITIES IN THE SINO-SAUDI RELATIONSHIP

1. Jon B. Alterman, and John W. Garver, *The Vital Triangle: China, the United States, and the Middle East* (Washington, DC: Center for Strategic and International Studies, 2008).

2. Yitzhak Shichor, "The Role of Islam in China's Middle-Eastern Policy," *Islam in Asia*, vol. 2 (1984), pp. 305–17; Yitzhak Shichor, *East Wind over Arabia: Origins and Implications of the Sino-Saudi Missile Deal* (Berkeley, CA: Institute of East Asian Studies [and] Center for Chinese Studies, University of California, 1989); Mohamed Mousa Mohamed Ali Bin Huwaidin, *China's Relations with Arabia and the Gulf 1949–1999* (London: Taylor & Francis, 2003); Ben Simpfendorfer, *The New Silk Road: How a rising Arab world is turning away from the West and rediscovering China* (New York: Palgrave Macmillan, 2011); Naser M. Al-Tamimi, *China-Saudi Arabia Relations, 1990–2012: Marriage of convenience or strategic alliance?* (New York: Routledge, 2013); Wu Bingbing, "Strategy and Politics in the Gulf as seen from China," in Bryce Wakefield and Susan L. Levenstein, eds, *China and the Persian Gulf: Implications for the United States* (Washington, DC: Woodrow Wilson International Center for Scholars, 2011), pp. 10–26; Abbās Varij Kāzemi and Xiangming Chen, "China and the Middle East: More Than Oil," *European Financial Review* (2014), pp. 40–44; Tim Niblock, "China and Saudi Arabia: the Shaping of the Relationship," paper delivered at the Gulf Research Meeting, University of Cambridge, 7 July 2010; Christopher Michael Davidson, *The Persian Gulf and Pacific Asia: From indifference to interdependence* (New York: Columbia University Press, 2010); John Calabrese, "China and the Persian Gulf: energy and security," *Middle East Journal*, vol. 52, no. 3 (1998), pp. 351–66; Makio Yamada, "Saudi Arabia's Look-East Diplomacy: Ten Years On," *Middle East Policy*, vol. 22, no. 4 (2015), pp. 121–39. For a good survey on the Chinese scholarship, see Li Caiyang, "Zhongguo-shate alabo guanxi yanjiu (1990–2009) [Sino-Saudi Relations Research 1990–2009]," Master's thesis, Yunnan daxue [Yunnan University], 2010. According to the author, much of the Chinese literature is largely oriented toward analyzing the economic aspects of the relationship, as well as providing basic sketches of the situation within the Kingdom to a largely unfamiliar audience.

3. Pew Forum on Religion and Public Life, *Mapping the Global Muslim Population: A Report on the Size and Distribution of the World's Muslim Population* (Washington, DC: Pew Research Center, 2009), pp. 13, 45.

4. Wang Meng, "Zhongsha guanxi de yisilan yinsu [Sino-Saudi Relations, the Islamic Factor]," *Alabo shijie yanjiu*, vol. 5 (2006), pp. 14–19; Dru C. Gladney, *Ethnic Identity in China: The making of a Muslim minority nationality* (Fort Worth, TX: Harcourt Brace College Publishers, 1998); Frauke Drewes, "Chinese Muslims Going

Global? The Role of Islam in Current Sino-Arab Relations," *China's South-South Relations*, vol. 42 (2013), p. 63.

5. Abdullah Al-Madani, "The Gulf in the Policy of 'Looking East,'" in *Gulf Yearbook 2005–2006* (Dubai: Gulf Research Center, 2005), pp. 297–305; Emilé Hokayem, "Looking East: A Gulf Vision or a Reality?" in Bryce Wakefield and Susan L. Levenstein, eds, *China and the Persian Gulf: Implications for the United States* (Washington, DC: Woodrow Wilson International Center for Scholars, 2011), pp. 38–44.; Joel Wuthnow, "The concept of soft power in China's strategic discourse," *Issues and Studies*, vol. 44, no. 2 (2008), pp. 1–28.

6. Joseph S. Nye, "Soft Power and American Foreign Policy," *Political Science Quarterly*, vol. 119, no. 2 (Summer 2004), pp. 255–70.

7. Wai-Yip Ho, "Mobilizing the Muslim minority for China's development: Hui Muslims, ethnic relations and Sino-Arab connections," *Journal of Comparative Asian Development*, vol. 12, no. 1 (2013), pp. 84–112.

8. Fahad bin 'Atiq Al-Maliki, "Sino-Saudi Relations through the visits of Saudi Kings to the Chinese Republic," *Hermes*, vol. 3, no. 2 (2014), pp. 89–114.

9. Ma Xiaolin, "Zhongguo meitizhong de shate alabo xingxiang [Saudi Arabia's image in the Chinese Media]," *Alabo shijie yanjiu*, vol. 1 (2005): pp. 30–37; Ma Lirong, "Lun xifang chuanmei zai zhonga hezuozhong de zuzhang zuoyong [Discussing the hindering effect of Western media on Sino-Arab cooperation]," *Alabo shijie yanjiu*, vol. 6 (2005), pp. 53–9; Chang Chung-fu, "Is China Islamophobic? A survey on historical and contemporary perspectives" (Conference paper, Reconnecting China with the Muslim World, University of Malaya, Kuala Lampur, Malaysia, 11–12 August 2015); Mohammed Turki Al-Sudairi, "Sino-Israel Relations from the Prism of Advocacy Groups," Durham University, al-Sabah Publication Series 8, November 2013.

10. Mohammed Turki Al-Sudairi, "China in the Eyes of the Saudi Media," Gulf Research Center Paper, February 2013, www.grc.net

11. Although often used as a derogatory and polemical term, Wahhabism refers to the predominating religious discourse in Saudi Arabia, and exhibits some difference from Salafism in terms of its greater attachment to the Hanbali legal school, among other features. For the purposes of this paper, however, the terms will be used interchangeably.

12. Raphael Israeli, *Islam in China: Religion, Ethnicity, Culture, and Politics* (Lanham, MD: Lexington Books, 2002).

13. Undoubtedly, there is a bias here toward using periodic divisions reflecting China's own historical development over the twentieth century. The reasoning behind this is that the domestic situation there has been far more pivotal in impacting which connectivities would emerge as opposed to others.

14. Edmund Waite, "The impact of the state on Islam amongst the Uyghurs: religious knowledge and authority in the Kashgar Oasis," *Central Asian Survey*, vol. 25, no. 3 (2006), pp. 251–65.

15. Jonathan Lipman, *Familiar Strangers: A History of Muslims in Northwest China* (Seattle, DC: University of Washington Press, 1997).

16. Ma Tong, *Zhongguo yisilan jiaopai yu menhuan suyuan* [The roots of China's Islamic sects and tariqas] (Ningxia: Renmin chubanse, 2000); Mian Weilin, *Zhongguo huizu yisilan zongjiao zhidu gailun* [Introduction to the China Hui Islamic religious system, 2nd edn] (Ningxia: Ningxia renmin chubanshe, 1999).

17. Ibid.; and Gladney, *Ethnic Identity*.

18. Alexander Stewart, "Where is Allah? Sectarian Debate, Ethnicity, and Transnational Identity Among the Salafis of Northwest China," Presentation at 44th Annual Conference of the North American Association of Islamic and Muslim Studies, Brown University, 19 September 2005.

19. "Qanadeel Al-Sheikh Baha Al-Deen Ma Zhixin tuner al-darb [The lanterns of Sheikh Baha Al-Deen Ma Zhixin light the way]," *China Today*, 2 December 2013, http://www.chinatoday.com.cn/ctarabic/se/2013–12/02/content_580838.htm

20. Ma Tong, *Zhongguo yisilan*.

21. "'Ma Youde shitiao' jingtian zhenxiang ['Ma Youde's Ten Laws' Shattering Truth]," *Zhongmu Wang* [27 September 2012], http://www.2muslim.com/forum.php?mod=viewthread&tid=408335; "Zhongguo muslin de mahapai [Chinese Muslims' Ma-Ha Sect]," *Baidu Tieba*, 5 March 2015, http://tieba.baidu.com/p/3618899151.

22. Anonymous interview, Lanzhou, Guanghe, Linxia, and Xining, 8–16 February 2014.

23. Long Ahong, *Long ahong* [Imam Long] (Linxia: Gansusheng linxiashi mingde qingzhensi [Linxia: Gansu Province Linxia city Mingde Mosque], 1996).

24. Elisabeth Alles, Leïla Cherrif-Chebbi, and Constance-Helene Halfon, "Chinese Islam: Unity and Fragmentation," *Religion, State and Society*, vol. 31, no. 1 (2003), pp. 7–35; Mohammed Al-Sudairi, "Chinese Salafism and the Saudi Connection," *The Diplomat*, 23 October 2014, http://thediplomat.com/2014/10/chinese-salafism-and-the-saudi-connection/

25. "Wahabiya de zhenshi mianmu (26) [The True Face of Wahhabism (26)]," *Iran Chinese Radio*, 2 July 2012, http://chinese.irib.ir/component/k2/item/41868-瓦哈比派的真实面目 (26)

26. Lipman, *Familiar Strangers*; and "Hu Songshan: zhongguo yisilanjiao zhuming jingxuejia" [Hu Songshan: Chinese Islam's most famous scholar], *Zhongguo Tonxin*, 23 March 2009, http://www.nxtx.gov.cn/show.php?contentid=345

27. Anonymous interview, Lanzhou, Guanghe, Linxia, and Xining, 8–16 February 2014.

28. Ibid.

29. Stewart, "Where is Allah?"

30. Ibid.

31. Gladney, *Ethnic Identity*.

32. Ma Tong, *Zhongguo yisilan.*

33. Andrew D. W. Forbes, *Warlords and Muslims in Chinese Central Asia: A political history of republican Sinkiang 1911–1949* (Cambridge: Cambridge University Press, 1986).

34. Ma Tong, *Zhongguo yisilan.*

35. Yang Guiping, "Dangdai sailaifeiye jiqi dui zhongguo musilin de yingxiang [Contemporary Salafiyyah and its Influence on Chinese Muslims]," *Huizu yanjiue,* vol. 1 (2013).

36. Leila Chérif-Chebbi, "Overlooked aspects of Islam: From Salafiyya to Tabligh, in Search of a Pure Islam," Conference presentation, Austrian Academy of Sciences conference, "Islam in China: Historical Bases and Modern Constellations," 11–13 June 2009.

37. Dru Gladney, "The ethnogenesis of the Uighur," *Central Asian Survey,* vol. 9, no. 1 (1990), pp. 1–28; Gardner Bovingdon, *The Uyghurs: Strangers in their own land* (New York: Columbia University Press, 2013).

38. Wang, "Zhongsha guanxi"; Yufeng Mao, "A Muslim Vision for the Chinese Nation: Chinese Pilgrimage Missions to Mecca during World War II," *Journal of Asian Studies,* vol. 70, no. 2 (2011), pp. 373–95; Linda Benson and Ingvar Svanberg, *China's Last Nomads: The history and culture of China's Kazaks* (Armonk, NY: M. E. Sharpe, 1998).

39. Shuja' Al-Baqmi, "Al-Filistiniyun wal 'Birmaweyun' wal 'Turkestaniyun' yagtahimuna barnamaj 'nitaqat' [The Palestinians, 'Burmese', and 'Turkestanis' enter into the 'Nitaqat' Program]," *Al-Sharq Al-Aawsat,* 6 March 2013, http://archive.aawsat.com/details.asp?section=43&article=719849&issueno=12517#.VpJVNDMrGZM

40. Bayram Balci, "Central Asian refugees in Saudi Arabia: religious evolution and contributing to the reislamization of their motherland," *Refugee Survey Quarterly,* vol. 26, no. 2 (2007), pp. 12–21.

41. Chancery (Jeddah) to Eastern Department, ES1016/2, 9 February 1950, "Proposals for an approach to the Saudis on the question of anti-communist measures in that country," FO371 82640 C652816.

42. Inayatallah Rahmatullah, "Al-Munadil wal Mujahid Al-Turkestani ... Mohammed Ameen Islami [The Turkestani Activist and Mujahid ... Mohammed Ameen Islami]," *Turkestan Times,* 22 December 2014, http://turkistantimes.com/ar/news-20.html; Inayatallah Rahmatullah, "Mohammed Ameen Islami ... Ramz al-kifah bi Turkestan Al-Sharqiyya [Mohammed Ameen Islami ... The Symbol of Resistance in East Turkestan]," *Asiyya Al-Wusta* [undated], http://www.asiaalwsta.com/chardetails_print.asp?CharId=12517; "Ahwal Al-Muslimeen fi Turkestan Al-Sharqiyya [The Situation of the Muslims in East Turkestan]," YouTube video, posted 8 February 2014, https://www.youtube.com/watch?v=V7VfD5jKIgc

43. Yitzhak Shichor, "Virtual transnationalism: Uygur communities in Europe and

the quest for Eastern Turkestan independence," in Stefano Allievi and Jørgen
S. Nielsen, eds, *Muslim Networks and Transnational Communities in and across
Europe* (Leiden: Brill, 2003), pp. 281–311; Gardner Bovingdon, *The Uyghurs:
Strangers in their own land* (New York: Columbia University Press, 2013).

44. Balci, "Central Asian refugees in Saudi Arabia."

45. Al-Sudairi, "China in the Eyes of the Saudi Media."

46. Brian Fishman, "Al-Qaeda and the Rise of China: Jihadi Geopolitics in a Post-
Hegemonic World," *Washington Quarterly*, vol. 34, no. 3 (2011), pp. 47–62.

47. Central Intelligence Agency, US Foreign Broadcast Information Service,
Compilation of Usama Bin Ladin Statements, 1994–January 2004, January 2004,
p. 114, https://fas.org/irp/world/para/ubl-fbis.pdf

48. Ibid.; and James Millward, *Eurasian Crossroads: A History of Xinjiang* (London:
Hurst & Co., 2007).

49. S. Frederick Starr, ed., *Xinjiang: China's Muslim Borderland* (London: Routledge,
2015).

50. Strategic Forecasting Inc., "China: Shining a Spotlight on ETIM," *WikiLeaks*,
https://wikileaks.org/gifiles/attach/28/28515_ETIM%203-part%20series%20
for%20c.e.doc

51. Mufid Al-Nuwaysir, "Hafeed Al-Imam Al-Bukhari alathi abhar Imbrator Al-Yaban
(The Grandson of Imam Bukhari who astounded the Emperor of Japan),"
Mudawanat Mufid Al-Nuwaysir (blog), 15 December 2013, http://mofeedsaad.
blogspot.hk/2013/12/blog-post.html

52. Mansur Bukhari, "Qadar al-hijra yulahiq al-shu'ub al-Turkistaniyyah bidayat kuli
qarnin jadeed (The Fate of 'Immigration' faces the Turkestani peoples at the start
of every century)," *Mansur Bukhari* (blog), 25 October 2015, http://mansour-
bukhary.blogspot.hk/2015/10/blog-post.html

53. Mao, "A Muslim Vision for the Chinese Nation."

54. Cemil Aydin, *The Politics of Anti-Westernism in Asia: Visions of world order in pan-
Islamic and pan-Asian thought* (New York: Columbia University Press, 2007).

55. Mikiya Koyagi, "The Hajj by Japanese Muslims in the Interwar Period: Japan's
Pan-Asianism and Economic Interests in the Islamic World," *Journal of World
History*, vol. 24, no. 4 (2013), pp. 849–76.

56. Mao, "A Muslim Vision for the Chinese Nation."

57. Huwaidin, *China's Relations with Arabia and the Gulf 1949–1999.*

58. Norafidah Binti Ismail, "The Political and Economic Relations of the People's
Republic of China (PRC) and the Kingdom of Saudi Arabia (KSA), 1949–2010,"
PhD dissertation, University of Exeter, 2011.

59. Al-Sudairi, "China in the Eyes of the Saudi Media."

60. 'Abd al-Nabi Al-'Akri, *Al-tanzimat al-yasariyya fi al-jazira wa-l-khalij al 'arabi*
[The Leftist organizations in the Peninsula and the Arabian Gulf] (Beirut: Dar
al-Kunuz al-Adabiyya, 2003).

61. Hashim S. H. Behehani, *China's Foreign Policy in the Arab World* (London: Routledge, 1985); Abdel Razzaq Takriti, *Monsoon Revolution: Republicans, Sultans, and Empires in Oman, 1965–1976* (Oxford: Oxford University Press, 2013).

62. Fengshan Ho, trans. Dr. Monto Ho, *My Forty Years as a Diplomat* (Pittsburg: Dorrance Publishing, 2012), p. 141.

63. T. Y. Wang, "Competing for Friendship: The two Chinas and Saudi Arabia," *Arab Studies Quarterly*, vol. 15, no. 3 (1993), pp. 63–82.

64. Ibid.

65. Rachel Bronson, *Thicker Than Oil: America's uneasy partnership with Saudi Arabia* (Oxford: Oxford University Press, 2006).

66. Muhamad Olimat, *China and the Middle East: From Silk Road to Arab Spring* (London: Routledge, 2013).

67. "1962nian taiwan canyu yemen chongtu: chuan shate junfu 'bang' beiyemen [In 1962 Taiwan joined the Yemen conflict: wearing Saudi uniforms to 'help' Northern Yemen]," *Feng Huang*, 2 April 2015, http://news.ifeng.com/a/20150402/43469868_1.shtml

68. Anonymous interview, Riyadh, Saudi Arabia, 14–16 March 2015.

69. Faisal bin Abdulaziz Al Saud, "Faisal's speech during his visit to Nationalist China-Taiwan," transcript, http://www.moqatel.com/openshare/Wthaek/Khotob/Khotub13/AKhotub144_8-1.htm_cvt.htm

70. Alles, Cherrif-Chebbi, and Halfon, "Chinese Islam: Unity and Fragmentation"; and Melvin Emer, Carol R. Ember, and Ian A. Skoggard, eds, *Encyclopedia of Diasporas: Immigrant and refugee cultures around the world* (New York: Springer, 2005).

71. "Ma Bufang," *Baidu Baike* [undated], http://baike.baidu.com/view/63211.htm

72. Anonymous interview, Riyadh, Saudi Arabia, 14–16 March 2015.

73. Ibid.

74. Peter G. Gowing, "Islam in Taiwan," *Aramco World*, vol. 21, no. 4 (July/August 1970), pp. 22–7.

75. Mohammed Al-Sudairi, "Saudi Influences on the Development of Chinese Salafism," Master's thesis, Peking University, 2014.

76. Anonymous interview, Riyadh, Saudi Arabia, 14–16 March 2015; and Gowing, "Islam in Taiwan."

77. Dru C. Gladney, "Muslim Tombs and Ethnic Folklore: Charters for Hui Identity," *Journal of Asian Studies*, vol. 46 (1987), pp. 495–532.

78. Ahong, *Long ahong* [Imam Long].

79. Chérif-Chebbi, "Overlooked aspects of Islam."

80. Kyle Haddad-Fonda, "The domestic significance of China's policy towards Egypt, 1955–1957," *Chinese Historical Review*, vol. 21, no. 1 (2014), pp. 45–64.

81. "Zhongguo Yisilanjiao zuzhi de jianli jiqi huodong [China Islamic Association's

Founding and Activities]," *Kan Zhongguo* [undated], http://www.showchina.org/zgwhxl/zgyslj/04/200703/t108783.htm

82. Min Junqing, "Xin Zhongguo Musilin di yici chaojin de qianqianhouhou [The Ins and Outs of New China's First Muslim Hajj]," *Gongchandang Xinwenwang*, 15 September 2009, http://cpc.people.com.cn/GB/165240/166717/10058445.html

83. Ibid.

84. Robert Vitalis, *America's Kingdom: Mythmaking on the Saudi oil frontier* (Stanford, CA: Stanford University Press, 2007).

85. Frauke Drewes, "Chinese Muslims Going Global? The Role of Islam in Current Sino-Arab Relations," *China's South-South Relations*, vol. 42 (2013), p. 63; Changgang Guo and Fengmei Zhang, "Religion and social stability: China's religious policies in the Age of Reform," *Third World Quarterly*, vol. 36, no. 11 (2015), pp. 2183–95.

86. Dru C. Gladney, "Muslim Chinese: Ethnic Nationalism in the People's Republic" (Cambridge, MA: Council on East Asian Studies, Harvard University, 1991), pp. 261–5.

87. Stéphane Lacroix and George Holoch, *Awakening Islam* (Cambridge, MA: Harvard University Press, 2011).

88. Lillian Craig Harris, *China Considers the Middle East* (London: I. B. Tauris, 1993).

89. Shichor, *East Wind over Arabia*; Cherif-Chebbi and Halfon, "Chinese Islam: Unity and Fragmentation."

90. Harris, *China Considers the Middle East*.

91. "'Minjian waijiao' lajin 'Zhongguo musilinsheng' yu musilinguojia de juli ['People's Diplomacy' has decreased the distance between 'China's Muslim Province' and Muslim nations]," *Renmin Wang*, 10 May 2008, http://politics.people.com.cn/GB/1026/7222816.html

92. "Al-'ilaqat al-Siniyya-al-Su'udiyya fi khamsa wa 'ishreena 'aman [Sino-Saudi Relations in Twenty-Five Years]," *China Today*, 27 August 2015, http://www.chinatoday.com.cn/ctarabic/se/2015–08/27/content_701697.htm; Ismail Hussien, "Marhala jadida fi al-'ilaqat al-Siniyya-al-Su'udiyya [A New Phase in Sino-Saudi Relations]," *Zhongguo Wang*, 5 March 2009, http://arabic.china.org.cn/china-arab/txt/2009–03/05/content_17382480.htm

93. Chérif-Chebbi, "Overlooked aspects of Islam"; Ma Lirong, "Yimeng, yihe yu zhongguo zhongdong renwen waijiao [MWL, OIC, and China's Middle East Cultural Diplomacy]," *Alabo shijie yanjiu* (2012), pp. 12–30.

94. Huwaidin. *China's Relations with Arabia*.

95. Anonymous interview, Lanzhou, Guanghe, and Linxia, 8–16 February 2014.

96. Alles, Cherif-Chebbi, and Halfon. "Chinese Islam: Unity and Fragmentation"; and Maris Boyd Gillette, *Between Mecca and Beijing: Modernization and consumption among urban Chinese Muslims* (Stanford, CA: Stanford University Press, 2000).

97. Mohammed bin Nasir Al-Abudi, *Dakhil aswar al-seen* [Inside the Walls of China; Journey and Discussion on the State of Affairs of Muslims, Vol. 1] (Riyadh: Al-Farazdaq Commercial Press, 1992).

98. Ibid.; Harris, *China Considers the Middle East.*

99. Ma Yibao, "Maserat tareekh tarjamat al-Quran al-Kareem lilugha al-Siniyya [The History of the Qur'an's Translation into Chinese]," *Zhongguo Wang*, 21 September 2010, http://arabic.china.org.cn/china-arab/txt/2010–09/21/content_2098 3354.htm

100. Al-Abudi, *Dakhil aswar al-seen*; Hei Liangjie, "Cong 'sange meixiangdao' shuoqi [Speaking from the 'Three Unthinkables']," *Renmin Wang*, 14 July 2010, http:// paper.people.com.cn/rmrbhwb/html/2010–07/14/content_569053.htm

101. Jacqueline Armijo, "Muslim Education in China: Chinese Madrasas and Linkages to Islamic Schools Abroad," in Farish A. Noor, Yoginder Sikand, and Martin van Bruinessen, eds, *The Madrasa in Asia: Political activism and transnational linkages* (Amsterdam: Amsterdam University Press, 2008).

102. "01 Sawaneh Al-Thikrayat * Al-Sheikh 'Adnan Al-'Ar'our [01 The Thoughts of Memory * Sheikh 'Adnan Al-'Ar'our]," YouTube video, posted 24 August 2011, https://www.youtube.com/watch?v=mW1EBm8GCqk

103. Anonymous interview, Lanzhou and Linxia, 8–16 February 2014.

104. "Shate Zhuming Xuezhe, Ge'erni [Famous Saudi Scholar, Qarni]," Youku video, posted 2014, http://v.youku.com/v_show/id_XNjEwMDAzMjY4.html?from= s1.8–1–1.2

105. "Al-Sheikh 'Aidh Al-Qarni yukharid lilmuslimeen bilugha al-siniyyah! [Sheikh 'Aidh Al-Qarni Tweets to Muslims in Chinese!]," *Sada*, 11 August 2015, http:// www.slaati.com/2015/08/11/p378199.html

106. "Islam on the Tibetan Plateau—Two Local Perspectives" (*WikiLeaks*, WikiLeaks Cable: 08CHENGDU39_a, 5 March 2008), https://wikileaks.org/plusd/ cables/08CHENGDU39_a.html; Anonymous interview, Riyadh, Saudi Arabia interview, 14–16 March, 2015.

107. Armijo, "Muslim Education in China."

108. Al-Tamimi, *China-Saudi Arabia Relations.*

109. "'Aidh Al-Qarni yamdah sha'bb al-seen al-adheem biu'jubah ['Aidh Al-Qarni praises the Great People of China with a miraculous story]," YouTube video, posted 13 June 2014, https://www.youtube.com/watch?v=J0J4VAVmEc0

110. "Liga khass ma' fadilat al-sheikh Saleh Al Taleb [A Private Interview with his Excellency Sheikh Saleh Al Taleb]," YouTube video, posted 5 August 2013, https://www.youtube.com/watch?v=6-yl7rt6GfI

111. Alles, Cherif-Chebbi, and Halfon, "Chinese Islam: Unity and Fragmentation."

112. Said bin Falih Al-Maghamsi, "The efforts of the custodian of the two Holy Mosques in supporting the study of the children of Muslims through scholarships to the Islamic University," *University Magazine*, no. 118 (2003), p. 1423.

113. Anonymous interview, Lanzhou and Linxia, 8–16 February 2014.

114. Ibid.

115. Al-Sudairi, "Saudi Influences on the Development of Chinese Salafism."

116. Mohammed Turki Al-Sudairi, "Sino-Saudi Relations: An Economic History," GRC Gulf Papers, Gulf Research Center, August 2012.

117. Ho, "Mobilizing the Muslim minority for China's development."

118. Anonymous interview, Beijing, August 2013.

119. Salomon Wald, *China and the Jewish People* (Jerusalem: Jewish People Policy Planning Institute, 2004).

120. Anonymous interview, Riyadh, Saudi Arabia, 14–16 March 2015; Abdullah Al-Dahas, "Dukhul ba'th al-'ummal al-siniyyin fi al-islam radd 'ala man kana ghaligan min istigdamihim lil'amal fi Makkah [The entrance of some of the Chinese workers into Islam is a response to those who were worried at bringing them to work in Mecca]," *Al-Madinah*, 31 August 2010, http://www.al-madina.com/node/262603

121. Al-Sudairi, "China in the Eyes of the Saudi Media."

122. "Tagheer Akhbari: Al-'Ahil Al-Su'udi Al-Malik Abdullah Al-Rahil wa Al-Seen [News Report: The Departed Saudi King and China]," *Renmin Wang*, 23 January 2015, http://arabic.people.com.cn/n/2015/0123/c31660–8840221.html

123. "Al-Islam fi Al-Seen: 23 milyon muslim wa 34 alf masjid wa 21 ma'hadan wa jami'a [Islam in China: 23 million Muslims, 34 thousand mosques, and 21 institutions and colleges]," *Al-Sharq Al-Aawsat*, 18 August 2009, http://archive.aawsat.com/details.asp?section=17&article=532276&issueno=11221#.V6M59tEkqTM

124. Khaled Almaeena, "China Visit Write-Up," Saudi-US Relations Information Service, 27 January 2006, http://susris.com/articles/2006/nid/060127-china-visit-over.html; "Samahat Al-Islam tajthub 600 Sini fi Al-Su'udiiya [Islam's tolerance attracts 600 Chinese in Saudi]," *Iqra*, 5 May 2015, http://iqraa.com/ar/News/50A113A101B115C105D53/%D8%B3%D9%85%D8%A7%D8%AD%D8%A9-%D8%A7%D9%84%D8%A5%D8%B3%D9%84%D8%A7%D9%85-%D8%AA%D8%AC%D8%B0%D8%A8–600-%D8%B5%D9%8A%D9%86%D9%8A-%D9%81%D9%8A-%D8%A7%D9%84%D8%B3%D8%B9%D9%88%D8%AF%D9%8A%D8%A9; "Shate zhichi Zhongguo yifa chengchu baokongfenzi [Saudi supports China's legal punishment of terrorists," *Feng Huang*, 18 June 2014, http://news.ifeng.com/a/20140618/40789575_0.shtml

125. Anonymous interview, Beijing, August 2013.

126. "Ihtimam al-mamlaka bi'shuun al-muslimeen al-Sineen dalalah 'ala takeed risalatiha itijah al-Islam [The Kingdom's attention toward the issues of China's Muslims is a confirmation of its Message toward Islam]," *Al-Bilad*, 11 February 2009, http://www.albiladdaily.com/%D8%A7%D9%87%D8%AA%D9%85%D8%A7%D9%85-%D8%A7%D9%84%D9%85%D9%85%D9%84%D9%83

%D8%A9-%D8%A8%D8%B4%D8%A4%D9%88%D9%86-%D9%85%D8%
B3%D9%84%D9%85%D9%8A-%D8%A7%D9%84%D8%B5%D9%8A%D9%
86-%D8%AF%D9%84%D8%A7%D9%84/

127. Drewes, "Chinese Muslims Going Global?"

128. Al-Tamimi, *China-Saudi Arabia Relations.*

129. Riyadh, Saudi Arabia interview, 14–16 March, 2015; Drewes, "Chinese Muslims Going Global?"

130. "Xinjiang: Amcit reports Hajj restrictions, missionary expulsions, harassment of employees," *WikiLeaks*, WikiLeaks Cable: 07BEIJING4871_a, 25 July 2007, https://wikileaks.org/plusd/cables/07BEIJING4871_a.html

131. "Surprisingly Small Increase in Chinese Hajj Pilgrims, Saudis Frustrated," *WikiLeaks*, WikiLeaks Cable: 07BEIJING7591_a, 21 December 2007, https://wikileaks.org/plusd/cables/07BEIJING7591_a.html

132. Al-Sudairi, "China in the Eyes of the Saudi Media."

133. Yitzhak Shichor, "See No Evil, Hear No Evil, Speak No Evil: Middle Eastern Reactions to Rising China's Uyghur Crackdown," *Griffith Asia Quarterly*, vol. 3, no. 1 (2015), pp. 62–85.

134. Timothy Grose and James Leibold, "Why China is Banning Islamic Veils," *ChinaFiles*, 4 February 2015, https://www.chinafile.com/reporting-opinion/viewpoint/why-china-banning-islamic-veils

135. Shichor, "See No Evil, Hear No Evil, Speak No Evil"; Fishman, "Al-Qaeda and the Rise of China"; Michael Clarke, "China and the Uyghurs: The 'Palestinization' of Xinjiang?" *Middle East Policy*, vol. 22, no. 3 (2015), pp. 127–46.

136. Yang, "Dangdai sailaifeiye"; Stewart, "Where is Allah?"; Chérif-Chebbi, *Overlooked Aspects of Islam.*

137. Waite, "The impact of the state on Islam amongst the Uyghurs."

138. "Xi Jinping: quanmian tigao xinxingshixia zongjiao gongzuo shuiping [Xi Jinping: Comprehensively Improve the Level of the New Religious Situation's Work]," *Xinhua*, 23 April 2016, http://news.xinhuanet.com/politics/2016–04/23/c_1118716540.htm

139. Mohammed Turki Al-Sudairi, "China as the New Religious Frontier for the Da'wah: Analyzing the Emergence of a China-oriented Missionary Impulse in Saudi Arabia" (unpublished).

140. Ibid.

11. CHINA'S UYGHURS: A POTENTIAL TIME BOMB

1. Stephen Blank, "Xinjiang and China's security," *Global Economic Review*, vol. 32, no. 4 (2003), pp. 121–48.

2. Stanley Toops, "Spatial Results of the 2010 Census in Xinjiang," University of Nottingham China Policy Institute Blog, 7 March 2016, https://blogs.nottingham.

ac.uk/chinapolicyinstitute/2016/03/07/spatial-results-of-the-2010-census-in-xinjiang/

3. Christopher M. Clarke, "Xinjiang—Where China's Worry Intersects the World," *Yale Global*, 19 March 2010, http://yaleglobal.yale.edu/content/xinjiang-where-chinas-worry-intersects-world

4. Population Census Office of Xinjiang Uyghur Autonomous Region, *Tabulation on the 2000 Population Census of Xinjiang Uyghur Autonomous Region* (Urumqi: Xinjiang People's Publishing House, 2002), quoted in Yufan Hao and Weiha Liu, "Xinjiang, increasing pain in the heartland of China's borderland," *Journal of Contemporary China*, vol. 21, no. 74 (2012), pp. 205–25.

5. Nicholas Becqueline, "Xinjiang in the Nineties," *China Journal*, no. 44 (July 2000), pp. 65–90.

6. Nicholas Becqueline, "Staged Development in Xinjiang," *China Quarterly*, no. 178 (2004), pp. 358–78.

7. Halford J. Mackinder, "The geographical pivot of history," *Geographical Journal*, vol. 23, no. 4 (1904), pp. 421–37.

8. Alice Su, "Harmony and Martyrdom Among China's Hui Muslims," *New Yorker*, 6 June 2016, http://www.newyorker.com/news/news-desk/harmony-and-martyrdom-among-chinas-hui-muslims

9. Ziad Haider, "Sino-Pakistan Relations and Xinjiang's Uyghurs: Politics, Trade and Islam along the Karakoram Highway," *Asian Survey*, vol. 45, no. 4 (2005), pp. 522–45.

10. John Cooley, *Unholy Wars: Afghanistan, America, and International Terrorism* (London: Pluto Press, 2002), pp. 57–8.

11. Hodong Kim, *Holy War in China: The Muslim Rebellion and State in Chinese Central Asia, 1864–1877* (Stanford, CA: Stanford University Press, 2004).

12. Hao and Liu, "Xinjiang, increasing pain in the heartland of China's borderland."

13. Sebastien Peyrouse, "Security and Islam in Asia: Lessons from China's Uyghur Minority," *FRIDE*, 18 July 2011, http://www.eurasiareview.com/28072011-security-and-islam-in-asia-lessons-from-china%E2%80%99s-uyghur-minority/

14. Baris Adibelli, "Sino-Iranian Relations since the Cold War," in Anoushiravan Ehteshami and Yukiko Miyagi, eds, *The Emerging Middle East—East Asia Nexus* (New York: Routledge, 2015), pp. 112–13.

15. James M. Dorsey, "China and the Middle East: Venturing into the Maelstrom," Working Paper 296, S. Rajaratnam School of International Studies, 18 March 2016, http://www.rsis.edu.sg/rsis-publication/rsis/wp296/

16. James M. Dorsey, "China and the Middle East: Tilting Towards Iran?" RSIS Commentary, 28 January 2016, https://www.rsis.edu.sg/rsis-publication/rsis/co16020-china-the-middle-east-tilting-towards-iran/

17. Ibid.

18. Nasser M. Al-Tamimi, *China-Saudi Arabia Relations, 1990–2012* (New York: Routledge, 2016), p. 62.
19. Jackie Armijo, "Islamic Education in China," Islamic Research Foundation International, Inc., 2009, http://www.irfi.org/articles/articles_551_600/islamic_education_in_china.htm
20. Ibid.
21. Michael Dillon, "The Middle East and China," in Hannah Carter and Anoushiravan Ehteshami, eds, *The Middle East's Relations with Asia and Russia* (London: Routledge, 2004), p. 51.
22. Ibid.
23. Baris Adibelli, "Cin'in Diplomatik Yenilgisi [The Diplomatic Defeat of China]," *Cumhurriyet Strateji*, no. 110 (August 2006), pp. 18–19.
24. Bill Roggio, "Turkistan Islamic Party emir thought killed in 2010 re-emerged to lead group in 2014," *Long War Journal*, 11 June 2015, http://www.longwarjournal.org/archives/2015/06/turkistan-islamic-party-emir-thought-killed-in-2010-reemerged-to-lead-group-in-2014.php
25. Ravi Shekhar Narain Singh Singh, *The Military Factor in Pakistan* (New Delhi: Lancer Publishers, 2008), p. 426.
26. B. Raman, "How China Forced Musharraf to Move," *Outlook*, 4 July 2007, http://www.outlookindia.com/website/story/how-china-forced-musharraf-to-move/235015
27. "The riots in Xinjiang: Is China fraying?" *Economist*, 9 July 2009, http://www.economist.com/node/13988479
28. Associated Press, "Thousands of Turks protest China violence," *Hurriyet Daily News*, 13 July 2009, http://www.hurriyetdailynews.com/thousands-of-turks-protest-china-violence.aspx?pageID=438&n=thousands-of-turks-protest-china-violence-2009–07–13
29. Andrew Small, *The China-Pakistan Axis, Asia's New Geopolitics* (London: Hurst & Co., 2015), pp. 67–8.
30. Al-Tamimi, *China-Saudi Arabia Relations*, p. 91.
31. Lilian Craig Harris, "China's Islamic Connection," *Asian Affairs*, vol. 8, no. 5 (1981), pp. 291–303.
32. Ibid.
33. Closed-door conferences and private meetings witnessed by the author in the period 2014–16.
34. Suhaib Anjarini, "Al-Baghdadi following in bin Laden's footsteps," *Al Akhbar English*, 2 July 2014, https://english.al-akhbar.com/node/20400
35. Don Mackay, "ISIS Militants in Iraq Proclaim New Islamic State and Pose Threat to All Countries," *Mirror*, 1 July 2014, http://www.mirror.co.uk/news/world-news/isis-militants-iraq-proclaim-new-3790221
36. James Griffiths, "Al-Qaeda magazine calls for Xinjiang to be 'recovered by the

Islamic Caliphate,'" *South China Morning Post*, last updated 21 October 2014, http://www.scmp.com/news/china/article/1621190/new-al-qaeda-magazine-calls-xinjiang-be-recovered-islamic-caliphate

37. Al-Tamimi, *China-Saudi Arabia Relations*, pp. 92–3.

38. Malcolm Moore, "Al Qaeda vows revenge on China over Uyghur deaths," *Daily Telegraph*, 14 July 2009, http://www.telegraph.co.uk/news/worldnews/asia/china/5822791/Al-Qaeda-vows-revenge-on-China-over-Uyghur-deaths.html

39. Zachary Keck, "China Doubles Down on Iraqi Oil Gamble," *The Diplomat*, 18 October 2013, http://thediplomat.com/2013/10/china-doubles-down-on-iraqi-oil-gamble/; Bree Feng and Edward Wong, "China Keeps a Close Eye on Oil Interests in Iraq," *New York Times*, 17 June 2014, http://sinosphere.blogs.nytimes.com/china-keeps-a-close-eye-on-oil-interests-in-iraq/?_r=0

40. Hassan Hassan, "Revealed: the plot to blow up DragonMart," *The National*, 9 July 2010, http://www.thenational.ae/news/uae-news/courts/revealed-the-plot-to-blow-up-dragonmart#full

41. Pu Zhendong, "Rise of ISIS surpasses other Middle East chaos," *China Daily USA*, 4 September 2014, http://usa.chinadaily.com.cn/epaper/2014–09/04/content_18546632.htm

42. Ibid.

43. Wu Jianmin, "One Belt and One Road, Asia's Stability and Prosperity," RSIS Distinguished Public Lecture, 12 March 2015.

44. Ibid.

45. Christina Y. Lin, "ISIS Caliphate Meets China's Silk Road Economic Belt," IDC Herzliya Rubin Center, 15 February 2015, http://www.rubincenter.org/2015/02/isis-caliphate-meets-chinas-silk-road-economic-belt/.

46. In discussion with the author, 24 June 2016.

47. World Uyghur Congress, "Seeking a Place to Breathe Freely, Current Challenges Faced by Uyghur Refugees and Asylum Seekers" (Munich: World Uyghur Congress, 2016), http://www.uyghurcongress.org/en/wp-content/uploads/dlm_uploads/WUC-Seeking-a-Place-to-Breathe-Freely-June–2016.pdf

48. Joshua Tschantret, "Repression, opportunity and innovation: The evolution of terrorism in Xinjiang, China," *Terrorism and Political Violence*, vol. 28, no. 4 (2016), pp. 1–20.

49. Ahmed Rashid, "Why Pakistan is Sinking," *New York Review of Books*, 2 April 2015.

50. Ibid.

51. Qiu Yongzheng, "Turkey's ambiguous policies help terrorists join IS jihadist group: analyst," *Global Times*, 15 December 2014, http://www.globaltimes.cn/content/896765.shtml

52. https://www.youtube.com/watch?v=8hTJr9rgCx0&utm (no longer accessible)

53. Popular Mobilization Front's Facebook post, 2 September 2014, https://www.

facebook.com/permalink.php?story_fbid=731771496858619&id=61107166
2261937

54. Associated Press, "China says Muslim Uyghurs have joined ISIS," *Haaretz*, 11 March 2015, http://www.haaretz.com/news/world/1.646317

55. Qiu Yongzheng, "Turkey's ambiguous policies help terrorists join IS jihadist group: analyst," *Global Times*, 15 December 2014, http://www.globaltimes.cn/content/896765.shtml

56. S. J. Prince, "WATCH: 80-Year-Old ISIS Soldier Gives Interview," *Heavy*, 2 June 2015, http://heavy.com/news/2015/06/oldest-islamic-state-isis-soldier-interview-video-turkestan-youtube-video/

57. Ibid.

58. Aaron Y. Zelin, "New nashīd from the Islamic State: 'Mujāhid'," podcast audio, *Jihadology*, MP3, December 2015, http://jihadology.net/2015/12/06/new-nashid-from-the-islamic-state-mujahid/

59. Stephen Chen, "'Islamic State hackers' attack top tier Chinese university's website urging holy war," *South China Morning Post*, 18 January 2016, http://www.scmp.com/news/china/policies-politics/article/1902268/islamic-state-hackers-attack-top-tier-chinese

60. Lin Meilian, "Xinjiang Terrorists Finding Training, Support in Syria, Turkey," *Global Times*, 1 July 2013, https://services.globaltimes.cn/epaper/2013-07-02/2F27552.htm

61. John Hall's image, http://www.guancha.cn/military-affairs/2015_04_23_317042.shtml/; John Hall, "Meet the Peshmerga's International Brigade: From IT workers to ex-soldiers, the men from the West teaming up with Kurdish forces to fight ISIS," *Daily Mail*, 21 April 21 2015, http://www.dailymail.co.uk/news/article-3049019/Peshmerga-s-foreign-legion-fighting-alongside-defeat-ISIS-workers-ex-soldiers-brave-men-world-teaming-Kurdish-forces.html

62. Information Office of State Council, "East Turkistan Terrorist Forces Cannot Get Away with Impunity," China.org, 21 January 2002, http://www.china.org.cn/english/2002/Jan/25582.htm

63. Yitzhak Shichor, "Ethno-Diplomacy: The Uyghur Hitch in Sino-Turkish Relations" (Honolulu: East-West Center, 2009), http://www.eastwestcenter.org/fileadmin/stored/pdfs/ps053.pdf

64. "Istanbul Names Park for Isa Yusuf Alptekin," *Eastern Turkestan Information Bulletin*, vol. 5, no. 4, August 1995, http://caccp.freedomsherald.org/et/etib/etib5_4.html#4

65. Shichor, *Ethno-Diplomacy: The Uyghur Hitch in Sino-Turkish Relations*.

66. Michael Clarke, "Uyghur Militants in Syria: The Turkish Connection," Jamestown Foundation, *Terrorism Monitor*, vol. 14, no. 3, 4 February 2016, http://www.jamestown.org/single/?tx_ttnews%5Btt_news%5D=45067&tx_ttnews%5BbackPid%5D=7&cHash=200344abdd89976c56dee55481597515

67. Selcuk Colakoglu, "Dynamics of Sino-Turkish Relations: A Turkish Perspective," *East Asia*, vol. 32, no. 1 (2015), pp. 7–23.

68. "Zhu in Turkey, Vows to Fight Terrorism," *China Daily*, 17 April 2002, http://www.china.org.cn/english/2002/Apr/30829.htm

69. In discussion with the author, 22 June 2016.

70. Shichor, *Ethno-Diplomacy: The Uyghur Hitch in Sino-Turkish Relation.*

71. Lucy Hornby and Piotr Zalewski, "China accuses Turkey of aiding Uyghurs," *Financial Times*, 12 July 2015, http://www.ft.com/cms/s/0/93607210285c-11e5-8613-e7aedbb7bdb7.html

72. Burhan Dogus Ayparlar, "Turkish PM Erdogan: 'Incidents at Xinjiang are almost Genocide,'" *Journal of Turkish Weekly*, 11 July 2009, http://www.turkishweekly.net/2009/07/11/news/turkish-pm-erdogan-incidents-at-xinjiang-are-almost-genocide/

73. "Turkey slams Thailand for deporting Uyghurs," *Hurriyet Daily News*, 9 July 2015, http://www.hurriyetdailynews.com/turkey-slams-thailand-for-deporting-Uyghurs.aspx?pageID=238&nID=85214&NewsCatID=510

74. World Uyghur Congress, "Seeking a Place to Breathe Freely, Current Challenges Faced by Uyghur Refugees and Asylum Seekers."

75. Ibid.

76. In discussion with Uyghur exiles, including World Uyghur Congress secretary Dolkun Isa, 24 June 2016.

77. Jonathan Kaiman, "China arrests 10 Turkish nationals on suspicion of aiding terror suspects," *Guardian*, 14 January 2015, http://www.theguardian.com/world/2015/jan/14/china-arrests-10-turkish-nationals-on-suspicion-of-aiding-terror-suspects

78. Ben Blanchard, "China passes controversial counter-terrorism law," *Reuters*, 28 December 2015, http://www.reuters.com/article/us-china-security-idUSKBN0UA07220151228

79. Cui Jia, "New anti-terror security guidelines made public," *China Daily USA*, 17 December 2015, http://www.chinadaily.com.cn/m/xinjiang/urumqi_toutunhe/2015–12/17/content_22744319.htm

80. Ibid.

81. "Satellite Spots Cross-border Tunnels," China Radio International English, 25 August 2014, http://english.cri.cn/12394/2014/08/25/2281s841656.htm

82. Eli Jacobs, "China's Underground 'Great Wall': A Success for Nuclear Primacy," Center for International and Strategic Studies, 25 October 2011, https://csis.org/blog/chinas-underground-great-wall-success-nuclear-primacy

83. Ibid.

84. Ucan, "China Losing Battle Against Extremist Islamic Teachings, Says Muslim Official," *Eurasia Review*, 30 March 2015, http://www.eurasiareview.com/30032015-china-losing-battle-against-extremist-islamic-teachings-says-muslim-official/

85. Xinhuanet, Full Text: "Historical Witness to Ethnic Equality, Unity and Development in Xinjiang", 25 September 2015, http://news.xinhuanet.com/english/china/2015-09/24/c_134655252.htm

86. "China's military in restive Xinjiang told to learn Uygur folk songs and dances," *South China Morning Post*, 16 September 2015, http://www.scmp.com/news/china/diplomacy-defence/article/1858710/chinas-military-restive-xinjiang-told-learn-uygur-folk

87. Ibid.

88. "Freedom of Religious Belief in Xinjiang," Information Office of the State Council of the People's Republic of China, 2 June 2016, http://www.china.org.cn/government/whitepaper/node_7238246.htm

89. Ibid.

90. Ibid.

91. Ibid.

92. Qiao Long, "China Enters Ramadan with Round-the-Clock Surveillance of Mosques, Uyghurs," Radio Free Asia, 6 June 2016, http://www.rfa.org/english/news/uyghur/ramadan-06062016113750.html

93. In interview with the author, 3 June 2016

94. Shohret Hoshur, "At Least Five Dead in Uyghur Prisoner Uprising," Radio Free Asia, 1 June 2016, http://www.rfa.org/english/news/uyghur/at-lesat-five-0601 2016164430.html

95. Martin Patience, "China Xinjiang: Muslim students 'made to eat' at Ramadan", BBC News, 11 July 2014, http://www.bbc.com/news/blogs-china-blog-28 263496

96. Jeremey Page and Josh Chin, "Xinjiang Authorities Ban Wearing of Face-Covering Veils," *Wall Street Journal*, 11 December 2014, http://www.wsj.com/articles/xinjiang-authorities-ban-wearing-of-face-covering-veils-1418303682

97. James Milward, *Eurasian Crossroads—A History of Xinjiang* (London: Hurst & Co., 2007), pp. 259–60.

98. Donald McMillen, "The Urumqi Military Region: Defense and Security in China's West," *Asian Survey*, vol. 22, no. 8 (1982), pp. 705–31.

99. Abdul-Reda Assiri, "Kuwait's Dinar Diplomacy: The Role of Donor-Mediator," *Journal of South Asian and Middle Eastern Studies*, vol. 14, no. 3 (Spring 1991), pp. 24–32.

100. Ilham Tohti, "Present-Day Ethnic Problems in Xinjiang Uyghur Autonomous Region: Overview and Recommendations," *China Change*, 22 April 2015, http://chinachange.org/2015/04/22/present-day-ethnic-problems-in-xinjiang-Uyghur-autonomous-region-overview-and-recommendations-1/

101. Zhang Xiaodong, "China's Interests in the Middle East: Present and Future," Chinese Academy of Social Sciences, 30 April 2009, http://iwaas.cass.cn/kycg/hjcg/2009-04-30/202.shtml

INDEX